ALSO BY JOSEPH W. NAUS

The Palsgraf Revelation

On Death, Four Short Stories (Fall 2020)

STRAIGHT PEPPER DIET

A MEMOIR

by Joseph W. Naus

K. M. PUBLISHING

Los Angeles, California

Story Editor: Alison Palmer
Copy Editor: Christine Van Zandt
Cover Design: Allie Paull
Book Layout © 2015 The Book Makers

Published by K. M. Publishing
www.josephwnaus.com

Printed in the United States of America
ISBN 978-0-9862833-9-0 (hardcover edition)
ISBN 978-0-9862833-0-7 (ebook edition)

10 9 8 7 6 5 4 3 2 1

Publisher's Cataloging-In-Publication Data
(Prepared by The Donohue Group, Inc.)

Naus, Joseph W.
    Straight pepper diet : a memoir / by Joseph W. Naus.

    pages ; cm

    ISBN: 978-0-9862833-9-0

    1. Naus, Joseph W. 2. Lawyers--California--Biography. 3. Alcoholics--California--Biography. 4. Sex addicts--California--Biography. 5. Autobiography. I. Title.
KF373.N38 A3 2015
340.09209794   2015936986

AUTHOR'S NOTE:
Anonymity — I respect the tradition of personal anonymity at the level of press, radio, and film, which is a principle of all 12-step recovery programs that are based on the original 12-step program, and thus I have not identified myself or anyone else as a member of any specific 12-step program. And while I understand that inferences can be drawn, none are intended.
PUBLISHER'S NOTE:
True Memoir — In light of the recent history of memoirs, particularly in this genre of memoir, the publisher feels that it is important to note that this is a true memoir. While we understand that perceptions of people, places and things are subjective, facts are still facts. The publisher has verified the truth of the basic facts of this text, by, for instance, reviewing many public and private government documents, some of which are included in the text itself.

Straight Pepper Diet relates to the phrase, *Sex is the spice of life*. As such, *straight pepper diet* generally refers to a voracious sexual appetite and overactive sex life. It is generally believed that the phrase was coined by Bill Wilson, the co-founder of Alcoholics Anonymous, in the book he authored, *Alcoholics Anonymous*, first published in 1939. The phrase *straight pepper diet* appears only once in *The Big Book* (as members informally refer to it), on page 69 of the fourth edition. As of 2011, over thirty million copies of *Alcoholics Anonymous* have been sold, making it one of the best-selling books of all time.

*Dedicated to those who attempt to take the next right indicated step
and to those who help them do so.*

ONE (PROLOGUE)

I'm sitting in my office at Yi & Naus, the two-man law firm, my partner Will and I started last year. I have no less than twenty phone calls to return, a dozen letters to write, and several motions to draft, but I've been staring out the window at the traffic passing by, several stories below, for nearly an hour. In my chest is a feeling of dread. This feeling varies in strength, but it never completely disappears. Today it's strong. Today, it took every bit of self-discipline I could muster just to drive into the office. As I stare downward, I keep thinking, do other people feel this shitty?

I can't let anyone know the way I feel. They'd think I was insane, or at best, clinically depressed. I'd be committed to an insane asylum like my grandma was, or I'd have to spend the rest of my life in a shrink's office zonked out on Valium talking about my feelings and walking around with a mannequin's smile. I'd lose everything. It's much better to conquer this on my own, just as I've done with everything else in my life. I'll try harder. I'll pull myself up by my bootstraps. I'm tough.

I hear Will's wingtips tapping on the hallway floor. He's heading toward my office.

"Hey champ," Will says.

I take a deep breath, force a smile, and swivel around in my chair.

"How was court? Did we win?" I ask.

"Kind of ..." Will replies.

"You know, Will, at Yi & Naus, victory is the only acceptable result," I kid.

Will chuckles but doesn't comment. The crease between his eyes reveals that he has something on his mind—I presume a warning or a reminder or something along those lines.

"Joseph, remember—tomorrow at 7:00 a.m., Brookside, Course Number One. Dr. Lee, could not be more important."

"I got it. I *totally* got it." I hold up my mobile phone. "It's even in here."

"Do you need a wake-up call?" Will asks.

"No, I'm good, dude. Really," I say reassuringly.

"Okay. I'll see you there." Will seems satisfied with my commitment to the gravity of tomorrow's meeting and breaks a smile. "Get there a little early and warm up that hor-rific swing of yours."

Will and I are a good team. He is extremely practical, and knows how to run a law office. I'm not, and I don't. Will likes to stay in the office doing transactional work. I'd rather be trying cases in front of a judge and jury every day. Law is business to Will. I practice law, because it's who I am. Will couldn't care less about being in the newspaper. I love seeing my name in print. It's proof of my success.

Last month I landed two cases from a friend I used to work with at Thomas & Colbert, who now works as in-house counsel at a Fortune 500 company. Among a dozen other cases, I represent a couple real estate investment trusts that are a constant source of business. Will has a few good clients, too, including two financial conglomerates who pay us a retainer that covers our entire monthly overhead. If things continue this way, we'll move to a bigger office, hire an associate attorney, and soon I'll be the rainmaking trial lawyer I've always wanted to be. Surely then my dread will finally go away.

The guy we're meeting tomorrow, Dr. Lee, a retired surgeon, is our biggest individual client. He owns a ton of property in Los Angeles, and he's rich, not first-class-plane-seat-rich but private-jet-rich. He's flying in from Singapore to visit his business interests and to meet me, the new litigation wunderkind who is handling most of his cases. I've dreamt of client meetings like this since I was first at Pepperdine Law, ten years ago. It's incredible: I'm meeting at a golf course with a client that pays me hundreds of dollars an hour to do what I love to do. I know how to handle this meeting. After I shank my tee shot into the water hazard, I'll refrain from throwing my golf bag in the lake, and, instead, brush it off and charm Dr. Lee with the story about how last week I showed up with the Los Angeles County Sheriff and a locksmith and evicted his tenants from the largest Chinese restaurant in Chinatown, and how I didn't know what to do with the lobsters in the tank, and how I had to turn off all the gas, because the sheriff threw out the kitchen staff while the burners were still going. Then I'll tell him about the deposition I took on one of his cases in San Francisco, and how I crucified the cross-defendant. Charming Dr. Lee will be easy. All I have to do is suit up and show up.

It's just past 8:00 p.m.; I've gotten nothing done at the office, and I'm driving back home to Santa Monica. It's been nearly two years since my drunk driving accident in Riverside, when I was working for Thomas & Colbert, and I still feel a little sketchy driving. I look over my shoulder and check the rearview and side mirrors over and over before changing lanes like I'm OCD. Sometimes I have to simply abort the mission and stay in my lane, even if it means missing an off-ramp or two. It doesn't make sense. There were no other vehicles involved in my accident. It happened because I was drunk out of my mind and tried to take a turn in an SUV at eighty-five miles per hour. But this fact doesn't stop me from breaking into a cold sweat every time I see a cop, or from panicking every time I'm approaching a yellow light at an intersection.

It isn't only fear of cops, Vehicular OCD, and a criminal record that I acquired after my drunk driving accident. Something far more disturbing has been with me since. It's the knowledge that there are two of me. There is the Joseph that lives life and does things, and then there is this other Joseph that constantly narrates my dread. The dread is shot-out nerves, reaching out, anticipating things going wrong, *terribly wrong*. It lives in my chest, and on full blast it radiates from the back of my eyes through my forehead and pulsates down my shoulders to my fingertips. I used to *feel* the dread, but now it comes with a narrator. No matter the subject of its diatribe, its basic message is the same: *You Are Fucked.* Sometimes there is a reason, and sometimes there isn't. The only time the narration stops is when I really lose myself in work, which has become exceedingly rare, or, when I'm fucking or drinking, preferably in combination. That's when the real relief comes. I used to mistake the relief as bliss, but now I know it's just a lack of pain—a temporary muzzle on the dread's narrator. When I'm done drinking and fucking, when I wake up, it comes right back at full volume, as if it's been saving up, waiting for me to wake up so it can lay into me. I so badly want it to stop. Sometimes, when I'm by myself at home or in the office, or sometimes even in the car, I shout out loud, *Shut the fuck up, and leave me alone!* And then I wonder if that makes me crazy.

Tonight, as with every other weeknight, I pull into the Chevron on Pico and buy a pack of Marlboro Red 100s and a lighter. I've wanted to quit smoking since I started. Smoking doesn't stop the dread, but it feels good and lowers the volume, and, even if it didn't, I'd still smoke, because I'm completely addicted. I can't go a night without smoking. Nevertheless, I throw away a lighter every night just after I declare that I will never smoke again, and that I'm serious this time. The clerk at the Chevron, a middle-aged Indian man with a kind smile, who I presume owns the station, pretends he doesn't notice the oddity of my buying a new lighter every night, yet he no longer asks me what color lighter I want. He knows I want the crayon-red Bic. If he doesn't have that color, I have to go somewhere else.

I drive through the Taco Bell on Pico, as I do nearly every night. The dread's narrator is clear and loud. Even my Snoop Dogg CD can't drown him out.

You're such a loser. You shouldn't even be eating fast food.

A half-hour later, I'm post-tacos, standing on my lanai, still in my suit. I'm chain-smoking and thinking. My neighbor passes by for the second time. I'm embarrassed. I avoid eye contact.

She thinks you're a maniac, a freak, standing out here chain-smoking all night. What's the matter with you?

I know. I feel like shit. This is the last night. As soon as I'm done with this pack, I'll never smoke again. I'll even throw away the lighter. I mean it this time.

Uh-huh. Yeah right.

Look, I graduated from law school and passed the California Bar Exam on the first try. I can fucking quit smoking if I want to. Tonight is the last night. Period.

Uh-huh. Yeah right.

Fuck you, if you don't believe me.

The sincerity of my declaration brings the sobering memory of what it feels like when I crave a cigarette and try not to smoke. I'm usually able to hold out for about an hour before I find myself standing on the lanai with a Marlboro Red 100 in my hand, hating myself … again.

God, I wish I could just feel good.

You know what? I want to go to the Liquid Kitty and drink Jack and Cokes at the end of the bar. That's what I want to do. I can stop and get another pack of cigarettes on my way. I haven't even thrown away my lighter yet.

That's a terrible idea. It's almost ten, and I have to be up at the crack of dawn to meet Will and Dr. Lee at Brookside Golf Course. Even if I go to bed now, I won't get eight hours of sleep.

But, it'd be a nice little walk. I'll just have a couple … a few, Jack and Cokes, and I'll be in bed by midnight.

I remember the last time I was going to try and only drink a few, a month ago at Ryan's bachelor party in Las Vegas. I ended up disappearing for nearly two days, and then I woke up, and I couldn't remember where I'd been. I had a pocket full of bank withdrawal receipts, adding up to nearly five grand, and a half-smudged telephone number written in lipstick across my back. I'm not even supposed to be drinking. That was part of the plea bargain on my DUI. I'm supposed to start AA and drunk driving school by the end of next week.

Yeah, that's right. I can drink tomorrow. I just need to finish this pack of cigarettes and go to bed. Just get to bed. Tomorrow, I can drive straight home from the golf course and go to a bar to celebrate my first day smoke free. I only have one cigarette left. I wish I had four or five. I'm going to make this last one count. I go in the kitchen, full of pricey unused stainless steel appliances, and mix myself a strong Jack and Coke.

The Liquid Kitty is dark, hiply curated, and the bartenders serve uniformly eye-watering strong drinks. I've only been here for an hour, and I am four Jack and Cokes in, and I'm not close to where I need to be. *M-something*, but not Mary, has ropy brown curly hair that is making me want to touch it. She's talking to me and sitting next to me at the end of the bar waiting for her drink. She works at an architectural firm in Century City, *Something & Something*. That's about all I hear over the music. She takes her soup bowl-sized chocolate martini and returns back to her gaggle of girlfriends. I drink another and tip five dollars. The gaggle leaves, and M-something leaves with them. She looks back at me and smiles, and then she's gone. She's a nice one, a sleeper, like Larisa, the twenty-one-year-old I just broke up with.

That tip was my last five bucks. Thank God I accidentally brought my ATM card in my summer jacket, even though I'd thought I'd only brought forty dollars to make sure I didn't stay too long. Forty dollars is not enough. I drink another. Now I'm where I want to be—in the warm, gooey, alcohol-induced, sweet spot. I smoke another. I drink, smoke, drink, and smoke. It's just me in here now, the sexy bartender, and a couple extras. She's nice to me but doesn't—*does not*—want to fuck me. I checked to make sure the last … *whatever day* it was I was here last … the day before yesterday? I could be such a great boyfriend to her. *She's so hot.* I drink, smoke, drink, and smoke. I could do this forever. She's *such* a good bartender. *I totally love her.* I can't remember her name. I knew it two drinks ago. Nick Cave or maybe Tom Waits plays on the jukebox, or maybe one of those other guys you have to be cooler than I am to appreciate. The guy she'll sleep with tonight, he'll be skinny with dark, perfectly disheveled hair, and he'll have tattoos up his arms. He probably has the entire Nick Cave and Tom Waits collection. *Fuck that guy.*

Things are going fuzzy and black and loud and jagged. I've been cut off from here before, maybe not the last time, but two times before that. I'm trying to stay mellow so she'll keep serving me. I order another and another. How many? Maybe nine or something like that, not a dozen. I've always been good with numbers, although things get a little fuzzy in the neighborhood of geometry. I think I just said that out loud, but I'm not sure.

Everything goes black.

❖   ❖   ❖

Black pavement, street lights, cars, the neon Taco Bell sign, the liquor store, the 10 Freeway underpass at Pico, the red neon of the porn shop. Visions streak by, and my feet thud numbly under me. I'm running wild. The cool summer night. My heart beats hard, and my lungs groan from inhaling two packs of cigarettes in a few hours.

I stopped somewhere on the way, and now I'm pounding on the door to the Oriental massage parlor. There's no back door; bad configuration. My vision is blurred. I can see if I close one eye. Things are not real. It's like a dream, but I can feel the warm summer air. Colors are snapping in my peripheral. Light and sound dart in an out of silence and shadows.

Again, everything goes black.

And then I'm back in the dream world. Now, I'm in a small dark motel room. It's factory-loud. It has to do with the Oriental massage parlor. A man is yelling. *Jesus Christ! Whoa!* I'm fighting, but it's as if I'm watching myself. I try to shut him down. I try to contain an angry screaming man. I'm naked, and my cock is hard. *Whoa!* I'm in trouble, and I need to get out of here. I was in the massage parlor bathroom. Now an Asian man swings wildly at me. He rocks me, and I see stars, flashing colors. I grab him and put him in a choke hold. Elbow –V to Adam's apple; cinch it in tight. He tries to scream, but he's losing air.

Shut the fuck up! I hear. It's me. I yelled that.

We are interlocked, flying around the little room. He's half my size. It's dark, and there is an industrial fan sounding like a prop plane. He won't shut up, but if I keep squeezing, I'll accidentally kill him on purpose.

Shut the fuck up, or I'm going to kill you! I yell again.

I let go. He gasps for air and wrestles with the front door.

I grab my clothes and back away from him into the bathroom. I lunge and fall out the bathroom window. I'm in a little alleyway between the building and a cinderblock wall. I climb clumsily, all angles. I'm out on the street, hopping, trying to get my pants on. I'm shirtless. I have no shoes. I'm on 32nd and Pico. I was in the massage parlor. There is Der Wienerschnitzel with its bright yellow lights.

Here comes the Asian man, and now he has a friend. They're pissed. One has a skateboard. One has a bat. I'm standing in the front lawn of a tidy little house across the street. They've cornered me.

They're yelling at me. I'm trying to get away. Screaming words are going back and forth. I can't understand what they are saying, and they don't seem to understand what I'm saying. This is not a dream and is getting more real every moment. I just want to get away. They won't let me go. I'm spinning; red and blue spots are floating in my vision. I think some of the lights are real, some aren't. I'm not sure which. My arms and legs are moving so slowly. My brain is telling my arms to move. They don't listen until a few moments later.

Thwack! Asian Man slams the deck of his skateboard right down on my head like I'm a giant tent stake he's trying to drive into the turf.

There are stars again. I concuss to blackness and then come back. I can't move. Like a cartoon character, he just hit me as hard as he can with a skateboard that is almost as big as he is, but I don't feel it, not at all.

Thud. Asian Man's friend hits me with the bat in my right arm. I heard it, but the feeling was as if my arm was wrapped by a giant pillow. I turn to the Asian Man, and he's yelling at me, something about Hawaii.

I try to reason with them, because I can't really see, and I can't really feel, and I can't really speak. I'm telling them about Hawaii and Volkswagens and fraternal brotherhood. They don't understand. I know what I'm saying, but it doesn't make sense.

Please just let me go! I yell.

I watch from somewhere just outside of me as they continue to beat me.

Thwack! with the bat.

Crack! with the skateboard.

The fifth or sixth strike to my head with the skateboard makes a new sound. Something gave way. All three of us react. The little Asian man looks concerned and backs off a bit, skateboard cocked above his head.

I want to go home now. I should have never left. I need to go home and sleep. I'm going to die if he doesn't stop. I try to move toward the street so I can run away, but they won't let me.

Asian Man does a little bullfighter parry. I'm the bull. Then again with the chopping motion.

Crack!

I'm gonna die.

I don't know if I just said that, but I know he realizes it and is thinking about whether he wants to kill me.

Thud! This one lands on my shoulder. Did he break my arm?

I gather all my will and decide to throw a kick. The thought passes my brain and travels down to my hapless limb, and the Asian man casually steps back as I fall. I'm a tranquilized bear. He's laughing, and his friend says something, something about stopping my beating.

Thwack!

Seriously man, you better stop.

I lunge toward the street while pulling up my jeans. I fall and drag my leg against the asphalt. It bleeds like a broken catsup bottle. I rise and hear sirens coming from all around, helicopter, *chop-chop-chop-chop.* I look back. People are gathering toward Pico. I'm running, barefoot and shirtless. I dive into a bush near the porch of someone's sweet little home.

Police show in force. They shine their spotlight. I don't want to get shot.

I'm here, I yell.

I stand and raise my hands in the air. They go berserk. Guns drawn, screaming. Get down, turn around! Handcuffs and pats and yelling and loud radios and spinning colors, as in my head when I was just in that dark room with the angry Asian man, spinning around like a fat palsied ballerina. The radios—loud and squawking: crackle, static, pop.

Stretcher, ambulance, and then blackness.

My contacts feel as if they've been transformed into miniature potato chips, fused to my corneas. My whole body buzzes from massive quantities of nicotine. My kidneys are pulsating, trying to escape through my back. My mouth is gummy from dehydration, and I am desperately thirsty. This is the all-too-familiar physical sensation I feel upon waking from a night of drinking. I know from experience that this is just the starting point. The real pain comes when my brain begins functioning. I want to go back to sleep before this happens.

Too late.

The realization that I've probably blown an appointment vacuums out my lungs. I try to regain my breath, and I'm hit with it. I was supposed to meet Will and Dr. Lee at Brookside. We have a 7:00 a.m. tee time. *Fuck!* Dr. Lee flew in from Singapore the night before last. *Jesus Christ!* I brace myself to open my aching eyes so I can see the alarm clock. Maybe things are okay. Maybe it's still early. I haven't heard my cell phone or my alarm clock. I take a deep breath and swing my legs around, while I pry open my eyes. My right leg slams into something hard. My ankle blurts out with pain. My wrist is held back, and I hear metal slide on metal. My vision is fuzzy, but I can tell it's dark outside and the lights are on in this room, very on. A firm hand presses down on my shoulder, easing me back into bed.

"Take it easy."

My eyes focus. There is a young uniformed police officer standing over me.

"Take it easy," he repeats. "There is nothing you can do right now."

Fuck. This is not my room and not my bed. It's a hospital bed. There is a cop standing over me, and I have an IV in my arm. *Very Fuck.*

I sit up, mouth agape, searching my memory for an explanation. It pours in like a horror montage: The Liquid Kitty; the front door of the massage parlor on Pico; a dark room with a loud industrial hum; swinging fists, struggling with someone in the dark, angry yelling; flashing red, green, and blue lights; sirens, cops, black handguns, *Get down!*, handcuffs; ambulance. It all had something to do with the Oriental massage parlor by my house.

I don't remember being with one of the girls. I remember the girl at the bar with the shiny hair, but she left with her friends. Nothing makes any sense. It wouldn't have been open after the Liquid Kitty closed. I know better than to go to a massage parlor at night. I've been to dozens of massage parlors, hundreds of times. I've never been late at night. But I must have.

The young cop says something, but I can't hear what he says through the blaring in my head. He has kind eyes. He leaves for just a moment and returns with a tall thin lady doctor, like one from a medical soap opera. She has a shiny instrument with a trigger. I'm sorry she has had to wake up to deal with me. She's probably married and has kids and lives in Beverly Hills. I picture her in bed with her husband when her pager sounds. He stirs and she kisses him, and she gets up and checks the number. It's a medical emergency, sure enough. She tells him, "Go back to sleep, honey; I'll be back soon."

She applies alcohol to my head with an oversized Q-tip. She has the fingers of a pianist. She holds the gun to my head.

"This is going to hurt, so brace yourself."

I grip the bed railings tightly and clench my jaw.

Chikew! The brassy sound echoes off the hard-lit sterile white walls. She stands back and observes me. She looks bewildered at my lack of reaction.

A memory pops. It was the two Asian guys in the front yard across from the massage parlor. They were yelling at me and taking turns whacking me. I remember thinking to myself that I should be feeling something; that if he kept hitting me he would kill me.

"That didn't hurt?" the doctor asks, rhetorically.

It didn't. She does it again and again. Each time the loud, brassy sound ricochets off the walls offending what should be the quietest time of the night. She is stapling my scalp back together, but the procedure is no more painful than a haircut. I open my eyes. She looks at me again. She's puzzled at my lack of pain, and she is disgusted by me. She is disgusted by me, because I'm disgusting. *You're right, Lady Doctor, and I'm sorry.*

It turns out I'm not in a hospital, just a medical room in the police station. The doctor finishes, and the cop takes me to use the phone. After my drunk driving accident, I never thought I'd have another "one phone call", but here I am, in the Santa Monica Police Station, in the same building where I had my first law school moot court competition ten years earlier. I've handled several cases in this building; I even know a couple of the judges.

I call Keri, my ex-girlfriend/criminal defense attorney, and after a disheartening number of rings, she finally picks up.

"Keri, Oh, you picked up," I say, relieved. "Thank God. Uh ... I'm in trouble, and I need you to come bail me out."

"Joseph ... *serious?* Are you drunk?"

"Yes, I'm drunk and no, I mean yes, I'm serious."

"Where are you?"

"Santa Monica jail."

Keri sighs deeply into the receiver. It's the sound of exasperated disappointment that I became so familiar with during our tumultuous relationship and during her handling of my felony DUI case.

"What are you being charged with?"

"I uh ... I ... well, don't know exactly ... probably ... uh ... solicitation?"

"*Solicitation of what?*"

"Uh ..." I realize there is no good way to say it, so I just say it, "prostitution."

"*Prostitution?*"—She sighs again, louder this time. "Joseph, *really?*"

"Well, I don't know, really. It could be anything. I was *really* wasted. Actually, I still am. I don't remember much. You'll find out when you get here. Just hurry up, and bail me out, okay?"

I'm taken to a holding cell. I'm by myself. There is a big steel door, and I stare at it wondering who will come through it. It's been at least two hours, and still no Keri. I shiver as cold alcohol and nicotine-laced sweat leaches out of my pores. A merciful lady cop brings me an itchy, gray, wool blanket and gives me a tight smile, as if she's looking at a rabid dog that used to be a cute family pet but now must be put down. The blanket doesn't stop me from shivering. As I sober up I begin to feel the gravity of my predicament. I'm in jail, and I'm probably in trouble again. *How embarrassing.* Pain radiates through to my back. I squeeze my arms tightly against my stomach to contain the pain. I wait and wait, but still no Keri. Maybe she's decided to let me sit in here a while to teach me a lesson. I should have told her that I need to get out as soon as possible so I can call Will and tell him I'm sick and can't make it to meet him and Dr. Lee—if it's not already too late.

I recall some mental snapshots of the night but nothing new. I'm starting to feel crawly. This is what happens after I binge drink. I need another drink so I can come down easy. I wish Keri would come get me out of here. I need a cold beer right away. I just want to shut my eyes and wake up in my bed. I shut my eyes, but I start to see a kaleidoscope of ants in red, and blue flashes of light. God, I just want to be in my bed. I wish I'd not gone out drinking. Just this once, I wish I'd done the right thing.

Keri finally arrives. The lady cop takes me to a visiting booth. Plexiglas separates Keri and me. She looks scared. Her full lips are white, and her eucalyptus-colored eyes washed gray. She holds her mouth tight.

"Goddamn, Keri, what took you so long?" I ask through the telephone receiver.

"I was meeting with the detectives. You wouldn't believe what I had to do to see you. They didn't want to let me see you."

"What? Why? I figured you were dealing with bail."

Keri is acting odd, even for this situation. She should be mad at me for waking her up, not to mention for getting arrested again after she finally settled my drunk driving case. There is something else, something grave; she looks like she used to look when we lived together in law school, and I'd hold her in the middle of the night after she'd woken up from a nightmare.

"What's the deal, Keri? When do I get out of here?"

She stares right at me, then down, then into my eyes again. I know that move. She's about to cry, but this time she doesn't. Instead, she shuts her eyes for a long moment. When she opens her eyes, she has her lawyer mask on.

"You don't understand," Keri says. "Don't say anything to anyone." She speaks with a slow solemnity that makes me realize that she must be right. Suddenly, things have become terribly serious.

"Keri, what am I being charged with?"

She takes a deep breath in through her teeth and then blows it out hard.

"You are being charged with Attempted Murder."

Part I

Joseph and his mom, Marie, lived in the Alley. The Alley housed a strip of one-story, duplex bungalows that were built in the late 1800s for the servants who worked in the homes that fronted Lime Street. Those homes, the backyards of which abutted the Alley, were massive three-story Victorians, owned by affluent Riverside families. The homes had long since been chopped up into single-resident occupancies and were visibly dilapidated. As was the entire neighborhood, the Alley was a mixture of drug addicts, welfare moms, parolees, and five-to-a-room Mexican families. After Marie's arrest, when she was twenty-five and Joseph eight, they moved to the Alley so that Marie could be close to the methadone clinic. Under the terms of Marie's plea bargain, in exchange for her guilty plea to solicitation of heroin, she was placed on probation and required to go on methadone. By doing so, she avoided a felony child endangerment charge and was able to retain custody of Joseph.

It was the middle of the night and pitch black in Joseph's bedroom when he got up to go pee. This was a near nightly occurrence, which was the result of his other nightly ritual. He'd stand at the kitchen sink and gulp two full tumblers of tap water just before his most cherished and long standing nightly ritual. Then he'd yell, *Mom, I'm ready for bed*, those words, exactly, every time; and Marie would come into his room, tuck him into bed, kiss him good-night, turn off the lights, and close the door behind her. He didn't know it, but his usual state of feeling was fear. Fear of the known and fear of the unknown. It sat in his stomach; it followed him while he walked the streets and rode his bike. Getting into bed, snuggling tight with his head under the covers after Marie kissed him good-night, it was the only time he felt safe. There was no nightlight in his bedroom. His old night-light was lost in the move from Sunnymead to the Alley, which was much more like a witness-relocation than a move. Marie even left their cat behind, and Joseph didn't even ask what happened to it.

Joseph felt his way to the bathroom door. The doorknob, which looked like a piece of glass that was cut to resemble a diamond, was a precarious device. The spindle was stripped, and if turned forcefully, it would fall out and crash onto the hardwood floor. The latch suffered from the mechanical equivalent of *rigor mortis,* and the door itself was so swollen it could only be partially closed with a move that involved popping one's shoulder into the door—a mini open-ice, ice hockey check.

Joseph opened the door silently. He had to. He didn't want to wake Marie up, not because she'd be mad but because Joseph knew, the way his lungs knew to breathe, that it was critical that he not cause any noise, not draw attention to himself, and most importantly, not cause a hassle. There is nothing important enough—not food, shelter, safety, or health—worthy of causing a hassle or drawing attention to oneself. This motto was engraved on the family crest that was far too much of a hassle to create. The concept had been passed down from Joseph's grandpa to his mother and now to Joseph. Although, he couldn't articulate it any more than a sea bass could address the topic of saltwater, it was this all-important principle, the prohibition against hassle and avoidance of attention and embarrassment, which subconsciously colored Joseph's every decision and his every move. He was a ghost and needed nothing—nothing at all. This was the real reason he didn't want to wake Marie, not just because she needed her usual fifteen hours of sleep.

It was too dark to see the bathroom floor. He could barely see the outline of his own feet. But he knew there was much more afoot than the faded yellow dirty tiles. Joseph slowly placed his left foot on the cold tile. He thought about what might happen, and the willies shot through him, as if he'd bitten into a banana peel. He followed with his right foot and then his left again. One more step and he'd be able to reach the light switch. He went for it. The sound was a crunch, like stepping on a light bulb, and then there was a *squish* as the gooey liquid shot out between his toes. For a moment he felt as if he might vomit.

Joseph turned on the light. The yellow tiles were eclipsed by a carpet of scurrying cockroaches. Like his mother, they did not like the light. They ran for shelter. They ran in and out the dirty grout and disappeared into the seams of the baseboards and the spaces where the silicone seal had rotted away between the bathtub and floor. Barging in on the cockroaches had become a nightly occurrence. He watched as the cockroaches scattered to the perimeter like marbles rolling away from a bulging center. The tile floor reappeared. Only one runt cockroach remained. There was always that one straggler cockroach that was left behind. Usually Joseph squashed it with one of his mom's old *Cosmopolitan* magazines. But that night he had a feeling, a strong feeling, that he shouldn't kill this underdog cockroach. Not only did he not want to kill it, he wanted it to survive. Joseph watched it navigate the edge of the wall beside the toilet until it disappeared into a crack in the baseboard.

There was no toilet paper left, so Joseph scraped cockroach exoskeleton and juice off the sole of his foot with the edge of a toilet paper roll. This one was big enough to have a personality.

Marie and Joseph stopped by a neighbor's house so Marie could get high before going to the methadone clinic. The neighbor was a straggly-haired, burnt-out Vietnam vet that seemed to always have Roller Derby on TV and a hot dog boiling on the stove. Joseph didn't mind stopping by, even though the cockroaches were so bad that they didn't even pretend to hide. Joseph always got a hot dog out of the deal, and Marie was calmer after she took a few hits from the bong.

They left and walked down the Alley hand in hand. Joseph looked down at a wide crack in the cement where a little dark puddle of dried blood marked the spot of Joseph's first fight. When they first moved to the Alley a few months ago, Joseph befriended a group of boys. He tried to fit in, but the whole thing made him nervous. Joseph was soft and white and quiet, and they were tough and brown and loud. Playing with them, he thought, was only slightly better than being by himself. After Joseph tagged the wrong boy in a game of team tag, the eight other boys turned against Joseph. The group's bully-leader called Joseph names, mostly in Spanish, although there were a couple insults in English, aimed at Joseph's prominent nose, something about a parrot. Despite Joseph's near-pleading apologies, the mood turned frantic as it became clear that the bully wasn't going to let it go. The other boys rallied around and began yelling and chanting. Joseph tried to get away, but all the other boys surrounded him and the bully in a half-circle against a wall of thick bushes. Without even an attempt at defense, let alone offense, Joseph ended up on the ground crying and bleeding, while the bully beat and kicked him under the chants of the other boys. The pain of the beating was dull under the humiliation. Joseph remembered the sounds of the yapping boys. Now, walking with Marie, he saw himself curled up on the asphalt with his eyes closed, accepting the barrage of punches and kicks. In the end, his only thought was that he just wanted to be in his bed under the covers. After that, Joseph never played with any of the brown boys again. If he wanted to play, he rode his bike across town where the rich white kids lived.

The methadone clinic was on the second floor of a three-story, boxy office building in downtown Riverside. Joseph enjoyed going to the methadone clinic. It was the only time he and Marie went anywhere together, except when their welfare check and food stamps came. The clinic office was full and quiet. Joseph and Marie sat in the last two unoccupied orange, yellow, and red fiberglass molded chairs that were bolted to stainless steel frames in groups of three. The drug addicts were all different: white, Mexican, black; young and old; male and female. But they were all from the same tribe. Their posture was an apology for existence. It was as if heroin caused a softening and general curvature of the skeletal system. Gravity was rough on junkies. They hung their heads, so their cigarettes pointed toward the ground, and they seemed to be guarding their chins with their shoulders like boxers. Their arms hung as if deboned. In their eyes was a look of defeat beyond defeat, especially in the old junkies, the ones with the gummy mouths; a look of people who had been irreversibly enslaved. To Joseph, Marie wasn't like these people. Sure, she was pale and skinny and smoked constantly and preferred to be in the dark, preferably asleep; she didn't eat or work, and she wore long sleeves even when it was hot out, and when she walked she shrunk into the scenery, but she wasn't like these people, these beaten junkies. She was beautiful.

There was a woman sitting in a gray metallic fold-up chair in the corner. She was a little older than Marie. Joseph recognized her. She was one of the girls that strutted up and down Market Street at night. He'd seen her leaning into the passenger side of men's car windows. Joseph relived the feeling he got when he'd see her and the other girls like her. It started as a burst of energy that shot through his entire body. Then the energy all gathered and settled into a tingly sensation in his stomach and below. Sometimes Joseph rode his bike by the girls several times, because he liked the feeling so much. The girl was much different here under the fluorescent lights. Her legs were bumpy, and her face sagged. The feeling wasn't the same. Joseph still got the feeling, but only from thinking about her out on Market Street. Joseph recalled the first time he'd seen girls like her. It was nearly a year ago on a trip with Marie to score heroin from the Mexicans in Casa Blanca. It was when Marie still had a car. The girls were on the corner by the bus station, all with big hair and exaggerated makeup, wearing skimpy skirts and dresses. They stuck out their asses and pouted for attention. That was the first time Joseph had the feeling.

The woman noticed Joseph staring at her. Her eyes were dim and revealed only exhaustion. She shifted her body so that she was facing away from him and wrapped herself tightly in her gray, hooded sweat-shirt. Her legs were exposed all the way to her ass, and the color of her skin reminded Joseph of Marie, when she was in the hospital with hepatitis. Marie's eyes were pee-yellow, and she had was so emaciated she looked like a cartoon zombie, with giant ears, like the mouse from "Tom & Jerry."

"Joseph! How are you doin' to-day?" the big black lady behind the counter asked.

"I'm good, ma'am. Thank you," Joseph replied.

"Look at those dimples," the lady said, looking at Marie, and pre-tending to squeeze Joseph's dimples from the other side of the Plexiglas that separated them.

Joseph smiled for her. He had show-quality dimples and was used to modeling them.

She reached through the opening in the Plexiglas and placed two Dixie cups down, one in front of Marie and one in front of Joseph.

"One for you, Marie, and one for you, Joseph."

Marie quickly emptied her cup, and Joseph did the same with his, which was full of delicious orange Tang.

"I'll see you next time, Joseph. You take good care of your mother, ya hear?"

Marie and Joseph left the methadone clinic and headed through the old outdoor plaza toward the bus stop. Downtown Riverside was a strange place, and Joseph knew every building, street, and store. It was in transition from rich to poor and from old to new. The old part included the Mission Inn, a resort hotel that boasted a presidential suite where Richard and Pat Nixon stayed on their honeymoon. The extra-wide Howard Taft chair was on display in the lobby. The Spanish-styled Inn was in disrepair and now more of a motel. Across from the Mission Inn was a massive modern library of bare concrete, which included a gallery space where Aunt Suzie, Marie's sister, sometimes showed her water-color paintings. There was also the normally empty Museum of Natural History, where Joseph spent hours roaming its dark, marble-floored halls, killing time and daydreaming about the Indians and their teepees and the dinosaurs. The plaza itself, its history still fully visible in the decaying storefront signage, some partially covered by realtor's "For Lease" signs, once was where well-heeled wives in dresses and hats shopped at fashionable boutiques. There were now only secondhand and knickknack stores run by Vietnamese women that spoke broken, angry English. *You no buy nothing, you go!* The plaza's walk was adorned with mature trees, rockscapes, a dry pond, and dry ministream water feature; but now the plaza had just as many slow-moving hobos barking out orders to squirrels as it did lawyers and businessmen, walking from office buildings to the courts and municipal buildings, which were now the sole going-industries of Riverside's downtown.

"Grandpa says it's dumb, right mom?" Joseph asked.

"Uh-huh," Marie answered, without realizing what Joseph was talking about until she felt the tug on her hand as Joseph moved them to get a look at the thirty-foot bright red modern geometrical sculpture.

"What is it, Mom?" Joseph asked.

"It's art, I guess," she said and shrugged, "I don't know."

Joseph remembered last Christmas when Marie's dad said that the sculpture was a ridiculous waste of taxpayers' money. Joseph kind of liked the sculpture. It was so different from everything else around it.

They continued past the Riverside Superior Courthouse. It was a traditional courthouse built at the beginning of the twentieth century and modeled after France's Gran Palais. It was solid white with a colonnaded entrance that led to a colorfully tiled decorative open rotunda. Standing high above the entrance atop the building were matching Lady of Justice statutes. To Joseph, it was the most magnificent building he'd ever seen. He often rode his bike to it and watched the lawyers and jurors come and go. The sight of it sent Joseph into a state of wonderment. Unbeknownst to Joseph, the basement of the grand courthouse was a jail where Marie had been after her first arrest for buying heroin.

"That's where they did *Kramer vs. Kramer*. Right, Mom?" Joseph didn't have to ask this. He knew it was true, because his Grandpa had said so on Christmas, right after he talked about the red sculpture.

"Yep. That's right," Marie responded. Her mind was clearly elsewhere, which made Joseph feel uneasy. He figured she was thinking about her usual problems: food and shelter. Joseph squeezed her hand and asked if she was alright. Marie didn't answer.

The bus stop was right in front of a three-story, glass building. It was tinted copper, but Joseph could still see the silhouette of people moving inside. There was lettering on the upper left corner of the building in a clean font that read, "Thomas & Colbert, Attorneys at Law." Joseph wondered if his friend's dad worked there. Collin's dad was a lawyer, and he lived in a big house in the neighborhood where Joseph started playing after his beating by the Mexican boy. Collin's dad came to Career Day at Grant Elementary School, which Joseph and Collin attended. He wore a suit and tie and shiny shoes, and talked about being a lawyer. That was when Joseph decided he wanted to be a lawyer, because, he figured, he couldn't be a lawyer and still be poor, and he'd get to go inside the Riverside Courthouse, where *Kramer vs. Kramer* was filmed.

Some poor people gathered around them waiting for the bus. This made Joseph nervous. He didn't like being around poor people. It was important not to spend time with them, act like them, or do the things they did. Joseph pulled Marie back so they were several feet away from the poor people waiting for the bus. Marie was smoking and deep in thought. Joseph gazed into Thomas & Colbert, watching the silhouettes of men at desks talking on the phone and sitting in big chairs. Some of them leaned back in their big chairs, which somehow emphasized their positions of power. Woman in flowing skirts and high heels walked in and out of the offices. Joseph could feel what it was like to be in there. Then the bus came.

Things were different since Marie was arrested and she and Joseph moved to the Alley. Before, when they lived in Sunnymead, Marie had her good days. Sometimes she cooked and cleaned the house. She hung out with Aunt Suzie and Uncle Billy and sometimes with the neighbors. Marie even worked as a cocktail waitress for a little bit. She was still losing, but at least she was trying. Now, she'd given up completely. She went to bed late and was usually asleep when Joseph came home from school after 3:00 p.m. She didn't cook or clean. The curtains were always pulled shut, and the hide-a-bed was rarely hidden. Joseph usually had to wash his clothes in the sink, because Marie almost never went to the laundromat—understandably, as it was a dangerous place in their new neighborhood. There was no food in the fridge, except for milk and bread, which Joseph would buy when he went to Sav-A-Minit to buy cigarettes for Marie. He'd buy each item separately so he'd have enough coin change leftover from the food stamps to buy cigarettes. They had a phone, but it never rang, and when it did, Marie never answered it. She was afraid it'd be Aunt Suzie or Grandpa. Joseph answered the phone, because he *hoped* it was his Aunt Suzie or Grandpa. Aunt Suzie never came to the Alley. And Grandpa only came to pick up Joseph to spend the night one Friday a month, but he never set foot in the door. Marie would stand at the screen door, revealing to her father only her shadowy silhouette, and then open the screen door just enough to let Joseph squeeze out and into the sun.

With the exception of their bimonthly walk to Sav-A-Minit, which coincided with receipt of welfare and food stamps, to buy TV dinners and black cherry soda, Marie had unofficially, and without any discussion, divested herself of the duty to feed Joseph. He was on his own, and it wasn't a problem. Joseph developed a system that included a series of alternating techniques, so that if one failed another could be utilized. It worked so well that Joseph had gone only one full day without eating twice since they'd moved to the Alley, and both these instances, Joseph recognized, were due to his own failures.

A primary source of food was the Boy's Club. During the summer, they had a sack lunch program that could get Joseph through an entire day. During the school year, they only handed out after-school snacks, usually celery sticks and peanut butter, not enough for the entire day, but a good supplement. The Boy's Club worked well, because none of Joseph's friend's from school, all rich white kids, went to the Boy's Club. Their parents wouldn't dream of letting their kids in the Boy's Club, and Joseph never mentioned the place. It was full of Mexicans and blacks and a few scraggly white kids.

Sav-A-Minit offered a secondary source of sustenance. Before Joseph's beating, one of the Mexican boys taught Joseph how to steal from Sav-A-Minit. The key was to buy something. So, Joseph would buy a few pieces of ten-cent candy and then stuff a few cheese and cracker packets, packages of graham crackers, and Butterfinger candy bars in his tube socks and jeans. The anticipation and the rush of adrenaline was an added bonus to the food.

There was also the Safeway grocery story. There he could steal food, ask women with kids, especially ones with strollers, for money, or turn in cans and bottles for change so he could buy food and candy. The bus station was also good hunting, but it was a last resort, because a lot of creeps hung out there.

During the school year, Joseph's primary technique was *sleepover hopping*. He had a rotation of four friends, whose parents let Joseph sleep over regularly. He did this so often that sometimes he wouldn't sleep in the Alley for three or four days at a time. Sometimes he called Marie to let her know, and sometimes he didn't. She didn't seem to mind too much.

Most often Joseph slept over at Collin's house. He became such a regular at Collin's house that Collin barely had to ask if Joseph could sleep over. Joseph even had his own tooth brush at Collin's house. Collin's family lived in what Joseph considered a mansion, like Aunt Suzie and Uncle Billy's house. It was a nice three-bedroom, two-story Craftsman with a yard and detached garage. It was at 773 Pine Street, which Joseph memorized the first time he stayed at Collin's house during the summer. Joseph used Collin's address so he could enroll at Grant Elementary, the same school as Collin and all the other rich white kids went. He had been signing Marie's name on his report cards, permission slips, late notes, registration forms, and anything else from the school that needed signing since they moved to the Alley.

One of the challenges of attending Grant and being in the fourth grade Gifted and Talented Education classes—"GATE"—and hanging with the rich kids was that Joseph needed brand-name clothes. If he wore Kmart clothes, everyone would know he was poor, and he knew that would ruin him. Joseph used the skills he'd acquired at Sav-A-Minit and Safeway to obtain the requisite wardrobe from Riverside's center of adolescent "haute couture": Miller's Outpost. He would go into the dressing room with a bunch of clothes, put on a couple items underneath the clothes he was wearing, and then walk out wearing them. It was very risky, and he was almost caught once. Joseph had just enough to pepper his wardrobe with a few key items: one pair of corduroy Lightning Bolt pants, two pairs of corduroy two-toned Ocean Pacific shorts, one Hang Ten half-sleeve shirts, and, his favorite, a Kennington terry cloth polo. The only thing missing were Vans slip-on shoes, but it was impossible to steal from the Vans store, so Joseph had to make due with knock-offs that his Grandpa bought him at Kmart. This was a source of constant embarrassment.

A couple days after Marie and Joseph went to the methadone clinic, Joseph went to Collin's house after school, and Collin asked his mom if he could spend the night. She said it was okay but wanted to talk to

Joseph's mom. Joseph doubted Marie would answer the phone but dialed anyway as if he was going to pass the phone to Collin's mom. This was the hard part. Even if Marie did answer, Joseph didn't like the idea of Collin's mom talking to Marie. He thought she'd find out about Marie and where Joseph lived, which would ruin everything.

Joseph dialed.

"It's ringing," Joseph said to Collin's mom as she stood next to him waiting to take the phone.

It kept ringing. Joseph worried that Collin's mom wouldn't let him stay if she didn't think his mom knew about it. He couldn't let that happen.

"Hi, Mom," Joseph said, pretending Marie was on the other end, "I had a good day at school ... uh, uh, yeah, Mom ... okay."

ring, ring

"Can I spend the night at Collin's?"

ring, ring

"Yeah, Collin's mom says it's okay."

Collin's mom impatiently motioned for Joseph to hand her the receiver.

ring, ring

"Mom, Collin's mom wants to talk to ... oh, you have to go? No, no real quick ... Oh, okay, I love you, too."

Joseph quickly hung up. Collin's mom stared at Joseph disapprovingly with her hands on her hips.

"I'm sorry. She was running late to work. She's a nurse. She told me to tell you thank you for letting me spend the night again."

Collin's mom wasn't buying it, and Joseph knew it. His face reddened.

"What's your phone number?" she asked.

Joseph told her, and she dialed. Joseph waited with his arms crossed. Marie didn't answer. Collin's mom cradled the receiver and stood thinking. Joseph wondered if she would make him leave. Collin wasn't even paying attention.

"You know our number. I want you to have your mom call me tomorrow when you get home, okay?" she instructed.

"Okay," Joseph answered.

Collin and Joseph retreated to Collin's bedroom. Collin's dad had a subscription to *Playboy*, and occasionally the timing would be right, and Collin would fish one out of the garbage can after his dad threw it away. Joseph would get the news from Collin during recess at school. "I got another one," Collin would excitedly report and then recite the calendar girl's bio: "She's twenty-two years old, 115 pounds, 36-22-34, enjoys skiing and horseback riding ...likes to walk on the beach ... Who cares! She has huge gazoongas!"

Joseph guarded the door, while Collin went into his closet and pulled out the newest addition to his growing collection of *Playboys*. They both sat against the door. Their plan was that, if someone tried to come in, Joseph would stay pressed against the door while Collin hid the magazine. They leaned against the door and gawked at the centerfold of Ms. September. She wore pink leg warmers and nothing else. She looked like Snow White but without a dress on. She had thick, black hair and pink nipples, and perfect liquid white skin, and she was curvy but thin too. Ms. September's lips were full and pouty like the photo was taken just before she was going to say a word that started with the letter "p." Girls didn't look like this, Joseph thought, except on television, like in "Three's Company", "Charlie's Angels" and "CHiPs".

The next day Collin's mom took Joseph and Collin to the Tyler Mall Movie Theater for a matinee to see *Flash Gordon*, while she and Collin's little sister shopped at the Tyler Mall. Tim, another friend from school, joined them at the movies. Joseph was really excited. He'd only been to the movies twice before with Aunt Suzie. When the boys got back, Collin's dad, the lawyer, was home. He was still in his gray suit, but his tie was undone and draped around his neck. Joseph, Tim, and Collin went to Collin's room. They took turns playing *Flash Gordon* versus *Star Wars* characters.

"I'm Emperor Ming. I'm going to destroy you, Flash Gordon!" Collin squinted with villainous boldness as he spoke to Tim, playing the role of Flash Gordon.

"I'm not Flash Gordon, faggot!" Tim responded. Tim was the most popular kid in fourth grade, and he was a red belt in karate and used words, like *faggot* and even *fuck*. Tim hung out with fifth graders a lot and even had a girlfriend. Joseph tried to pretend he wasn't scared of Tim, but he was.

Tim and Collin spent a few minutes sword fighting with Collin's two plastic *Star Wars* light sabers, and it looked like Emperor Ming, now played by Tim, was going to win, but then Joseph joined the fracas.

"I'm Darth Vader, and you're a bogus butthead," Joseph declared in his deepest voice, imitating the heavy-breathing villain.

Despite Tim's physical dominance and dread at losing at anything, he conceded the superiority of *Star Wars* over *Flash Gordon*, which was not even a point of contention, and allowed Darth Vader—borrowing Flash Gordon's *Star Wars* light saber from Collin—to cut off Emperor Ming's head and then Flash Gordon's. Joseph declared the obvious: *Star Wars* rules and *Flash Gordon* sucks!

And then they switched it up so that everyone was a *Star Wars* character, which led to Joseph's character's quick demise, by decapitation, followed by a fierce battle between Tim and Collin, which became heated. Tim was a tournament karate fighter, but Collin was bigger and a CYA club soccer standout and all-around good athlete. Neither liked to lose, and it got ugly. Joseph stood by uncomfortably, hoping it would end without Collin's mom intervening or anyone getting too mad, and most importantly, without his involvement. It was when Han Solo, a.k.a. Collin, had nearly submitted Luke Skywalker, a.k.a. Tim, via a full nelson that Collin's dad opened the door carrying a pizza box and wearing a baseball cap backward like a catcher. Collin let loose of Tim, and they both sprang to their feet.

"Yo. Yo. Yuze guyz ordered a pizza pie?" Collin's dad asked, imitating a guido.

"Dad, don't be stupid," Collin said, still out of breath.

"I don't know what you are talkin' 'bout. My name's-a-Anton-i-o, and I got a delivery of a pepperoni pizza pie for some guy named Collin ... but if uze guyz don't want this delicious pizza pie, I bet I could find somebody who does."

Collin's dad walked out and shut the door behind him, and for a second, Joseph and Tim thought Collin blew it, and that they had forfeited the pizza. They both looked at Collin with disappointment.

"Dude!" Tim said.

"My dad's just being stupid," Collin assured Tim and Joseph.

Collin's dad opened the door, still in character.

"It's uze guyz again! I must be lost ..."

Joseph and Tim laughed. Collin rolled his eyes.

"He sounds like Vinnie Barbarino!" Tim said pointing at Collin's dad.

"No," Joseph said, "Bowzer from Sha Na Na!"

Even Collin started laughing.

"I told uze guyz," Collin's dad said, pretending to be confused, "I'm Antonio, and I gots-a-delivery of this here uh-delicious pizza pie. You gonna eat it or you gonna sleep with the fishes. Am I makin' myself clear?"

Collin's dad winked at Collin. Joseph wondered what it would be like to be Collin. Tim had a piece of pizza in his mouth before Collin's dad shut the door behind him. They played some more, and later, Collin's mom and dad made root-beer floats for the boys and Collin's little sister. In the morning, Collin's dad made pancakes. It was one of the best times Joseph ever had. For a little while he forgot about the Alley.

Collin asked if Joseph could stay the night again, but Collin's mom said he couldn't, because they had too much to do. Collin's piano teacher came over, so it was just Joseph and Collin's mom in the car. She didn't say anything on the entire ride over, and he could tell she was concerned about something. She pulled up across the street from the house where Joseph usually had her drop him off.

It was a nice little house with a big porch. Joseph picked the house as his fake house, because it was nice and looked like no one was ever home. Collin's mom dropped Joseph off at the fake house several times before, usually with Collin and Collin's little sister. Joseph would walk up the steps and wave good-bye and wait for Collin's mom to drive away and turn the corner, before he left and walked the half-mile back to the Alley. But this time, someone was home. It was an elderly Mexican woman, and she was playing in the yard with two toddlers. They must have been her granddaughters.

"Your mom and sisters?" Collin's Mom asked. She raised her eyebrows, but her voice was more sad than sarcastic.

Joseph had no answer. He stared into his lap.

"Where do you *really* live?" she asked.

Joseph felt shame wash over him, and he squeezed the muscles in his face as tight as he could to stop from crying. He paused to gather himself. He pretended he hadn't heard her question.

"Thanks for the movies ... for letting me spend the night ... and the pizza," he said, pausing to squeeze back the tears.

Joseph diverted his eyes and jumped out of the car and briskly walked off.

"Joseph please ... What's the matter?"

Joseph turned and waved good-bye as he crossed the street. She followed him and rolled down the electric passenger window of her Mercedes sedan.

"Joseph!" she shouted out the passenger window. "C'mon, Hon. Get in. I'll take you home."

Joseph ignored her and kept walking, and then darted around a corner so that she couldn't follow him. As he walked, he thought of how he would never see her again and that he would never sleep over at Collin's again, not after what had just happened, not now that she knew.

He thought about how she was so different from his mom. She was probably ten years older, and she had so many things. She spent more time cooking than Marie spent awake. Joseph loved Marie more than anything, and he knew she would be more like Collin's mom, if his dad hadn't left Joseph and Marie when Joseph was six weeks old. Joseph's dad was mean and drank beer, and, Joseph thought, *so what if he bought me a bike?* Collin had a bike and a piano and two *Star Wars* light sabers, and a dresser full of Ocean Pacific, Lightning Bolt, and Offshore clothes. Collin even had two pairs of Vans. Collin lived in a house in a nice neighborhood. Collin had a sister and got to play soccer, and his mom packed his lunches. Collin didn't even think all that stuff was a big deal, because he was so used to it. Collin's dad even bought pizza and made funny jokes. Joseph's dad didn't even pay child support. Joseph knew that because he heard Marie on the phone with Grandpa, asking for money, and that's what she said. Joseph knew it was all because of his dad.

He crossed the street at Lemon and walked around the block to avoid the house where the Mexican bully that beat him up lived. He was sure it'd happen again if the bully saw him. Joseph crossed through a partly boarded-up apartment complex that his grandpa said looked like Beirut, and climbed the wall where the coin laundry room was and went through a field. There were certain houses and blocks near the Alley that were best to avoid, especially on foot.

Joseph reached the corner just before the Alley, where he saw red lights spinning off the mulberry bush at the mouth of the Alley. He'd seen lights like that many times before. It was either a police car or an ambulance. Someone overdosed or one of the old people died, he thought. Joseph ran toward the lights to see what was going on. Three police cars were in front of their apartment. He ran past the cop car blocking the entrance to the Alley, and a cop half-heartedly tried to stop him. Two police units were squeezed in the driveway. Marie stood at the front door, smoking and staring at the cops' feet. Broken, green, clear, and brown glass was everywhere. The concrete was covered with sheets of it, and splatter marks covered the off-white stucco wall of the apartment. It was obvious to Joseph that the Mexican men that always drank at night, the ones Marie always ignored when they whistled at her and said things in Spanish, had thrown beer bottles against the apartment.

Joseph felt his face redden and his insides drop heavily. Something was terribly wrong.

"Mom!" Joseph screamed.

He tried to run into the house, but one of the police officers that was talking to Marie turned and blocked the door. Marie was draped in Joseph's brown cowboy blanket, the one Aunt Suzie took to summer camp when she was a kid. Marie's face was pink and puffy, and one eye was swollen shut. She was smoking hard. The living room was torn up and the bedding on her hide-a-bed was tangled up into a ball.

"Joseph, it's alright," Marie cried out. She broke through the police officers. "He's my son."

She hugged Joseph tightly.

"Mom, what happened? Are you alright? I was at Collin's ... I'm sorry ..."

Marie began to cry. "It's alright. It's not your fault," she said and hugged him tightly. "I love you."

A lady police officer took Joseph away. He sat in the front seat. He asked what happened to his mother and where they were going. The lady cop kept her eyes on the road and said, "Don't worry. You're going to be alright." They rode in silence, and only the occasional squawking of the police radio interrupted the silence.

"Four-eight-two, do you copy? Four, eighty-two," the police dispatcher over the radio sounded.

"Copy, go ahead." The lady copy responded.

"We have Suzie Waltson on the way to take custody of the minor on the 261. Copy that?"

Joseph was staring out the window listening in his periphery, but the sound of his aunt's name over the radio brought him to attention.

Apparently, the lady cop was affected, too, because she fumbled the radio handset awkwardly and said *dammit,* while trying to respond before the dispatcher continued.

"283 is taking victim to Riverside General for a rape kit. No perpetrator in custody..."

The dispatcher's voice cut off when the lady cop spoke into the handset.

"Copy. I'm with minor child. Radio silence on details, copy that?"

"Sorry. Copy that," the voice over the radio sounded back.

THREE

It was the beginning of my junior year in high school, 1987. My mom was off heroin, but she was still a chain-smoking depressive that preferred sleeping and TV to all else. We moved from the Alley to the gnarliest apartment complex in the city, ironically named *The Tennis Club Apartments.* The reference to "tennis" had to do with fenced-in patches of cement, where dirty toddlers played crash derby with shopping carts, while their adolescent older brothers practiced their tagging skills on the previously green cement surface. Red spray paint was for Bloods and blue was for Crips. Presumably, there used to be nets, but all that was left on each "court" were two stubby posts. The apartment complex was a hodgepodge of white trash, black gang-bangers, speed freaks, and Mexican families.

We lived with Carlos, my mom's boyfriend. He was bipolar, and his Social Security Disability paid the rent. Carlos wasn't so bad when my mom met him in the Alley six years ago, but since then his marijuana habit had evolved into a meth addiction, his general stupidity had transmuted to full-fledged paranoia, and his fondness for guns had become an obsession. Carlos usually woke up around noon. His day then consisted of paging through back issues of *Guns & Ammo* and *Soldier of Fortune* and watching late night TV. He had an *Of Mice and Men*-Lenny-like sidekick named Brian. Brian wasn't mean spirited like Carlos, but he would do anything Carlos told him to do. Long after my mom had gone to bed for the night, Carlos, and sometimes Brian, would sit in front of the TV with TV trays, atop of which would be splayed parts from a disassembled radio, blender, speaker, minivac, pistol, rifle, motorcycle engine part, or stereo component. Whatever it happened to be on a particular night, it was going to be torn apart, cleaned, re-rewired, and re-rebuilt. With the exception of the guns, which Carlos was in the business of selling, the items had little chance of ever functioning correctly again.

I spent as little time as I could at the apartment. I got up early and walked to my best friend Rex's house so I could get a ride to school with him and his mom. I left school before last period so I could make it to work by 3:00 p.m. I'd walk to the apartment, which was two miles; then I'd ride my ten-speed to Parker's Sporting Goods. It closed at nine, and we'd usually count out, lock up, and get out by 9:30. Half the time, I'd ride to Rex's house and sleep there, and the other half I'd go to the apartment. If Carlos was home, I'd crawl in through my bedroom window. I'd go to sleep and do it again. I usually worked a full day, and a half-day on the weekends, so there wasn't much time for anything else. I made enough money to pay for all my own food and clothes, and I was saving for a car. When I wasn't at school or work, I was usually at Rex's house.

Rex looked like me. We were both tall, blonde, and had blue eyes. He played guitar and was into music and was always turning me on to different bands. He had crates of albums and a turntable that used to be his dad's. We listened to punk rock, speed metal, rap, and reggae. We sat in his room and just talked and listened to music: Bad Brains, Youth of Today, Excel, Metallica, Slayer, Van Halen, Agnostic Front, Suicidal Tendencies, Dead Kennedy's, Blast!, NWA, Run DMC, Minor Threat, Jimmy Cliff, and Peter Tosh. We'd talk about which girls we liked, which ones were the *finest* and why, and what we were going to do when we got jobs and what cars we were going to drive. We were both going to be lawyers, and we were going to buy matching black BMW M3s.

Rex knew everything about me except one thing. It was something I didn't tell anyone. It was what happened with Vanessa. It was last year before I was dating Beth. I called the 976-SURF line to check the surf, and after I hung up, it suddenly occurred to me to call a 976 sex line. After a couple tries, I found Vanessa at 976-TITS. The whole thing lasted only a couple minutes, but it was like I'd discovered the perfect drug.

I felt so naughty as Vanessa described to me her enormous … soft … milky … double D … tits and then how she was sucking my big … fat … hard … cock. My only response was a muffled uh-huh, uh-uh, uh-uh. I'd masturbated hundreds of times before, but this was something different. My whole body became my cock. I'd never felt anything so powerful. Every bit of pure pleasure was extracted out of every cell of my body, and then I squeezed the receiver so hard I thought it would crack. Vanessa continued describing a blow job, now adding slurping sounds. I let my muscles relax, caught my breath, and came back out to the world. I was immediately engulfed in shame and disgust. And then I realized that my 976 call was going to show up on my mom's phone bill. No problem, I reasoned, it just happened once, I'll tell her it was a misdial … It will never ever, ever happen again.

Fifteen minutes later: I already did it once, I thought, what does it matter if I do it one more time? I tried to call Vanessa, but it was a different girl. I frantically kept on dialing, trying every seven number combo I could think of. 976-HOT-FUCK, 976 BIG TITS, 976 HOT XXXX, 976 HORNY69, 976 PLAYBOY, 976 69WHORE, 976-REDHEAD, 976-WHATEVER.

I spent the next month chasing Vanessa, trying to get that feeling back. I came every time, and it was good, but it was never the same as the explosion I'd had with Vanessa. Each time I called I'd swear on a stack of babies that I'd never ever, ever—and this time I mean it—call again, and each time I meant it—I really meant it. After an ordeal with the phone company, which involved me intercepting the eight hundred dollar phone bill and calling the phone company pretending to be my dad, and settling for a couple hundred bucks, a 976 phone block was put on our phone. I knew I couldn't be trusted, so I was relieved.

❖   ❖   ❖

Rex and I were waiting in the snack bar line at lunch talking to Beth and Elsa. It was a Friday before a football game, and they both had their cheerleading uniforms on. Beth had blue eyes, hair the color of fire, and freckles across her little nose. I had a huge crush on her, and I was long overdue to ask her out.

"Are you going to the game tonight?" Beth asked me. Her question took a long time to register, because all I could think about was how much of a wimp I was for not asking her out.

"Oh, yeah…" I responded, as if I'd just decoded her question. "I mean, no, I have to work."

"Oh … well, Elsa and I are going to be at Rocky's Pizza after …" she trailed off.

I could feel Rex and Elsa, both who knew that I'd had a crush on Beth for months, stop talking to each other, and subtly focus on me to see if I was going to ask Beth out.

"Oh, that'll be fun," I said.

I wanted to kick myself for wimping out again. What the hell was a matter with me? I'd never kissed a girl let alone had sex. Rex and Elsa continued the conversation, trying to steer it back so I could have another opportunity.

"Well, after your work, we could probably stop by Rocky's. Right, Joseph?" Rex asked.

"Yeah, I uh—" Midsentence I felt a shove from behind. I turned and saw the back of a letterman jacket. It read, "Bomb Squad," and had an embroidered graphic of a squadron of World War II planes dropping footballs. It belonged to Clarence, our football team's star receiver.

I cleared my throat to get Clarence's attention. He turned around.

"Yeah," Clarence said defiantly.

The look in his eyes was not one of contrition. I wish I wouldn't have reacted, but it was too late.

"Dude, you bumped into me, and we've been waiting in line for a long time.." I said and paused to look back at my friends for some type of support, "... It's not cool to cut in front of us."

Clarence pushed his nose right into mine and said, "What the fuck are you going to do about it faggot?"

I stepped back. *"Dude,* why are you getting all—"

Clarence pushed me with both hands so hard I fell back and flipped head-over-heels, off the concrete and into the soppy grass. I stood up as quickly as I went down and brushed myself off. The knees of my jeans were thick with mud. Clarence glared at me, saw that I wasn't going to retaliate, and turned back away. Rex and Beth continued chatting, obviously trying to act as if nothing had happened. I stared at the ground, turned red with humiliation. I fought back the tears. I couldn't speak. I just nodded as Rex and Beth continued talking, although I couldn't make out a word they were saying. The bell rang before we even made it to the front of the line, but I didn't go to class.

I spent the rest of the day and night in my room at the Tennis Club Apartments thinking. I kept reliving it, re-feeling how humiliated I was. What would have happened if I wouldn't have backed down? Maybe he would have punched me in the face. I've been punched in the face before. It didn't hurt that much, not as much as being a coward.

I sat up in bed, in the dark. I punched myself in the thigh as hard as I could. It hurt. I could really feel it. I did it again. Then I started thinking of bullies: the Mexican kid who punched me in the Alley, the kid who called me "welfare boy" in front of all the other kids at soccer practice. Then I started thinking about my dad and Carlos, men I hated. It was pitch black, and my brain was so loud I couldn't hear the TV from the living room anymore. I slammed my head back against the wall and dented the drywall. Carlos hollered something over the TV. I started breathing hard. I was so tired of being afraid of everything and everybody. I was so tired of working so hard and never getting anything. None of my friends had to work a full-time job. They didn't have to pay for their own food and deal with their mom's scumbag boyfriend. They got to play sports, and their parents paid for it and drove them. *I'm fucking tired of this.*

I woke up the next morning and called Rex and let him know I wasn't going to school. Later, I called Tony, my manager at Parker's Sporting Goods, and told him I was sick and wouldn't be coming in. I got on my bike and rode a couple miles across town and joined Gene Brigham's Kung Fu San Soo. It was a dojo with a weight-lifting gym, and I started lifting weights right there and then. I had no idea how to do it. I just copied a guy in the gym. As I pressed on the leg sled and pushed on the bench press, I thought, *never again, never again.*

Never again would I be afraid to fight. I decided that I'd rather die fighting than be humiliated by anyone ever again. I decided that if I wanted something, I was going to ask for it, and if that didn't work, I was going to fight for it, and if that didn't work, I was going to take it. Fuck embarrassment. Fuck being afraid. *Never again.* It was the fall of my junior year of high school.

It's the end of my senior year. I am different now. Things are different. I have a car. I'm dating Beth. I'm lean from lifting weights. I stopped playing kung fu, and now I train kickboxing and Muay Thai. Rex and I built a kickboxing gym in his garage. We have weights, a heavy bag, a double-end bag, a speed bag, and mirrors for shadow boxing and jumping rope. We spar until one of us can't go on, usually Rex. For months now I've wanted someone to pick on me at school, preferably Clarence. I wanted revenge. I kept waiting for the opportunity. I waited for him to cut in line or pick on someone I knew. I kept waiting, and it seemed like I'd never get the opportunity. Then, as I walked to my locker, I saw Clarence in the snack bar line talking to another kid I knew who used to come into Parker's Sporting Goods. It was perfect. I cut right in line in front of Clarence. I put my back to him and started talking to the kid I knew, loudly.

"What's up, man? You don't mind if I cut in do you?"

He just raised his eyebrows and shook his head. I think we were both waiting for Clarence to react.

"Hey, man, what's up?" Clarence challenged aggressively, with a just a hint of hesitation.

I turned to Clarence, and leaned in close enough to kiss him. I felt crazed. I stared at him unblinkingly.

"Nothing, man. Nothin's up? What's up with you?" I said.

Clarence stepped back from me and looked at his friend and said, "Dude's weird." Clarence handed his friend some change and said, "get me some Corn Nuts." And then he left. I stared him down as he walked away.

Now I do everything as if failure will kill me. I have a 4.0 GPA. I lift weights and train kickboxing until my body won't go on. When Rex and I surf, I pretend that I'm going to drown if I don't catch the wave. I go to work early and leave late. I hustle from the minute I clock in until the minute I clock out. I have a gorgeous, sweet girlfriend who I'm madly in love with and hope to marry. Things couldn't be better. I know I'll never be poor or afraid again.

It's the summer before college, and I spend most of my time with Beth at her parents' house. Beth has an older sister that still lives at the house, but she spends most of the time at her boyfriend's house, so sometimes when she's gone, I spend the night in Beth's sister's room. Beth's dad, Dale, is a truck driver from Missouri. I think he's been through the ringer in a past life. He has a tattoo of a woman's name, Cathy, or maybe Cyndi, on his arm crossed out, then another crossed out, L-something short, probably Lisa, and then an eagle and crest type thing trying to cover the whole mess up. Dale is so reformed from something, sin, I suppose, that he's become a fire-and-brimstone Southern Baptist preacher. The problem is that nobody shows up in his church, which is a room he rents at the Masonic Temple every Sunday morning. I attend out of respect, but it's downright embarrassing to attend a church with only six people sitting in the stackable plastic chairs that second as pews. This number includes both of his daughters, his wife, who plays the piano, and both his daughters' boyfriends. The only person outside the family is one of Dale's fellow truck drivers and his wife, and every once in a while, a black woman and her two young boys.

I like Preacher Dale, though. He is a man of God, and he's got no quit in him. It doesn't matter how many people show up Sunday morning, he's firing the Good Word like a rusty shotgun. We're all *sinners in the hands of an angry God* in Dale's church. I've been a proud atheist since I read a book my mom had when we lived in the Alley, something about Darwin and the Galapagos Islands, but Dale has knocked me down one notch into an agnostic. I don't care if he's delusional or not; Preacher Dale is a good man. He gets up early and studies the Bible. He's a teamster and shows up for his job driving a truck for Weyerhaeuser every day. When he isn't at work or studying the Bible, he is working in the yard, washing the cars, or changing the oil. He wears thick red suspenders, Wrangler jeans, and boots. Preacher Dale takes care of his two girls and his wife. He builds stuff. He's been in the army. That's where he learned to tie a Double Windsor. Dale taught me to tie a Double Windsor, how to shave, how to change my car's oil, how to change a flat tire, and even how to properly wash and wax a car. I even help Dale in the yard sometimes, and he showed me how to adjust the choke on the lawn mower.

I'm technically still living at my mom's apartment, at least that's where I keep my stuff. I bought my first car during my senior year, a 1979 Honda Civic hatchback with a rebuilt engine. It's house-painted light blue. You can even see the grooves from the brush strokes. Even

Preacher Dale says the paint job is the worst thing he's ever seen—*beyond repair*, even rubbing compound won't help. It's so great to have a car. I take Beth out to the movies; I drive to work, and sometimes I pick my mom up from work. She hasn't had a car since we lived in the Alley when I was nine years old, so to be able to jump in a car and go anywhere I want any time I want is extraordinary.

My mom isn't an unemployed junkie anymore, but she's still as miserable as I've ever seen her. She works at a day care center and is always exhausted. Her feet and back hurt all the time, and she's constantly worrying, because she doesn't make enough to pay the bills. On top of all that, she has to deal with Carlos. When I asked her why she doesn't leave him, she says she can't afford to. He pays the rent.

It's a rare weekday when I'm not working, so I drive down to give my mom a ride home from work. I'm standing in the lobby, and through the glass wall, I can see my mom in the infant room. She has a kid hugging her leg, and she's holding another kid on her hip, while changing another kid's diaper. She sees me and smiles. She comes out and gives me a hug and then clocks out. We walk out to the parking lot. It's burning hot out.

"Are you alright, Mom?" I ask.

"Oh yeah," she says as she lights a cigarette so she can get one down in the parking lot before she gets in my car. "It's just so exhausting. I only have one helper, and I used to have two, and I have three more kids. They gave me a tiny little raise but then added three kids and took away one of my helpers."

She drops her cigarette in the parking lot and squishes it with the toe of her shoe. I open the car door for her and let her in. When I get in the driver's side, she's crying. I can't remember the last time I saw my mom cry, maybe not since that day when all the cops were at our apartment in the Alley.

"Mom," I say, "you just need to tell them that it's too much, that they have to get you a helper."

She rolls down the window and lights up another cigarette. She knows she can't smoke in my car, but I don't say anything.

"It isn't that. It's Carlos. He's getting so mean. I'm worried."

I pull the car over on the dirt to the side of the road by the In-N-Out Burger. I can smell the beef grilling.

"What's going on, Mom?"

She stares out the window.

"I told him I didn't want the guns in the house. He got really mad, but I went to sleep. Then he woke me up in the middle of the night, and he had a knife pressed up against my neck."

She starts crying hard and pushes her hair back and shows me the red mark on her neck.

"It's all the speed he does."

I'm frozen with rage.

"Joseph, are you alright?" my mom asks.

"I'm so sorry, Mom. I've been spending all my time at Rex' and Beth's. I'm going to kill that son of a bitch."

I hug her tightly. I expect her to respond, to tell me not to do anything rash, but she doesn't. She smells like cigarettes. It reminds me of when I was a kid.

❖   ❖   ❖

It's 6:00 a.m. They aren't supposed to be here until 7:00. I am ready. I don't have anything that I don't mind leaving behind, except some clothes and an old metal box with some pictures of me and my dad and mom when I was a baby. I have my birth certificate, Social Security card, and a couple boxes of books. I easily fit everything I have in the back seat of my Civic.

Rex arrives first in his VW Westfalia camper van. Then my Grandpa arrives in his minitruck. My Grandpa hates confrontation, so I am surprised when he doesn't say anything about the fact that Rex is carrying a bat. Then, Scott and Kevin pull up, both friends since elementary school. We all huddle up.

"Okay," I say, "I'm going to go in and lightly tap on my mom's door. She is going to get up and go to the bathroom and get dressed. Once she is dressed, she'll come out the front door and leave with Grandpa. Then we go in and move all the furniture out. It's all my mom's, so just grab everything."

"What about Carlos?" Scott asks.

"My mom says he only has two handguns in the bedroom and that she got rid of the bullets."

"If he tries anything, I've got this," Rex says, as he takes a practice swing.

"He has a lot of knives," I say, "but I've got this." I pull out the hunting knife my dad's brother, Jimmy, had inexplicably sent me for my birthday a few years ago.

"They drew first blood," Scott kids.

We get my mom out and on the road, and I'm happy that she looks more relieved than scared.

Then I hear, "What the hell is going on?"

Rex and my Grandpa have the couch lifted up in the air. Carlos, with his skinny little legs, is in his robe. He's furious.

"My mom is moving out," I say.

He sees the knife in my hand.

"Oh, you and your little high school friends are tough, huh? You little fuckers are going to come into *my* house ...Where is she?" Carlos shouts.

"She's gone and never coming back," I say.

Carlos darts back into the bedroom. I hear him tearing the room apart looking for his guns.

"Where the fuck?! Goddamn bitch!" he shouts.

Rex and my Grandpa rush out with the couch.

Carlos comes out dressed and brandishing a switchblade.

"Carlos," I shout as loud as I can, "We are leaving! It's done."

Carlos is far enough away that I can bail if he lunges at me with the knife. I slowly back out the door. The police arrive and are talking to my Grandpa. They take Carlos into his bedroom and start asking him questions. I can hear him yelling at them, *my house!* One of the cops comes out and tells us to leave, and we do.

As I drive down the freeway, with the windows down and the warm air pressing hard, in a slow lane caravan between my best friend in his orange VW camper van and my Grandpa in his little brown minitruck stuffed with my mom's worthless furniture, it occurs to me like a sudden pleasant memory: I don't live at the Tennis Club Apartments anymore. I'll never have to live in such terrible conditions again. This thought fills me with joy, and I can't stop smiling.

❖   ❖   ❖

Preacher Dale and Beth's mom let me move in to their home with Beth for the summer until I move to the dorms at Cal State. I spend my time working at Parker's Sporting Goods, lifting weights, and kickboxing and hanging out with Beth. Life is as easy as it's ever been for me. I haven't seen Carlos since the day we moved my mom out. I think he's probably in jail, or better yet, prison.

It's triple-digit hot. We have the swamp cooler on. Dale and Beth's mom are at work, and Beth and I are making out furiously in her sister's bed.

"Joseph, hold on," Beth says, "I heard something. Is my dad home?"

"What?" I ask, still panting.

"The door."

Every once in a while he'll surprise us and come home early, but we haven't been caught yet. I look through the front door peephole. My heart stops. It's Carlos and his sidekick Brian, and Carlos has a black handgun held against his stomach under his open leather jacket.

"Joseph, we know you are in there," Carlos announces.

Brian is snooping around the outside trying to see in the windows.

I crouch beside the couch.

"I think I saw him," I hear Brian say to Carlos.

I can see Brian craning his neck to see in at me through a space in the shutters. I scamper along the carpet to the back bedroom, grab Beth, and put her in her sister's armoire.

"Don't come out until I tell you. Carlos is outside."

I shut the door carefully and scamper back into Beth's parents' bedroom. I grab Preacher Dale's "midnight special," a cheap .38 revolver. I crawl out to the living room and look through the front door peephole. They are both standing there murmuring. Carlos pounds on the door again.

"Joseph, we just want to talk to you."

I hear Carlos whisper to Brian through the paper-thin front door, "I know that little *motherfucker* is in there."

The doorknob jerks back and forth violently above my head. I think they're going to kick it in. I hold my breath, and quietly place the nose of the .38 into the door right at Carlos's chest. I'll put three holes in each of them if I have to.

"He's in there," I hear Carlos say to Brian, "His car is in the fucking driveway. Let's just break in."

The doorknob rattles again. Then they go silent. The door swells inward as if Carlos is leaning on it to see how much pressure it will take to break it down. I pull the hammer back, and it clicks into place. I'm shaking. I hold my breath.

"Carlos," I hear Brian say with a hint of desperation in his voice, "I'm not going back to jail for this."

A few seconds later, I hear Carlos start his motorcycle. All the muscles in my body unclench as I hear the engine's whine fade. They drive off.

Then Rex calls. He's pissed. He just got home, and his mom is upset, because Carlos and Brian came to his house. I can hear his little sister crying in the background. I listen as Rex rants furiously. Beth is sitting next to me. I look at her and smile softly. She's so beautiful and so sweet. I love her so much. I can't believe I brought this into her home. I can't believe I brought this into Rex's home.

❖   ❖   ❖

It's been two nights since Carlos showed up at Beth's home. My fear has morphed into anger and is now a barely controlled rage. Exacting revenge against Carlos is all I think about. It's all I *can* think about. So, I'm stalking him now, lying in wait, waiting for the best possible moment to send a message that couldn't be clearer: *Don't ever fuck with me, my friends, or family again.*

As he's done, ever since I can remember, every night at around eleven, Carlos walks from the apartment to the liquor store to buy his Mickey's forty-ounce beer and a pack of menthols. It's a quarter-mile walk straight up the road. It's only lit on one side, and the other side is an unlit dirt sidewalk. He always walks in the dirt on the dark side.

For the third night in a row, I sit in my car in the dark waiting for Carlos to come walking back from the liquor store. I start to think about the last two years of training. I moved from kung fu to kickboxing, and started training under a bona fide psycho named David Morrow. David wasn't interested in meditation or belts or exotic animal names, such as Crane and Lotus and Monkey. He taught his students how to fight. Most people that came into David's gym left without asking for a refund. I loved it. I bashed my shins until they were hard as bats. I learned how to throw punches like a boxer. He taught me how to break someone's arm, choke them to death, and smash their larynx. He taught me the most powerful strike in the world, the Muay Thai leg kick. I practiced it so much that it became second nature. I'd spar with people and make them quit. David used to put me in the ring with a gangbanger named Harvey, a certified Crip, with jail tattoos and cornrows to prove it, whose Grandpa was a professional boxer. Harvey was a superior boxer, and he was mean as the pit bull he kept tied up outside the gym. He regularly beat the shit out of me. David would only stop it when I was going to get hurt, but David would never let me quit. I knew I couldn't become a better boxer than Harvey, so I started keeping him on the outside with my jab and my kicks. After a few months of sparring with Harvey, of getting pummeled, I started to give almost as good as I got. After a while, I learned to keep him off me most of the time. I started working his legs with Thai kicks. I had vicious Thai kicks from either side. I learned to rotate my hips and lag my shin behind and then whip it around the way a golfer swings a driver. I bashed Harvey's legs over and over. I loved the dead-smack sound it made. One night, during a sparring session like so many others, I finally beat him. I made him quit. He took a knee and David stepped in. I can't remember being prouder.

Harvey was sitting against the wall rubbing his legs, while I unraveled my hand wraps. "Nigga, come here," he said. Before that night, Harvey hadn't said one word to me. I half expected him to tell me he was going to kick my ass, but, instead, he bumped fists with me and gave me a nod. David walked over to us.

"Took you long enough," David teased me.

"This mothafucka *right here*," Harvey said to David. "*Man*, he got a leg kick like a goddamn baseball bat. You turned this nigga into a straight, white-boy killa."

I look out over my dashboard into the dark. No Carlos yet.

My thoughts returned to David and Harvey. I'm sure both of them will die or end up in prison pretty soon, but I still love them. I love them because they showed me that pain doesn't hurt. *Cowardice*, now that hurts, and it doesn't heal. It festers and grows until I can barely stand looking at my eyes in the mirror.

It seems darker and quieter out. I roll down the windows. I am both calm and excited. David teaches, *Don't think about doing it, do it.* He means you have to strike before you think about striking. I know he's right; this isn't a movie. And, for all I know Carlos is carrying a gun, and I know he has a knife. He always has a knife.

I see a shadow slowly emerge. I know his slinky stride. He has on his leather bomber jacket. I see the glow of his cigarette. It brightens when he brings it to his mouth. He follows it with a swig from his paper-bag-wrapped beer. I can hear my heart pounding in my inner ear, and my armpits are filling with cold sweat. I have my hands on the car door handle as he gets closer and closer. He stops no more than thirty yards in front of my car. He pushes out his face, like he's straining to see me.

"Joseph ... Joseph ... Is that you?" Carlos yells.

Real violence isn't much like kickboxing. It's more like deboning a chicken for the fryer. It's wet and messy, and things crunch disgustingly. Crunch, crunch, crunch.

FOUR

I'm driving back from Cal State listening to KROQ. The DJ somberly announces that Kurt Cobain died and plays "Polly" in honorarium. I make this half-hour drive nearly every day; that's when I think. Today I think how perfect my life is, that I'm finally safe, that I'm only twenty-one, and my whole glorious life is laid out before me. I'm going to be wildly successful. Soon I'll be married. I asked Beth to marry me on Christmas Day. She cried tears of joy. I love her. She's so sweet and beautiful. I'd do anything for her, and she'll make the perfect wife and, eventually, a mother.

There is an accident, and the freeway traffic is nearly stopped. I can see glass and a bumper in the emergency lane, and a Highway Patrol officer lighting and dropping brilliant flares to divert all four lanes to one. It's a rare day, because I have nowhere to be after class. Another Nirvana song. I turn it up. I like to think about my résumé and how impressive it is. It makes me feel safe. It makes me feel further and further from The Alley and the Tennis Club Apartments.

I have a 3.7 GPA, 3.92 in my major; I'm the founder and president of the Pre-Law Association; I'm Phi Kappa Phi; I'm on Moreno Valley's Ecological Protection Committee—the youngest committee member in the history of Moreno Valley; and, after my rookie performance on Cal State's Model United Nations team—where we won the first of any championship in the history of the university—I was nominated to lead the team as the head delegate in this year's competition in New York City. I was elected to the Student Union Board. I won several scholarships this year, including one from the Secret Service and one based on my twenty-page essay on Law & Morality, "I Know It When I See It: Pornography Under Miller v. California." I still kickbox and occasionally teach Muay Thai and kickboxing classes to kids when David is traveling to a fight or choreographing a fight scene for a movie. On top of all that, I landed a job with "Tito" Gonzalez, one of the top trial lawyers in the country.

Traffic has come to a complete stop. I crank the AC fan up. I think of how satisfying it is to mentally pitch my résumé. I can see the Vanir Tower in my rearview mirror. It's a golden-glassed, high rise in downtown San Bernardino. Tito's office occupies the entire top floor. Tito has taken me under his wing. I told him about my mom, and although he's been a millionaire for decades, he was an orphan. I spend as much time as I can with Tito. On the days I work, we are usually the last ones in the office, often leaving hours after all the other attorneys and staff have gone home. Tito had me organize his press clippings for a speech he was giving in honor of some award he was getting, and he was described more than once as the *quintessential gentleman*, loved by everyone, even the attorneys he battled against. I want to be just like him, and I'm on my way.

Traffic is starting to move. I read the off-ramp sign, "University Avenue 3 miles." Instantly, the warm secure feeling I have evaporates. This is how it happens. University Avenue is where the hookers walked when I lived in the Alley. I get the rush. A little extra air in my chest, a buzz, a flow of blood. I try to ignore it, just keep driving, but I know it's futile. When I'm at Beth's and no one is home, I'll get the thought, and then the rush, and within five minutes I'm at the video store renting porn. The embarrassment of facing the store clerk with *Anal Asians 5* is almost unbearable. I get home and masturbate in utter fear that someone will return home unexpectedly. But the fear makes it even better. The orgasm is volcanic. The shame immediately following is cavernous.

"University Avenue, 1 mile," I read the next sign aloud.

Just get in the fast lane and drive by. It's no use. I submit.

The rush is so much more than with porn. The anticipation is unreal. I drive west toward the Alley, toward the bad side of town. I see a group of Bloods hanging out on the corner wearing red Pendletons, wife beaters, and sporting drippy, shiny hair. They watch as I drive by. I'm getting closer. I pass the donut shop, and finally I see one. She's a curvy Mexican, and she's wearing a skirt that is barely covering her ass. My heart pounds. I can feel the nerve endings rise on my forearms. I slow to get a good look at her. She sees me and looks back to see if there is a cop around and then waves me to pull over. I do as she says. I watch her approach in the side mirror. I'm so excited I could burst. My cock is already hard. She's twenty feet away. My window is down, and I can hear the click of her heels on the sidewalk. I'm about to hyperventilate. I step on the gas and speed away. In my rearview mirror, I see her throw up her arms and flip me off. Jesus Christ, that was fucking close.

The Rose Way Convalescent Home smells of ammonia and old people. The floors are a shiny black-and-white checkerboard. I don't sign in. I just wave at the Filipina nurse that hovers over a computer behind the reception counter. She's friendly enough, and I've learned from experience that, if I walk in with authority, I don't have to sign in or deal with any visiting hours' nonsense. I used to hope I'd see some sexy nurses. *Not happening.* They're all middle-aged Filipina women, with roughly the shape and sex appeal of pumpkins.

I stand just outside the doorway. Runner is pleading with an orderly. "Just get me some, and I'll get you some cash when my lawyer comes."

"No more until I get some cash. Nigger, you already owes me five dollas," the orderly responds.

"Yo, Runner!" I holler jovially as I burst into the room. I hand a twenty over to James—according to his name tag—a shady little black orderly whom I recognize from my last visit. "Here is what he owes you plus fifteen more. Get him what he needs. Please."

Runner had alcohol running through his veins before he was born. He was taken away from his mother and put in foster care when he was a toddler. He was never adopted, and so spent his childhood bouncing from one foster home to the next, and then from one group home to another. Runner is a fuckup for sure, but nothing serious enough to land him in California Youth Authority—at least, not yet. Tito is Runner's lawyer, and that's how I know Runner.

About a year ago, Runner ditched school after first period, scored some booze, and got drunk with some other low-level delinquents at an abandoned house. He came back on campus to catch the school bus. It was San Bernardino High School, a gang-infested ghetto school. One of the school cops saw him, and tried to chase him down to make sure he got detention for ditching. Runner didn't want to get caught drunk, so he ran. Within a couple minutes, the whole school police force was in hot pursuit. Runner dropped his shoe while he climbed the school's chain-link fence. He picked up his shoe and started running toward the neighborhood homes. A cop announced over his walkie-talkie that "the suspect" was carrying something in his hand, which got passed on as, "He's carrying a weapon," which got passed on as, "The suspect's got a gun." Runner scrambled to get away, hid in a backyard, and then, thinking he had an opening to get away, burst out of the bushes directly into the line of a cop running at him. They collided, and the cop's drawn service revolver fired right through Runner's C3 vertebra, as the cop fell on top of Runner. Now Runner is not only a hope-to-die alcoholic but a quadriplegic, too. I know all this, because I've spent many hours analyzing and summarizing boxes of deposition testimony, police reports, photos, and videos. I even went to the scene on my own and took photos and created a diagram.

I don't pity Runner. I just figure since we come from similar places, and I got lucky and he didn't, the least I can do is get him a drink and visit him once in a while. I figure I'm pretty qualified to hang out with Runner. My Uncle Billy is a quad, so I know a little about what it's like. I help plan for the time when Runner gets out of here—plans about getting a van with a lift and shopping for his apartment and making sure it's wheelchair-accessible. I also worked at a group home for a couple semesters before I got the job with Tito, so I was around kids like Runner. I know they are going to act how they are going to act. It's way too late to change that. The only thing anyone can do for them is to be the adult who isn't going to lie to them or abuse them. When Runner asks me when I'm coming back, I tell him I don't know, unless I'm absolutely certain when I'll be back. He isn't much for expressing feelings, but I know he appreciates me, even though I'm just another privileged white boy in his eyes.

"The People's Court" is on the TV over the bed. Daytime television depresses me, but I don't fuss with it. I just sit down in the chair next to Runner. Sometimes he doesn't say anything, and I just start doing my homework, while he stares at the TV. I think he just likes having someone here. We sit in silence for a couple minutes before Runner comments.

"I seen this one before. This bitch talkin' 'bout she don't owe no money to this motherfucker, but Judge Wapner ain't even hearin' it."

Runner is full-bred Tomahawk Indian, with a widow's peak and hair as thick as shoelaces, but to see him, one would swear he was born in East LA to the Garcias. And to hear him, one would think he was born in Watts to the Washingtons.

"How you hangin' in there, Runner?" I ask, even though it's a stupid question.

"Good, good, man. You know ... when's Tito comin'? You don't be tellin' him about that shit, right?" Runner says, referring to his drinking.

"What are you talking about, Runner?" I say and smile at him knowingly. "I'm off the clock. I was just in the neighborhood and thought I'd say hello. You think Tito's gonna pay me to sit here with you and watch Judge Wapner?"

"Tell Tito I need some money, okay?"

"That's between you and Tito. I told you, I'm just here to say hello, because I was in the neighborhood."

"A'ight," Runner says and pauses in thought. "You still with your girl, the one you showed me the picture of, the fine one with the red hair?"

James, the orderly, walks in with a paper bag with Runner's booze and sets it on Runner's stomach.

"Jimmy, you best not be holdin' out on me," Runner says as James ignores him and walks out.

"Pull the curtain and pour it in there," Runner orders me.

I pour nearly a quarter liter of vodka into a big red plastic tumbler. Runner has to manipulate himself to get it wedged into his curled-up hand so he can work the straw. He's highly motivated.

"A'ight then," Runner says to me as I get up to leave. He is in a state of relief after his first long drag from a giant plastic sippy-cup straw.

Only when I reach the parking lot into the fresh air do I realize how horrible it smelled in there. I have two hours to kill before I have to be back at Cal State for cellular biology class, and then a model-U.N. planning meeting. Two hours to kill. Recognition of this fact causes a domino effect in my mind. *Oriental massage parlors.* One summer my dad showed up and took me for a couple weeks. I was about thirteen. He had a fence company, and I spent most of my time working. The fenceyard was in a bad area of Pomona, and when we'd drive home in his truck, we'd drive by a sparse, spread-out dirt area, where there was a string of little homes that had been converted into Oriental massage parlors. They were so quiet and odd. I didn't exactly know what they were, but I could tell it was something on the outskirts of society, and I could feel the energy. Toward the end of the workday, I'd start to look forward to driving by. Once I saw a man exit from a rear entrance, and a little Asian woman in a short tight dress closed the door behind him. It sent a wave of adrenaline through my body. Just the thought of driving by sent a charge through me.

I leave Runner with anticipation coursing through me.

I drive down Baseline. Baseline in San Bernardino is just like University Avenue in Riverside, but even more seedy. I love driving down this street and seeing the homeless, gangbangers, porn shops, liquor stores, patrolling cop cars, gun stores, pawn shops, and the few nicer businesses hanging on to the past.

I see one. *Here we go.* A tall blue-black girl struts in high heels, bare legs, and a short, tight, spandex skirt. Her big, round ass sways and bounces up and down, back and forth. She looks over her shoulder at the passing cars, trying to bait a john. Girls like her can sense guys like me from three blocks away. She stops and walks toward the curb and puts her hand on her hip at a drastic angle. I slow and roll down my passenger window to get a good look. I start to tingle; my pulse races.

"You need a date, handsome? I got whatchoo need," she taunts and struts with her ass raised like a cat.

I nod. She motions for me to pull around the corner.

I turn the corner and park about a half-block down. I see her walking toward me in the rearview mirror, her head swiveling around looking for cops. I think of Beth. She's so sweet and innocent and beautiful, and I love her so much. It would kill her if she knew I was doing this. *Just pull away*, I think to myself. *Just pull away.*

We are in a one-bedroom apartment that apparently doubles as the world's saddest nursery. She doesn't say anything. She pulls her skirt above her hips, flops out her heavy breasts, and squats down in front of me. My pants are down, and my cock is pointing at her accusingly. She spits on it and grips it with both hands like she owns it. It feels so goddamn good I have to grit my teeth not to scream. Energy surges through me. She feels me cumming and blocks the blast with her cleavage. It hits so hard it splatters. I go weak. She squeezes the remaining droplets on to her left tit as if it's the last bit of toothpaste.

I pull my pants up, and she disappears into the bathroom. Panic and dread envelop my body. Her boyfriend is going to walk in with a gun. The cops are waiting outside. I can't believe I'm doing this. My whole future is fucked. I'll never get into law school. I see Beth's blue eyes crying. I hear the toilet flush just as I shut the door and race down the steps into the neighborhood. It looks so much worse shaded in guilt. I repeat my new mantra as I walk as fast as I can to my car: "Never again, never again."

❖　　❖　　❖

It's one of those perfect California mornings. Only Beth and I are home. We just had sex, and she's glowing like she's plugged in. She's in her aerobics outfit, and we are having breakfast before she leaves to teach a class. I try not to think about what happened, but I can't help to wonder what the fuck is wrong that I would rather fuck a skanky prostitute than make love to this gorgeous woman. Beth usually lifts weights after she teaches aerobics. I wonder if I have time for porn.

"Are you going to lift after class?" I ask.

"Why don't we go to the movies?"

I nod in agreement. I'm actually relieved that I'm not going to have to deal with the stress of racing to the video store, jacking off, and hiding the video before she gets back. Beth pages through the newspaper in search of the movie section.

"Can you believe this?" she says, and slides the paper in front of my cereal bowl.

It's a young politician with his wife and daughter, smiling, in the foreground of city hall. Next to it is a grainy mug shot of the same man. The headline reads, "Councilman Arrested During Prostitution Sting." I feel a rush, and I can feel my face turn red. For a second I think Beth knows. My life is about to end. I try to act nonchalant, *wow ... that's crazy*, as if the subject were absolutely foreign. Beth kisses me on the lips while she gathers her things.

"Yeah, so sad. I feel bad for his poor wife."

Beth walks out. I read the article. There is nothing in it that isn't obvious from the headline and the photo. I can't imagine the conversation he had with his wife. I can't imagine what it must have been like to face his colleagues. He's fucked, and I am, too, if I don't stop. That settles it. I'm done. I'm not going to ruin my life, and I'm certainly not going to hurt the angel I'm about to marry.

Between small industrial buildings and undeveloped barren lots, there's a string of Oriental massage parlors dotting Highland Avenue, right outside the San Bernardino city limits: Sunset Spa, Oriental Massage, Japanese Acupuncture and Massage, among others. They are the solution to my street-hooker problem. I park in the back of my favorite, Oriental Massage. As with all of them, Oriental Massage is run with the quality control and efficiency of a McDonald's franchise. Each mama-san asks the same questions. I always give the same answers. Mama-san and her girls never let customers see each other. Protocol must be followed.

I walk across the cool dark lobby to the glass window and ring the bell. A stocky Chinese woman slides a clipboard under the glass. I write "Michael Smith" and scribble a series of illegible numbers and letters in lieu of my license number.

"Thirty-fy dolla. You come here befoe?"

I slide two twenties under the glass.

"Many times. Is Sunny here?" I say, trying not to let my voice tremble.

"You like Sunny," she says with a tone somewhere between statement and question.

Mama-san walks around and unbolts the interior gated door and hands me a five-dollar bill. I follow her down a dim hallway of shut doors. The smell of wok-cooked Chinese food wafts heavy in the air. We walk past the small room where the girls hang out. They peer out at me as I walk by. I presume this is part of the protocol to make sure customers who say they've been here before actually have and to make sure we go back to the same girls. There are four girls sitting on a couple thin mattresses eating out of bowls with chopsticks, while watching a video that sounds like a Chinese soap opera. Each girl wears lingerie, except Sunny who is wearing red terry cloth short-shorts and a baby doll T-shirt. She smiles at me. It feels as if I've been injected with an epidural of adrenaline. I'm going to be fucking her really soon. Cold sweat flushes out the pores on my forearms like gas out a fuel injector.

Nearly identical to the dozens of other massage rooms I've been in since I stopped picking up street hookers—a run that has lasted nearly a semester—this one is a clean little room with wood paneling, a chair, a small end table with a lamp, and a bottle of baby oil. The massage table is a small, thin mattress on the ground with clean white sheets. I quickly strip down naked and neatly place my clothes on the chair. I place two twenties and the five-dollar bill conspicuously on the end table. I lie on my stomach and place the ever-present threadbare hand towel over my calves. Then I wait. I tremble so hard that I erupt into a full body shiver that I must tamp down. I anticipate. I think one of two things is going to happen: either cops are going to burst in, and I'm going to end up in jail, or Sunny is going to walk in, and I'm going to get a little bit of heaven.

"Fuck ... I can't believe I'm doing this again," I mutter to myself.

Sunny walks in and dims the light. She's changed into red lingerie and stilt heels that elevate her to five-foot-five. She mounts me atop my ass and applies baby powder. Her expert hands glide across my body.

"You no come here long time," she says without pausing the flow of her hands.

She creates long flowing patterns with her hands, so that with every pass near my nether regions, I become more and more eager, until the anticipation is breathtaking. I am so entranced there is delay between input and output in my brain.

"Oh, uh ... sorry, Sunny. That just feels so good. I've been busy. How are you? I missed you."

"You no come here see other girl?" she asks, as she drags the tips of her long, thick hair down my neck and spine, and then slowly down my ass in between my thighs. Goddamn.

"No, only you, Sunny." I look back at her to bring home the point.

Sunny places her palms on my ass cheeks and pushes all her weight down, opening up my ass. She plunges her tongue through the condom she holds between her lips and into my ass. All I can do is pant and whimper with pleasure so intense I can barely stand it.

"You like it, baby? You like Sunny tongue in you ass?"

I can't speak. I moan something affirmative. Do I like Sunny's tongue in my ass? It's a rhetorical question, but I want to say, "Don't ever take your tongue out of my ass." Sunny turns me over and proudly observes the glass erection she's created. I could carve ivory with this thing. With ninja-like precision, she slides a pink condom onto me with her mouth. She mounts me for a while. Then I fuck her ankles-to-ears missionary for a while. God bless her for leaving her heels on. That is a straight pro move. The coup de grace is doggy-style. Her ass is so small that when I thrust as far as I can, I can feel the end, and she winces just a bit and reaches back to try and restrict me.

"Jesus fucking Christ!" I yell a little too loudly as I pound into her arched ass. The cum starts in my toes and shoots through my body like electricity looking for escape, until it finally fires out my cock. It's over. I have to be still, or I might die. I roll off her and collapse. Sunny is all business. She jumps up and throws a robe on, and gathers the condom with a towel. She's out the door.

It's just me and my abject dread. It fills me up. How can I have done this again? Why have I done this again?

Sunny cleans me up with a warm towel. I dress. She puts my shoes on, as usual, which makes me feel uncomfortable, as usual. I just paid you to fuck me and stick your tongue in my ass, but having you put my shoes on just seems so chauvinistic.

"Thank you, Sunny," I say sheepishly.

"You visit come soon."

No, Sunny. I'm never coming back. This is the last time I'll ever do this. Never again . . .

"See you next time, Sunny."

FIVE

I've been working here at the gym where Beth teaches aerobics during the weekends for the last couple months. It's easy, and I get to work out for free. It's nearly eleven p.m., and it's empty except for one girl, Melissa. Melissa doesn't really work out. She just saunters around the gym swaying to the music, toying with the equipment, absorbing attention. I've been jerking off to fantasies of Melissa —bent over the tanning bed, blowing me in the locker room—since she joined three weeks ago. Melissa is a sex-bomb: tits, ass, and hips spilling out everywhere.

I make my regular announcement: "Just to let you know, you've got about five minutes to finish your workout. I'm closing up."

She's facing me using the pectoral deck machine. She smiles at me and asks, "What are you doing after you close?"

I'm not expecting this question. "Uh, nothing, the usual, going home."

"Oh ...," she responds, open-endedly.

Melissa walks up to the counter as I count out the register.

"Can I borrow a pen and a piece of paper?" she asks.

She writes something down and folds it up into a triangle and hands it to me. I stare at her heart-shaped ass as she walks out. Anxiously fondling the note in my fingers, I watch her back out a blue minitruck, barely missing a car crossing behind her. Her car stereo blasts through the glass doors of the gym. Her truck's headlights beam through the gym's glass wall and swipe across my chest as she exits the parking lot.

❖   ❖   ❖

It's exactly midnight according to my car's digital clock. I unfold the note and read it again. "*Meat* me in my bed at midnight, 3359 Oleander (across from JFK Elementary)."

"Meat me," I say under my breath and chuckle.

I take a deep breath and get out of my car. Melissa's truck is in the driveway across the street. An "Air Force Wife" sticker is affixed slightly askew across the window of the truck's cab. This, and the surprisingly large wedding ring she always wears, are both subtle clues that I shouldn't be here. I can't help but think of the photo of me reenacting my proposal to Beth on Aunt Suzie's lawn last Christmas, me on one knee, Beth beaming in the Christmas-day sun. I get back in my car. I can't do this. I love Beth. She's my fiancée. I've done this before with a few girls at Cal State and the hookers and the massage-parlor girls, but I promised myself I would never do it again. *Never again.*

Just get in the car and drive home. Why can't I get the feeling I want from Beth? I know I can't. I'll never get that feeling from a woman I love. I could never look at that beautiful face and want to fuck her like I want to fuck Melissa. I can't keep doing this. I'm going to get caught, and my whole life will be over. Just start the car and drive away.

I think of Melissa's curvy body and that slack "Fuck me" mouth of hers, and a wave of dense energy begins to flow through me. My breathing becomes deliberate.

I knock lightly on the door. It's a brand new fungible mini-mansion tract home. The front lawn glistens with impossibly plush sod, the seams of which are still clearly visible in the half-moon's light. White, vinyl-framed windows, so damn many, the type that slide open like ice on linoleum, still have fresh UV-rating stickers in the bottom corners.

The door opens slowly inward. A fat, orange, tabby cat slinks around Melissa's bare feet and calves. She's wearing a white, silky Japanese robe with a red-and-white, koi-fish print.

"Shhhh. They're asleep," Melissa whispers.

"They who?" I whisper back.

Her mouth is slightly open, and her robe is wide open. Precious tight-knit, white panties fight to restrain a springy dark thicket. Melissa's sporting 70s porn bush: It's quite a contrast from Beth's precision orange strip. Her tits hang heavy; pink, puffy nipples, framed in tan areolas, point at my ascending erection. "My mother- and father-in-law," she replies, matter-of-factly. "Mack is in the Gulf."

Mack is in the Gulf. *Oh, Jesus Christ!* Her husband. She says *Mack* so intimately, as if I know him. You know, Mack? Your buddy, Mack! Let's say a prayer for Mack. God, please bring Mack home from the war in Iraq safely.

I can't do this. This is so wrong.

Melissa extends her hand across the doorway, exposing her breasts. "C'mon," she whispers.

I feel the wave of lust sweep through me, and I take her hand. She leads me in the near-dark up the stairs and into her bedroom. We punish one another for an hour. At one point she straddles my face and pinches my nose shut, while she grinds her pussy into my mouth. I struggle for air. She slaps my face. I turn her over and use the strap of her robe like a horse's rein to pull her head back, while I fuck her ass from behind. We nearly faint.

I escape in a rush, in the usual bath of guilt and self-disgust, and on my drive home I feel a dread that is even more intense than usual. I think of my mom, and I wonder if this feeling is like the one that made her unable to get out of bed for years. I think of Beth and how she is as beautiful as I am ugly, as precious as I am rotten, as honest as I am a wretched liar.

It's late and everyone is in bed except Beth who is up waiting for me.

"Hey, baby, did you have fun with Rex?" she says and hugs me and gives me a soft kiss.

I panic as I realize that I rushed out of Melissa's so abruptly I didn't even wipe the pussy off my face.

Beth must not notice, because she doesn't react.

"It was fun. Rex is good."

I am absolutely worthless.

❖   ❖   ❖

It's my first night in New York City. James and Keri and I decided to go to Mahoney's Irish Pub instead of joining the rest of Cal State's Model United Nations Team for a Broadway musical, *Cats* or *Les Mis*, or some other ridiculousness. Mahoney's is a simple bar with a jukebox that seems to vacillate endlessly between Rolling Stones' classics and Billy Joel's greatest hits. It is loud and packed with locals. I've had several beers, a couple courtesy of two thirty-something women with Brooklyn accents that flirt with me and ask me to repeat, *Awesome!*, *Surf's up*, and *No way, Dude* in my nasally SoCal drawl—which I didn't know I had until I got to New York.

"I can't believe you smoke," I say to James as he lights another cigarette. "What the fuck is the matter with you?"

James and I fuck with each other like this, but I really do find smoking abhorrent. I'm an athlete. The idea of purposely ruining this body I've worked so hard for is unimaginably stupid to me. "They turn your teeth yellow; they're expensive; make you breathe like your eighty years old, and eventually will kill you."

"Fuck you," James retorts. "I smoke because I want to."

"Yeah, fuck you," Keri repeats without conviction.

I smile at her.

James orders a round of Jack & Cokes. I can't believe how good they taste. I had no idea. I just turned twenty-one, and I've had a couple beers here and there, but I've never really drank before. James and I drink another round of Jack & Cokes, our third. Keri bowed out after the first and is now nursing a Sprite. I'm silk and velvet, swirling around amidst the music in the center of the world. Everyone likes me. I'm finally undeniably funny and handsome and successful and everyone in here knows it. I love them all. I've never been this relaxed. This must be how it feels to make it. This is the way I want to feel forever.

Keri is half-dancing while sipping her drink, taking it all in. She wears jean coveralls that reveal a couple inches of curvy milky white hip, and her eyes are an impossibly light shade of green. She's shy and awkward, and the smartest girl I've ever met. I love being around her.

"The bars don't close here," Keri says.

"What do you mean?" I shout over the glorious jukebox and clanking bottles and happy voices.

"They don't close until the morning," James says. "It is not like in California."

This is good news. To know that this semi-orgasmic state will continue for hours is almost too good to take. Everyone in here is my friend. I walk up to a table on the way to order another drink and just start talking. I have no fear. They love me, especially the girls. So, I drink, and I talk, and I flirt, mostly with Keri. She and I keep getting closer. Our hands brush, and it sends a mild wave of pleasure up my arm and down my spine. I use the crowdedness to edge in and put my hand on the small of her back. I'm not scared.

I want to stay until the morning and through the night, but after a couple hours, James and Keri insist we leave. We spill out onto the street. It's black and wet and the skyscrapers are indescribable, and my breath forms clouds, and even the bums huddled in the stoops are like exotic birds. Steam rises from vents just like in the movies. Cabs roll by. Their tires peel little streams of water. I want to live here forever and go drinking at Mahoney's Pub every night.

James and Keri light up cigarettes. The orange tips are so beautiful, and the smoke swirls into the cold night air.

"Let me have one," I say to James.

"Seriously?" James asks in earnest.

Oh yes, I am serious. It's the obvious thing to do. I don't think this; I feel it.

James hands me a Marlboro Red 100 and lights it for me. James and Keri watch me curiously as I smoke the first cigarette of my life. It's glorious. The combination of Jack & Cokes and Marlboros is simply perfect. I'm clutching a full Jack & Coke, probably my fifth. I didn't mean to walk out with the drink, but I feel so lucky that I did. It's like finding a twenty in the laundry. I look up along the face of a high-rise and blow out the smoke. It's as if I were always meant to smoke and drink, and I've just now discovered it. It feels so good. It's so natural. I smoke cigarette after cigarette on the way back to the hotel. Keri and I sit in the stairwell of the hotel smoking and talking and flirting until it is almost light. It's the best night of my life, and I'm completely in love with Keri.

I spend the rest of the week consumed with the consumption of Jack & Cokes and Marlboro Red 100s, and spending time with Keri. Twice I take walks and stop at a bar and have several drinks before sauntering around Times Square. I smoke and take it all in. I especially love the red color and the seedy energy of the peep shows and porn shops. I don't dare go in, but I don't need to. New York City is truly the greatest city on earth. We win the Model United Nations competition, the first national championship in the history of Cal State. It's in all the local newspapers. I couldn't care less.

I'm mostly sobered up by the time we land back in California. Beth is waiting at the terminal. I see her before she sees me. She is wearing black leggings, with high leather boots and a tight sweater. Her fire-red hair jumps out in the crowd. When our eyes meet, she lights up. I try to return her enthusiasm as the guilt gurgles up between my stomach and chest. I fear she'll sense my love for Keri. I could never tell her about the prostitutes, but if I told her about the girls from the gym and the ones from Cal State, I know she'd forgive me. I haven't even kissed Keri, but Keri is the one she could never forgive me for.

Beth jumps in my arms and wraps her legs around my waist. I kiss her deeply and swing her in a circle. We've never been apart for more than a day since we started dating four years ago. I love Beth. I really do. She's changed who she is for me. I thought, if she were thinner and dressed sexier, I'd lust for her the way I lust for other women. I need that. Beth worked out constantly, became a vegetarian, and dressed in miniskirts and tight leggings. She was undeniably beautiful and sexy. But, it didn't work. I'm still the same. So I have to go.

I twirl Beth around, and on the first spin I see Keri greeting her parents while trying not to react to Beth and my postcard reunion not forty feet away; on the second spin, Keri looks right at me. It's just a glance, yet undeniable. The guilt in my stomach becomes a tumbleweed of nerves. I pretend nothing is wrong as it spreads out. I put Beth down. I get a feeling in my forehead and my temples like I want to cry, but I know I won't; I know I can't. I never cry. I wave good-bye in the general direction of the team, specifically to get a look at Keri. She looks away.

I watch myself break up with Beth. It's disgusting. I can't believe I'm doing this. I steel myself. When I tell her, she cries so violently she heaves as if her chest is going to crack open. My voice never wavers. I watch myself place a stiff arm around her, and when she finally stops bawling, I say things like, *you're a wonderful person, but I'm just not in love with you anymore.* I hate myself for this. I gather my things and leave before her parents come home from work. I want to tell Preacher Dale that I'm sorry I hurt his daughter, that I appreciate him taking me into his home and treating me like a son; but I can't. I can't spend another moment looking at Beth's swollen, bloodshot eyes. I have to leave. I'm a liar, a cheater, a coward. I don't deserve to be here.

I stay in a motel near Cal State. I sleep, drink, and smoke and visit the massage parlors. I pick up a sickly skinny woman from the bar next to the motel who likes to suck cock while she smokes. The more I drink, smoke, and fuck, the darker my mood becomes. I ponder the idea of suicide. I think of my dad. He slit his wrists when he was nineteen, not long after I was born. His sister found him in the bathroom and wrapped a towel around his wrists. He survived. The truth is: I don't want to live right now, but I'm not ready to kill myself. I can always play that card later. That's something I've known for as long as I can remember, probably since I learned about my dad's suicide attempt. On day four, after a fourteen-hour slumber, I get up and leave. I've got Keri and Pepperdine Law waiting for me. Things are going to be different.

SIX

I'm sitting in the Pepperdine Law School cafeteria. Through the wall of windows is a cloudless sky and the Pacific Ocean, blue as far as I can see. I've only been in law school a couple weeks, so the whole thing is still blowing my mind. It's empty in here except for me and Jennifer. Jenifer is Jewish. Jewish people are a new thing for me. There are no Jews in the Inland Empire, at least not that I know of. Jennifer talks a mile a minute. She has flawless white skin, big dark eyes, and long dark hair. She's a third-year student, randomly assigned as my Research and Writing Mentor. She's on track to be valedictorian and has a job lined up at Quinn Emanuel, one of the world's most profitable law firms.

"... and after my morning run and breakfast, and no later than seven a.m., I start my studies," Jennifer says. She emphasizes *seven a.m.* As if that exact time is the real key to her success.

Jennifer walks me through her day in a hushed tone, as if she's revealing the secret to success that will undoubtedly propel me to professional stardom. Basically, this is her secret: *Study your ass off constantly.* She reminds me of me when I used to work with foster kids when I was at Cal State. I was so excited. I thought that since I came from the same type of screwed-up childhood they did, and since I *made it*, that I could just tell them what I did, and the light would miraculously flash in their eyes, and they'd suddenly become honor students instead of inmates.

I spent my three years at Pepperdine Law fighting myself. I knew who I wanted to be, but I just couldn't do it for more than a couple days at a time. I'd have three days of depression, when the best I could do was go to class, sleep, drink, smoke, and jack off to porn. Then I'd give myself a pep talk and get all riled up and promise myself that I was going to be the man I was supposed to be. For maybe a week, I'd study hard, eat well, and exercise. I'd spend hours in the library, then surf and play basketball. I'd stop smoking, stop watching porn, and only have a couple drinks at night. I'd get that feeling I so craved. I felt good. I felt like *I was good*. I'd breathe in the ocean air and see the unbelievable beauty of Malibu—the mountains and the ocean. And then it'd be over, and I wouldn't know what happened until it was too late. I'd get a craving for porn or cigarettes, or I'd hook up with a classmate and feel horrible since I was still with Keri, and the whole thing would unravel. I'd be right back where I started. Each time, the depression got worse, because I hated myself for promising to change and not keeping my promise. I'd miss class and spend the whole day in bed only getting up to drink, smoke, and masturbate.

The law made perfect sense to me. I didn't have to learn to think like a lawyer, because it came naturally. So, without applying myself fully, I was able to stay in the middle of my class. This made me feel even worse, because I knew that if I could ever get myself to study consistently I'd be at the top of the class.

Keri followed me to Pepperdine Law after my first year, and we moved in together. We lived in a tiny studio almost hanging over the ocean. I knew she was what I needed. If she were with me all the time, I'd be fixed. And it worked for a while. I loved her so much. Sometimes when I'd come home and see her sitting on the couch studying, I'd be overwhelmed with joy. I felt safe. I knew that if I had her, I'd always be okay. She's so smart, lovely, and loyal. I thought we'd get married and have great jobs and live the privileged lives of two successful lawyers. I decided to be a good boyfriend and a good student. No more porn, cheating, smoking, drinking, or oversleeping. *Never again*. It wasn't too late to make the most of my law school career.

I lasted about a month, and then I got even worse. Watching Keri work her ass off and take advantage of everything law school had to offer while I struggled to get out of bed to go to class ramped up my depression to a whole new level. We only stayed together for that whole year, because she was so busy studying and working on law review articles that she didn't have time to deal with me. We broke up the summer after her first year.

On occasion, I was able to motivate myself to do something more than the minimum. During my third-year after Keri and I broke up, we teamed up and entered a big moot court competition. Despite my sub-lackluster law school career, I was still intent on becoming a trial lawyer like my mentor, Tito. I put everything I had into that competition, and I felt good again. We won. In fact, with the exception of one relatively close round in the semifinals, when I showed up hung over, we dominated every round, including the finals. The Chief Justice of the California Supreme Court presented us with the award at the Annual Law School Dinner at the Biltmore Hotel in Los Angeles. It was my only moment of glory during my three years in law school, and I was barely sober enough to navigate the stairs up to the stage. I've seen the black and white professional photos of Keri and me shaking hands with Chief Justice Ronald George—Keri and Justice George looking elegant in black tie and dress, and me dressed like an Armenian pimp—but I only recall the event like one recalls a childhood memory.

I graduated, took the Bar, and passed. I was finally a lawyer.

After I received official word that I'd passed the Bar, I got a job working with a sole-practitioner, who'd worked in North County San Diego for twenty years. He had a couple other businesses, and he had so many clients he couldn't handle them all. I hit the ground running, so much so that I couldn't even wait for the swearing-in ceremony. I had to be sworn in by a judge that was about to hear a motion I was scheduled to argue the same day on a multi-million-dollar quadriplegic injury case. I won. I floated out of the courthouse. Life was good. Things were going to be different.

I found an apartment one block from the beach south of the Oceanside pier. Oceanside was a seedy town that fed off the skinny jarheads from Camp Pendleton Marine Base. It had been that way for sixty years, and it was still that way. But it was changing. There were still hookers, strip clubs, porn shops, massage parlors, smoke shops, and dive bars, but the property developers were slowly edging in, starting at the water's edge. When I was a kid, I used to visit my Grandpa and grandma when they visited Oceanside for the summer, and they would tell me not to go north of the pier. Of course, I did. I remember playing with a boy my age whose mom was a hooker. He and I used to play in a roach-infested diner, while his mom was upstairs taking care of business and shooting dope. That motel was razed, and replaced by the condos where my Grandpa now lives (Grandma died of liver failure from drinking at age 56): a green and white sixty-unit complex with balconies, underground parking, and twin Jacuzzis. But, it's still Oceanside, so the Homeowner's Association had to install an automatic electric gate, because they kept finding hookers blowing their johns in the guest parking.

❖   ❖   ❖

I didn't make the most of Pepperdine Law, but I passed the Bar, and I am a lawyer now, and I have a good job. I figure: I was born to be a lawyer, not a law student.

I have a big beautiful office in a Spanish-style building, with room for my desk and a little bookshelf stuffed with the California Codes, *Witkin's Summary of Law*, and *Miller & Starr's Real Property Guide*. I even have a small conference room table. French windows open out to the perfect weather of North County San Diego. Lanny, my boss, and I share a secretary, but since Lanny isn't in the office that much, she is primarily dedicated to me. Lanny has quickly realized that I don't need supervision, and I have even started bringing in some of my own clients. Pat, our secretary, used to be a federal judge's courtroom clerk, and she is an ass-kicker. We crank the work out. I meet with Lanny from time to time to get direction on a case or to let him know what is happening. I am eager, and I overstep my authority every once in a while, but Lanny doesn't get too worked up about it. He's mostly happy to have a lawyer that wants to work and can handle matters without bothering him. Lanny doesn't like to go to court, so I am in court quite often, which is rare for a young civil attorney.

I join the San Diego Trial Attorneys and the North County Bar Association, attend their events, and even have a couple articles published in their journals. I've been appointed to the Ecological Protection Committee Board for the City of Oceanside. I've gotten to know two of the bar owners at the local bars I frequent, and they have both started coming to me for legal advice. Bars, I've come to realize, are a constant source of legal work. After a little more than a year with Lanny, I am getting regular calls and referrals and bringing in half the cases on my desk.

I'm so focused on my career that I'm mostly keeping it together. I've been smoking a lot, and I drink a lot too, but I've nearly abstained from prostitutes. I do occasionally meet a girl at a bar and get laid. I also have a growing porn collection. There are prostitutes on Hill Street just three blocks from my apartment, and it can be tough to resist, but after a couple close calls getting caught while being blown in my car, I decide it's too risky. It's been over a month now. I did try the local massage parlors, but the protocol is different from the ones in the Inland Empire. Maybe it has something to do with the marines, or maybe some deal they have with the cops, but the massage parlors here max out at hand jobs, and that's just not enough. I'm managing on a cocktail of porn, cigarettes, and alcohol, with the occasional one-nighter.

What I really need is a girlfriend. If I find the right girlfriend and settle down, I won't need any of my vices.

❖　　　❖　　　❖

I am sitting at the Fire Stop Bar drinking with the owner and bartender, Johnny Law, when I first see Caroline.

"Johnny!" she yells as she excitedly trots up to the bar. She climbs up and kisses Johnny on the cheek. "How are you?" she asks, but apparently doesn't expect an answer, because she says without pause, "I'd love a Rum and Coke."

"Of course, darling," Johnny says, smirking, as if he is familiar with her routine but willing to play along. Johnny grabs a glass and turns toward me, "Joseph, this is the lovely Caroline. Caroline, this is Joseph."

"Hello, Caroline," I say casually, trying to mask my excitement.

"Joseph is my lawyer," Johnny explains.

"Oh my," Caroline responds. I can't tell whether she is being sarcastic, maybe because I am transfixed by her dark green eyes. "Johnny could use a lawyer," she continues and laughs. She's wearing a tight black T-shirt, and when she laughs her perfect breasts jiggle.

"Please watch my purse, boys. I'm going to use the ladies room."

A trail of eyes follows. She's model skinny, has long black hair and, in heels, is only a couple inches shorter than me. She walks dramatically, and she sucks up energy like a little hurricane.

"Who the fuck is she?" I ask Johnny.

"You like?" Johnny asks while pouring me another free Jack and Coke.

"What's not to like?"

"I've known her for a couple years. She's young, probably too young to be in here. She used to go with Bobby Metz."

I've never met him, but I know Bobby is a pro surfer that owns a local surf shop.

Caroline and I sit at the end of the bar drinking and smoking until Johnny closes up. She talks and talks while I gaze into her eyes. We pound Long Island Iced Teas. She tells me everything, her whole life story. She's not like any of my ex-girlfriends. She's like me. Both of her parents are alcoholics. She's been on her own since she was sixteen. She's in junior college and works in a coffee shop. Her car barely runs, and she's always behind on her rent.

I'm in love.

She drives me down PCH to her apartment in a Ford Festiva that is held together by surf stickers. She keeps bumping the highway divider. I think she's kidding, until I notice she has one eye closed and is squinting through the other. She lives in a tiny converted motel room in Leucadia, a pot-smoking, long-boarding, hippie holdout. Her place is half-quaint, half-pathetic. We make out for a while, but she is so hammered, she passes out. I take off her shoes and tuck her into bed. I lie on the floor and think about our future.

The next morning by the end of breakfast, we are a couple. She moves in the next day. Her car dies, and I give her my 1968 stock-white Camaro RS, and I lease a new truck for myself. We are going to save each other. I tell her this. I'm tired of the drinking and smoking and one-night stands. I tell her I want us to get a Christmas tree, go to family functions, go to lawyer-event dinners, and volunteer together at the Boys & Girls Club. I tell her we are going to be *wholesome*. We make a pact. We even join a gym together. Caroline and I agree to drink only a couple beers during the week and only go out and drink on Fridays and Saturdays, to do no hard drugs, and to keep the smoking to a half-pack a day.

Things are good. I'm sleeping only with her, and I don't even do porn. We've tamped down our drinking and smoking, and we are both working harder. I feel so much better. We rarely fight, and when we do, it's usually about her phone calls to her father. He lives close by, but she never sees him, and she assures me that I will never meet him. She says,

"Daddy would kill me." She says it like she's a five-year-old, child's voice and all. I sit on the couch watching Wimbledon. I mute it so I can hear her. I don't know why. It's always the same thing, and it twists my guts and makes me want to cry and then beat her father to death, who I picture as the drill sergeant in *Full Metal Jacket.* Caroline always has a couple drinks before she calls him, and lights up a cigarette before dialing.

"Hi, Daddy," she says with her little girl voice.

***

"Yes, Daddy ... with my boyfriend ..."

***

"Daddy, don't say that ... Daddy, please ..."

***

"I'm not a whore. Don't say ..."

***

Caroline burst into tears and cries into the phone. I walk over to pull the receiver out of her hand and hang up the phone. She turns away from me so I can't. I can hear him screaming through the receiver.

"Daddy ... Why can't you just love me ..."

I put my arm around her and try to hold her while I pull the phone away. She resists violently, and I have to pry the phone out of her hand. I listen to the receiver. Her dad speaks coolly and cruelly like a TV Nazi. *... and that makes you a whore,* he finishes and hangs up. Caroline runs into the bathroom and locks the door. She knows to lock the door now. Last time I opened the door she had her finger down her throat and was kneeling at the toilet vomiting. I sit at the bathroom door and try to console her, but she's bawling so loudly I'm not sure she can hear me. I tell her, *please, baby, don't do that thing with your finger.* She just cries.

Twenty minutes later she opens the door, and she's silent. She hugs me and kisses me on the neck. As gently and loving as possible I give her my usual spiel about how well my *pretend-he's-dead* technique works with my dad. She doesn't even argue. She's in a trance. That night we make love, and I feel the cuts on her inner thigh. She winces at my touch. I finish. I go to the bathroom and make a warm, wet cloth to clean my cum off her stomach and pussy. I gently wipe her clean. Then I take a cotton swab and dip it in hydrogen peroxide and clean the several long cuts on her inner thigh. Somehow the cuts are beautiful in the candlelight. I dab them with Neosporin. I kiss her good-night and tell her I love her. I roll over, blow out the candles, and stare up toward the ceiling. I think: my girlfriend's bulimic, anorexic, alcoholic, *and* she's a cutter. We are going to fix each other.

❖   ❖   ❖

"Suzie, Oh, my God! Look at you! Did you color your hair? You look so beautiful!" Caroline croons to my Aunt Suzie. She hugs Suzie and kisses her on the cheek, and then pulls my mom into the hug.

"Marie. Look at you," Caroline continues, "Your sweater is so adorable! Have you lost weight? You look amazing."

My Auntie Suzie and mom lap it up like puppies at a milk bowl. It irritates me. It's like Mexican TV, when the guy in the bee costume shows up out of nowhere and everybody is laughing—I don't get it. Caroline's spell is even more effective on men.

It's Christmas, and my Grandpa has just pulled up to Aunt Suzie's driveway. Caroline is the first to meet him at the door.

"Bill!" She runs and hugs him. "How are you? You look so handsome! Joseph, doesn't he look handsome?"

"Hello, Grandpa," I respond deadpan. "Yes, indeed, you are looking good, Grandpa."

"Such a handsome man," Caroline says.

I want to scream, enough already!

I scan the room, while Caroline is hugging my Grandpa. I want to see someone's eyes roll, some indication that I am not the only one thinking she is more than just a little over-the-top. Nothing. All glazed-over puppy-dog eyes. My Aunt Suzie, Uncle Billy, Mom, Grandpa, they all fucking love her. I love her, too, but I know who she really is. All they see is this version. Maybe I'm jealous, I think. If I could woo a jury the way she woos my family I'd be the best trial lawyer in the country. Actually, maybe I do have a little Caroline in me. I won my first trial just a month ago. It was a case I shouldn't have won, but I did, because the jury liked me, especially the jury foreman, a cute Black-Asian girl who gave me her number after the trial. Caroline is going on and on about how handsome Grandpa looks in his Christmas sweater, a hideous thing, and I am reminded of Caroline adjusting my tie just before I left for my closing argument at my first jury trial, *my handsome man,* she said.

We eat turkey and then open presents by the Christmas tree. Caroline wrapped everyone's gift differently and wrote out sweet little cards. Everyone is happy. I feel serene. I feel safe. Everything is right on track. This is what I've always wanted. Caroline and I, we are wholesome. One day soon we'll be married and live in a beautiful sun-filled home like this one, and we'll have a kid and a couple Labradors. I want to feel like this forever.

Caroline makes her round of elaborate good-byes, and we drive back to Oceanside. Neither of us have smoked all day, so we are both itching for a cigarette. And, we reason, we might as well get a drink, too. I park the car and quickly unload the Christmas presents, and we walk briskly to the Fire Stop Bar. Johnny Law is there bartending. Caroline gives him a tin of chocolate-chip cookies my mom baked. The only other people in the bar are marines. We joke with Johnny that we couldn't leave him alone on Christmas. We drink hard and fast. By midnight we are wasted and horny.

We stop by the porn shop on the way home. It's Christmas, but after five Jack and Cokes, it seems okay. We make the all-male patrons, mostly jarheads, uncomfortable with our tipsy pointing and laughing. Some leave. The clerk asks us to do the same. We buy *Best of Christy Canyon, Volume 1* videotape and a battery-operated dildo with a remote control.

It has a clear tip that is filled with colored beads and a remote that adjusts the speed at which the tip both rotates and gyrates. Protruding out of the base of the dildo is an extension shaped like a snake tongue that vibrates. It's meant to sit right on the clit when the dildo is inserted. It's a *goddamn* utilitarian work of art.

I always feel athletic when I drink hard. I carry Caroline piggyback all the way back to the apartment. We fuck and drink a half pint of vodka. Our new superdildo is not as great as we'd hoped. We play the video. For a few moments I find myself in that state of drunkenness, that place just before I blackout, where I float above myself and observe me. There I am. Caroline is riding me. Sometimes she fucks to get me off, but this is all for her. Her perfect tits jiggle, and she grinds away. Christy Canyon, my favorite porn star, is on the TV screen, moaning. A big-haired blonde has her face buried in Christy's bush. Caroline grinds away. She digs her nails into my chest. There is no way I'm cumming again. My cock is numb. I envision our upstairs neighbor, a little bubble-butted surfer girl, and wonder if she'd join in with us. Christy Canyon says, "Oh God … stick your tongue in my ass." Caroline trembles, cums and collapses. I stare at the ceiling. I feel disgusting. I wish we had come home, made love, and gone to sleep. This is not a wholesome Christmas.

It's been over a month since Caroline left for a semester of college and, supposedly, an audition as a runway model in London. By the time I dropped her off at LAX, she'd whittled her 5'10" frame to 115 pounds. Her C's are now B's, and she's pale and gaunt. She looks like the girls in the Robert Palmer video, "Simply Irresistible." If she were a few years younger, she'd probably have a shot at modeling. I didn't want her to leave, but I also figured it'd be good for her to travel. Our wholesome living plan wasn't working out very well anyway.

I try to fill the void left by Caroline by working harder. I do well for a couple weeks, and then I start arranging meetings and court hearings in Los Angeles or Orange County early on Fridays, so my weekends start around noon. I go berserk on the weekends—drinking, smoking, porn, prostitutes—and then I pull it together and work hard on the weekdays. It's not long before I start drinking and smoking during the week, and after a while I fill every minute I'm not working or sleeping with some combination of my cocktail of debauchery.

I'm exhausted.

I'm at the Fire Stop Bar hanging with Johnny Law and some of the strippers from Candy Land. Johnny lets them drink for free on Sundays to attract jarheads. Cindi, who introduces herself to me as *Cindy-with-an-I*, talks to me rapid-fire. She's done several lines of coke with Johnny, and she just keeps talking. I nod my head and admire her skirt, which is hiked so high I can see her little white cotton triangle. She says she knows Caroline, knows I'm Caroline's boyfriend, and knows that I'm Johnny's lawyer. I'm relieved for a moment. I figure her knowing Caroline is extra insurance that I won't end up fucking her—even though she's a petite little blonde, wearing a stripper-modified, Catholic schoolgirl uniform, and there is nothing I'd rather do right now than fuck her. Cindi rambles on through several more drinks and places her hand on my thigh and drags her fake red nails up and down. She giggles and says, "You know, Caroline's not here, but I am."

I feel my cock rise, and I have a fleeting idea that just maybe I can reverse this decision, kind of like when I tell myself I'm not going to drink or smoke anymore. But that's ridiculous. I can't stop time. It's already done. Cindi and I are wrapped together like snakes as we rush to my apartment. She just keeps talking—all the way to my bed.

Cindi is the best kind of whore. She needs every hole filled. We fuck like grubby acrobats. I lose track of time, but I think it's not too long before I need to get up for work. I cum for the last time. She lies with her head on my chest and tells me about her eight-year-old daughter, who rides horses. I can barely contain the disgust I feel for myself. I want to wash off the last month since Caroline left. Here I am with Cindi, lying in the same bed Caroline and I make love in. Cindi tells me sweet stories about her eight-year-old daughter, and all I can do is nod and say, "Ahh," and try to pretend I don't want to crawl out of my skin.

Eventually she shuts up, and we both pass out.

The big, red, digital numbers on the clock read 5:45. The numbers reverberate in my conscious, and I silently churn them until the relevance attacks me. I wrestle the sheets and blankets and whip my legs up, grabbing the alarm clock.

"5:45!" I shout.

There is a wrestling and a sleepy voice that I don't recognize.

"It's so early," the voice says.

It's Cindi. The night comes rushing back.

"Oh Jesus Christ!" I yell.

I jam a suit on.

"I've got to go," I say. "Uh ... uh. Thank you." I kiss her cheek. She barely moves.

I jump in my truck. I am supposed to be in Los Angeles for a hearing at 8:00. It's a two-hour drive, and I'm probably not going to make it. I can call the clerk and ask to be put on second call.

My boss Lanny calls, and I nearly swerve off the freeway trying to answer my mobile phone.

"Yeah, Lanny. What's up?"

"Where are you?" Lanny says curtly.

"Uh ... you want to go to the court hearing with me?" I ask.

He does.

Lanny has this annoying habit of telling me that he is going to handle a court hearing but that he wants me to be prepared for it just in case he can't go. I've learned over my two years with him that this means there is a one-in-fifty chance that he'll actually go. But, apparently, this is that one-in-fifty. *Bad timing.* This is a big federal case that I've been handling by myself against two of the biggest law firms in Los Angeles. I've come within inches of hitting a home run and winning a summary judgment motion on a tenuous argument. The clients love me. I'm more than irritated that Lanny wants to get involved now, today of all days.

I meet Lanny in the parking lot. He's standing in front of his truck with the engine running.

"Do you have the file?" he asks.

"Of course, Lanny" I say. I've never seen him this angry.

"I told you I was going to the hearing," Lanny snaps at me. "I came in early, and the file wasn't there."

I feel the heat rise up in me, and I go on the offensive.

"You *always* say you are going to go, Lanny. I didn't know you were *really* going to go this time. I took the file home over the weekend to prepare for the hearing."

Lanny is a really sweet guy, so this is a surprise to me. I wonder if this has something to do with me recently asking him if he wants to be partners. Maybe he's worried I'm going to leave and steal his clients. Whatever the case, I'm pissed. I work too hard and bring in too much money to put up with this shit.

"I go to *all* the hearings, Lanny. I write *all* the motions," I say sarcastically.

This is true, and although I've slacked a little the last month, I still average at least sixty hours a week. I recently worked thirty hours straight, spent the night at the office to finish a motion, and then drove it down to downtown San Diego to file it, all because Lanny had failed to tell me until the last second that he'd attended a telephonic hearing and the judge wanted the motion filed by Monday. I had to pull over and sleep on the side of the fucking freeway. This thought makes me even angrier. And Lanny probably thinks it's no big deal, because he doesn't have the faintest idea how much time goes into a hard-hitting motion. He only writes two-page, bullshit motions. And I won that fucking motion, too, which was a malpractice case against him, no less.

"Here," I say, and push the file into his chest.

Lanny is red with anger. He's twenty years older than me, but he's one of those stout, eastern European, tough motherfuckers. For a second I think I might have to fight him right here in this parking lot.

"Go home, Joseph," Lanny says, "Take the day off. We'll talk when I get back."

I can't believe he just said that. I don't even respond. I'm seething. *Fuck him.* I'm done. I park my car, walk up to my office, and load all my stuff into three banker's boxes.

SEVEN

I am ready to start all over with Caroline. I've even been faithful to her since I moved from Oceanside to Riverside four months ago for my new job with Thomas & Colbert. Yes, I've been drinking and smoking a lot, and my massage parlor habit is up to a few sessions per week, and my porn collection is impressive, but I haven't had any one-night stands or picked up any prostitutes, except one—one prostitute and that's it. And that was an isolated incident, just a car blow job, and I'm blocking it out of my mind, because I promised myself I wouldn't do that anymore. Although I do think of it from time to time, and it worries me a bit.

I can't wait for Caroline to come home from London. I've already fucked up two relationships with women I love. I'm not fucking up another one. I'm going to make this work. Caroline is young and beautiful, and she's a fighter. I love her. She has her issues, but I know she wants a wholesome life just like me. We'll put Oceanside behind us and start fresh. We'll stop all the partying and drinking and smoking and drink like normal people. Maybe we'll even go to church and volunteer at the Boys & Girls Club. At Christmas we'll decorate a Christmas tree, and at Thanksgiving we'll cook turkeys for the homeless, shit like that. It's going to be perfect clean living as soon as she gets home.

I rented this big expensive brand-new apartment. Caroline's going to love it. I've carefully unpacked her clothes and placed them into the drawers of the new IKEA dresser I spent an absurd amount of time assembling. We talk on the phone often. She calls drunk, asks me to wire money, says she can't wait to see me.

❖   ❖   ❖

I am in bed sick when Caroline unlocks the door.

"Joseph?"

I don't answer. I want her to come into the bedroom and take care of me.

"He's asleep," she whispers into her cell phone, "Yeah, yeah, yeah … Kathy, Jesus. Don't worry about it. I'll tell him I promised I'd come to your birthday party … I know it's not, Stupid … Don't worry, we'll be *part-y-ing* tonight *girlfriend* … gotta go."

Caroline came back from London, but she never came back to me. She keeps making excuses to stay in San Diego: Her mom is sick, then her dad needs her help moving, then she's getting her school transcripts, and her stepsister *this* and her good friend *that*. She's been home for two weeks, and she's only spent the night in our bed once. One excuse follows the next. Caroline is a terrible liar. She knows I know she's lying. She can't help it. I get it. She doesn't really have a choice. It's the way she's built.

Caroline walks into the bedroom. Her musky perfume is familiar. I pretend I'm asleep. She lies on the bed and strokes my hair. I am so mad, but it feels so good. My grandma used to come into my room and stroke my hair just like Caroline is doing. I'd be so mad at her for causing a drunken scene at a restaurant, and ruining dinner and humiliating Grandpa and me, that I'd want to turn away and tell her to leave me alone, but I couldn't. Her touch felt so good, so I'd just lie there in the dark and pretend I was asleep.

"Are you awake?" Caroline whispers.

"I feel terrible," I moan with a little added drama. I snuggle up to her. "I'm so glad you're finally here to take care of me, baby."

"Oh, baby, poor baby," Caroline croons, "Can I get you anything?"

She goes into the kitchen. I hear the freezer door open, which means she's getting some vodka for herself. She comes back with orange juice for me and a screwdriver for her.

"Baby ... Don't be mad, okay? ... I know you are sick, baby, *my handsome man*, but Kathy's birthday party is tonight, and I promised her I'd go." Caroline purses her lips into a pouty face. "She's my little sister. I don't want to leave, but I can't not go to my little sister's birthday party, can I? I promised her, baby."

I am fuming with anger, but I want to give her a way out. I sit up against the headboard. Tissues spill out from the folds of the comforter.

"You've been finding an excuse not to stay here for weeks," I say. "What is the problem, Caroline? I know you don't want to live in Riverside, but this is where my job is, and I support us. I pay for that cell phone you talk on and that car you drive and this apartment and that overpriced fucking perfume you're wearing."

I'm more hurt than angry. I know there's no changing Caroline's mind about anything. I know she has no choice but to lie. We both know she's going to lie.

"I know, baby. It'll be different soon," she says.

"I need you to stay here with me. *Today.* I'm sick, and I need to be better by Monday for work. I have two depos scheduled. Please don't go, please." I'm one notch above begging. I want her to change her mind. She doesn't know what's at stake. "Call your sister, and tell her you can't go, because I'm really sick. I am *really* sick. Please, baby," I plead. I want her to turn the corner on this lie so badly. I know she won't. A good liar never turns back from a lie.

I hear the door shut and her key chain jangle, as Caroline locks the dead bolt from the outside. *Tap-tap-tap*, down the stairs. Caroline says she'll leave her sister's party early and be back tonight.

Right.

I sleep and sleep. I wake just before 2:00 p.m. the next day. Caroline isn't back and hasn't even called. I am still green-sick. *That's it,* I conclude.

She's made her decision. I drag my body to the hardware store and buy a new dead bolt and install it. I pack all of Caroline's belongings into the same boxes I unpacked them from five months ago. I drive ninety miles to her mom's house in Oceanside. Her mom is pacing and beside herself, as I unload Caroline's belongings into the middle of the living room. She calls Caroline over and over and leaves frantic messages. I want Caroline to answer, but I know she won't. If she were to answer and come over and sincerely apologize, I might forgive her, but I know it's for the best, because she isn't going to change. Caroline's mom tries to talk me out of leaving her daughter.

"It isn't even Kathy's birthday!" Caroline's mom blurts out, and then realizes she may have made a mistake—maybe I didn't know it wasn't Kathy's birthday. She stumbles around some explanation about maybe they are out celebrating Kathy's birthday after-the-fact.

"When is Kathy's birthday?" I ask. She pretends she doesn't hear me, changes the subject, and trails off. I see the same expression Caroline gets when she lies, and I realize that Caroline's mom is a liar, too. Of course she is.

I drive home in an emotional and physical haze. I barely make it. I sleep until I hear keys jangling and the door rattling the next day. It takes Caroline a while to figure out the key doesn't work, and a little longer that the lock has actually been changed. She freaks out. She calls my cell phone over and over, but I don't answer. I lie in bed and stare at the little numbers on the little screen as my phone rings impatiently. She can hear my phone from outside the door. She bangs on the door.

"I know you're in there!" Caroline yells. "Please, Joseph. Please … Why are you doing this to me?"

She cries. It's authentic. She's like me, and is scared to hell, above all else, of being poor and alone. I can hear it. She's just realized that her safety net has been cut wide-open. She doesn't have a place to stay or a man to take care of her. She thinks of the car I pay for, that spending the night at her sister's isn't open-ended. She cries and cries. I can't take it anymore. After about ten minutes, I open the door as far as the chain will allow.

"You fucking lied to me!" I yell at her. "I heard you, Caroline. I heard you on your cell phone tell Kathy ... It wasn't even her birthday!" I want Caroline to know that I gave her chances and she chose to blow them off. "I'm here sick as a dog ... You've only spent the night here once since the night you came back, and you lie to me just so you can go *fucking* party with your sister!"

"But ... I just ... I just wanted ... No-oh, no-ho-o, no ..." Caroline begins howling, "No," and sobbing uncontrollably. She collapses into a pile at the base of the door.

"You just wanted what, Caroline ... to go drinking instead of staying home with the man you say you love? I *begged* you to stay. I wouldn't have even cared that you lied about your sister, if you just would have stayed. I take care of you! I pay for your food, your cell phone, and the rent ... and the money I wired you in London. I can't fucking believe you."

I let it linger. She's sobbing hard enough to crack a rib, "Oh God ... no ... no ... please, God, no. Please don't leave me ..."

My chest and my heart and my lungs are empty. I want to implode, to rip my skin off. It's that kind of pain; my organs are crying. It makes me want to kill myself. I am past angry. I am a void. I could almost cry. I can't believe she lied to me like that, treating me like a fool, using me. How could she be so uncaring? I just can't go back. I just can't forgive her. It's over.

She cries into the crack in the front door. I shut my bedroom door and pull the covers over my head. The sound is wretched, like a dying animal's, because in her mind that's what she is. Finally, after fifteen minutes and a visit from a neighbor and then the apartment's security, she gives up, then *taps-taps-taps* down the stairs and drives away. Yesterday: I am dreaming of our new life together, of asking her to marry me, of proudly holding hands at a luncheon with other married couples from Thomas & Colbert. Today: she's banished from my life.

I'm too sick to jack off, drink, or smoke. I go fetal until I fall asleep.

❖   ❖   ❖

Thomas & Colbert is the largest, oldest, and one of the most prestigious law firms in the Inland Empire. They own a mid-century, three-story, glass and steel building in downtown Riverside a couple blocks from the federal and county courthouses. It has its own law library. There is a wall in the stairwell where quirky pictures of all past and current partners hang, dating back nearly a hundred years. Thomas & Colbert's reputation, especially the partners, is impeccable. I know about Thomas & Colbert from when I worked for Tito. He had several multimillion-dollar catastrophic-injury cases, for which Thomas & Colbert represented the corporate defendants. Tito wrote me a letter of recommendation addressed directly to the managing partner of Thomas & Colbert, Jack Clinton, which couldn't have carried more weight if it had been authored by Jesus Christ. Tito's status, even among his adversaries, is legendary.

The fact that I'd clerked for Tito and thus been exposed to huge liability cases, before I'd even stepped foot into law school, wasn't the only reason Thomas & Colbert wanted me. The amount of experience I had at Lanny's was extraordinary for a two-year attorney. I'd been in every court—state, federal, appellate, administrative, bankruptcy—and handled the gamut of civil litigation cases, both plaintiff and defense, from medical malpractice to elder abuse to personal injury to contracts to real estate to civil rights. I'd been published twice, had a successful jury trial, took dozens of depositions, handled mediations and arbitrations, and had a long law-and-motion résumé and appellate briefs with several victories. The advantage of having worked for Lanny was that I did everything. First-year attorneys at firms like Thomas & Colbert wouldn't even argue a motion they drafted, let alone try a jury trial by themselves. Just a second-year attorney, I had more experience than most big-firm lawyers had after five years of practice. On top of that, I'd graduated from Pepperdine, Jack Clinton's and a couple of other partners' alma mater. And, most importantly at Thomas & Colbert, still a country club firm at heart—I was tall, white, bright, and polite.

After a couple months, I am one of the top billers, and they give me a big corner office with a couch and a dedicated secretary. The senior partner assigns me a case while he is on leave, because his mother died, and the case gets some media attention, because it is a First Amendment libel lawsuit between two millionaire candidates running for office. I write, argue, win a motion, and get the case dismissed. I read myself quoted in the *Riverside Press Enterprise*: "'We won, because my client has a right to free speech under the First Amendment. It's as simple as that,' attorney Joseph Naus said." They announce my victory over the inter-com at Thomas & Colbert, "Your attention please. We'd like to take a moment to congratulate Joseph Naus for his victory in the *Barry* matter. Congratulations, Joseph."

Yes, Caroline is gone now, and I am starting over, but things couldn't be any better.

My plan to achieve domestic bliss with Caroline in this new location has failed before it even began, so I decide to try something new: *Fuck every girl that will let me.* I start with Tracy, a fellow Thomas & Colbert attorney's secretary. She is a twenty-five-year-old divorcée with a daughter. She has long blonde hair and matching legs and is tattooed everywhere clothes typically cover. Then, I add Jill, one of the partner's secretaries. She is bookish but ravenous, and more than once we fuck on the giant Thomas & Colbert conference room table on a Sunday—a source of great pride and amusement for me during the weekly Monday morning attorney calendar meetings. Then there's Elvira, a fourth-year attorney at Thomas & Colbert. She has a perfect bubble butt. Then, there is Jena, my favorite. She is a paralegal at a neighboring firm. Her dad is a well-known legal malpractice lawyer. He was in the Korean War and married a Korean woman. Jena is the blessed result. She has full lips and almond-shaped eyes with a wide cat smile. She is mischievous and curvaceous, has the ass and legs of a German high jumper, and she fucks like she is trying to hurt me.

Then there are the massage parlors. I handle cases at the Palm Springs Courthouse, sixty miles east, so I drive out there, make my court appearances on two cases at once, and come back to the office around lunch and already have ten hours billed. I stop in at Royal Massage in San Bernardino, next door to the massage parlor I used to go to when I was at Cal State. I've found a girl named Sunny who speaks fluent analingus and has big natural tits.

I feel a terrible sinking guilt the moment after I collapse after fucking Sunny. The feeling is diluted somewhat by the thought that I just billed ten hours and thus am an industrious scumbag and not a slothful scumbag. On the weekends, sometimes I hit two massage parlors. I have the money, and it's much better than porn or fucking Jena, Jill, Elvira, or Tracy. They'd think I was a freak, if I asked them to do the things that Sunny does, except for Jena; I don't even have to ask her. But even with Jena, it's just different. There isn't that insane charge of anticipation I'd get while on my way to the massage parlor. Sometimes I'll be driving down the road, and out of nowhere I get the feeling, and it's over. My car just goes. My stomach quivers with anticipation, and beads of sweat rise up on my forehead. I become possessed. Once it starts, there is little that can stop me. Next thing I know, I'm lying in one of the familiar bare rooms waiting for a petite little Asian woman, Spring, Sunny, April, May, or June. Next thing I know, I'm glazed in sweat, and we're done, and she's left to get me a warm towel. Next thing I know, *here I am again*, soaking in guilt and self-loathing and wondering how I could have broken my promise not to do it again … again.

And then there is Dante.

My apartment is a few blocks away from a cheesy nightclub-sports bar, Calypso Beach Bar & Grill. Coincidentally, Jena had worked there as a bartender before I knew her a couple years ago when Calypso only employed bikini-clad twenty-somethings. I start drinking here after work and befriend the owner, a twenty-five-year-old Mexican hustler named Jose. Jose and his wife have an impressive stack of cards, each card financing the other. I am Jose's off-the-record lawyer, and I point him in the right direction on employment issues, Alcohol Bureau Control matters, contracts, and on various other legal issues. In exchange, I get some cash, an endless bar tab, and get to play the big shot in his nightclub. This is how I meet Dante. She is a petite, light-skinned, black girl with big beautiful brown eyes and freckles sprinkled across her nose. She has the body of a sprinter—literally; she is fresh out of college where she sprinted on the track team. The first night I meet her I am drunk out of my mind. It's dark, and the club is packed. A bad reggae cover band is playing. Jose introduces us and tells her to constantly serve me Jack & Cokes. I flirt with her and tip her five dollars every time she brings me a drink. Just before the club closes, she hands me a drink. I hand it back to her and tell her to hold it. I lift her up and carry her to the dark kitchen. We make out.

We leave for Las Vegas after her shift. I am on the verge of blacking out, but I don't. Instead I remain in a surreal world, just on the edge of reality. I never drink and drive, so Dante drives my car the whole way. We stop for gas and snacks. The road is empty. It's not long after 9/11, and Las Vegas is still dead. I lose chunks of time during the three-hour drive, but I am cognizant when I tell her that she is perfect, and that we should get married. I mean it. Why not? We check into the New York, New York Hotel. It's nearly empty and everyone stares at us. I wonder if it's because she's so gorgeous or because she's black.

She is flawless and tight. I'm just drunk enough to treat her like a whore. For hours, I build up to orgasm and then release and cum and start over; each time, it builds a little more. This is going to be the best orgasm I've ever had. She reluctantly lets me fuck her in the ass. It hurts her. I can tell this is her first time. It's so intense that my grip on her hips leaves bruises. I feel the absence of all feeling except pure bliss as everything I've ever felt gathers in my balls and then fires out of my cock. I cum in her face in three distinct streams, the first of which actually splatters. I collapse, and the feeling of disgust and guilt enters me before I even unclench my ass. Dante says nothing and yet I can feel her trying to pretend it's okay.

She goes to the bathroom. I keep my eyes closed. I hear the faucet, the flush, the faucet. When she returns to bed smelling fresh I pretend I'm asleep. She lays her head on my chest, wanting to talk. I fall asleep.

"Good morning, Joseph," Dante says, all pep, and then goes into the bathroom.

I remember that she doesn't smoke or drink, so we were clearly in two different states last night.

"Dante ... what a crazy night, right?" I emphasize the word, *crazy* and pretend that I'm groggier than I actually am.

"Yeah," she responds over the faucet noise, "Wow, my mom isn't going to believe it. *Married.* She'll be so mad."

Fuck, I think so loudly that I wonder if she hears me think it. Dante really thinks we are getting married. *Fuck. Fuck. Fuck.* I don't know whether to pretend I don't remember what happened last night or whether to be honest about it. Part of me just wants to go along. Hell, she is young and hot. She can't be too much crazier than Caroline, and I was going to marry Caroline. *Don't be ridiculous. This is crazy.*

"Uhhm ... Dante ... I'm not sure that ..."

She can't hear me over the shower and interrupts me.

"So where are we going to do it?" she shouts over the shower. "Don't we have to get a license or something? I mean, you are the lawyer, Mr. Naus. Mrs. Naus ... *Misses* Naus."

It's a long drive back.

❖   ❖   ❖

For the better part of a year, while working at Thomas & Colbert, I've been dating five women; drinking heavy every few days; secretly chain-smoking a pack of cigarettes every night; and visiting massage parlors a couple times a week. I want to stop. I'm exhausted. I just go from fix to fix. I want to meet a girl I can eventually marry and settle down with, as I was planning to do with Caroline.

I meet Alison through an online dating site. She thinks I am everything she wants: a pull-out-your-chair and open-your-door-for-you, tall, clean-cut, suit-wearing, career-driven lawyer. She is sold the first time we meet for lunch. I actually don't like her that much, but the *idea* of her is perfect. Alison is definitely girlfriend material. She's a Pulitzer nominated *Los Angeles Times* reporter working the Inland Empire bureau, and her office is three blocks from Thomas & Colbert. She's petite, cute, wicked-smart, a redhead from Alabama with huge, natural tits. Her liberal views are harsh—something akin to reverse fascism. Being around her taxes me. At any moment she may catch me saying something politically incorrect, maybe admiring a fur coat, or referring to my black friend as *black*. Obviously she'd have strong opinions about my porn collection, my binge drinking, my pack-a-day cigarette habit, let alone my penchant for anal sex with Asian prostitutes, so I have to carefully hide these things from her. Alison is kind of a bitch. I decide she is the one I should settle down with.

It's time to get serious. Enough fucking around. Here's the plan: Alison and I will date for a while. I'll taper off my drinking until I reach the point where I can just have a couple beers or glasses of wine. I'll quit smoking altogether. I'll slowly rein in the massage parlor visits, and eventually quit them all together. No earlier than six months from now, and no later than a year, we'll move in together. Then, no more than two years from then, we'll get married, at the Mission Inn in Riverside. By then, I'll be close to making partner, and I'll have become more active in professional organizations and politics. I'll probably have my eye on a city council seat or maybe a county supervisor position. She'll have published her first true-crime novel and will have progressed in her television news career. Maybe she'll even have a regular spot on a news show, or even her own show by then. We'll be a serious power couple.

❖   ❖   ❖

Riverside's Annual Orange Blossom Festival will be my last blowout before I turn my life around and settle down with Alison. I tell Alison that I have to work, so I can't take her, and I make a deal with my friend, Danny. I pay for all his drinks, but he has to drive my car. Danny is broke and alcoholic, so it's a good deal for him, even though he already has two DUIs. It's a good deal for me, because I never drink and drive. It's one rule I've made for myself that I will not break.

We arrive in the heat of midday. It's over a hundred degrees. We walk and drink and smoke and watch and flirt with skinny young girls in short shorts and curvy moms. And then we drink and smoke some more. We watch local rock bands and hop from bar to bar. I lose some time in the gray of my mind after we drink whiskey and smoke cigars at a cigar bar. There are some junior-college girls. One sits on my lap. It seems much later now. It's dark out, and I find myself dancing in a packed, dark club. I'm not sure that I'm dancing with the girl whose back is to me, until she presses her ass into me and glances back and smiles. There are more drinks, shots this time. And then much later I am walking with Danny. My ears ring. The courthouse looks beautiful at night just like it did when I was a kid, riding my bike by its majestic white stairs, dreaming of walking in the door with a briefcase and wearing a tie. Everyone has gone home except us and the bums. Only the trash remains.

The warm night air sets me free. I run around yelling, as I often do when I reach the dreamy state of intoxication. I run up the steps of the courthouse like Rocky. Danny tries to rein me in. I lead us in a friendly altercation with a group of bums under the outdoor chandelier of a bright, white, colonial-style title company building, just across from Thomas & Colbert. I talk of Vietnam as if I'd been there. I channel the Vietnam vet my mom used to smoke pot with in the Alley. *Yeah, Ting Cri was a drag, man.* I promise them Danny and I will be back to help them later, and I mean it. I really mean it, *man.* They are drunk or crazy or both, so they understand me. I run away excited with the prospect that I'll soon be helping these bums start new prosperous lives, not unlike what I'm about to do for myself.

We arrive back at my SUV. It's the only vehicle left in the parking lot. Danny refuses to drive. He is in the passenger seat, and I am driving. I'm talking about the bums, and how we can help them. Energy pulses through me. I feel like I could take on the world. We rage down the 91 Freeway. We reach eighty miles per hour. The speed feels good. I crank up the music as loud as the speakers will go. Social Distortion blares out of the speakers, egging me on to go faster. Danny says, "Careful, man".

Fucking pussy. If you wanted to drive, you should have.

Danny grabs the dashboard as I whip around a solitary car on this barren freeway. We reach ninety miles per hour. I sing along to the blasting rock of Social Distortion,

"Sick boy ... na nah na nah na nah ..."

I follow the cambered transition from the 91 northbound to the 60 eastbound at around eighty-five miles per hour. And then I'm no longer steering. Centrifugal force and inertia are in control. My SUV slides and then rolls over to the driver's side. I'm in a three-dimensional, slow motion kaleidoscope. I'm sideways, held in position by my seat belt. My head is inches from the ground. I'm in a drive-through car wash, but instead of water and brushes, we are rushing through the foliage and skinny trees on the side of the off-ramp. We slide, mowing over the little trees. A pure sheet of bright white smashes me in the face. I see stars. It feels like being kicked in the side of the head with a roundhouse in that spot just behind the ear that makes the brain go haywire for a couple seconds. And then everything stops. Time stops so I can appreciate the precise wrinkle of space between the car wreck that is officially over and the aftermath that has officially begun. With clarity purer than I ever thought possible, I hear the voice in my head speak.

This is not all right. This is not all right.

Yeah, I know. You're right, Joseph. This is not all right. This is what you've been waiting for, right? You knew something had to happen.

The deflated white bags, those are the airbags. I've never been hit so hard, not by kick or punch.

Am I still alive?

I'm still alive.

The music is still blasting, now over perfect silence.

"Sick boy. Nah-na-na-na ... Sick boy."

My arms work. I can feel my breath.

Danny, oh fuck, Danny.

"Danny, are you alright?" I ask.

He isn't responding. He's slumped. His eyes are shut. He's hanging limp against the seat belt. My body jerks to life in a panic.

"Danny!" I yell over the raging music. "Fuckin' Danny, man! Don't do this, c'mon, man!"

It feels so strange to be in a car in this position. My entire body weight is strung tightly against the seat belt. Tiny bloody glass cubes and debris from the rear are strewn about the front of the car. A solitary softball cleat, several golf balls, empty 7-Eleven coffee cups, CD cases. I reach across Danny and pull myself up by the handle above his door to create slack in my seat belt. I struggle against the tension and manage to unbuckle myself.

"Danny! C'mon, man!" I scream desperately. "You have to wake up, man, c'mon!"

I try to open Danny's door, but I can't. There's blood on me, but I feel fully alert and feel as strong as I've ever felt. I turn toward Danny; I hang by the handle above his door, and kick across his body through the broken passenger side window. I keep kicking until I clear the window space. With each kick, little cubes of glass rain down on us. A couple pieces cling to the blood on Danny's lips. He doesn't react.

"Danny. You fucker! Wake up!"

It hits me. *He may not be unconscious. He may be dead.* This can't be happening. This can't be happening.

I grab Danny by his hair and shake him hard. "Danny, Danny. C'mon, Man, c'mon. You are alright!" I shout desperately over the music.

"Sick boy ... nah, na-na ..."

Danny stirs, opens his eyes, and mumbles a few cuss words.

Oh God ... fuck. Thank you, God.

I crawl out through the passenger window, straddle the doorframe, and help pull Danny up through the window. The headlights shine so quietly, and the music is distant out here. The front passenger wheel spins eerily. I jump off onto the grass median. Danny sits on the curb, bent over in pain. He's broken something, but he's alive. Every window I can see is broken. The underside of the SUV is so foreign, so ugly. It should never be seen like this. It's a full moon, and the polished white paint reflects the moon light. My vehicle is crumpled and mangled and has lost half its length.

Within a couple minutes, we are in a much different scene. Reality has reacted, and we have a show going: tons of spinning red and blue lights; orange cones; official trucks and law enforcement vehicles; white, medical, and black and tan uniforms. Danny is carried off on a stretcher and swallowed up in the back of an ambulance. I watch it drive away. A CHP officer has me blow into a Breathalyzer. Then he cuffs me.

"Check it out," he says. He shows his partner the reading, "point-two-nine."

"Nice," the partner says sarcastically. "Oh, Man, that's a good one," he says as he searches my wallet. "Even better, look at this," he holds up my business card, "He's a lawyer. Joseph W. Naus, *Esquire*. Thomas &

Colbert," he reads aloud and then turns to me, "I have a feeling this type of thing is frowned upon at the firm, Mr. Naus."

Keri bails me out and picks me up the next day. We go to the junkyard to get my personal belongings. I'm still wearing a blood-splattered, blue hospital shirt. A leathery old man in blue coveralls walks us out to my SUV. It looks deathly in the blaring sun. We stare, shake our heads, and make disapproving comments like Grandparents watching MTV for the first time. Every window is shattered. Every panel is crinkled like an accordion. The back axles are snapped, and the rims lie flush against the ground. Each door is wedged shut and held closed with twine. The hood is folded in two and angled toward.

Keri and I and the old man in the coveralls take it all in for a second. I see my reflection in the cracked side mirror and stare at myself for a few beats. A swath of hair is stuck to my forehead from dried blood. I have swollen, black and blue eyes, and my big nose is split on the bridge.

The old man in coveralls says, "Goddamn," with great sincerity.

PART II

EIGHT

This is not part of the plan. It hasn't even been two years since I left Thomas & Colbert and Riverside to get a fresh start in Los Angeles. I left Riverside in shame—a fallen legal star—after my drunk-driving accident. After that, I lost my swagger. I couldn't look any of the partners in the eye, so I had to leave. But then everything fell into place for a perfect new beginning. I got a great job with a prestigious law firm making even more money. I moved into a beautiful condo in Santa Monica. After a year at the new firm, I left and started my own practice with a buddy from law school: Yi & Naus. We opened up an office in Pasadena and even had a satellite office downtown. Now I'm making even more money. I have a beautiful young girlfriend, Larisa. I have it all. But I didn't leave my feelings of dread in Riverside, and I didn't leave my cravings there either. And no matter how much money I make, I still wake up in the morning with the feeling of dread, and I still try to make it go away however I can: porn, prostitutes, massage parlors, binge drinking, cigarettes, one-night stands. And so, here I am again, after a blackout, in the back of a police car.

I'm not sure what happened last night. I have a vague idea. It has something to do with a massage parlor. But it doesn't quite add up. Whatever it was, it was bad, really bad. So bad, that Keri says I'm being held for Attempted Murder. *Attempted Murder.*

I am pretty sure I'm being taken to Twin Towers, which is the main Los Angeles County jail. It's a giant beige concrete horror-of-a-structure on the north side of the 101 Freeway, just north of downtown

Los Angeles. It has vertical slits of windows running up and down its three-foot-thick walls. I've never been before, but I drive by it on my commute from Santa Monica to my office in Pasadena. I always think of Chan Heng when I see it. She was one of my first clients. She'd been misidentified by the police and arrested and taken to Twin Towers. Her English was broken, and she never could explain to me why Twin Towers was so horrible, but I could tell from her eyes that the very thought of it upset her.

It's late at night, and there is no traffic on the 10 Freeway. The lights of the downtown skyscrapers are getting brighter as we get closer. I don't remember the back seat of the patrol car in Riverside having molded plastic seats likes this. Maybe I left in an ambulance? I was insanely drunk. These two standard white cops, transporting me from Santa Monica jail to Twin Towers, are talking about me like I'm not here.

"... so he climbs into the apartment and attacks this guy who is asleep ... puts him in a nigger hold and almost kills him."

The cop driving is talking to the passenger-side cop, who is half listening, while he's punching buttons on a lit console unit.

"A sleeper hold?" he asks.

"Yeah, a straight nigger hold," the driver responds. "Not a headlock, not a full nelson, a nigger hold, just like in the academy. The victim lived in the apartment, he described it exactly. It was a classic nigger hold."

"Is he an ex-cop or something?"

"No. Get this," the driver cop says and chuckles, "he was butt naked with a hard-on."

"Get the fuck out of here!" the cop says and laughs, "They are going to love him at Central."

"And he's not an ex-cop, even better ..."

The radio interrupts, crackling with a dispatcher's voice, and the passenger cop picks up and tells her in cop-speak we are en route to Central Processing.

"... yeah anyway, so he's not an ex-cop ... he's an attorney, a fuckin' lawyer!" the driver says, as if "he's a fuckin' lawyer" is the punch line of a hilarious joke.

They laugh. Driver cop looks in the rear view mirror, and passenger cop turns around.

"Hey, counselor, counselor! Are you a *faggot?* Your Honor ... May I approach the bench and ... suck your dick?"

They laugh like they think this is the funniest thing they've ever heard. I think of sitting in Dr. Mansky's office at Cal State, telling her how absurd it is that cops in California don't have to have college degrees. She laughed, but I was serious. Then I think of what the cop just said, "Some guy's apartment." This is new information. "Some guy's apartment" isn't the massage parlor. That doesn't make sense. How did I end up in some guy's apartment?

At Twin Towers, I'm placed in a holding area, and then two sheriff's deputies that look like they are training for the next Mr. Olympia usher me and a group of other losers around a maze of shiny, concrete floors with colored stripes.

"Blondie!" a deputy yells, "Get to the head of the line!" I look back. I don't know whether he's talking to me. There are other white guys in line with light hair. I can't see everyone. I keep walking.

"Blondie! Asshole," the deputy yells again. He grabs my cuffs and yanks them. I pretend it hurts. I'm sure it should, but my body is so tired and dull that it has little pain to give.

He pushes me to the front of the line where his fellow deputy is leading us.

"Suicide risk," he yells.

My group finally reaches a large processing room. There are a couple hundred people in here. The others in my group immediately disperse like we've just arrived at prom, and they are going to meet with their friends. Some of the inmates sit on benches; some are corralled into cells at the back of the room. At the head of the room, there is a raised platform like a large judge's bench with computers and printers. Half a dozen deputies are gathered on and around the platform. Behind the platform are offices where civilian-clothed workers and doctors and nurses work. There is a steady flow of names announced over the speaker and inmates going in and out of the large room. A black deputy walks me to a bench right next to all the other deputies and handcuffs me to the railing of the bench. I am the only prisoner that is handcuffed of a couple hundred in the entire room.

I stare at the TV at the front of the room and try to ignore everyone. *48 Hrs.* is on, but right when Eddie Murphy is about to sing "Roxanne"—when Nick Nolte is going to get him out jail—the DVD stops, and the screen reads, "REMOVE AND CLEAN DVD." I just stare and wait until it starts again. It plays, and then stops again while Eddie Murphy is singing. I am so tired. I think of that time I worked overnight to finish a summary judgment motion when I worked for Lanny. After being up for over thirty hours, I started to see things in my peripheral vision, and it made me lurch. It's hell in here. It really is. And yet, most of the inmates seem so comfortable. They are in hell, and that's just the way it is for them. These cops work here. This is where they go to work every day. It's so loud, and the hatred bounces of the walls. There are no clocks, because there is no time in here. I have nowhere to go. I'm here in *Fuckedville.*

I think of my bedroom at the Tennis Club Apartments. There was that one time when I'd been saving and saving to buy a car, and I wanted a car so badly that it was all I could think about. One night, I dreamt that I'd finally bought a car. It was such a realistic dream that when I woke up in the morning and the car wasn't there, I was surprised. It actually took me a few moments to realize I'd been dreaming, that I didn't own a car yet. I wish I were dreaming now. I'd wake up in my bed in Santa Monica. *If only.*

My right hand is so numb I can't feel it anymore. The cuffs tightened when the deputy yanked me to the front of the line. He must have meant to do it. I have been here through three movies now, and a new shift of deputies has arrived for work, and *48 Hrs.* is back on.

"Naus! Joseph Naus!"

My name is called, and I shout to the deputies at the desk.

"Officers ... that's me, but I'm handcuffed."

An irritated deputy comes over to unhook me, and he's yelling at a little dark-black guy.

"Trustee! What the fuck is a matter with you? High-priority sitting here on regular list. You are supposed to tell us."

I'm escorted to an office. A standard-looking middle-aged office lady is sitting behind a desk. She's reading a piece of paper.

"Joseph Naus," she says, mispronouncing my last name. "Suicide risk?" she asks.

"Uh ... Mrs.?" I respond.

"Don't worry about my name," she says, "Just answer the question."

I want to explain to her that "suicide risk"—whether she raised her tone at the end of "risk" or not is not a question; that I presume she wouldn't have this high-dollar, coveted job, if she hadn't been to college; that I would presume that basic knowledge of how to structure a question was probably a prerequisite to graduation. But then, I think, it's probably best if I keep that to myself.

"Okay. Look," I say, deciding to explain to her my thought process regarding suicide, "I have pretty much had a good life. I've been to Europe. I've had a fairly successful legal career, and have been with some beautiful woman, in fact, a lot of them. I've surfed and skied. I mean you know ... *bummer* it had to end this way, but that's the deal."

"Mr. Naus," she says, mildly irritated—as if *she's* the one having a hard day—"I just want to know whether you feel like taking your own life?"

"And I told you. I already have," I say.

"Does that mean you're going to try and kill yourself?"

"I guess, yeah," I say and pause for thought, "That is what it means. Why would I want to continue to live? It's game over."

"Do you have a specific plan on how you are going to kill yourself?" she asks.

I can hear *48 Hrs. Nick Nolte says the "n" word a bunch of times in that movie*, I think to myself. It's surprising. You'd never get away with that these days in a mainstream comedy. I look out the little wire reinforced-glass window back out in the bullpen of hell where I just came from. I don't know what I expect to see out there that will help me answer this lady's question.

"I've never been here before," I tell her. I'm trying to specifically answer her question. "You know... I mean ... I guess if I find a place to jump, I'll do it. Let's just say that. I mean, *no doubt.* If there were an open window behind you, I'd have already jumped."

My answer, apparently, is enough for her. She summons the trustee and a deputy sheriff.

"He's fifty-one-fifty... in a wheelchair," she announces to the deputy and trustee.

I know what *fifty-one-fifty* means. It is the California Welfare and Institution Code section that allows the government to place someone in protective custody, if they are an immediate danger to themselves or others, even if they haven't committed a crime.

I sit on a bench outside the lady's office waiting for the trustee to get me a wheelchair and think of Miguel, one of the kids I worked with at Olive Crest Group Homes. They used to page me when there was an emergency, and this time the emergency was Miguel. When I pulled up, he was in the middle of the street swinging a fence plank at anybody who came near him. When I got closer, I saw there were two nails protruding from the end of the plank. A couple of the female counselors were trying to talk him into putting the plank down, a board he'd ripped from a five-foot wood fence, but when they got close he'd take a swing at them. It was funny looking, because the plank was as big as he was. A bunch of neighbors had gathered on the fringe of the scene. I timed his swing and tackled him just after he swung. I had him pinned in the middle of the street when the police arrived. They wanted to arrest him, but the other counselors and I talked them out of it. I drove Miguel to the loony bin and 5150'd him. Two days later I picked him up, and he acted like nothing had happened. I worked at that particular group home often, and I became friendly with him. I thought I could help him by just telling him that he could do whatever he wanted if he tried. I learned quickly that it didn't work that way.

I 5150'd Miguel again after he'd been transferred to another Olive Crest Group home, this one out in the boonies. This time, he broke into a counselor's car, a guy who was in the process of becoming a cop. He sliced open the ragtop of the guy's convertible with a box cutter, popped the trunk, and stole a box of .22 bullets. Then he took them in the house and cranked up the oven full blast and put them in the oven. I wasn't there when it happened. I just got paged afterward, but I heard all about it. Apparently, bullets don't bake well. A couple bullets were still lodged in the walls of the living room when I got there.

Miguel was a tiny little Mexican kid. He was thirteen and weighed all of eighty pounds, but he was tough. Still, he cried streams when his mom didn't show up for a scheduled visit. His mom was a tweeker, all skin and bones and rotted teeth, and she used to rent him to pedophiles. And Miguel, all he wanted was for her to visit him once every other week in the group home. After the .22 incident, Miguel did some time in juvenile hall for some other prank. I wonder where he is now.

I am being pushed in a wheelchair up into a cement corkscrew corridor by the trustee. The corridor is divided by a red line. A handcuffed chain gang, led by a deputy, passes by. They are in blue uniforms, like nurses' uniforms but with "L.A. COUNTY JAIL" screen-printed vertically on the legs. I look at my intake wristband. It has a tiny, pixelated picture of me. Even in the tiny photo, you can tell I was the abject loser of a serious fight. I realize I am in a wheelchair, because the lady saw that I was limping. I hadn't noticed. I can vaguely see my reflection in an interior office window. The flesh around my left eye is so swollen that it changes the shape of my profile.

The trustee orders me up and leaves with the wheelchair. The deputy and I are in a brightly lit hallway with fishbowl-windowed cells on either side. I strip to my boxers. The sheriff hands me a plastic-y orange quilt-y thing to wear. It's heavy. It's the tormented offspring of a bulletproof vest and a mover's blanket. It's a Psycho-Robe, specifically designed to thwart clever suicide attempts. The glass door clamps shut behind me, and there is only the whoosh of the aggressive air-conditioning system and the smell of what I surmise is a combination of blood, spit, piss, shit, ammonia, bleach, and just a hint of semen. There is also the raging fluorescent light.

This cell is designed to prevent suicides. The face is all glass, and there is a large rectangular block of cement in the middle that joins the floor as if poured together. Atop is a half-inch thick, blue pad. In the corner, on the opposite side of the glass door, is a stainless steel combo toilet-sink-water fountain. I pee for a minute straight. I try to block out the crazed black man in the cell across from mine who is furiously masturbating at me. I lie down on the blue mat and squeeze my eyes shut, trying to block out the light, but it's too bright, so I use the Psycho Robe to cover my eyes. I am shaking and sweating cold nicotine-laced droplets of alcohol. I can smell it coming out of me. I hurt almost everywhere. My body throbs. My head is pounding, and I see tens of little crawling starfish coming in and out of my mind's vision. I reach down my left leg. It's all dried blood and scabs, like a piece of sandpaper. I scratch my head and catch a fingernail in a staple, tangled with hair and dried blood. I curl into a fetal position as tightly as I can, and I squeeze my eyes shut.

Oh my God. How the fuck ... I whisper to myself.

Anxiety rushes in. Everything rushes in. My mind races with it all. I don't want to think about it. I just want to sleep. *I just want to sleep.* The little starfish, crawling in between the blood vessels in my eyes, keep me conscious. I think out loud: *I am being charged with attempted murder, and my career is over and I am fucked, and I have lost it all, and I am going to lose my place, and I am going to lose my car, and I am fucked, and I've let down my girlfriend and my law partner and Mom and Dad and Keri and Aunt Suzie and Uncle Billy and Grandpa, and I am going to die, and this is it, and I have to figure out how to kill myself, and can I do it? I'll die in jail, and my mom will cry at my funeral, and I won't be able to console her because I'll be dead and all my friends will be sad and embarrassed and ashamed including Tito and Lanny and everyone I've ever known and why? Why? Why?*

I think of heroin. I'm going to die like this, and I'll never get to shoot heroin. I hate needles, but if I could, I'd gladly shoot up and overdose on heroin right now. I don't think I can smash my head in here and die. It has to be possible, but I don't think I can do it. If I had enough Jack Daniels, I could drink myself to death. I could do it. I've come close before.

I squeeze my eyes harder. The starfish get brighter.

Beth. I picture her with her fire hair and her sweet smile. It was ten years ago we were together. She was so pure. I'm so sorry I left you like that. But everything worked out for the best for you. You got away from me.

Beth's dad, Preacher Dale, preached that every man has a moment where he knows God. He preached to his embarrassingly small congregation with every bit of will he had. Stuffed in that cheap suit, trying to stay focused on the word of God and not how few people showed up to his makeshift church. Wherever *two or more* are gathered in his name, he preached, and we barely met that attendance requirement. I remember Preacher Dale raging on in that sinners-in-the-hands-of-an-angry-God tone about the troops in the foxholes during World War II. I pictured them on the beach with barbed wire, bayonets, and limp bodies akimbo, legs and arms scattered everywhere. Dale said they all hunkered down in the foxhole and prayed to almighty God with intensity and sincerity, whether they were lifelong atheists or baptized angels. Atheists prayed to God while Nazi bullets flew over their heads and hand grenades exploded all around: "God! Save me and I'll never sin again. Oh, God, please, don't let me die! Just please, God, get me out of this war."

I get on my knees to pray.

Dear God, I begin and then pause.

Fuck you if you thinking I'm going ask you to save me. You don't exist, and if you do, you're an evil bastard for letting it come to this. I've been asking you to show yourself since I was a kid. Remember? Remember when you let my mom get raped in the Alley? It wasn't enough that she had to be a junkie? Fuck you. Fuck you. Fuck you. Amen.

The door cracks loudly. I open my eyes to see a middle-aged man in cheap casual-wear step in my cell, flanked by a deputy. He introduces himself as a psychiatrist. I go to shake his hand, but I pull my hand back when the deputy shakes his head at me.

"I see you are religious," the psychiatrist says. "It's good to have religious beliefs in difficult times." He speaks as if he's reading out of the DSM IV. I don't even answer him.

"You're an attorney?" he asks as he scans some papers, "and you want to kill yourself? I mean, do you want to kill yourself?" he asks.

"I'm being charged with attempted murder, and my life is pretty much over, so yeah, I want to call it quits. It's been a nice ride, and it's over," I say deadpan.

He motions for the cop to leave the cell, and he looks over his half-glasses at me.

"Look," he says likes he's about to tell me a secret, "You may want to kill yourself, but if you keep saying it, you are going to stay in here until you stop saying it. And everyone wants to kill themselves, if they stay in here long enough."

We both look at the crazed masturbator, who is now slapping his flaccid penis against the glass as if to confirm that this psycho cell is not the place to be.

"Here, take this," he says and hands me a cup with a pill in it.

"What is it?" I ask and then reconsider, "You know what, never mind. I don't care."

"It's lithium," he says. "It's natural, a salt."

It could be rat poison for all I care. I swallow it. He says he'll be back tomorrow.

Keri's white skin and wispy, light blonde hair contrast with her solid black skirt-suit. Her face is puffy, and she looks tired. She's chewing gum. I wonder if she's been smoking or if it's allergies or dealing with me, probably a combination of all three.

"You wouldn't believe what I've had to go through to get in here," she says through the dirty glass into the phone, "Fucking county jail bureaucracy. They tried to say I couldn't see you, because you're fifty-one-fifty. Fuck that. I had to make some veiled threats."

Our eyes fully meet, and I'm back in our little apartment in Malibu when she was a first-year law student at Pepperdine. She came home early and caught me jacking off to some amateur porn photos online. Our eyes met then, too. She pretended she didn't know what I was doing, but I knew she did. I felt shame like I'd never felt before.

"You like my new jacket?" I ask. I stand up a bit and model the orange atrocity. "It's a Psycho-Robe. I think by Armani. Fashion first, safety second. Absolutely impossible to commit suicide in this. I've been trying desperately since I got here." I try to laugh, but I start to crack. I haven't cried in so long. It would feel so good. Maybe it'll happen this time.

Keri averts her eyes and takes on a lawyerly tone.

"Okay. Your bail is set at a million dollars, but I'm trying to get it reduced. You'll go to court tomorrow."

"A million dollars!" I shout into the handset, "Why a million?"

"I already told you it was a million dollars, don't you remember? In Santa Monica?"

"I guess," I answer, "actually … not really, Keri."

"You were obviously still drunk," she says, "You kept repeating yourself … Anyways, you've been charged with a host of crimes. Each one has a bail amount, and the DA added them all up, and it comes to a million."

A deputy comes up behind me and announces, "Time's up."

"More than attempted murder?" I ask.

The deputy stands me up, so I stretch the receiver trying to hear Keri's answer as I am pulled away from the phone.

"We'll talk about it at the arraignment," Keri says and hangs up while giving the deputy a dirty look.

I'm back in my cell with my Psycho-Robe and the lights and the stink, but the masturbator is gone. *One million dollars*, I say aloud and think about what that means. I know what that means. It means I'll have to come up with one hundred thousand dollars cash and collateral of nine hundred thousand dollars. That is not within the realm of possibility, not even close. Keri is a savant of sorts when it comes to technical legal arguments, but even if she were to get my bail cut in half, or even down to two hundred and fifty thousand dollars, there is no way I could come up with it. I curl up, squeeze my eyes shut, and pull my Psycho-Robe over my face. Then I realize exactly what my bail means. It means I'm not leaving here. I'm not leaving here. I'm going to die in here. All the alcohol is out of my system. I haven't had a drop of alcohol, a cigarette, an orgasm, or coffee in two days. Has it been two days? I can feel all my wounds. I can feel the weight of realizing I'm probably going to die in here. But still, no tears.

❖   ❖   ❖

I'm on the sheriff's bus driving down the 110 Freeway past downtown on my way to the LAX courthouse. I'm in the VIP cage just behind the driver. I presume it's where they keep the suicide risks, the snitches, the high profile fuckups. It's just as well that I'm in here as the other fuckups can't get to me. I can see out the window. It's the same view I've seen so many times, the downtown LA skyline. It doesn't feel the same as when I see it from my SUV on the way to my law office. Now, I'm on the outside looking in to the city, not a part of it. I'm *rollin' in the gray goose*, just like Snoop in *Murder Was the Case*. I met Snoop when I visited Judge Rich's courtroom, the judge who taught my Trial Techniques class. Snoop was in trial facing life in prison, but he didn't look scared at all. Not me, I am scared. I can't believe this is happening. I just want to wake up.

LAX Courthouse is a great, glass and steel, modern high-rise that towers over the 405 Freeway. We drive down into the subterranean parking, and I'm taken off the bus first. I'm cuffed and shackled. All the other inmates wear orange, but I and the guy I'm cuffed to wear brown. We even have our own deputy. I hear my name.

"Naus, that's me!" I shout louder than I intend.

This causes the dozen deputies and sixty inmates to hush to a near silence. *Fuck, I shouldn't have done that.*

"Who the fuck told you to open your fucking mouth?" a deputy barks at me while walking across the landing toward me.

I stare forward at the elevator. The scrawny guy cuffed to me whispers, "Don't say anything."

The deputy grabs the back of my neck and shoves my nose into the wall.

"*You* shut up," he tells me and then turns toward the deputy running the elevator, holding a clipboard. "Naus is in Dept. 9, first group. They are waiting, and Judge Stevens is pissed."

We are shoved in the elevator and then marched into a windowless holding cell with one of those stainless steel combo toilet-sinks. After a few minutes, I'm taken into a busy courtroom. They are waiting for me. Still cuffed, I sit next to Keri. My mom is in the audience. She is white with worry. She has that strained look on her face, the one that induces her to smoke a cigarette like she is trying to suck all the tobacco out in one drag. I start to panic. I can't hear much over the chaos in my head. It sounds like an amplified beehive. I've never had a panic attack, but this is what I hear they are like. My senses go numb, and my body tries to escape my skin. It's just too much. I can't have done this to my mom and my Grandpa. This can't be happening. The buzz gets louder. I can barely hear over it. I may pass out. Keri speaks and then the DA and then judge. They are all women, talking about me—which can't be good. I can only hear some words and phrases: *flight risk, stacking, bail is set at one million, suicide risk,* and then, *flight risk* again.

I've had two plans for suicide, I think, since Keri and I broke up seven years ago. Actually, that's not right, I think, I have always had plans for suicide.

The DA is still talking. I can see her talking, but I can't hear her. Sometimes she looks over at me. She is skinny and cagey like a Los Angeles coyote.

First, there is the New York plan. Gather all the money I can and just drink at dive bars and do coke and smoke cigarettes and bring girls back to my hotel. Run out of money, and then dive out a hotel window. There is something romantic about dying in the cold. It reminds me of that Kafka book I never finished.

Keri is doing her thing. I can hear something, something about *stacking* and *flight risk*. My mental dialogue is much louder than the courtroom drama that is unfolding in front of me, about me.

Then there's Las Vegas. It's a good place to die. Maybe I don't want to die in the cold, and it would be much better to jump into the Grand Canyon, and there are endless hookers in Vegas. Wander around

Freemont Street in old downtown where the destitute work and hustle. I'd fly into the Grand Canyon. I wonder if I'd be able to enjoy the fall. Will my contacts come out? Maybe I should wear my racquetball glasses.

"Mr. Naus ... Mis-ter. Naus," the Judge repeats, "Do you agree to this? Do you understand these rights?"

I see that she's talking to me, but I don't know what to do. I turn to Keri. She whispers in my ear, "Just say yes—just say yes."

I stand up. "Yes, Your Honor," I say. I realize I've said this too loud from people's reaction. It's because I have to shout over my head noise.

I'm ushered out by the bailiff. I try to see my mom, and Keri says something to me about visiting me. My mom is standing up. My Grandpa has his arm around her. She looks so white. She's crying. She looks right at me and mouths, "I love you."

NINE

I'm traveling back through the maze from LAX Court back to Twin Towers. I'm taken from one cell to the next. I'm given peanut butter and jelly in strange little packets and a tiny carton of milk. Each cell has the same new cast. I'm in my third or fourth cell since I left the courtroom. The benches are all taken by Mexicans and Salvadorians that banter without pause. I crouch in a corner. A lanky white guy with meth cave-mouth and spastic mannerisms edges toward me and tries to catch my attention. I pretend I don't hear him. He starts jabbering at me and the wall about how *the war* is about to *pop off* at Twin Towers. I've seen enough jail documentaries to know he could be right.

Now I'm on the big, silver, sheriff's bus on the freeway back to Twin Towers. The Los Angeles skyline is on my right. It's full of people in offices that are now very different from me. I can feel them looking down on me with pity. *Sad, disgusting*—that's what I am to them. A couple days ago I was worthy of envy, at least externally.

Back at Twin Towers: another cell, another hall with colored lines, more handcuffs, yet another cell, and another group of miscreants to be wary of. Another shift of khaki-uniformed sheriff's deputies replaces the previous. They are fungible, all thick with muscle, their shirtsleeves taut on their biceps. Even the women's arms look unnaturally thick.

I'm too exhausted to remain terrified.

I don't know what just happened in the courtroom. I think Keri had me plead "Not Guilty." My mom was pale and old with worry. She's only forty-nine. My Grandpa, his expression was the same as always.

He never gets emotional, or at least he doesn't show it. Keri was being *Attorney Keri.* I don't know what she said. My head was so loud that I could barely hear anything.

I take a deep breath, and I think. I think: *How can this be happening? How is this possible? This can't be happening.*

The sound of an old man's voice snaps me to.

"You got it bad, huh?" he asks.

He and I are the only ones left of the dozen that were in here an hour ago. He has gray, tight curls and tired, brown eyes. He could hide paper clips between the wrinkles in his face.

"I'm in here, so yeah. I'm not doing so well," I reply.

"I meant *yo* head. You all up in *yo* head."

I pause to mentally translate.

"Yeah, you're right. I'm just going crazy in my head," I answer. And he's right, I think. I'd be better off if I could stop thinking.

He gestures toward the sack lunch that is tucked up against my hip. "You goin' to eat any of that?"

I hand him the sack. He digs through it.

"So, where we going next?" I ask, "Do we get transferred to a cell in general population or something?"

He squints at me and chews a big bite of a small apple. He takes his time gnawing it down. I'm strangely eager to hear his response. He picks some apple chunks from his teeth with his tongue and clears his throat.

"Nah, man, we's goin' home as soon as they finish up the paper-work." He pauses as if he's done, but then blurts out like he wants to be heard outside the cell, "Lazy motherfuckers ain't in *no gat damn* rush to be doin' any-thang."

I chuckle and nod my head as if to say, "Good one."

"I ain't bullshittin' you, boy. This here is *Release.* I been here before, believe-dat. Too many times. We's about to get up out of here."

"Seriously?" Now he has me wondering if he could be right.

"I done told you. Yo wife or yo momma or yo somebody done bailed yo ass out." He gulps down a tiny white and pink carton of milk. "Whatchew in here fo' anyways? A deuce, a DUI, right?"

I chuckle my way into a nervous laugh and shake my head. "I wish I was in on a DUI. I'm in here for attempted murder." I notice a slight edge of pride within me when I say this. I like the shock factor. It feels like when I tell someone I was raised by a junkie mom.

He laughs back at me. "Nigga, *please*. Gat-damn. You look like you done cheated on yo taxes." He looks at me sideways and twists up his lips. "Nigga, please, you ain't no *killa*."

He lies down on the bench, and I follow suit. After a few minutes I start to nod off, but I know I can't fall completely asleep. Several minutes go by in silence.

"Naus. Joseph Naus!" Authority shouts my name. A huge deputy stands at the cell door and stares at me rock-faced.

The old man strains to sit up. He grins at me.

"*Ahh-ite*, killa. You stay good," he says softly.

I'm standing in front of Twin Towers. It must be midnight or later. I'm wearing a tissue-thin, jail-issued, royal blue jumpsuit. There are only a few cars on the road, mostly taxis. A bail bondman's neon sign glows blue and red across the street. The city's skyline rises above. A tranny that was processed through Release along with me is getting in an old Toyota sedan with a Tibetan flag sticker on its back window. It's driven by a Puerto Rican woman. The car tilts toward the driver's side from the woman's weight. The tranny pulls up her tight patent leather miniskirt nearly to her hips in order to get in the passenger seat of the car. I think: it must be strange to be a tranny and have friends and family to deal with. Eventually, it must become routine like anything else. "Oh, what a pretty dress. Have a good time tonight, *Mijo*," I imagine the fat lady in the driver's seat saying to her would-be daughter while watching the 11:00 p.m. local news, spooning ice cream straight out of the carton.

The sight of the patent leather skirt riding up the tranny's hip as she gets in the low car reminds me of so many hookers wobbling in their heels at my passenger's side window. The rush of adrenaline, the orgasm so powerful it's forever etched in my cerebral cortex: I shudder at the memory. And I cringe at the thought of the thought I'm having.

Keri pulls up to the curb in her silver Toyota 4Runner.

We drive in silence for a while. It scares me, but I still love this city. Its lights are crisp in the predawn. It readies to wake.

I feel like I've been kidnapped by terrorists, and I've finally been rescued and flown home.

"Jeez … you smell *so* bad." Keri gives me the full dramatic facial twist and nose pinch.

"I guess it's true. You can't smell yourself," I respond.

I haven't showered since I was arrested. I must smell of alcohol, nicotine, and fear. I smell my pits. They're intensely pungent.

"So … they dropped all the charges, and this is all just a bad dream?" I ask.

"Yeah, and Brad Pitt is marrying me, and he wants you to be the best man," Keri responds without taking her eyes off the road.

"So, what happened at the court hearing?" I ask.

"Your case—it was originally written up by the detectives as attempted murder, because of that little choke move you put on homey. But the DA didn't file it as attempted murder. They are charging you with a whole bunch of other crimes. They were supposed to give you the bail amount of the highest charge, if all the charges occur out of the same incident, as opposed to a … like a crime spree. They made some futile bullshit argument, but I won, and the judge agreed, and the bail is a hundred grand."

We transition from the 10 West to the 405 North, and Keri turns to me, "You owe me ten grand."

"I'll gladly pay you in the morning," I say. "You know I was thinking about buying one of those new Range Rover SUVs."

Keri continues talking as if I hadn't said a word.

"Your Grandpa put up his house for bail."

That stings. I can't believe I've dragged my Grandpa into this. He is regularly hounded, because he cosigned on my law school loans. Now his house is on the line.

"What if I kill myself?" I ask. Keri is the one person who knows that I'm not kidding.

"Why don't we just see how this turns out," Keri says without pause. "At least pay me before you off yourself."

I cover my face with my hands as we get off the freeway. I feel embarrassed to be anywhere near the Liquid Kitty, the condo, the massage parlor, West Los Angeles, the world. It's as if the entire night were telecast on a giant jumbo screen, and everyone was watching. Everyone knows what a fuckup I am. If they weren't all asleep, they'd be throwing rotten fruit at Keri's car for bringing me back to the neighborhood. Keri pulls up to the curb at her apartment, a couple miles from my condo.

"We are going to your place and spending the night. You are in my custody. *I'm serious.* You are going to rehab tomorrow at noon."

"Rehab?" I ask. This is the first I've heard of it even though it was obviously discussed at my bail hearing or arraignment or whatever it was.

"It's a condition of your bail. You can either go to rehab or go back to jail."

The commercial that I always saw on our little rabbit-eared, black and white TV, when my mom and I lived in the Alley, popped into my head. It's a close-up of a guy bent over a highball whiskey. He's smoking a cigarette, and the smoke is swirling up into the air. He says he'll quit tomorrow, and then there is a voice-over that echoes: *tomorrow ... tomorrow ... tomorrow ... tomorrow.* I guess tomorrow is when I'm going to quit, too.

"So what are the new charges?" I ask, "I mean, it's not attempted murder, right? I mean, those guys nearly killed *me*."

I was supposed to start classes and AA ... *fucking* yesterday. *Jesus*. I just thought of that. I am supposed to start electronic monitoring, DUI classes and AA classes or meetings or whatever those people do, as a condition of my probation. I could have to go to jail in Riverside for two years on a probation violation on my DUI.

"I'm exhausted," Keri says. "We'll talk about it tomorrow. I'll give you all the details then. Right now, just know that you are going to rehab for the next thirty days—at the very least. All you have to do is *be* in rehab."

The condo feels different. I don't belong here anymore. It rejects me—as does the entire neighborhood. I've violated it. I know this is the last night I'll ever spend here.

I wait for a half-hour and make sure Keri is sound asleep. The wood floors creak. I scour the suits hanging in my closet for cigarettes. I only manage four until I hit pay dirt on one of the last suit pockets. Thank *fucking* God. I have sixteen cigarettes. I carefully empty them all into one pack. I tiptoe downstairs and turn the living room light on to the lowest dim. In the kitchen, in the bottom cupboard, is a half-gallon jug of Jack Daniels with a couple fingers left in it, maybe three shots if I'm lucky. I open the fridge and light spills out into the kitchen. There is one backlit, glorious, green-glassed Rolling Rock. I set it back in the refrigerator. I don't drink alcohol for the taste. I drink to get drunk, and there isn't enough alcohol in this house to get me anywhere close to drunk.

I smoke each cigarette one by one, lighting the previous with the next. I drag down my last one until the fire-orange tip dies. I crush it out and go upstairs to my room. I climb up on the stepladder and push a cardboard box full of papers to the side. There are a couple dozen porn videos. The boxes are so distinct. I can spot one a hundred yards away. I've thrown at least this many away every few months for five years. Just the sight of them makes me hard. I stuff them all in a trash bag except my two favorites: *The Best of Christy Canyon* and the hardcore Vivid one with voyeur scene. I shove Christy in the VCR and kill the lights. I double-fast-forward to the scene. Practiced, I time it perfectly. Christy's on top with those natural D's swinging mirrored clockwise. She's a master of dialogue, and has the best fuck-face in porn.

I give the Vivid girls a go. They are the modern hardcore types, sexual athletes, with the rock-hard abs and fake tits. They fuck angry. They are captured with slick camera angles and high-quality sound.

I rest for a minute and then go down to the parking garage and bury my porn stash along with the evidence of my chain-smoking session in the bottom of the dumpster.

Good-bye.

I wake in my bed, and for the slightest moment I think I'm in my pre-personal-catastrophe life. But then I hear Keri on the phone, and I recall my reality and cringe. Keri takes me to the police station. It's bright out, and the sun exposes me. I despise the cheery brightness of Santa Monica, and I know everyone that sees me knows what I did. They know who I am, and what I've been doing in their pristine city.

The desk cops are all business. They could care less about me, and I'm grateful for that. Keri does all the talking. My stuff is in a ziplock bag. I wait until I'm back safe in the 4Runner before I open it. Keri gets us to the 10 Freeway headed back downtown. She turns the radio on to cut my edginess. I open the bag, and along with my wallet, cell phone, and keys: there they are, five crisp, twenty-dollar bills. I immediately realize what this means: I stopped at an ATM after I left the Liquid Kitty. Five twenties is what I always withdraw when I go to an ATM before I go to a massage parlor. Forty gets me in, and the rest is for "tip." I am always in full-heart palpitating anticipation when I go to the ATM. I've done it over a hundred times. *I know*: I pulled out this one hundred dollars for the same reason I always do. I get that feeling I get, and I go on autopilot to the massage parlor to get my fix. My stomach dances just thinking about it. I've never been to a massage parlor past dark. I know they all close by six or seven. I have no idea why I would think they were open at two in the morning on a weekday. I can only assume that I was so insanely drunk that I was in some type of walking fantasy. I recall being in the apartment and the beating I took after, but my memory is that of a strange dream. I have no recollection of going to the ATM, but I know which one I must have gone to, because it is the only one between my condo and the massage parlor.

"I'm going to give you my online bank information," I tell Keri. "You'll need to pay my bills anyway. I guarantee you there will be an ATM withdrawal of a hundred dollars, just before my arrest at the Savings & Loan, whatever it's called, the one right across the street from the massage parlor by the Wienerschnitzel."

Keri turns off the radio. "I love Wienerschnitzel's fries," she says, "They're so good ... Why would you go to an ATM?"

"First, you are correct. They are delicious, especially when paired with the chili cheese dog, no onions. And second, I must have been in some weird walking fantasy. I must have thought I was going to go to the massage parlor."

"It costs a hundred dollars?"

"When they have sex with you it does."

Keri scrunches her face in disgust, "Oh Jesus. Joseph, *seriously?*"

"Welcome to Pasadena Recovery Center!" a great big black lady announces as she bounds out from behind the office door into the waiting area. "You must be Joe, and you must be Keri." She moves in for a hug, and I don't know what to do. It's too late to stab out the handshake. She's nimble for a lady who's big enough to double for a '70s black sitcom mom. She hugs me like a pro, one of those full body hugs. I try to relax, but I can't. This must be how my Grandpa feels when I hug him. It's like holding a cat that wants to get away. Then, when I say, "I love you," he looks so uncomfortable he might turn and run.

"I'm Florence. I'm one of the counselors here," she announces, as I think, you can't seriously be named *Florence.* "We are going to get you checked in. Then I'll show you around."

She is sincerely cheery, as if she's welcoming me to the first day of summer camp, and we are going to be canoeing any minute now. "You can say good-bye now," she tells Keri, "Remember, he can't have any visitors for the first week."

Keri is nervously chomping her gum like she's the one going into rehab. It reminds me of when I first met her and fell in love with her. She was always chomping gum, and she wore mascara that filled in the corners of her eyes. I always wanted to clean it out like I did the sleep from my mom's cat's eyes. Keri gives me a one-armed hug and then hands me a manila envelope and darts out the door.

Florence picks up my heavy suitcase like it's a bag of rice cakes and leads me into the office. She opens it and rummages through it expertly.

"*This* you can't have," she says, holding up a bottle of mouthwash.

"Why? What does this institution have against minty fresh breath?"

"Oh you funny, huh? Minty fresh breath," Florence repeats. "Mouthwash has alcohol in it, funny man."

I'd actually heard that before. It was in a documentary about an Indian tribe. I recall a shaky, handheld video of an Indian in his trailer trembling and drinking mouthwash chased with hair spray.

"And why would you bring these in here?" Florence says as she swivels her head as only a black woman can. A string of shiny, gold, condom packages hangs from between her thumb and index finger.

This catches me off guard. *Fuck.* "I didn't pack those," I say, "I mean, they are mine. They were just already in the suitcase. I didn't bring them. I did obviously *bring them* but ..."

"You can't use them in here. You will get kicked out for any horseplay in here." Her mouth forms a barely perceptible smile. She rolls them up and puts them back in my suitcase. I know Florence is thinking of sex. Nobody can hold up a string of condoms and not have, at least, a thought about sex. I wonder if she's thinking about the last time she had sex. I bet she's a hammer in bed.

Pasadena Recovery Center is a flat-roofed, former convalescent home built in the 1950s. It could use a remodel. Florence leads me from the entryway down a hall. The tile is dirty-white from wear. On one side of the hall is an interior patio and on the other side are double doors. She opens the door to give me a peek. On one side of the room, there are a half dozen round, cafeteria-style dining room tables and chair sets. On the other end of the room there is a piano in one corner, a large-screen television, and several couches. There are about twenty people seated in a loose half-circle. A little guy is crying, and everyone is looking at him. A moment passes. He gathers himself and says, *But one day at a time, right?* Some of the others nod aggressively. One woman rolls her eyes. Then the crying man says, *Thanks for letting me share.* This is followed by a smattering of applause, and a couple hushed NPR-radio-toned voices, *Thank you, Bruce.*

Florence takes me down the men's room hall and shows me my room. Unless they were going for a mid-century Russian dormitory theme, there has been no attempt to decorate. It's as institutional as a welfare office. There are identical steel-framed beds against opposite walls. They both have white sheets and thick gray wool blankets. The floor is the same white tile as the hallway. The room shares a showerless bathroom with an identical room. Opposite the door to the hallway is a sliding glass door, which is bolted shut with long screws blocking the slide rails.

"Why don't you get settled, and I'll come back later," Florence says.

I nod.

"Okay. Are you alright?" She looks at me and tilts her head to the side.

There are several ways to answer this, none of which seem appealing, so I go with the most efficient.

"Fine. I'm just uh ..."

"I'll come back." She stops in the doorway and turns back apparently remembering something. "This door is *never* to be completely closed, okay?"

I turn the lights off. A little natural light seeps in through the sliding glass door and under the heavy curtain. It's July-hot outside, but the tile keeps it fairly cool in the room. I heave my suitcase on the bed and begin unpacking. The dark wood drawers of the built-in dresser are empty save a few pennies, lint, and a little forest-green booklet entitled, *Los Angeles Area Meeting Directory, Alcoholics Anonymous.* A page is earmarked. It reads, *Monday Night Discussion Meeting (Reservoir and Alvarado), 8 p.m.* In the margin someone has written, *mtg sucks—bunch of stupid hipsters.* In the closet hangs a lonely T-shirt. It's navy blue and worn thin. Screen-printed on the front in red and white are half-opened church doors. Above the doors is a stylized N.A. logo. Below the N.A., it reads, *Victory Through Surrender.* I smell it. It's clean. I put it on, and it fits perfectly. I wonder what N.A. stands for? Something anonymous, I suppose.

I finish unpacking. I sit on the bed. The manila envelope Keri handed me before she rushed off sits at my side waiting for me. I take a deep breath and pick it up. I hold it and close my eyes. Inhale. Exhale. Repeat. It's a criminal complaint. *The People of the State of California vs. Joseph William Naus.* Apparently, the entire State of California is after me. I read:

Count 1: First Degree Burglary

Count 2: Criminal Threats

Count 3: False Imprisonment

Count 4: Attempted Forcible Rape

Count 5: Forcible Sodomy

Count 6: Assault with Intent to Commit a Felony (Rape, Sodomy, or Oral Copulation)

I can't believe what I've just read. It's as if I'm watching this all happen to someone else. But I'm not. It's me. It's me here in the dim room sitting on a hospital bed in a rehab facing six felony counts, three of which are sex crimes. I lie down. I can't believe it's worse than attempted murder. How do you get worse than attempted murder unless someone dies? Attempted murder is way better than this. Attempted Forcible Rape? *What?* Keri said there was a guy in the room. *Attempted Sodomy?* Did I try to fuck some guy in the ass?

"Oh, Jesus Christ, you've got to be kidding me. Attempted Sodomy? Rape?" I realize I'm saying this out loud, when I hear footsteps and chatter coming from the hall.

I envision my Criminal Law professor from Pepperdine, Dr. LeSmyth, with his neatly trimmed beard. The first time he called me, he stumped me with a question about the distinction between specific and general intent crimes. It was embarrassing standing up, a class full of students staring at me while I stammered, trying to recall the answer. But the next time he called on me, I was ready. I never thought his lesson would be so personally apropos.

"Mr. Naus," he announced in his booming voice.

My heart raced. I stood.

"What are the elements of a burglary, Mr. Naus?"

I took a deep breath. Eighty sets of eyes were on me, all waiting to see the to-be-humiliated-or-not-to-be-humiliated drama unfold. Okay, I know this, I thought. "Uhm ... it is the breaking ... and entering ... of the dwelling of another ... at night ... with the intent to commit a felony or theft therein."

"Ah, good. You've memorized the common law definition of burglary. Good, good," Dr. LeSmyth said with a bit of sarcasm. He turned away. I was relieved. I began to sit, but he turned back for more. I rose back up.

"But that isn't what this case we've been discussing teaches us, is it, Mr. Naus?"

I shook my head. I knew exactly where he was going.

"So what is it?"

"It's that ... that the intent to commit the felony occurs at the time of the breaking and entering."

"Go on, Mr. Naus ..."

"Right, of course ... the point is that you could be breaking into an empty house, but if you think there is a bunch of diamonds in there even though there aren't, you'd still be committing a burglary. What we learned from this case is that factual impossibility is not a defense to burglary."

So in the *Naus* case, I think, as if I'm explaining my current status as a defendant to Dr. LeSmyth: the DA obviously thinks that I entered the premises with the intent to commit a felony, presumably a rape, even though there wasn't a woman in the premises to rape. As I also learned in your class, it is legally impossible to rape a man. A rape can only occur between a man and a woman. Now, the DA here either has a wicked sense of humor or is covering all her bases by also throwing in a sodomy charge, which, of course, is a crime, unlike rape, which can happen between a man and another man. I, of course, Dr. LeSmyth, do not have sex with other men. And, of course, once all the facts are cleared up and known—that I was drunk beyond capability of reason, that I'm straight, and that I clearly intended to pay for sex with a prostitute—all these heinous charges will be dropped. I envision Dr. LeSmyth, saying, in a very dignified manner, "Yes, of course, Mr. Naus ... all just an unfortunate misunderstanding."

The massage parlor is housed in an old hotel. It's in a C shape, and the massage parlor is in the bottom leg of the C. The rest of it, I presume, is either an operating motel or converted apartments. I don't know, but I must have gone in the wrong window—as if there was a right window to go into. I vaguely remember being in the back and falling out a window. Maybe I came in a door and left out a window. I cannot remember. Was I so horny that I was going to break into the massage parlor hoping one of the girls stayed there and wanted to do some after-hours business? Was I not willing to take no for an answer? *Am I a rapist? No! I'm not a rapist.* But maybe drunk enough, I am capable of anything.

The last time I'd brought a girl home from the Liquid Kitty was just a few days ago. I thought for sure I was getting laid, and she denied me. She was so sexy: Spanish, tall, and dark with a curvy figure. We made out for a good half-hour, and we were both drunk. She said, "No," and I stopped. Your Honor, I stopped!

Is this the defense I'm reduced to? *Look, Your Honor*, I could have raped this girl the other night, and I didn't. Surely if I were a rapist, I'd have raped her! *Right?* In fact, Your Honor, I could have raped a lot of girls!

Of course, even in a comedic fantasy hearing, I knew the situation here was completely different. Here, there was no rational thinking involved. If I had been conscious, I obviously wouldn't have done the things I did. I actually recall those nights and those women who decided not to have sex with me. Those memories are not like some vague dream with shifting characters and strange floating environs. This was different. This was a bizarre collision at the intersection of my blackout drinking and prostitution habit.

❖   ❖   ❖

"So you're an attorney. My daughter's an attorney," Dr. Blume says, gazing over his glasses, before returning to reading my file.

"Yeah, for now," I say. And then it dawns on me why the plaque in the garden near PRC's entryway with the crafty lettering reads, "Blume where you are planted."

Dr. Blume owns this joint. He's a psychiatrist. He's white, bald, plump, jovial, relaxed, and kind—an aging cherub. I can't imagine him as a young man. He's always been this age.

"Oh my, this is quite the story," he says and sets my file down, "No matter. You are here now, and we are going to help you get your life back in order."

"Great," I say. He's so nice, so I try not to sound sarcastic, but I'm not thinking of getting my life back in order. That's absurd. I'm thinking suicide is a real option. It feels real. It's a logical option at this point. I could be dead soon.

"You look like someone assaulted you—not the other way around," Dr. Blume says with a little chuckle that develops into a cough, "How are you feeling?"

"Physically, I'm fine. My head hurts, and I'm sore, and my legs are bashed up, but it's no big deal. I do feel like the words are taking a little bit longer than usual to get out of my mouth. That's a bit scary."

"That's typical of binge drinkers. You took some blows to the *ole noggin,* too. Binge drinking can be significantly more harmful than daily drinking."

He goes back to my file for a long while and then breaks the silence abruptly.

"Are you an alcoholic?" Dr. Blume asks and leans forward in his office chair and looks right at me.

"Uhm ... well, I don't exactly ..."

"Okay. Let's go back a step. I don't always know where clients are, you know. Most people that come in here have been in rehab multiple times. But, this is your first?"

"Yeah. People come more than once?"

Dr. Blume laughs heartily as if I told him a good lawyer joke.

"Do you have any addiction in your family? Pills, drinking, anything?" He has a fresh notepad out.

"Yeah, my mom was a heroin addict—a long time ago."

"Oh," he says. This catches his attention, and he starts scribbling.

"And my grandma, she was an alcoholic," I report.

"Was …," he starts to ask a question but stops and scribbles some more. "Did she get sober?"

"No, she's dead. She died in '89. She was fifty-seven. Liver, kidney, lung cancer. It all gave up on her."

"Mmmm. Uh-huh. Which grandma?"

"My only grandma," I answer.

He looks at me quizzically, and then I realize why.

"I mean uhh … my dad's family was kind of out of the picture. But, you know, my dad, he's a drinker. I've not seen him much, but I don't think I ever saw him go a day without a Budweiser. But, you know, I don't think he's an alcoholic. He used to do heroin with my mom, I know that."

"Okay. Well you obviously indicate significant family history … brothers and sisters?"

"No."

"Oh," he says and scribbles again as if my lack of siblings is extremely important. I envision his barely legible doctor's cursive scratch, *narcissistic only-child of junkie parents. Doomed.*

"Any attempted or actual suicides in the family?"

I don't expect this question. I recall a yellowed Polaroid of my dad and me when I was born. It's the only picture I had of him when I was a kid. He's nineteen, long blonde hair, rugged, and thin; wears jeans, boots, and a short-sleeved striped shirt. He's lying down on the couch and holding me on his chest. He's half asleep or maybe nodding out from dope. That's how I always picture him. Once I pressed my mom on what happened. Why did dad leave when I was only six weeks old? I wanted details. She finally gave them to me. She told me we had been burglarized the second night we moved into a slum apartment in a black neighborhood in Riverside. My dad came home drunk again, and he was furious that she'd locked the door. He was screaming, *It's my fucking house* and *I pay the fucking rent.* I was in a bassinet that Grandpa had bought for them as a wedding present. I woke up crying. My dad threw a vase against the wall near me, and it shattered into shards of white porcelain, some of which fell into my bassinet. My mom said she told him she'd call the police if he didn't leave. She'd never told him to leave before, but seeing the shards of porcelain all around me in my bassinet made her furious. He left, and he didn't come back.

A few days later, my dad's sister, who was my mom's closest friend in high school, told my mom that she'd found my dad in their family home's bathroom slumped over on the floor. He'd taken a razor blade and sliced his wrist. I always picture him on the floor of the bathroom in a huge puddle of blood. For some reason in my mind he has a belt around his upper arm as if he were shooting dope. I wonder how close he came to dying. Was it one of the drama-suicide attempts, or was he really going for it? I like to think he was really going for it.

"No. No attempted or actual suicides in the family," I tell Dr. Blume, "Not that I know of." I wonder why I lie about this. I'm so proud of my mom for being a teenage junkie, but dad gets no credit for a teenage suicide attempt.

"Many addicts and alcoholics report a feeling of powerlessness—that they reach a point where they have no control over their actions," Dr. Blume explains. "There comes a time where they no longer choose whether they want to drink or drug or gamble or whatever, as we say, their 'drug of choice is,' it is something they are compelled to do. Have you ever felt this way about alcohol or anything else?"

I lean back in the chair and sigh. I know the answer. I just don't know what to tell this nice man. I remember exactly the first time I felt the powerlessness he's talking about. It was years before I'd taken my first drink or smoked my first cigarette. I was chasing Vanessa on the 976 lines. It's been fifteen years since Vanessa and the 976 lines, but it's always something. I spend so much energy trying *not* to do things. Recently, it's been the cigarettes and the binge drinking the most, but sex is always in there. Even if it's just porn, I always hate myself for it and want to quit. The massage parlors were the worst when I lived in Riverside. Hookers, massage parlors, porn, one-nighters, cigarettes, food, alcohol, it's always something—something that I can't stop doing even though I hate myself for doing it.

"No," I tell Dr. Blume. "No, I have never been unable to stop when I want to."

"No?" he questions. He's surprised I say this. "You've never crossed that line? Never promised yourself you wouldn't do something and then did it, because a part of you wanted to do that something so badly?"

I consider the absurdity of my answer and decide to give him a better one. I decide to steer clear of the hookers and massage parlors. I don't want him thinking I'm a sex addict that was so strung out I tried to rape someone. It's not true, but I do see that there is some logic in such a conclusion.

"I mean, I *guess* I have. I've felt that way with cigarettes. I tell myself I'm quitting smoking, and then I throw away the pack. But, I always end up smoking again. You know, sometimes I smoke instead of going out to drink. But with drinking, I love to drink, but I don't do it every day. Some days I don't drink at all. I just, you know, I just need to control it better."

Control it better. Did I really just say that? I become frustrated with my answers. They are not reasonable. I can't seem to say anything convincing to Dr. Blume. I try again; this time I try to hover a little closer to the truth. "Once I start drinking, and say I want to limit it to just four or five mixed drinks. But instead, I'll drink … usually … maybe ten or so … much more than I should. Sometimes I drink so much I don't remember what happened. I mean, I don't remember anything for big chunks of time."

"Uh-huh," Dr. Blume responds. He is back to reading my file and taking dutiful notes. I want to tell him the truth: that I've desperately wanted to stop smoking, drinking, and going to prostitutes for half my life, and I'm completely strung out on all of these things. And I hate myself for being so weak that I can't stop.

"I'm not an alcoholic like my grandma, you know?" I say, trying to offer something Dr. Blume will find acceptable.

He looks up and doesn't say anything for a second, just smiles softly. Suddenly, I don't like him as much as I did a couple minutes ago.

"Alcoholism is a self-diagnosed disease," he says as if it's the truest thing ever uttered, "Not that we professionals can't come to a reasonable judgment based on a patient's history and behavior, but it doesn't really matter what we think, because unless you think you're an addict, there can be no recovery, because you don't believe there is any disease to recover from."

He's lost me, and I'm suddenly overcome with fatigue. Did he say *disease?* Like cancer? AIDS?

"One more thing, and you can get back to Group," Dr. Blume continues, "Have you experienced depression?"

"Depression ...," I ponder aloud.

I don't need to ponder it. I used to think about suicide all the time, but now, now that I'm really considering suicide, I know it wasn't real. I was terribly depressed. I hated myself, but I was never really willing to kill myself, because I always believed life was worth living even if I didn't want to live at that moment. I always believed that if I worked hard enough I could achieve my goals and conquer my demons. I've had twisted, dark feelings that made me not want to face the day many times: the times I cheated on Beth, every time I picked up a street hooker, the endless times I promised myself I'd never go to a massage parlor again, or binge drink again, or smoke again. Every time I lied to myself, it felt worse and worse. After fifteen years of it, my soul has been stripmined.

Before I can answer Dr. Blume, Florence knocks and opens Dr. Blume's office door in one motion and declares a minor emergency: someone just had another seizure.

"Okay. I'll be there in a second," Dr. Blume tells Florence and then turns back to me. "Well, Joseph, whether you are clinically depressed or not, we won't know for a while, but you quite obviously have situational depression." He hands me a sample pack of Lexapro. "I want you to take these right now, and then you can get them at the med counter in the mornings from now on. These will smooth out the highs and lows and help you be able to better deal with everything you're facing."

I nod. We stand and shake hands. He pats me on the back like my Grandpa used to do, before I unilaterally instituted a policy of hugging. Dr. Blume lies to me and tells me everything is going to be alright. I eke out a smile.

TEN

I wake up to Florence singing, *Rise and shine . . . Rise and shine* as she traverses the hall and pushes the doors open. There are groans and growls. It takes only a moment for me to realize where I am and for the wave of dread to crash upon me as I realize why I am here. I have a roommate now, an OxyContin junkie named Otis, or something. Otis-or-Something stirs a bit from the morning commotion. He's been in bed since he arrived here late yesterday morning. He's facially asymmetrical and severely scrawny, and he twists and violently flips and flops in his bed, swaddled in his blanket, a makeshift straight jacket. It's a wonder he hasn't toppled to the floor. This is the first time I've really understood that some people use prescription drugs like alcoholics drink beer and junkies shoot dope. Although I do recall thinking Tylenol with codeine was a fair trade-off for the pain and expense of having three impacted wisdom teeth extracted, it never occurred to me to take it other than as directed.

I'm on shower duty. The newbie gets it for a week. I don't mind. I've never minded cleaning, unless it was my place I was cleaning; then, it never seemed worth the hassle. The showers here are like locker room showers but with individual stalls. I use an industrial mop, yellow gloves, and bleach spray. Each stall has a heavy black rubber mat, and I throw each one out and scrub it and mop underneath. The whole process takes a half-hour. I'm sweating, and it doesn't smell like alcohol. It's been a week since I last drank. I haven't gone a week without a drink in many years. I feel stronger. I look in the mirror above the sinks. I touch where the scabs were on the left side of my face. They've reduced to reddish spots the way puddles evaporate after a rain. My eye is no longer black and blue. It just looks irritated, as if I've worn my contacts way too long. I run my fingers over the row of staples in my scalp. They're hard and foreign. My fine blonde hair is entangled, and some hairs are sprouting through the scabs at the base of the staples. I test out my right leg with a little knee bend. I'm barely limping. My leg has nearly healed from the bat beating. It reminds me of my first sanctioned kickboxing bout at Nationals, when the guy from Benny Urquidez's Jet Center's kickboxing gym bashed my left thigh with his right shin until I could barely walk the next day. *I still should have won that fight.* I knocked him down in the first round. It still pisses me off. I look closely in the mirror. A puffy, beaten, red-eyed boy-man looks back at me.

"Jesus Christ, what the fuck happened to you?" I ask myself aloud.

A gigantic black man with caramel skin, a big gut, and braided hair walks in. He gives me a sideways glance, and I try to act nonchalant as if I were squeezing a blackhead off my nose and not talking to myself in the mirror. He's one of the ex-cons from the prison-release program. I can see his knobby little dick bob in the mirror as he strides past. I think: *It must suck to be a big black guy and have a small dick.*

I dress and go to the back of the line to get my daily happy pill, which, according to Dr. Blume, should be kicking in soon. I'm anxious to see if I'll feel anything. There are four guys in front of me. They walk up to a half-door and initial a paper on a clipboard with a pen that is connected with string and masking tape and take their medication in front of the rehab counselor. I don't have a good look at the rehab counselor, but I hear her raspy voice, and recognize it isn't Florence or the old lady that did it yesterday. I reach the front of the line. A thin, flat-chested, Thai girl with long shiny, straight black hair smiles at me.

"What'll you have?" she asks, "Ha-ha, just kidding. We haven't met. I'm Kib."

She extends her hand over the half-door. She wears metallic bangle bracelets and several small silver and turquoise rings. Her nails are short and natural. She shakes my hand. She has a strong grip. I think I read somewhere girls that have strong grips have good relationships with their fathers. Or maybe I didn't. Maybe I read that people with strong grips have self-confidence, that women with self-esteem have good relationships with their fathers. I've combined the two into one barely defensible, pop psychology factoid. This is the type of shit I think about sometimes. I'd use it as a pick-up line, and it'd probably work, too. *God, I hate myself for being such a cad sometimes.*

"I'm Joseph. I just got here a few days ago."

"Oh, you're the lawyer," Kib says and turns away to get my medication. She continues talking. "I was working the night shift, so you're sleeping when I'm here, but now I'm working day shift."

Kib wears a striped vintage Hang Ten T-shirt that doesn't quite reach the waist of her low-rise jeans. Her skin is Vietcong dark. She's either Vietnamese or Cambodian. I've had sex with over a hundred Asian woman, most of them were massage-parlor prostitutes, most Thai or Chinese, but some from Vietnam and Cambodia. They all knew how to touch in a way that made me ready to explode before we even started having sex. I wonder if Kib knows how to do that.

Of course she doesn't, because she's not a Goddamn sex slave. What's a matter with you? You think those girls wanted to be fucking you? You're disgusting.

"Here you go," Kib says and hands me a tiny paper cup with my little blue happy pill.

I lock eyes with her as I toss the pill back. She smiles and bats her long eyelashes. I know that smile, and I know that look. If we were in a bar, I'd be thinking I was about to close the deal, and I'd start buying her drinks.

"I'm not supposed to be dispensing meds," Kib says. She leans forward over the half-door counter so she can confide. "I'm not a certified counselor. Inger didn't show up, so they told me to do meds today."

"Well, you seem to be doing a good job," I say at a near whisper. "And I won't tell anyone ... Kib."

Look them in the eye, and say their name decisively. Did I originally learn that at Parker's Sporting Goods or from selling shoes at Harris'? I knew it way before I went to law school. It's definitely a sales thing, but isn't everything a sales thing, really?

Kib is still grinning as she comes out from behind the counter and locks the door. We walk down the hall toward the group room together. She's thin, and she naturally switches her hips when she walks. I let her get ahead of me a bit so I can watch her ass. It flares out from her waist, and she has that diamond space between her crotch where her thighs meet—the best absence of space.

I join the couple dozen other patients in the dining room. I load my tray from the rolling buffet carts. It's like a Vegas breakfast buffet: scrambled eggs, fatty bacon, little sausages, roasted potatoes, toast, cereals in plastic dispensers, coffee, and orange juice. I eat more in one meal at PRC than I used to eat in two days, especially during the weekends when drinking, smoking, and fucking superseded all else.

I sit at a round table with Cindy, Roy, and Jack, my new trudging buddies. Cindy nearly drank herself to death from a quart-of-vodka-a-day habit. She went from the emergency room to the psych ward to PRC a couple weeks ago. She's eighty-five pounds of venom and plays bass guitar in an all-girl power-pop band. With tattoos, jet-black hair, and Bettie Page bangs, she's a proud lesbo with a sense of humor that'd make Redd Foxx blush. Her favorite shtick is to say shockingly disgusting things nonchalantly. Roy is her quiet comrade. He's married to a famous Jewish comedian who, I presume, is footing the bill. Roy is Gothic-white with dyed jet-black hair. He's the well-read, artsy type that looks like a character from a Jerry Stahl novel. He likes Joy Division, retrospectively, of course, and bands I've never heard of. And yes, he told me, he knows where the name *Joy Division* comes from. *Doesn't everyone?* I've never seen him wear anything that isn't black. He seems asexual. I'd like to drink with him. I'm sure he'd tell me about some amazing books to read and albums to buy, and I'd write them down on a cocktail napkin with a pen I'd borrow from the bartender. I'd find a way to drop his wife's name to impress a girl I was trying to fuck.

I sit down and dig into my cheesy scrambled eggs.

"I see you've met Kib," Cindy says coyly.

I know what's coming, one of her routines, so I chew and swallow my eggs quickly, so I don't choke.

"Yes, I've met Kib, Cindy," I respond.

"I do declare," Cindy says, batting her eyes, in full shtick mode. This is her *Gone with the Wind* Southern belle persona. "Kib's as fine a treatment center staff member as one could find. Isn't that right, Mr. Roy?"

"That's right, Miss Cindy," Roy responds in a southern drawl. "Kib's salt-of-the-earth here to help us floundering addicts and alcoholics find … well, find … *ourselves* and to find God—Jesus Christ, our Lord and savior. AYYY-men!"

"Yes, Mr. Roy," Cindy continues, "I do agree that you are correct in your assessment of Ms. Kib … such a *fine* young lady. She's here to be of service—and I do mean *service*—to you, to me, and to everyone that crosses the threshold of this fine institution. Don't you agree, Jack?"

Jack, who is intentionally ignoring Cindy and Roy's improv skit looks up at the sound of his name, and nods as he slurps a few remaining Cheerios from a large bowl.

"Yes," Cindy continues, "she taught Jack the AMA model of addiction, as well as sharing her own story of triumph." Cindy nods in grand, mock earnestness, and then turns to me. "And do you know what else, Joseph?" Cindy asks. Her eyes are wide and unblinking.

I shake my head.

"Not only is she a fine employee …," Cindy pauses for dramatic effect, leans forward and looks at Roy, Jack, and then me, each in the eye, one by one, "… she's *a cum-gurgling slut who loves nothing more than getting on her knees and draining cocks.*"

Roy and I burst out laughing.

"*Jesus Christ*, Cindy, do you have to talk like that?" Jack asks.

"It's true, Jack. You need to know the truth, Jack," Cindy responds.

Jack leaves.

"Yes, indeed, you are correct, Ms. Cindy. She's a *cum-gurgling slut.* That's exactly what she is. It's so true, and we don't hide from the truth here, Joseph," Roy says.

"*Truth*, Joseph, it's what will keep you clean and sober and free from sins against man and God!" Cindy concludes.

After breakfast, the twenty-plus residents of PRC meet for Group. It's an hour of comedy. I sit in the back behind the couches with Jack on my right and Roy and Cindy on my left. Everyone is gathered in a big half-circle. An old woman, Ingrid, moderates the group. It starts with a prayer. A gambling addict named Alfredo makes a show of replacing the word, *God* with *doorknob* during the prayer, much to the chagrin of Ingrid, who is beside herself with disgust for this act of insolence.

"Winner gets a dollar," Cindy whispers to me, Jack, and Roy. "Jack you in?"

"Yeah, I'm in," Jack responds. "The phrase that pays is 'half measures', right?" Jack whispers across me back to Cindy.

"No, no," Cindy corrects Jack, "it's *let go-let God.* Got it? *Let go, let God.*"

"I'll go seven," Jack says.

"Gimmee six ... no, no, make it eight," Roy says.

I take five, and Cindy goes with twelve. The object is to pick the number of times the given recovery phrase, in this case *Let go, Let God*, is said during the hour-long group. Winner gets the four bucks, which in rehab equates to a pack of cigarettes. Anyone who is betting doesn't count, so, for instance, Jack can't raise his hand at the end of the meeting and say the phrase until it gets to the number he wants. However, as I learned yesterday, we can say anything, including the phrase itself, to influence someone else to say it.

It's been fifty minutes of painful bullshit from whining addicts, most of whom have been on the rehab circuit the majority of their adult lives. The magic phrase has been repeated eight times, so Jack and I have already lost. There are only ten minutes left before the meeting ends, and we pray out. Alfredo, a chubby thirty-something with a permanently backward Yankee's cap and a too-tight undershirt, is near tears as he recounts his wife leaving with his five-year-old son and his mother-in-law, after he spent all night at the Commerce Casino and dropped two weeks' pay after being up three thousand dollars on blackjack.

"I couldn't leave. I just *couldn't* leave ... so, then, she did. She left with Jeremy. My wife and son left me ..." With the dramatic subtlety of a Mexican soap-opera star, he trails off and mumbles into his hands; then, after a few moments, he suddenly straightens up, as if gathering strength, and says, "One day at a time ... one day at a time."

I can't see any tears, but he acts as if he's wiping away shot glasses full of them. Cindy rolls her eyes. Most of the patients clap, myself not included. I'm going to need to see some real tears if Alfredo wants an ovation. His couch neighbor puts her arm around him and consoles him Oprah-style. He sops it up like invisible tears on an invisible handkerchief.

I'd love to depose Alfredo, I think. I'd tear him to shreds. You have to set up liars, and then let them impeach themselves. They'll do all the work for you if you let them.

Kib is just outside the sliding glass door near the ping-pong table smoking a cigarette. I glance at her. She glances back. I get goose bumps.

Cindy raises her hand to make a last-minute attempt to influence the outcome of our game.

"I just want to say, when I'm having a hard time, I just keep repeating, 'Let Go, Let God', because whatever you are going through, God can make it better. Does anyone else do that? That's all I wanted to say, 'Let Go, Let God'. Thanks for letting me share."

Gina pops her hand up. Gina is a pretty, upper-class Hispanic housewife from Valencia. She's going through a divorce. She was arrested after chasing her husband on the freeway with her two young kids in the back of her SUV, which apparently is a very serious felony. Being at PRC is part of her sentence. She loves boxed wine with the driving passion that matches my love of Thai hookers and Jack Daniels. She's big on drama and shares at every Group, three or four times a day.

"Thank you for calling on me," Gina says. She turns to Cindy with a glaring show of emotional solidarity, which includes a closed-eye nod and then a pulling of the hands into her heart. "Cindy, I just …"

Ingrid interrupts Gina abruptly. "Gina, there is no cross talk at Group!"

Gina's eyes flash rage at the interruption. It belies her candy-sweet delivery, and reminds me of how my alcoholic grandma would switch from sweet to evil in a solitary second. Gina takes a moment to gather herself.

"Okay, Ingrid, thanks for that gem of wisdom regarding cross talk. So, *so* helpful," Gina says as cuttingly sarcastic as possible. "As I was saying, before being interrupted, thank you, Cindy. I'm there too. *Just let go and let God.* Amen, sister. You are so right. I have to just let go and let God. I have to …"

Gina begins to cry. Jack, Roy, and I pass our dollar bills to Cindy.

"Well played," I whisper to Cindy.

Group time expires, and Gina sobs as the group joins hands and prays out with the Serenity Prayer.

I'm oddly nervous sharing at the afternoon group. There is no escaping sharing, because it's a round-robin format, and we don't end until everyone has shared. Today's topic is *gratitude,* a recovery classic. When my turn comes, I'm feeling at a loss for words, an extreme rarity.

"I'm Joseph, and I'm ... uh ... I have problem with my drinking, as most of you already know. Among other things, I'm here, because I got arrested for ... uh ... getting into a fight while I was in a blackout ..."

"Are you an alcoholic?" someone behind me asks, apparently concerned that I haven't officially identified as an alcoholic. Everyone identifies as an addict or alcoholic when they share. It's customary. *I'm so-and-so, and I'm an addict/alcoholic.* I must hear this a hundred times a day. I feel a rage at this. I want to tell whoever just said that to shut up and stop interrupting me, and then I want to bash his skull in. It passes, and, instead, I respond reasonably.

"I don't really know what that means. *Alcoholic.* I didn't drink every day. You know, I'm not sure. So, anyway, gratitude. I'm grateful for not being in jail, and being alive ... I guess. I could have been killed the night I was arrested. Or I could have killed someone. So, I'm grateful for that. That's all I got."

Jack speaks next. He's pollyannaish, as usual, and claims gratitude for every individual thread in each and every sock in his sock drawer. The counselor moderating is nodding her head in approval like a goddamn bobblehead. Anyone with a cerebral cortex can tell Jack's full of shit.

I should be grateful, I think, as I tune out Jack's ramblings. I can think of logical reasons why I should be, but I don't feel grateful. I want my fucking turn back. I want to tell everyone that I hate gratitude. The very word makes me sick. Next person to utter the word g*rateful* has to go in the kitchen and place their hand in the deep fryer. I wish those guys had killed me that night. I wish anything had happened differently the night of my arrest, anything but Assault with Intent to Commit Rape. I'd rather be charged with robbing a bank and killing every motherfucker in it. *Fucking gratitude.* Fuck your gratitude. When are these fucking happy pills going to finally start working anyway?

Kib is out smoking a cigarette again. I turn toward her, directly away from the next whining share. I want her to see that I'm looking at her.

Kib, now she is something to be grateful for. I should have said that. *I'm grateful for Kib.* Look at her ass in those jeans. Look at the way she stands with one hip jutting out when she smokes. How's that for gratitude? You want me to choose a God of my understanding? Kib is my God.

Group finally ends. I smoke five cigarettes end to end and go into the bathroom and jack off to a fantasy of fucking Kib in the med closet. I shut the bedroom door and crawl into bed. I wake up six hours later. I've missed lunch and dinner and all the Group sessions. I'm surprised none of the counselors woke me. People are watching some Jim Carrey movie on the big screen in the Group room. Gina is all snuggled up in a blanket on the couch. I wish I could join her. I'd so love to be curled up with her under that blanket. I need to smoke. I go out to the center patio and join Jack.

Jack is a giant man in his mid-forties. He dresses like an '80s frat boy. He played inside linebacker for the Cornhuskers back in the '80s. Jack was destined for the NFL until he snapped his knee during the last game of his sophomore season. It was one of those plays where the announcer says, *You might not want to watch this.* After the injury, Jack hit the weights and the juice and rehabbed like a maniac for two years. He developed a steroid habit and a Vicodin habit. He re-injured his knee during the first play of his first game back. No NFL for Jack. He was devastated, and he was never the same. He's spent the last twenty years chasing prescription drugs and washing them down with whiskey.

Jack sits at a plastic table playing Solitaire by himself in the interior patio. He's concentrating as if there are serious stakes.

"Who's winning?" I ask.

"Me," Jack responds, "always."

I sit in a covered patio swing a few feet away, and light up a cigarette. Jack is constantly trying to get away from cigarette smoke, which is a tall order in rehab. Normally, I'd put my cigarette out, but my life is no longer normal. I have to smoke. It may be the only thing between me and a well-secured noose.

Jack's eyes don't leave the rows of layered cards. "So what's your story, man?" he asks me. "I told you mine. What's a guy like you doing in here?"

"A guy like me?" I say half-jokingly. "You should talk. You look like you should be at a country club, not rehab."

Jack wears his usual: leather boat shoes, no socks, khaki shorts, and a Red Nebraska Cornhuskers polo shirt, the nice kind the coaches wear. His hair is perfectly groomed. He's clean-shaven, and wears smart, tortoise-shell glasses.

"I'm on Bruce's dime getting back in shape," Jack says, referencing an earlier conversation, when he explained to me that he met Bruce, this crazy, little, middle-aged union baggage handler in a bar in Phoenix. Bruce loved hanging out with an ex-college football star, and so he paid for Jack's pills and alcohol for a week. Then Bruce told Jack the reason he was off work was because he was on leave to go to rehab to save his job. Bruce offered to pay for Jack's flight and a month at rehab if he came with.

"Getting back in shape for what?" I ask.

"To go back out," he says matter-of-factly. "I'm not done yet." He looks up from the cards. "How's that for rigorous honesty?" He goes back to his game and continues talking, as if to the cards. "I'm going to get some money together and go down to Mexico. I hear there are places where you can get Vicodin for fifty cents a pop, stay in a hotel on the beach, and drink beer all day for practically nothing. Not to mention, the little *senoritas* wearing bikinis."

I can tell Jack is full of shit when he shares in Group. His shares don't pass the smell test. Maybe I've become adept at spotting liars, because I've spent a good part of the last ten years analyzing people's testimony and taking depositions, but it seems obvious he's just parroting all the recovery terminology he's learned from going in and out of 12-step meetings and rehabs over the last two decades. Nevertheless, I'm still surprised to hear him tell me he's just here at PRC refueling for his next drug run.

"Wow," I say. "Well… I guess sitting on the beach with senoritas and beer does sound kind of good, especially given my current situation."

Jack stops playing Solitaire for a moment and looks up at me. "No doubt, right?"

I picture the scene for just a second. Unlike Jack, I've been wasted in Mexico many times. The *idea* of partying in Mexico is much better than the *reality* of partying in Mexico.

"I swear, this whole pill thing is new to me," I say. "I mean … I do remember my mom selling Valium that she got from a psychiatrist, but the idea of doing prescription pills for fun … it was never even on my radar."

"You don't know what you're missing, counselor."

"Yeah?"

"From what I've heard you'd be better off with a Percocet habit than drinking the way you did. I've never heard of a lawyer breaking and entering in the middle of the night in a blackout, or rolling cars off the side of a freeway at ninety miles an hour. Pills just make you feel better … a lot better." Jack pauses and lays down a seven of spades on an eight of diamonds. "You know that feeling you get when you've had four or five stiff drinks?"

"Uh-huh," I respond and try not to think about the taste, which has developed on my tongue at the mere thought of a stiff drink.

"That's the way you feel the whole time. A little Dilaudid, OxyContin … Demerol. You wouldn't need to drink like a maniac."

Now I'm curious.

"Everybody talks about OxyContin. What's that like?" I ask.

Jack leans back in his chair and takes a deep breath, apparently recalling an OxyContin-induced euphoria.

"It's like …," Jack lowers his voice when he notices Kib walking over, "… like that," he nods toward Kib, "like what you want to do to her … but the orgasm doesn't last ten seconds, it lasts ten hours."

Kib sits down next to me on the patio swing. She pulls out a cigarette. I light it.

"What lies are you telling this poor newcomer, Jack?" she asks and winks at me.

"I was telling Joseph here how the 12-steps saved my life, and how they can save his, too."

Jack gathers his cards and makes a show of coughing from our cigarette smoke. "I'll leave you nicotine junkies to hammer another couple nails in your coffins. You know Bill Wilson died of lung cancer, right?"

Kib flips Jack off and starts the patio swing going by kicking her feet playfully. She's wearing slip-on Vans with no socks.

"What were you guys really talking about?" Kib asks.

For an instant I weigh my desire to be completely honest with her versus any negative ramifications that might result. There is something about *id-level* honesty that often helps me get laid, or, at least, admired by some women.

"He was telling me how he wants to go to Mexico, drink beer, and take cheap prescription pills, you know, like Dilaudid, Percocet, and OxyContins, I believe. He mentioned bikini-clad Mexican woman. He didn't come out and say it, but if my intuition serves me, I'm thinking he wants to have sex with them. In fact, I'm pretty sure."

Kib laughs. "You're crazy," she says.

"I am crazy, hence why I am in here. And, if I can be even more honest—what is it the 12-steppers say, *rigorously honest?—*" I finger quote, "Jack's plan doesn't sound half bad. All except the pills. I don't really care about the pills."

"So you like Mexican girls in little bikinis?" Kib asks and nudges me flirtatiously.

"I'm just a huge fan of girls in bikinis, not just Mexicans."

She pulls out another cigarette, and I light it. "I have stretch marks, so I wear a one piece, but I still make the boys look."

"I'm sure you do." I lean back and frame Kib with my fingers like a photographer. "I can totally picture you in a bikini."

It's getting dark out, and the sky is gold and pink. Most everyone is in the group room watching TV. Through the sliding glass doors, I can see the flickers of light and activity and people walking down the hall. Some glance at Kib and me on the swing. The people who really run this place are gone for the day. The rules are relaxed. I feel good, gently swinging and smoking with Kib. I feel good knowing this pretty girl likes me, is charmed by me.

"You're a lawyer, right?" Kib asks.

"Yes. I am for now," I say.

"Can I tell you something? You promise not to tell anyone?"

"Sure. I'm used to keeping secrets," I say, trying to act nonchalant.

"You promise?" she asks.

"It's a legal duty," I respond. "You know . . . the attorney-client privilege?"

"Okay." Kib scans the area to make sure no one is close enough to overhear. She squeezes my hand and says, "You promised."

"Yeah, I promise," I assure her.

"I was at a party on the beach up, uh, you know, uh, like up near, like uh past Malibu with my friend Suzette. We swam, you know, had some beers, then, a bonfire. Everyone had blankets, and it was fun. Just mellow, you know? Then Bill, this guy Suzette likes ... he's a stockbroker or something ... he rolls up a joint and starts passing it around. I don't smoke all the time or anything but ... and then, out of the frigging nowhere one of those jeeps pulls up—like a *Baywatch* lifeguard jeep with its lights and you know, everything. And of course, I'm holding the joint."

"Oh, damn," I say with as much sincerity as I can muster. "Did David Hasselhoff jump out and save you?"

"*Shut up!*" She realizes she said *shut up* too exuberantly, and looks around to see if anybody heard her. "I'm serious. This isn't funny." She smiles. "Anyway, I got a ticket, a *frigging* ticket, for having the marijuana. It wasn't even mine ... I have to go to court in a couple weeks. I could *like totally* lose my job."

God, how I wish my big problem was getting a ticket for smoking pot.

Cindy slides open the patio door, Scrabble box in hand, and Roy is a couple steps behind her. They walk toward us. At this point Kib and I are almost touching. Kib scoots away from me a bit.

"You want in on Dirty Scrabble? Double points for anything phallic," Cindy says and then directs her attention to Kib. "You owe me a cig, girlfriend, and, I'll take payment ... uh let's see ... how about uh ... now."

Kib rolls her eyes at Cindy's histrionics and hands Cindy a cigarette.

"I better get back in and see if Alfredo has destroyed anything," Kib says. She grips my thigh and pushes herself up off the swing. Her touch sends a wave of pleasure through me. "Talk later," she says and walks away.

"Talk later?" Roy asks coyly. "Correct me if I'm wrong," he continues, "but did Kib put her hand on your thigh?"

We both look to Cindy and wait for her to respond. It's sure to be good.

"She's a nice girl, isn't she, Joseph?" Cindy starts her shtick in a saccharine, matronly tone. "And you like tight Asian pussy, don't you, Joseph?"

I grin and nod affirmatively, playing along, as if I were a child and Cindy an elementary-school teacher that asked if I liked cake.

"We all do," Cindy continues. "Right, Roy?"

Roy nods earnestly.

"I mean ... I'll be honest, Joseph, tight Asian pussy is one of my favorite things," Cindy says.

"Oh, me too," Roy says.

"But you have to be honest with yourself, Joseph. You have to be honest with *you*. You have to admit that you love tight Asian pussy. Say it Joseph: I ... love ... tight ... Asian ... pussy."

"I don't think I'm ready yet, Cindy," I respond jokingly, but also think how Cindy doesn't realize how apropos this is.

Cindy gives me a heartfelt nod. "Okay, Joseph, we are here for you, when you're ready to admit you're powerless over tight Asian pussy."

"Okay, enough already, Cindy," Roy says. "Let's play Dirty Scrabble. Now, before we start I need to know what all the double-point phallic words are. Dick, cock, penis, schlong ... schlong's a word, right?"

"Of course," I interject.

"Schlong's not a word," Cindy barks at me. "I thought you were a lawyer. Didn't they teach you in law school that schlong is not a word? And don't change the subject. What were you and little Miss I-work-at-a-rehab-and-dress-just-a-tad-slutty-and-flirt-with-all-the-cute-boys talking about? *Hmmm?* Were you talking about her tight Asian pussy and—"

"Cindy, where are your manners?" Roy interrupts. "If you are going to inappropriately sexualize Kib, be specific about it. I believe the correct terminology is tight Vietnamese pussy. She doesn't like being thrown in with all the other Asians, any more than you like being thrown in with all the other carpet-munching dykes."

"You know, Roy," Cindy retorts softly. "I know where all this aggression is coming from. It's because you'll never be able to please your wife the way I can." Cindy frowns and lowers her chin, feigning a sad face, "Ahhh, poor Roy..."

"Roy's right," I declare. "Say what you mean, mean what you say, but don't say it mean. You shouldn't talk about Kib like that."

"Very nice, Joseph," Roy says. "I see you've been paying attention at the Al-Anon meeting."

Roy and Cindy lay out the Scrabble board, and I watch them play while I smoke cigarettes and occasionally mediate a minor Dirty Scrabble dispute. Is the word *balls* dirty? And, if so, is it phallic and thus deserving of double points or just phallic-adjacent? After twenty minutes they take a break, and Cindy turns her attention to me.

"So why don't you identify as an alcoholic in Group?" Cindy asks.

"Sometimes she'll get serious on you," Roy quips.

"No, *for reals*," Cindy says, "I fuck around a lot, but I almost died from alcohol poisoning. If I don't get sober ... *fuck man*. The doctor said I could have died. I was drinking a fifth of vodka every day. I barely weighed ninety pounds."

The mood turns heavy.

"I didn't even drink every day," I say, feeling as if I have to defend myself. "I'd go days without drinking sometimes and, you know, it's not like—what—I mean, sometimes, I'd go to dinner with my girlfriend's parents or something, and I'd just have one glass of wine." I pause and think of my grandma who died in her fifties. "Yeah, my grandma was an alcoholic. She drank like you did, every day."

"I didn't take drugs or drink every day either," Roy says, "but I'm an addict because once I get something in my system I don't know what's going to happen. Sometimes everything is cool, and sometimes I end up jumping out of a moving car." He pauses for emphasis. "I kid you not. I jumped out of a moving car just on a whim ... I was that drunk and high."

"I don't know," I say, "I just feel like I have control. I just can't say I'm addicted or can't go without it."

"Whoa, whoa, whoa," Cindy starts, "I've heard your story. You're a *fucking lawyer*. You wreck a car and get a DUI and then keep drinking and then break into some building in the middle of the night and start a fight with someone you don't know. You are questioning whether you are an alcoholic?" Cindy asks, incensed.

"It's a self-diagnosed disease, give him a break," Roy says to Cindy.

"I know, Roy," Cindy says, truly irritated, "this is my fifth rehab, remember? He's a ...," Cindy starts to answer Roy but then changes her mind and goes directly at me. "You are a classic binge-drinking alcoholic, and you are going to die or kill someone or both, if you keep drinking..."

My roommate is still for a change. It's dark in our room. A soft light breaches the gap between the door's bottom and the tile floor. I hear faint sounds of stirring and late night TV from the group room. It comforts me like the parties at my Aunt Suzie's house when I was a kid. I'd sleep in her and Uncle Billy's water bed. Ranger, their black Labrador, would lie with me. I could hear the music and the laughter. My aunt and mom would check on me every once in a while. I felt safe, because I knew I'd be waking up at Auntie Suzie's house.

I need relief. I masturbate quietly under the covers. Kib in a white bikini. The orgasm relaxes me. I'm comfortable in this hard hospital bed, and I'm tired. I close my eyes. But the racing thoughts come like the alcohol spins used to.

A black twister of fear and regret and anxiety, a frantic mix of everything that makes me feel desperate and horrible. Put it all in a blender, add black dye, and pour it in my brain: Caroline crying on the phone; Keri looking at me through Plexiglas at jail; the psycho ward at Twin Towers with spots in my peripheral all around and the little spiders crawling on my skin; my SUV on its side with tires spinning and sirens; Preacher Dale and his .38 special, and me handcuffed to a hospital bed again. How am I going to pay my bills? What about my clients? My Grandpa and Tito and everyone, jail, my mom, assault, criminal threats ... rape, the broken bottles in the Alley ... the cop cars, bent spoons, and cigarette burns.

The racing thoughts, they're worse than the spins. If only I could stick my finger down my throat, vomit, and feel better.

My eyes blast open. I can hear my heart bashing against my chest.

Jesus Christ. Cindy says I'm a binge-drinking alcoholic, a *binge-drinking alcoholic.* What the fuck does that mean? What the fuck does it matter? It's too late for me. I'm through. Game over. I just want to go to sleep.

I close my eyes and think of Dr. Blume's kind cherubic face. I ask him, *Why wouldn't I want to commit suicide?* His response is a question: Are you okay right this very second? Right here, right now, are you okay? If the answer is *yes*, then you are okay.

Right here, right now, I think, *I'm okay.* I keep repeating it to keep my racing thoughts away.

ELEVEN

The one-day-at-a-time mind trick coupled with Lexapro is quite the sedative. I know my life sucks, and it isn't that I don't care; it's just that I'm—strangely—okay right now. Yes, I'm being charged with a host of felonies; yes, I have a law practice with cases that are ticking away, and I have no idea how or if I'm going to manage them; yes, I don't know where I'm going to live when I get out of rehab; yes, I have so many problems they all melt together into one thick dark fudgy *fuck-it* sandwich. But, I feel like I'm a separate entity viewing myself from above.

I should be crying until I run out of tears, but there is a certain freedom in knowing that my life is so inexorably ruined that all I can do is what's in front of me this very second. That's what they say in here: Just do what's in front of you. And some days, the only thing that is in front of me is a big plate of macaroni and cheese, some ping-pong, and endless group therapy and 12-step meetings. I have so many problems it takes me a few hours just to list them. I know this, because Florence had me do it. It felt great. I just wrote them all down, page after page. Then I rose up off the ground for a bird's eye view. *Look at all those problems that guy's got!* That is one hell of a list.

I'm in the perfect mood to finally read the police report Keri brought me two days ago. I asked her why it was still entitled *Homicide* if they weren't charging me with attempted murder. She explained that the police make a recommendation of what to charge, and then the DA makes the actual decision. So, the most heinous charge the police recommend is what is on the police report. *Please Keri*, I think, *can't you convince them to change it back to attempted murder?* I just want to be charged with attempted murder. Please, I just want to be an attempted murderer. This rape and criminal threats and sodomy, it's unseemly.

HOMICIDE/ATTEMPTED MURDER 7/23/2003. The report is fifteen pages. If it weren't me I am reading about, I'd want this guy to get the electric chair. What a scumbag. Do they still use the electric chair in California? Or is it lethal injection? For me, I want the guillotine with a crowd of French people screaming horrible French things at me, throwing moldy baguettes at my exposed head.

The gist of the fifteen pages of single-spaced, Arial font, narrative is this: After making a commotion at the front of the closed massage parlor, I crawl in through the back window into a bathroom. I take off my clothes and walk out into the apartment. There is a loud industrial fan going. The bathroom and the apartment are meticulously neat with sparse furnishings. There is a guy in a bed with a sheet over him. He has long hair and a goatee. He wakes from the smell of nicotine, alcohol, and sweat. I jump on him and hit and choke him.

Yes, *seriously*. That's what it says.

We are up and about in the dark room fighting. He hits me. I hit him. I tell him, *Shut up or I'll kill you.* At some point he notices that not only am I naked, but also that my penis is erect.

Then I put the poor guy in a "carotid artery restraint hold." The cop writes he's been a defensive tactics instructor for ten years and knows this hold can be fatal.

It's good to know my years of martial arts training finally paid off. I can picture my first kung fu sensei, saying, "If you ever break into a man's house naked, in an alcoholic blackout—*don't judge, it's going to happen, it's just a matter of* when *it's going to happen not if it's going to happen* —and your victim just won't shut his goddamn mouth long enough for you to explain your hard-on and unfortunate breaking and entering, use this hold, the carotid artery hold, aka, the *rear naked choke*, aka,

Mata Leao, Portuguese for *choke the lion.* Remember, eight seconds and he'll pass out from lack of oxygen, fifteen and you may kill him, so be careful."

The report continues: the victim says he *breaks free* of the choke hold. This seems doubtful. A rear naked choke isn't something somebody typically breaks free of. It's like being handcuffed. The only way you get out, especially if you aren't a trained fighter, is if you are let out. I imagine I let him go, because I thought if I didn't I'd kill him, but who knows?

He runs out the front door and I, the *perpetrator,* go back out the way I came in, the bathroom window. He and a neighbor chase me down across the street and, the police report says, *contain me* until the police show.

Contain in police jargon must mean, *bash over the head with a skateboard.* Actually, I don't blame them at all for that. If someone broke into my apartment, I'd probably have done worse.

Here is where the report gets interesting. First, the DA failed to redact the victim's name in one spot. His name is Winston Jones! The little Asian guy's name is Winston Jones? Obviously, I'm wrong. He's not Asian. I try to picture his face. I can't. I wonder if I just presumed he and his buddy are Asian, because of the massage parlor?

Winston wrote down in the police report all the things he says I said. Besides for everybody's favorite home invasion line, *Shut up or I'm going to kill you!* I allegedly also said, in response to his questioning about my inconspicuous nakedness and hard-on, *I thought you were a girl,* and *My friends told me that a hot girl lived there.* I was also going on about being in a fraternity with him and his buddy, *You are my brothers,* and rambled something about a Volkswagen, and said, *This would never happen in Hawaii.*

The stuff about the girl doesn't seem right. Obviously I was there to get laid at the massage parlor, hence the hard-on and the one hundred dollars and the fact that I was there. But why would I lie about friends telling me a girl lived at his place? It was almost as if I was trying to convince him I wasn't gay. And maybe I didn't say anything about the massage parlor, because, in my drunken state, I thought admitting that would get me in trouble. And, I've never been to Hawaii, nor have I ever been in a fraternity, and the only Volkswagen I'm familiar with is the Baja Bug that my mom had when I was a kid, so I can only presume that all that was just the ramblings of a mad-man.

The police report also had copies of all the various cards in my wallet, which I apparently left splayed open in the apartment.

I wonder how many attempted rapists are card-carrying members of the ACLU and Amnesty International.

Winston identified me by the picture on my driver's license. The police report quotes Winston as saying, *Yes, that's him. He still has that boy-band hair.* Oh Winston! How cruel. I know. I know. Even after only several days of rehab, I know: It only hurts, because it's true. The truth is I *do* have boy-band hair. But why did you have to say it, Winston? Besides breaking into your apartment in the middle of the night and waking you to the stench of my alcohol and nicotine-laced sweat, choking you, punching you, threatening your life, and putting you in a deadly choke hold while naked, what did I ever do to you to deserve such harsh criticism?

The report also includes a supplemental report about a detective going to the massage parlor to investigate whether I'd been there before. Of course, *mama san* says she's never seen me in her life. Even for a cop with no incentive to help me, it seems more than a little disingenuous to be asking a pimp to corroborate my story that she is running an illegal brothel and that I'm a customer.

❖   ❖   ❖

It's Saturday night, family night at rehab. It's an Indian summer. PRC is energized with people: anxious wives, doting moms, shamed dads, ambivalent brothers and sisters. Larisa is here. She has decided to give me a second chance in my time of need. She's forgiven me for breaking up with her so cruelly, a couple weeks before my arrest. I had to. She wouldn't let go, and I needed to be able to drink and play without interruption. Breaking up with her was a better option than cheating on her. I promised myself I'd never do that to another woman again.

She wears a short jean skirt. She's so cute and spunky with her short, sandy-blonde hair, and bright blue eyes. I call her Speck, because she has a brown speck in her right eye. I'm the only one who calls her that. She's nearly twelve years younger than me. Larisa's a rich Palos Verdes girl, but she's had her problems, too, including a stint in a bad-girl, rehab school with Paris Hilton, when she was only sixteen. Now, at twenty-one-years-old, she's getting her life back together and about to enroll in nursing school. I was never in love with her, but I do love her.

Larisa sits next to me and kisses me on the cheek. Her pale freckled Italian skin glows. Her face is classically pretty, like a 1920s flapper. I look down into her lap. Seeing her athletic legs crossed, her little mini-skirt barely covering her panties, I can't help but to think that this is not only the longest I've gone without drinking, but also the longest I've gone without sex since I was eighteen.

Dr. Blume stands behind a rickety lectern and speaks to a crowded room of mostly anxious family members. Everyone loves Dr. Blume. He's the perfect Grandpa, kind to the bone. And he's got a PhD and MD.

"The American Medical Association recognizes addiction as a disease," Dr. Blume declares as forcefully as his cherubic face will allow.

There is a little grumbling in the audience. I'm having a hard time swallowing the concept myself. It sounds like a great excuse for a bunch of degenerates. I'm pretty sure this is a ploy by the AMA to the get the insurance companies to pay for rehabs. Dr. Blume sets a cardboard-backed picture onto an easel. At first glance, it looks like an abstract painting on a shiny black canvas.

"I know the concept of addiction as a disease can be tough to accept, because society has deemed addiction a moral issue. No one goes to visit a cancer patient in the hospital and chastises them for not showing up to work, or their kid's soccer game, because they have cancer."

Alfredo's dad stands up, outraged, and shouts, "My mom died of liver cancer."

Alfredo, normally filled with Jersey-bravado, shrinks in embarrassment. His dad is a walking stereotype.

"Are youze telling me that some *frigging*—excuse my near French," he says and looks down at his wife for confirmation that referring to *frigging* as near French, is, indeed, clever, and she giggles and nods up at him in a touching show of solidarity, "Uh-hum …drug addict who keeps doin' it and doin' it, because he wants to get *frigging* high and doesn't want to face life like the rest of us peoples is the same as a cancer victim?"

Florence pops up from next to the podium to defend Dr. Blume. "Sir, we'll have time for questions after Dr. Blume is finished speaking."

Alfredo's dad looks like he belongs on the set of "The Sopranos," but in a straight-up fight, Florence would take him.

"Thank you, Florence," Dr. Blume responds, mediating. "Florence is right—thank you—but that is a great question, and I'll just go ahead and address it right now, because that attitude is exactly what we are talking about tonight."

Alfredo's dad sits down. There will be no super-heavyweight bout between Alfredo's dad and Florence tonight.

"What the medical community has proven without a doubt," Dr. Blume says, "is that there are physiological differences between an addict and a nonaddict, just like with cancer. The difference is that a cancer patient, at a certain stage, may have no viable option for survival. An addict, given the opportunity, can recover. But that doesn't change the fact that addiction is a disease, not a moral issue." Dr. Blume points to the red, blue, and black printout of an MRI film on the easel. "The right is the frontal cortex of a normal person shown alcohol. This is a person who drinks from time to time, enjoys it, but doesn't *need* it. The left is the frontal cortex of an alcoholic when a drink is put in front of him. Keep in mind, he hasn't drunk anything. He's just been shown the drink. You see all that red? That is high energy. When he sees that drink, he goes into a *primordial* state. He sees red. He *has* to have it. It's the same way your brain will light up when put in a dangerous situation. Mr. Szarrto," Dr. Blume addresses Alfredo's dad, who is clearly impressed that Dr. Blume knows his last name, "if you left here tonight with your lovely wife, and *God forbid*, a robber approached you at your car with a knife, you'd do anything to protect your wife, right?"

Alfredo's dad puts his arm around his Gucci-clad, thick wife who mock-waits for his response, as if she is going to chastise him for anything short of an enthusiastic, *yes*. "Of course, I would," he proudly responds.

"Of course, you would," Dr. Blume repeats. "And at that moment when you saw your lovely wife in danger, the frontal cortex of your brain would light up like a Christmas tree. You'd have no choice in the matter. You couldn't control it anymore than you can control when the sun comes up. And it's no different for Alfredo, if I were to put a line of cocaine in front of him."

Alfredo laughs nervously. Even though he's in here for gambling not drugs, unbeknownst to his dad, he just tested dirty a couple hours ago. Alfredo's dad nods his head, satisfied, if not impressed.

"Now let's talk about my favorite addiction study of all time ..."

Dr. Blume describes a double-blind experiment, in which mice were given increasing doses of cocaine until they were hooked. All of the mice reacted the same way once they were hooked. Even if they were starving, they'd choose cocaine over food. If they didn't get cocaine at the regularly scheduled time, they'd go crazy, jerking around the cage in a flutter. And the most convincing part was that they'd cross over an electrified metal plate and get electrocuted to get coke. They'd do this, even if the last mouse to do it was electrocuted to death.

My first thought is, who would do this to these cute little mice? I picture a white mouse wiggling its cute little nose. Poor guy, all strung out. After the experiment did they send them to rehab? Are there little mice rehabs? Or do they just party until they die? The little emaciated mice, in a cage, all around a black leather couch, wearing dark glasses, chopping up fat white lines on a glass table, and taking turns snorting them up their tiny little nostrils with miniature rolled hundred-dollar bills. Stacks of untouched cheddar-cheese blocks in various degrees of mold surround them. "I'm Just Waiting for the Man" is playing in the background on a miniature turntable.

Do we really need to kill a bunch of mice to realize that addicts are possessed by their need for their drug? Spike Lee taught us that in the '80s.

Dr. Blume continues. He's on a roll. Some of us tune out, presumably daydreaming about coked-out mice. Larisa has her head on my shoulder and is nearly asleep. Dr. Blume is so kind and friendly he's given an unusual amount of leeway by a tough crowd. I tune in when he says that heavy daily-drinking alcoholics can die from withdrawal, and that is why drugs and even small doses of alcohol are used for detox. He talks about dt's, delirium tremens, and the crawling bugs on the skin. I think of the psycho cell I was in at Twin Towers when I was first arrested, and how I had a similar sensation. I felt like spiders were crawling on me. I wondered if I was having dt's. Dr. Blume ends, finally, by reading from the *Big Book*, which is what the alcoholics use at their meetings. I was given one at check-in. I've read some of it since I've been here. It's a strange book written by a stockbroker and a doctor in the 1930s. I haven't read this section. It's about Dr. Jekyll and Mr. Hyde, and the gist is that a real alcoholic, unlike a heavy drinker, loses all control once he starts drinking, and can act in *disgusting* and *antisocial* ways when he drinks. That's me, I think, *disgusting* and *antisocial*. I presume by *antisocial* this doesn't mean playing golf in cut-off jeans, but *antisocial*, as in psychopathic. I make a mental note to look this up. I'd like to know if there is something out there that would explain my behavior, whether it be plain old madness—*antisocial*—or bumbling aspiring rapist—*antisocial and disgusting*—even if it's a book written by a couple dead God-loving drunks.

Bob looks like a pre-Vegas, pre-anabolic-steroid Carrot Top, but instead of freckles he has pockmarks and crevices. He wears thick Buddy Holly glasses and an Indiana Jones hat. Bob used to be the singer of a fairly successful band whose only big radio hit was a joke song called "Sammy Hagar Weekend." Bob and his band died out due to Bob's heroin and alcohol habit. He's best friends with one of the most famous rock star junkies in the world, so even though he's a dirt-poor musician who drives a rehab van, he does things like fly to Paris in a private jet and stay in the penthouse of a five-star hotel to watch a rock show. Today's not so glamorous. Today he's taking me to see Dr. Rothberg, a renowned psychiatrist with a CV the size of a phone book, whom I've paid five thousand dollars to tell the DA the obvious: I'm not a violent sexual predator.

"So where to today, LAX Court? Your attorney's? Lawyer AA?" Bob asks. He has been chauffeuring me around, mostly to meaningless court continuances, since I arrived.

"We are going to the Valley, Sherman Oaks, to see some overpaid PhD expert witness who is going to tell everyone I'm an alcoholic, maybe even a manic depressive … *whatever*, just not a violent sexual predator," I tell Bob.

Other than Dr. Blume, Bob is the only one I've told my whole story to. Bob's a godless 12-stepper, which I don't understand, because the whole 12-step program seems to be littered with God-this and God-that, hallowed be thy name.

"Violent Sexual Predator," Bob repeats contemplatively. "That could be a movie ... with Arnold Schwarzenegger. *Violent Sexual Predator*," Bob enunciates in better-than-average Schwarzenegger voice.

We ride in silence for a few minutes. Bob stops at his favorite gas station that sells the cheapest cigarettes in town.

"Dr. Blume was talking about that whole Dr. Jekyll and Mr. Hyde, addiction-is-a-disease stuff last night at Family Night. What do you think about that?" I ask.

Bob is thoroughly enjoying his cigarette, and he seems halfway out the window. Raggedy Ann hair whips underneath his hat. I wonder how it stays put. He contemplates my question almost long enough for me to decide he's decided not to answer. Bob is always smiling. He's an old junkie who threw away a promising music career and now works in a rehab, barely making ends meet, but I get why he's happy. He's free. He works an easy job, makes music, and he doesn't spend his time copping dope. I remember being free like that. It was when I was sixteen and worked at Parker's Sporting Goods, before the prostitutes and before the alcohol and cigarettes.

"I don't understand how the program works," Bob says, "I just do it. It's a program of action not thought. I don't believe in some bearded cloud-God up there deciding whether I get a record deal or not. So what if I do? I used to break into my best friend's house and steal his shit and pawn it for heroin. I used to steal from my mom for heroin. I'd have done anything for heroin. And I'm sure I've done worse drunk. I just don't remember."

"Yeah?" I ask.

"Yeah, that's not me," Bob says. "I would've never done those things had I not been strung out."

We ride quietly for a few minutes. It feels good to be on the freeway and not be in handcuffs.

"One time we were playing in one of those big music festivals in Europe. I'm so drunk I'm jumping around on stage. I break my leg, and I don't even know it. Do you know how badly a broken leg hurts? People go into shock from it, and I didn't even know it was happening ... yeah, Dr. Jekyll and Mr. Hyde. That was me."

"What about prayer?" I ask coyly. "I mean do you get down on your knees every night?"

"Yep. Every day I pray to a God I don't think exists. *Here's what I know.* Doing what is suggested means I don't have to stick a needle in my arm, or neck, for that matter. It means I don't have to take a drink. It's the only thing that ever worked. So, yeah, I pray, and I do the deal, not perfectly, but I do it."

Bob drops me off in front of a high-rise office building on Ventura Boulevard, only a couple miles from the apartment where I lived my third year of law school, the one I used to think about jumping off when I was drunk.

I'm sitting in Dr. Rothberg's office waiting for him to finish typing on his laptop. I'm surprised at how young he is—mid-forties, tops. Handsome, trim, well-tailored suit. *I fucking hate this guy.* He asks me a bunch of questions, and he reviews the MMPI test that I took while waiting. MMPI is Minnesota something or other. It will tell him whether I'm a psycho or not. He asks questions, but only looks up when I say something juicy, like when I tell him my mom was a junkie and that my grandma died in a fierce competition between lung cancer and cirrhosis of the liver in her fifties. He's not so impressed that I graduated from Pepperdine Law. He probably doesn't even know anyone over twenty-five without a graduate degree.

We play a game: He says words. I repeat.

He says, "Rope, tiger, pencil, stick, shark, helicopter, giraffe."

I say, "Rope, tiger, uh ... giraffe, uh ... pencil."

"Okay," he says, "you've got it now. Let's try again. Rope, tiger, pencil, stick, shark, helicopter, giraffe."

"Rope, tiger, pencil, uhm ... *fuck* ... stick plane, giraffe, pencil."

This game sucks. I used to be able to count cards at a single-deck blackjack table and add five-digit numbers in my head. I'm only thirty-two years old. Now I can't remember a few words?

He goes again, "Speaker, stereo, tape, cup, glass, home, apartment, light, lamp."

I try again, "Speaker, stereo, tape player, uh … lamp and glass … then … uh … house."

He does it again and again, and on my best try I'm a five out of seven. He seems surprised, not in a good way like when he found out my mom was a junkie and my grandma died of alcoholism.

He explains that he'll have to review the MMPI, the history he's noted, and various other things from the police report before he can do his report. He tells me he's interviewed my mom, Larisa, Keri, and Will. He says it's pretty obvious that I don't qualify as a Sexually Violent Predator.

"What's interesting," he says, "your history of concussions from the car accident, your boxing career coupled with the systemic binge drinking has caused … I don't want to say *brain damage*, but your short-term recall is not close to what I would expect from a practicing attorney. Did you pass the Bar on the first try?"

I say, "yep" but I think, *Of course I did, you pompous asshole.*

"Now there is no way of knowing what additional damage was done on the night of the incident from the blunt head trauma," he says, "but given the staples in your head, what is in the police report and your state of mind that night, I can only surmise it was significant."

"*Jesus.* How bad is it?" I ask. I'm a bit alarmed as I realize that my thinking has been fuzzy, and how much difficulty I've had getting words out. I haven't noticed how bad it is, because I haven't been working.

"Your short term memory will slowly come back," Dr. Rothberg says reassuringly. "It may not be one hundred percent for a while, but it will slowly come back as long as you stay healthy. My initial assessment is that your progressive alcoholic binge drinking and extremely high tolerance, coupled with your mild brain damage from multiple significant head trauma, predisposed you to cognitive and behavioral dysfunction."

He looks at me through his smart glasses, telling me I have brain damage. That is why I can't remember seven words. I could have been just like him: mid-forties, sitting pretty, charging people outrageous sums of money, because I'm so goddamn smart. But now, apparently, it's amazing that I can tie my own shoes. I'll soon be slobbering on myself when I try to say a word involving more than one vowel. I want to jump over his cherrywood desk, use his head to bust the window open, and then throw him ten stories down onto Ventura Boulevard. I picture him falling like that scene from ... *fuck, I can't remember* ... was it one with Mel Brooks? No, it was with *whatshisname* ... fuck, uh, goddammit ... *The Fugitive.* Thank God I remembered that.

"So I've had so many concussions and all the blackout drinking ... I just basically lost my mind that night? Is that right?" I say dryly, trying to recap in lay terms.

"Yes, basically," he says as he looks down at his watch. It's the same way I used to look at my watch when the amount of time a client had paid for was nearing an end.

I want to beg him for another chance at the seven-word game. *Dr. Rothberg please. I'm just tired, stressed out. I can do it. Just give me another chance. Please!* I pull at his sleeve as he nudges me out of his office. Can't we just go to lunch at your country club and forget about this whole *mild but significant* brain damage thing?

On the drive home, I think of every phone call I've had since I've been in rehab in which I couldn't recall a name or a date. Maybe I don't have any memory at all. I just have a bunch of ideas about what I think probably happened, and my imagination fills in the blanks to keep my memory from panicking. Maybe that's why I thought my victim, Winston Jones, was Asian. I've been a brain-damaged attorney. No wonder I drank so much.

We're in deadlocked traffic on the 405 in this big, white, generic passenger van. It's hot. Bob has the window down and is smoking. Framed by the hat, the glasses, that crazy red hair, is a little Buddha grin. He seems so fucking content. I get it. He's okay right now. I guess I am, too. I'm pretty sure there is a time in my future where I'm not going to be okay. But right now, right here, everything is okay. *Hell,* right now, this very moment—not what I think is going to happen to me or what probably will happen to me—but right here, right now, it's pretty good. Bob doesn't say anything. DJ Rodney on the Rock is on the radio playing Bob Marley. Bob turns it up, rolls down my window, and lights a new cigarette off his and hands it to me, and then we sing along.

Caroline visits.

She looks like she's going to the Kentucky Derby. She's relapsed into fashion hell, but instead of a Social Distortion groupie like when we met, she's now San Diego trophy wife chic. She has a big straw sun hat with huge dark sunglasses, and a flowery sundress that is a bit too high on the thigh. She's wearing four-inch wedges that match the straw hat in color and texture, and absurdly making her barely shorter than I am. Her breasts are squeezed up and out. They are still magnificent. She walks in like she's expecting paparazzi. The Group Room is full, and everyone stops and stares at her. The black wife at the table next to me is hush-yelling at her skinny white husband, about having to take care of their vending machine business and the baby while he's in here again; even she stops the berating she's dishing out to watch Caroline float in like Princess Di. I'm equal parts embarrassed and proud.

Caroline hugs me and kisses me on the lips, which surprises me. I haven't seen her in several years. She's called me a couple times. The first call was about her first DUI, the second about her second DUI, and the last to complain about her new rich boyfriend. She calls late and drunk, crying.

She squeezes my cheeks between her fingers. She has square-tipped fake nails. They match her cherry-red toenails.

"Oh my God! What happened to you?" she says, dramatically.

I give her the short version, but it doesn't seem to register. She stops listening after the first minute.

"But why are you here? This place is so … *dirty*."

"I don't have a choice, Caroline," I respond with irritation. "Didn't you hear what I just told you? I *have* to be here. Obviously, I have a problem with alcohol."

Now I remember what it's like talking to her. It hits me like a gust of wind.

"But you aren't an alcoholic," she says matter-of-factly.

"I don't know, Caroline. I mean alcoholism is a disease. You know me. I never drank and drove. We always walked or took a cab when we were together. I would never risk anyone's life. But I did. I nearly killed myself and my passenger in my DUI."

Caroline looks confused.

"Can you take off the sunglasses, please? And the hat? Are you going to a polo match after this?" I ask sarcastically, and I immediately feel guilty.

She takes off the hat, and tears well up in her big, crystal-green eyes.

"I just wanted to look good for you," she says, her voice cracking.

I forget how quick she is to tears and how it breaks my heart instantly. It's just like when she was outside the door at the apartment in Riverside, begging me to give her another chance. I never needed a drink so badly. Seeing her makes me want a drink. I want a Jack and Coke with ice in a huge glass tumbler. It would make everything better.

"I'm sorry, baby," I say, trying to stop her from crying. "You drove all the way out here to see me. I'm sorry." I hug her. She feels good. I can feel the wetness of her tears through my T-shirt. "You have to understand, Caroline. I'm going through a lot here."

I hand her a napkin so she can dry her eyes.

"Caroline, what I was trying to say is, the way I act when I drink and get blasted, *it's not me*. I wouldn't risk anyone's life by driving drunk in a blackout. I wouldn't crawl into someone's window in the middle of the night. That's not me. Alcohol makes me a different person. I'm like Dr. Jekyll and Mr. Hyde."

"Who?" she asks.

"Dr. Jekyll and Mr. Hyde. You know ..."

I stop. By the look on her face I realize she doesn't know, which reminds me how much younger she is than me and how uninterested she is in most subjects, literature included.

"It's a reference to a story of a doctor who was a good guy, but he had a monster that would come over him and take him over, kind of like a werewolf. It was a metaphor for split personality or whatever. I don't think I ever actually read it ... it's just in the lexicon ... a phrase."

Caroline dabs at her eyes with the edge of the napkin and sniffles and says, "I don't know what you mean. What's a lexicon?"

"I have a disease," I say. "Alcoholism. That's why I do these horrible things that I don't want to do. I did a horrible thing, and it may have ruined my life. I can't drink anymore. I think ... I mean, I am an *alcoholic*."

There, I said it. I'm not sure I believe it.

"That is crazy, Joseph. You just got a little too drunk, and this," she says, waving her hands around, "is all a big misunderstanding. You just need to drink less." Caroline widens her eyes for emphasis.

"Oh, I just need to drink less! Of course, why didn't I think of that?" I respond angrily. "I rolled a car off the side of the freeway and could have easily killed my friend, not to mention myself. I had to spend a year and ten grand to fight that case, and then I continue blackout drinking while I'm on probation for a DUI, which by the way was one inch from being a felony DUI, and then I break into someone's house in the middle of the night in a blackout and am being charged with six felonies! And you think I might want to *tone it down a little* on the Jack and Cokes? *Really? You think?"*

The room goes hush, and everyone stares at us. I'm yelling. She's crying. She's crying like a child. *Fuck.* Why did I do that? My chest cracks open again. I hate seeing her cry, especially when I'm the cause. I wish we could just go to a bar and drink and smoke like we used to.

"Do you have a cigarette?" she asks between sniffles.

We go out on the patio and smoke together just like when we lived in Oceanside. I wish I were back in Oceanside, and we could try again. God, how I wanted to fix her. I wanted to fix *us* so badly. I wanted to take this crazy, unrefined, sexy Irish girl and turn her into my perfect little lawyer's wife. We'd buy a house, get a dog, and stop fucking up. We'd have perfect Christmases and host Thanksgiving dinners, pass out candy at Halloween. We'd go to bed early on the weekdays. She'd wear tasteful dresses and drink one glass of wine at dinner. What the fuck happened to us?

We hug. I apologize. I thank her for visiting, and I give her gas money. I watch her walk out to the parking lot. She's backlit. The sun shines through her skirt and between her long legs, creating a precise silhouette. She is beautiful.

TWELVE

———————

I'm lying on my back on an examination table staring up at Dr. Singler. He rolls up a hand towel as he explains what he's about to do: remove seven huge staples from my scalp.

"Open up," he says and presses a tightly rolled hand towel in my mouth like a horse's bit.

I try to say, "What's this for?" but the words come out inaudibly muffled.

"So if you bite down hard, you won't break a tooth," Dr. Singler says.

As I ponder the nature of a procedure that is so painful that I might bite down so hard that I'll break a tooth without a bit in my mouth, Dr. Singler, an octogenarian, begins to tell me a story from when he was a medic in World War II.

I stop listening at the point when he extracts from his old-timey medical case a gleaming, chrome, surgical staple remover, the size of a plumber's wrench. I envision him trying to save a young Brit soldier's life on the beaches of Normandy, but I'm not exactly sure there *were* Brit soldiers on the beaches at Normandy.

Dr. Singler grins softly at his shiny new toy. I am more than a little reluctant about this procedure. It doesn't seem consistent with modern medicine.

"This is going to hurt quite a bit, young man, *quite a bit*," he says. "We cannot risk giving you any pain medication this early in your recovery, Old Boy, so I'm afraid you'll simply have to grin and bear it."

At least I don't have to leave rehab to have this procedure. Rehab is my cocoon. I know I'm going to have to leave here soon—face the world—but I don't want it to happen any sooner than absolutely necessary. The thought of dealing with an outside doctor or a hospital is far worse than dealing with Dr. Singler here. The phrase I've heard and read no less than a dozen times daily since my arrival at PRC passes my mind's lips, *just let go.*

"Try to relax," Dr. Singler advises.

He digs and digs with the nub of the staple remover. It takes several seconds to edge it in through my hair and scab. It feels like he's doing it from the inside of my head. I feel nauseous. He squeezes the handle, expanding the nose of the staple remover. It pulls the staple and a chunk of my hair with it. My eyes water. It smarts like hell. I close my eyes, bite down, growl, and squeeze my legs as hard as I can.

OhmyGodOhmyGodOhmyGod. This is definitely my new, *that's the most painful thing I've ever felt* feeling. I'm queasy. *Just let go,* I think.

Dr. Singler holds the first staple out and examines it approvingly. I open my eyes and see it upside down and blurred. It's too long and thick to have been in my scalp. It's gnarled with hair and scab. He sets it in a stainless steel tray. It *tinks* as it hits the tray. Six more to go. *Just let go.*

I think of someone asking Florence in group therapy, *what if right here, right now sucks?* We all laughed, but it was a good question. Florence said that we should be fully present, even in painful situations, that it's better to live in the *now* even during the bad times. They are only bad, because we judge them that way. We really don't know.

Each staple hurts a tad less than the last.

I wake from a nap after my encounter with Dr. Singler. It's after lunch and before the last Group. There are a few people in the center courtyard. Jack is talking to a new guy about USC football. I say hello, and take my seat on the swing by myself. I love smoking out here. I don't have anything to worry about right now. It's just me and my cigarettes and then whoever wanders out. I see Cindy and Roy through the glass doors that go into the dining room. They are carrying a board game, probably for another round of Dirty Scrabble. Kib walks down the hallway talking on a cordless phone. She sees me, stops, and smiles. She hangs up and hooks the cordless phone on the waist of her low-rise jeans.

"I need a cigarette!" she declares playfully.

I hand her one and light it for her. She takes a deep drag, and blows out the smoke with an exaggerated, *aaahhh.*

"It's like, *look lady,*" Kib says to me regarding the phone call she was just on, "I'm sorry your son's in rehab, but he'll be out when he's out. You know the visiting hours. What else is there to talk about?" She shrugs her shoulders and turns her palms skyward. "So what's going on with you, Mr. Joseph?"

"Dr. Singler took my staples out," I report.

"Let me see," she says. I bow my head and part my hair so she can see.

"Oooohhh. That must have been fun." Kib runs her fingers through my hair as she inspects the wound. I melt. She squeezes and rubs my neck and says, "Poor, baby."

I wish I could tell everyone in the entire rehab to leave, so she wouldn't have to stop. I can't imagine how I could ever get tired of her. She has that mother's touch, strong hands that really *feel.* There is something about being a mom.

We see Florence walk down the hall. Kib removes her hands from my scalp, slides over, and stands up. Florence opens the heavy slider enough to get her head out, peers at Kib and then at me.

"Joseph, Dr. Blume is ready to see you."

I put out my cigarette and hop up to go so that she can't shut the slider before I get there. "Look, Florence. I got my staples out. I was just showing Kib," I say. Florence is smart enough to know I am just trying to make an excuse for why Kib had her hands in my hair. Florence purses her lips. Her eyes are flat.

"*Uh-huh.* She ...," Florence says, furrows her brow, and looks at Kib, "... seems very interested in you. C'mon, Dr. Blume is waiting."

I follow her down the hall and into Dr. Blume's office. He's on the phone, but waves me in. I sit down. Florence leaves and shuts the door behind her. Dr. Blume is talking to someone about me.

"He's in here right now. Yes ... Yes ... I'll make sure of it. He'll be here ready to go. Uh-huh ... okay ... you too ... thanks." Dr. Blume sets the receiver down and turns to me. "That was Dotty from The Other Bar, it's AA for lawyers. You haven't been to any outside meetings yet, so this will be great. She'll be here tomorrow at 11:30 to take you to a nooner not far from here. Good woman."

"Great. Thanks." I don't ask Dr. Blume how this came about. I called Jim Heiting, the President of the California Bar Association, right when I got here. I used to have cases against him, and we worked out at the same gym when I was at Thomas & Colbert. He's a nice guy. I figure this has something to do with me leaving a message for him. *The Other Bar.* What a horrible name. I remember hearing that name and thinking the same thing when I was at Thomas & Colbert. They used to make us do continuing legal education seminars, and every year we did one on alcohol and drug addiction. I remember having felt weird during one of the presentations, because I had had quite a few drinks at lunch when some of us had gone to watch the second round of the Masters on TV at a local steak and beer joint. I was still a bit buzzed, and I was craving more. There was a crackhead lawyer who told us how he'd been living in the streets of Long Beach dumpster diving. He passed out an AA Twenty Questions quiz on a narrow slip of paper. I checked *yes* to nearly all the questions, which was supposed to lead me to the conclusion that I had an alcohol problem, but I dismissed it as overly inclusive. I remember sitting at the bar that night telling a girl I was seeing, that anybody who was ever in a frat would answer yes to at least fifteen of those stupid AA questions. *Who hasn't had a complete loss of memory, or felt remorseful, or craved a drink the next morning after a night of drinking?* She didn't answer me. She just asked me if I was ever in a frat. That irritated me, because she knew I hated frats.

"How are you doing, Joseph?" Dr. Blume asks over his glasses.

"It's kind of weird. I know my life is pretty much over, but I think the Lexapro, and being in here away from the office and just accepting that I can't do anything about my criminal case, I kind of feel okay right now."

"So the medication is working," Dr. Blume concludes. "Well, that is a sign that you have *clinical,* as opposed to *situational* depression." He flips a page in my file. "We talked about that when you first came in, that obviously you were going to be depressed given how you ended up here. Anyone would be depressed under the circumstances. And, people forget that alcohol is a depressant, especially in excessive amounts. I talked to your attorney ..."

"Which one, Mark or Keri?" I ask.

"Keri," Dr. Blume responds. "And from what she says about your drinking habits, *excessive* is a hell of an understatement. Now, what are they telling you about your situation?"

"Frankly, Keri is telling me not to kill myself, to hang in there. I don't really see any reason to kill myself just yet."

"So you're doing good?" Dr. Blume asks.

I muffle a laugh. I think he's joking, but he's not.

"I know I'm ruined," I confess. "And I'm scared, but I don't feel that thing where I can't get out of bed and I dread every moment. Lexapro is truly amazing."

"Yes, go on," Dr. Blume prods.

"Well, I heard this lady say it during that mixed A.A-A-la, Ala ... What is it?"

"Al-Anon," Dr. Blume answers.

"Right, Al-Anon ... She said that she used to mix up being suicidal with the feeling of not wanting to live. In other words, she didn't want to die or kill herself, but she didn't want to live either. She was stuck in the middle waiting for something to happen. I realize that's how I've felt most of the time over the last ... *fuck* ... years and years."

"At least, now you know what the problem is," Dr. Blume says.

"Now, I understand you want to set up some type of work situation."

"Yes, sir."

"Well, you've been here for twenty-eight days, which is the usual full stay, and I know you are going to be here longer, because of the situation with your bail. But, can't you at least wait another month?"

I explain that I can't pay for rehab if I don't work. He agrees to let me go to work from noon to eight Monday through Friday, and tells me I'll be randomly tested for alcohol and drugs when I return. Florence is at the door, letting him know a pharmaceutical rep is waiting for him—probably the reason I'm getting free Lexapro samples.

"Florence is your counselor, right?"

"Yes."

"I'll tell her, and she'll let everyone know and have you sign in and out and such."

I nod and remember something I wanted to tell him. "Oh, and Dr. Blume, thanks for that little seminar at Family on Friday night. That Dr. Jekyll and Mr. Hyde thing really helped me."

"You related to that, did you?" Dr. Blume asks.

"Yeah, I did. I feel so horrible about doing things that my rational mind tells me I'd never even consider. I guess I've always figured maybe I am really bad at the core, and alcohol just brings out the real me. I don't know if I believe the Jekyll and Hyde thing or the disease model, which seems to me one in the same, but I like it better than the view I had. I sure want to believe that I'm not a bad person but just have a treatable disease."

He shakes his head in contemplation and opens the door to let me out. He's looking even more cherubic today in his camel-colored cardigan. He puts his arm over my shoulder and leads me out.

"You know that Dr. Jekyll and Mr. Hyde reference came from a book that has saved millions of people's lives." Dr. Blume stops and looks at me. "Really. If I were you, I'd consider it the gospel on the subject of addiction. *Shit* ... forget everything else."

"The AA Big Book, right?" I ask.

"That's right. Read it," he says as he ushers in a sharply dressed pharmaceutical rep. "Oh, Joseph. One more thing. I want you to do something for me. I want you to meet a longtime family friend, Todd. He's in need of some help, and I think you are going to be able to help him."

"Okay," I respond, trying not to look too confused.

I've heard all the AA rhetoric about being of service to others, but I have no idea how Dr. Blume thinks I could possibly help anyone other than by being a horrible cautionary tale.

But what I'm really thinking about is what I just told Dr. Blume. Saying it aloud has brought it home for me. I've been in purgatory, a place between not wanting to live and yet not willing to kill myself, for years. Maybe that's why I was compelled to get high through alcohol and prostitutes. Or maybe I was in the purgatory between not wanting to live and yet not wanting to kill myself, because I got high through alcohol and prostitutes and hated myself and because I couldn't seem to will myself to stop. I don't know. I don't know if it matters. I feel kind of good right now, like I've been in training for a fight against an opponent I know is going to kick my ass, and the fight has been called off. It's crazy. My life is ruined, but, right now, I actually feel better than I've felt in a long time.

❖ ❖ ❖

Kib is handing out meds again. I make sure I'm last in line. Jack and I talk about how much we hate USC football. He gets his cup o' meds from Kib and grins at me as he walks away. I feel strange talking to him.

I'm not used to someone being taller than me. Kib looks tired, and she's wearing a threadbare, tight, boy's T-shirt. She's delicious.

She says *hi* and it's as sexually charged as *hi* can be. She pulls her hair together and over her left shoulder and twirls the tips.

"I'll have the usual," I tell Kib and instantly regret saying something so cheesy.

She turns and gathers my Lexapro from a plastic Tupperware with NAUS written on the lid in black marker.

"I've got to go to court next week," Kib says. "I'm so worried. What if Dr. Blume finds out?"

My brain churns. I must take this opportunity. "I don't see how he'd find out. I mean, you aren't a counselor. Even if he did find out ..."

"I guess not but ..." Kib pauses as one of the new clients walk by.

"Look," I say, "Dr. Blume is letting me go to work from twelve to eight every day. You get off at six, right?"

A couple guys who just came in from the parole program walk by, both in jeans and white T-shirts. Kib is quiet, pretending to wrestle with the Tupperware lid. I just wait.

"My mom babysits my son, so I have to get home, but on Wednesday my ex has him. I could come by," she says cautiously.

We both know what I've just asked for and what she's agreed to, but we try to act nonchalant.

"We could talk about your situation, which I'm sure is no problem, and if you want to make a little extra money you could help me with filing stuff on an appeal I'm working on. I could only pay you twenty dollars an hour, but it's easy work."

"Joseph Naus to the front desk," crackles over the intercom.

"I gotta go. But that's great. We'll have fun," I say awkwardly, and then pop the little white Lexapro pill.

Florence calls me to the office because the lady from The Other Bar is on the line. I'm meeting her at a meeting where addict lawyers gather. I presume it's like the meetings here, but I'm not sure. I've only talked to this lady on the phone. She's so sweet it's kind of irritating. She says things like, *we couldn't be more pleased to have you join us*, and *we'll love you until you learn to love yourself.* She says these things over the phone. I've never met her in my life, and she says she's going to love me until I learn to love myself?

It's my first day back at work, and I'm driving the three miles from PRC to my office. It's unnerving. After my DUI I nearly had an anxiety attack every time I needed to change lanes. I was sure there was always a tiny little car filled with a delicate family of unbelted children in my blind spot. I'd look in the mirror, look behind me, then slow down and do it again, then put my blinker on for a full five seconds before I slowly eased over—all the while sweating like I was on a treadmill in a steam room.

There is a cop behind me. There must be one patrol car for every stop sign in Pasadena. It's amazing. I turn down the radio. *Be cool*, I think. They know. They know I'm the attorney-murder-rapist guy. They are just waiting to catch me and throw me back in jail. He's on his radio right now talking with dispatch, *Yeah, I've got him. He'll fuck up if I follow him long enough.* I'm breathing hard, and thinking about it is making it worse. I put my right blinker on to get over to the first lane even though I need to take a left. There is a car in my way. I don't know what to do. Should I speed up and change lanes or slow down? Either way is suspicious. This cop has surely already run my plates. He's just waiting. He already knows I'm driving suspiciously. I have to do something. I have to act. My blinker has been on too long. I press on the gas and accelerate in front of the little old lady from Pasadena. I take a right in front of her on to a side street. I pull to the curb and turn the ignition off. My heart is pounding, and I can feel the veins in my neck pumping. I look in my rearview mirror, expecting the cop to pull in behind me. I see the black and white. I hold my breath. He passes. *Goddamn.* I'm okay, for now.

I park in my designated spot in the underground parking at the boxy, three-story office building where Yi & Naus is located. Every person I pass—in the garage, on the elevator, in the lobby—they all know about me. They're thinking, *there's that guy*, the one that went crazy. How can he be here? Should I call security? Shouldn't he be in jail or in an insane asylum? But nobody I pass says anything. They are all too polite, or maybe they are scared, but they know. They must know. I think they know.

Will stands over his desk packing his attaché. I feel sick when I see him. Just over a month ago I came into the office, and we had lunch at this little Thai place just down the street in Old Town. I couldn't believe things were going so well, that we were making money, that I didn't work for a boss, that I could walk to Old Town with my law school buddy and have lunch.

"Hey, champ," Will says, "How you doing?" He means it literally, *how am I doing?* I can't tell him I almost had a nervous breakdown, because I drove near a cop car. No matter how I feel, I have to tell him I'm doing okay. I've done him enough damage.

"Good. You know, as good as can be under the circumstances," I say as cheerily as possible.

He looks up at me wanting more.

"I'm ready to get that KET appeal hammered out," I say, "piece of cake. We will win this one for sure."

"Clarence will love you forever if you pull it off," Will says, referring to KETs part owner, part retired counsel, Rolls Royce owner, and aficionado. Will is such a pragmatist I know he doesn't care that Clarence thinks I'm a genius and Will's a hack, even though I've only been on the case for a couple months and Will has been working with KET for years. I'd be pissed if I were Will. But Will is just happy our best client is happy, because that means those checks keep coming. Unlike me, Will doesn't define himself as an attorney. It's just what he does for a living.

"Yep," I say, "I'm going to get *their motherfucking money. We going to get yo money!*" I mimic a skit from In Living Color." I'm not sure Will recognizes the reference, but he laughs anyway.

"I'm going to KET's office right now," Will says and pats me on the shoulder and walks out. I open my office door and sit at my desk. There are two banker's boxes with all the correspondence, pleadings and discovery for the KET appeal. Next to that is a blue litigation file for a real estate arbitration I need to prepare for Ken from Flyer Motor Homes, next to that is another blue litigation file with a plaintiff's personal injury case I need to get filed, and then next to that is a file with a demurrer to a complaint I filed on a real estate case for an attorney I used to work with from Thomas & Colbert. There is a stack of pink telephone note call slips. The top is dated yesterday, "Ken called again—wants to know what the FUCK is going on with both of his cases. He paid the seventy-five-hundred-dollar retainer." It's in Will's handwriting. The light on my desk phone blinks with messages. I swivel my chair to the window and look out over Marengo Boulevard into the park with the band shell. Cars whiz by below. It's sunny out. The Pasadena Court is one block east and my home, a rehab, is eight blocks north.

I shut my office door and lock it. I pull out a bottle of baby oil from my desk drawer and find some vintage Christy Canyon on the Internet. I jack off for relief. Then I go down to the parking garage and find a nice hidden nook and smoke. I go back to my office, jack off again. Then I go down to the garage and smoke. Then I go back up and jack off again. I lock up, smoke and head back to PRC. It's the best I can do. I'll try again tomorrow.

Today's going better. On the drive in, I took an alternate route, but I still ended up being followed by a cop. I didn't panic; just pulled over immediately and regrouped. I've been at the office since one o'clock. I take all the files off my desk and all the telephone messages and make a list. I just have to do one thing at a time. Start with the first thing on the list; that is the only thing that matters. *One thing at a time.* "#1: Ken: Review Ken's files; call Ken." I review Ken's files. The first is easy. Ken was rear-ended on the freeway by a lady in an SUV. She hit the back of his classic Jaguar hard. He called me when it first happened. I told him he ought to just do it himself, and he tried, but the insurance company fucked with him, so now he wants blood. I've already sent the nasty demand letter, and I have plenty of time to file the suit.

Case Number Two. This is an arbitration involving a rental house Ken bought, one of a dozen. A big chunk of it was an addition that wasn't permitted, and the sellers didn't disclose that to Ken. It wasn't a strong case, especially since Ken had already made a couple hundred thousand on appreciation and, after fixing it up, had rented it out for twenty per-cent more than the mortgage payment. Ken didn't want to hear that bullshit, and he was right, theoretically. But, the arbitrator is going to be a human, so I have to let Ken know his damages are questionable.

I set the file down on my desk and scribble some notes. Ken is prob-ably the only client I'll tell about my *situation*. Ken and I are friends. He likes me, because, when I worked for Thomas & Colbert and he was the General Manager for one of Flyer Motor Homes' largest manufacturing facilities, I came out to visit the plant. He thought I was just doing it to pad my billable hours, but when I told him I was doing it on my own time, that I just wanted to see how the manufactured homes were built so I could better defend a case where it was alleged that a home was manufactured improperly, he thought I was the only honest lawyer on the planet.

After Ken left Flyer Motor Homes and started his own manufactur-ing company, and I left VSB and opened Yi & Naus, I took over all his le-gal work. Ken is a lot like Tito, an extremely hardworking, honest, and smart Mexican-American family man. He is loyal above all, and since the day we met he's treated me like I was part of his family.

I pull up Ken's number on my cell phone and stare at it, not quite ready to press *call*. I need a cigarette or several before I do this.

After half a pack in the parking garage, I come back up and call Ken. I come clean. He's shocked. He tells me how he used to drink hard and smoke, but when he got married he made a decision to stop, and he hasn't smoked again or drank excessively again. I don't know what he's getting at. Is he saying, that's how I should have done it? Just quit? And why in God's name would anyone quit drinking if they didn't have to? That's just stupid. I need to get off the phone. I can barely listen to him. I'm thinking about that little bar between here and rehab. I've never been there, but I bet it's dark, and there's a pool table, and during the day it's just a few drunks sitting on shiny, dark red, vinyl barstools. I want to be there right now, smoking a cigarette and drinking a Jack and Coke on ice, strong enough to cut rust.

"So where are we?" Ken asks. "... Joseph?" Ken practically shouts. I hold the phone out from my ear.

"Uh ... we are ... not filed yet, still negotiating with Farmers Insurance. I'll get some action ..."

"No," Ken interrupts. "Aren't you listening? *Where's my shark?*" he says rhetorically. "The house, where are we on the house?"

"Shit, Ken, I just told you I had to go to rehab. I've been a little pre-occupied. I'm still your shark, and I'm about to leave some shark teeth in those pricks. We just have to set an arbitration date. Give me some dates next month when you are available."

I hang up with Ken. He's a bit agitated, but he's cool. He's coming to the office next week. I'll have everything worked up by then. I look down to my list for the next to-do. "Appeal –Opening Brief due 9/14— 10 DAYS!"

Fuck. Ten fucking days! I have to get an appeal out in ten days. I open up my Internet browser. I'm going to relieve some stress. No, Kib is supposed to come. There is a possibility that she won't flake and that I'm going to fuck her on this very desk. I think of that drink in the inside of that dark bar I've never been in. I go down to the garage and smoke a few more.

I open up the banker's boxes filled with the documents for the appeal. I lose myself in legal arguments for a while, but then my cell phone takes me out of my trance. It's Kib. Perfect timing. Will just left.

I meet her down in the garage and have her park in Will's space. When I get to her car, she is hurriedly putting on makeup. She gets out and hugs me. I keep my arm around her and walk her to the elevators. She's rambling about how annoying work at PRC is. My arm slides down and my hand is on her bare hip. My blood is flowing. I show her the law library, the kitchen, the conference room, Will's office, and then mine. I sit her in my chair and I lean over her from behind and show her the time line I've created for the appeal. I show her the stacks of paper and tell her I need six copies of each page that is tagged. She smells good, a sultry perfume with a nicotine base.

This is going to happen. It's going to happen *now*. In just a few moments I'll be fucking her. It's no different than if I were lying on a massage table waiting for Sunny or June or Mae. A rush of heat swallows me up.

"Remember when you were rubbing my hair the other day when I was showing you where the staples were removed?" I ask.

"Uh-huuuuh." She nods and smiles widely. She knows exactly where I'm going. "You liked that, huh?"

She pivots away from the desk toward me and reaches out her hands. I kneel down and put my head against her stomach below her breasts. She holds my head, scratches and rubs, carefully avoiding the area where the staples were. I'm melting again. I pull up and kiss her. Her lips are satiny from lip gloss, and her mouth tastes like mint gum and cigarettes. Her tongue is meaty. My fingers slide into the roots of her hair from the base of her neck. I lift her off the chair, shove my laptop out of the way, and sit her on the desk. I yank her pants off and spread her legs. I look at her dark skin and her glistening little thicket of hair and think: There is nothing better than this, nothing.

THIRTEEN

———————————

Every time I enter this rickety two-story, Victorian sober living house, I wonder how many guys have overdosed in it—at least a dozen. The first day I was here a guy left on a gurney. He was the house manager. He had a heart attack while drinking, smoking crack, and jacking off to porn.

I'm on my way to PRC to pick up Todd and take him to an Other Bar meeting. Part of the agreement with Dr. Blume to allow me to leave rehab and move into a sober-living is that I had to get a 12-step *sponsor* and a *sponsee.* My sponsee is Todd, and my sponsor is Vinny. Vinny's got five years clean and sober, he's a paralegal, and he used to be the singer in a minor rock band. He's probably the nicest guy I've ever met. He doesn't mind me calling him. In fact, he *wants* me to call him, says it takes his mind off his own problems. We meet and talk regularly. I go to his house. It's weird. He treats me like I'm his long lost little brother. The whole concept seems ridiculous. I have no idea why some guy, who no longer drinks or gets high, would want me calling him complaining about my problems. But there is something that works about it. Now, if a day goes by that I don't call Vinny, it doesn't feel right. There is something comforting about telling Vinny about my problems and getting his advice, which is usually some real basic shit that has nothing to do with the problem. I tell him, *They won't drop the rape charges, and I'm going to get disbarred!* and he tells me, *Pray that God gives you the strength and guidance to take the next right indicated step.* What the fuck? Why would I do that? I'm not religious, and neither is he, but he says, *Pray to God.*

He says you don't have to be religious or believe in God to pray. I ask, "Why pray if you don't believe in God?" He says, because that's what his sponsor told him to do, and it worked. It's the same bullshit Bob tells me. *Fucking atheists praying to God.*

Dr. Blume has a real soft spot for Todd, and he insisted that I be his sponsor. Todd is the son of a gazillionaire. He's in law school and about to flunk out. He grew up in one of the most exclusive neighborhoods in Los Angeles, a gated paradise with horse trails called Hidden Hills. Dr. Blume's kids and Todd are the same age, and they grew up together. Todd is a ruggedly handsome, Greek-American surfer and meth addict. But meth isn't what landed him in jail and then rehab. Like me, he goes psycho when he drinks too much.

I pull into PRC's parking lot and walk toward the front entrance. Todd is sitting on the curb crouched over with his hands covering his face.

"I have a pass to go home this weekend," Todd says. "My mom wants to see me, but my dad is acting like I can't spend the night at the house. Can you believe that?"

"Yeah, I can believe it," I say. "You were in a drunken rage-slash-meth psychosis last time they saw you, right?"

"I know. But they know it wasn't me. It was the alcohol and speed."

"They just need time," I say. "If you can't spend the night, that's alright. Visit them during the day, and leave and spend the night at rehab. You're paying for it anyway."

"Actually, they are," Todd confesses.

We pull to the curb across from the church where the Other Bar meeting is being held. We are early, so we walk into the walled courtyard and sit on an ornate cement bench. The walls block the street noise from Colorado Boulevard. It's a sunny little sanctuary.

"My sister's a bitch," Todd begins, "and my brother-in-law and brother just go along with it."

Todd delves into a five-minute tirade on his favorite subject: His sister and brother are stealing his inheritance. They run his dad's restaurant equipment distribution company, and he gets none of it. He used to work there, but they drove him out. True, he didn't show up at work because he spent much of his time reverse engineering VCR remote controls, and dismantling microwave ovens in his room after snorting foot-long rails of crank, but it wasn't just that, *they were out to get him.* I let Todd vent for a while, and softly remind him of his part in his problems, and then change the subject.

"How's law school?" I ask.

"Shit ... I'll probably get kicked out of this crappy school, too. I'm trying to study, but these fucking groups at PRC take all my time. That's one thing speed did for me. I could study."

"Yeah, so many speed freaks in the Ivy League grad schools, especially Wharton."

"Huh? Yeah? Like at Harvard?" Todd asks. He's so entangled in his head, he doesn't even notice my sarcasm.

"Nothing," I say. "I'm just joking, being sarcastic. I'm pretty sure in the long run meth is really bad for your brain."

Todd sits doubled over with his hands in his face, rocking a little. I know how he feels. It's a fucked up feeling, like the world is suffocating you, and the harder you try to escape, the tighter the grip gets on your neck. However, I feel pretty good right now because I'm thinking about Todd's problems and not mine.

"How can it be any worse?" He asks rhetorically. "I'm about to get kicked out of another law school. I'm thirty-two. I have no girlfriend. I have no place to live. I have no job ..." Todd's voice cracks, taken over by an emotion somewhere between sadness and exasperation. "Fucked, *totally fucked,*" he recaps.

I pat him on the back. It feels weird, but I know that is what I'm supposed to do, because that's what Vinny does with me.

"Todd. I'm thirty-three," I say, "I'm facing six felonies, including two sex crimes. My girlfriend and I broke up, because she couldn't handle the stress of watching me lose everything. I'm practicing law while living in a *goddamn* sober-living. I spend every waking moment working, or in a 12-step meeting. I'm paying for expert witnesses, an investigator, attorneys, sober-living, court-ordered therapy ... you name it. I could go on and on ... my point is: Things could be worse."

"I know. I know," Todd responds.

"One thing I learned after spending the last nine months living in rehab, 12-step meetings, Other Bar meetings, Lawyer's Assistance Program meetings, and therapy ... outpatient etcetera ad nauseam is that *compare and despair* doesn't do anybody any good. There is some guy out there that did worse than both of us, and he didn't get arrested, just went to AA, and now everything is cool; and there is some guy out there that didn't do half the bad shit we did, and he's dead."

Todd nods.

"Yeah, like that guy during my first year at Syracuse," Todd says, "poor bastard goes to a frat party, drinks too much, and dies suffocating on his own vomit ... never even went to his first class."

"One of the first days I was at PRC," I say, "they brought in this panel, and this black lady was on it. She says, 'I'm Ramona, and I'm an addict,' and then within the first minute of her story she says, 'I just got tired of sucking cock for crack."

"Sucking cock for crack!" Todd repeats.

"At least, you're not sucking cock for crack, right? I mean—*you're not*, right? You're not sucking cock for crack, right?"

We laugh as Dotty, the secretary of The Other Bar meeting, walks up. "What's so funny?" she asks.

"Nothing," we say in unison.

There are a dozen of us—active lawyers, disbarred lawyers, a paralegal, and Todd, the sole flunking law student—sitting in an oblong circle in flesh-colored foldout chairs in a small room next to the gymnasium of this little church. There is a worn piano in the corner. Dotty reads things from a notebook that are always read at the beginning of the meeting. God this and God that. Then people share. Jill is a nutcase with big fake tits and bloated lips. Her hair is short and dyed blonde. She is still wearing her yoga gear and obviously spends a great deal of time at the gym. She's divorced and working part time doing plaintiffs' wrongful termination cases. She talks about how she's been depressed, and her doctor is tinkering with her bipolar meds. She's still dealing with the divorce, but getting over it, she says, even though it has been three years ... and twenty-four days.

Jill passes to James. James is an aging hippy. He was disbarred many years ago. He's Mexican-American, has a beard, has been married for twenty years, and has two kids. He says he loves his job but wants to re-apply to the Bar. Dotty quietly encourages him, nodding steadily. She's about the sweetest woman I ever met, but her constant nodding and almost aggressive concern and empathy freaks me out.

"I want to hear from our newcomer," James says, referring to Todd.

Dotty, who is seated to Todd's left, pats Todd's right hand atop his knee and whispers, with the utmost sincerity and support, "Go 'head, Todd."

"Uh ... thanks for having me here," Todd says nervously. "My sponsor, Joseph here, brought me, and I'm real grateful. I'm just trying to keep from comparing myself to others, but I keep thinking I got fucked. Oh shit, this is a church ..."

"Say what you need to say, Todd," Dotty whisper-speaks. A couple others join the sentiment.

"Okay, sorry," Todd continues. "I'm just ... my sister and my dad and my brother-in-law they are all just like coming down on me. My mom drinks all day, and nobody is giving *her* a hard time ... of course she's not getting arrested ... I'm trying to study for night law school while I'm at the rehab. It's so loud ..." Todd goes on until someone softly knocks on the wall, indicating Todd has rambled too long.

After the meeting, Todd and I join Dotty and a few others at a restaurant across the street. I order the beef dip with cheddar cheese, fries, and a Coke. I've got to stop eating like this, but then again, that's the least of my worries. I'm eating this beef dip, and the conversation is just a hum. Someone at our table says, *you can't fix a broken brain with a broken brain.* I wonder what my life would be like right now if I'd gone to therapy. Would I have allowed someone else to fix me? Would I have gone to rehab? 12-steps? Taken antidepressants? *Not likely.* If I had been willing to get help, I'd have gotten help. Instead, I just kept trying to fix my broken brain with my broken brain, thinking I'd defeat my problems by pulling harder on my bootstraps.

The hum of conversation at our table and the ambient noise of this busy restaurant are comforting. Todd seems to be enjoying himself, and for once he's not grinding away about his family. So maybe I'm being of service to him by taking him here. That's what Vinny says to do. Stop thinking about yourself and be of service to someone else.

❖   ❖   ❖

"All rise. The California Second District Court of Appeal, Fourth Division, the Honorable Judges Slevin, Tasky, and Stevens residing. You may be seated," the bailiff pronounces, and then less officially says, "Please turn off all cell phones, pagers, or any other electronic devices." Three black-robed judges walk out to the bench and take their seats. My opposing counsel, a thirty-year litigator who has been on this case since it was filed six years ago, stands. I stand and take a peek back into the audience. My client is trying to un-stuff himself from a theater-type seat to stand as the judges enter.

"You may be seated," the bailiff says.

Opposing counsel and I remain standing, waiting for the judges to address us.

I'm here for oral argument on a case that I won in the trial court for one of our big clients. The client's in-house counsel and Will had just about lost the case before we partnered up, and I took over and found a novel legal argument that turned the case from a loser to a winner. It was one of my finest moments as a lawyer. Our client went from most certainly losing hundreds of thousands of dollars to most certainly winning hundreds of thousands of dollars. That's why he drove his Rolls Royce all the way from his mid-century, modern mansion in Palm Springs and is sitting in the audience grinning from ear to ear.

This appellate hearing should be nothing more than a coronation for me. And yet I'm sweating through my suit jacket. I feel like everyone in here knows what I've done. They've read the police report. They talked to the police, the DA, and the victim. It's absurd, I know, but there is a part of my brain that won't be surprised if I'm arrested just for being here. There has to be a law against an attorney with pending sex crime felonies arguing a high-dollar appellate court case—as if nothing has happened. Everyone knows, but they are pretending they don't.

"Mr. Seyomer," the lead judge says into her microphone, "I'd like to hear from you ... How can you possibly distinguish this claim from the *Rutter* decision cited by Mr. Naus? Isn't it clearly analogous?"

The judge might as well have said, *Mr. Naus, you win.*

I'm trying to listen to opposing counsel wage his last stand, but I'm floating in the absurdity of my being here. If these judges knew that tomorrow I'd be attending my own felony preliminary hearing, not for some complicated white-collar crime, but for breaking into someone's house naked, they'd tell the bailiff to handcuff me.

After several minutes of spirited but futile argument by my opposing counsel, the lead judge turns her attention to me. I swallow hard. I've long since sweated through my suit coat jacket. I so desperately want to leave here and find some quite place to smoke alone.

"Mr. Naus, would you like to address Mr. Seyomer's points?" she asks.

I look directly at her to see if she knows about me. There's no reason for her to know. But can she see it on me? Can she see that I don't belong here—that I'm a fraud?

"No, Your Honor," I answer. "Unless the court found any of Mr. Seyomer's points persuasive or the court has any questions of me, I don't see any value in reiterating what's in my brief."

The judge on the right of me clears his throat and covers his microphone so that the court reporter doesn't take down what he's about to say and says to the lead judge, "Apparently, you can't entice Mr. Naus to pry defeat out of the jaws of victory."

The court denies the appeal. We win. The bailiff calls for everyone to stand, and the judges disappear into their chambers. I shake opposing counsel's hand. I'm not smug about it. Soon he'll know what a loser I am. He'll read about me in the *California Bar Journal* and the *Los Angeles Daily Journal*, and how I was disbarred for being a psychopath, a drunk, a sex criminal, *a loser*. When he reads about me, I want him to be surprised, not happy.

I walk out with my client. He hugs me and shakes my hand. His hands are thick and meaty.

"Fuck those guys," he says gleefully. "They thought they won, but here we are."

I smile and nod and pretend that my skin isn't crawling, that I don't want out of this building so, so badly.

It's the day after the appeal I argued downtown. Now I'm at another court for my own felony preliminary hearing. I've been here in the parking lot for a half-hour. I've already smoked eight cigarettes, and I've nearly finished my second twenty ounces of coffee, thick with cream and sugar. I hate this place. I've been here over a dozen times since my arrest. The LAX Courthouse: every time I pass it on the 405 I feel a sickness in my stomach and mutter to myself: *fucking Death Star.*

Keri meets me in the front. It takes fifteen minutes to get through security. A fat black lady, stuffed into black polyester pants and a white uniform shirt, drones on about pocketknives and shoes and electronic devices. She repeats it verbatim every two minutes. Keri and I take the stainless steel elevator up to the ninth floor. Two uniformed cops are in the elevator. Keri talks to a DA she knows. He assumes I'm in court as a fellow attorney, not a defendant. I want to scream and burst through my skin.

The ninth floor is bright from the sun's rays, which penetrate at a sharp angle. To the north is a wall of glass revealing a spectacular view toward downtown with a sprawling South Central Los Angeles in the foreground. There is a row of identical double doors a hundred yards across the entire floor, each leading to separate courtrooms. Keri and I walk toward Judge Mader's court, and I see Winston, my *victim.* It must be him. I've read the police report, and Keri described him to me. He's got long hair and a goatee. He's small and thin and dressed as formal as a wardrobe can allow without owning a suit. He's holding his girlfriend's hand. She's an adorable little Japanese girl. She's barely five feet tall. They couldn't be a cuter couple, which somehow makes me feel like even more of an asshole. I lock eyes with Winston for a moment. His eyes look angrily at me. I don't look away. I try to look humble and contrite. I want to say: *I'm here. I'm facing this. I'm sorry.* Keri told me he has enthusiastically supported my prosecution. He told the DA, "What if my girlfriend would have been with me that night?" He's right. I get it. If he'd broken into my house drunk and naked with a hard-on when Larisa was there, I'd have beaten him within an inch of his life. He had every right to kill me. *Fuck, I kind of wish he had.* I have no recollection of him whatsoever. I terrorized this twenty-something guy for no reason.

"People versus Naus," the court clerk calls out formally.

"Mark Ackerman for the defendant, Joseph Naus," Mark announces and stands at the defense table. Mark is one of the top criminal defense attorneys in the country. He's polished but not slick, aggressive but never offensive.

"Deputy District Attorney, Carmen D. Villa, on behalf of the People."

This is the woman who is trying to kill me. She's a wiry blonde with a heart of onyx. Her demeanor is high-grit sandpaper. She hates me more than I deserve to be hated. It's as if I raped *her* before I broke into Winston's apartment. Vinny told me to pray for her. It's a 12-step program thing, he says. Pray for the people you resent most, and eventually you'll be free of the corrosive resentment against them. Out of respect for Vinny, I do it. Every night, I do it. *God, let Carmen D. Villa get everything she wants in life, and keep her and her family safe.* That's on a good night. On a bad night it's, *God, let that horrible bitch who is ignoring the fact that I am clearly not a rapist but who is trying to ruin my life for her professional advancement ... get everything she wants in life and keep her and her family safe. Amen.*

I sit between Keri and Mark at the defense table. DA Villa calls one of the responding cops to the witness stand. He parrots the police report. My humiliation is absolute. I'm doing all I can to keep from burying my head for the remainder of this hearing. If I could flush myself out of here down a nine-story toilet, I would. The cop is talking about *me* doing all this horrible stuff. *It's all me.* None of it is even disputed. I'm the guy, *right fucking here.* I'm the psychopath. I want to stand up and scream: Yes, it's me, and I did it, but I didn't do it! The clerk, the judge, the bailiff, the court reporter, Mark, Keri, all the other attorneys, all the people in the audience, a dozen or more, they are looking at me: the rapist, the psychopath who crawled into someone's apartment in the middle of the night.

"Do you swear to tell the whole truth and nothing but the truth, so help you God?" The clerk swears in Winston.

"I do," he says. I realize that this is the first time I've heard him speak.

Winston Jones is the perfect witness. He testifies as if he has no axe to grind. He's just here doing his civic duty, helping out ol' lady Justice. DA Villa guides him through his story. There is nothing new. It's the same thing that is in the police report, same thing that the cop just testified to. I look at him. I want him to get in my brain and see that I'm not a rapist, just a crazed drunk. I want him to at least admit that my being a rapist doesn't make sense. But, he doesn't communicate with me telepathically. Instead, he just keeps on testifying.

I'm fried. This is much too much to take. The humiliation has turned to numbness. I'm mentally drooling. There is a buzz in my head. I daydream, wondering if I can make a go of it in Mexico. I think Jose, my former client, is hiding out in La Bufadora. I could go down there and work with him, finally learn Spanish, drink, surf, and eat lobster. Winston and his girl could hang out with us; they'd see that I'm really a good guy. I'd take them to the La Bufadora blowhole and buy them some of those cheap street tacos. I wouldn't drink around them. I wouldn't want to scare them.

Mark begins to cross-examine Winston.

"Did Mr. Naus do anything sexual to you, touching you in your private areas or anything like that, yes or no?"

"No," Winston says calmly.

"Did he try to get you to touch any private part of him, any of his genitals, or private parts?"

"No."

"So Mr. Naus didn't do anything sexual in nature to you that night, right?"

I mentally cringe. I think Mark has made the rookie mistake of asking one too many questions.

"No ..." Winston says with a slight pause, "well, besides for being naked with a hard-on in my apartment."

A few people in the courtroom chuckle quietly, including me.

Mark concentrates the rest of his examination on establishing that Winston and his buddy beat the shit out of me, and they were in no danger and that I said crazy things that made no sense—the stuff about Hawaii, and a Volkswagen and being brothers. Winston agreed that I'd said all of it, and that I was obviously extremely drunk.

At the end of the hearing, Mark makes an oral motion to dismiss the sodomy charge. The judge grants the motion. So, *great*, I'm no longer being charged with trying to butt fuck Winston. I wait outside the courtroom while Keri and Mark talk settlement with DA Villa. I look out over Los Angeles. The cars move on the freeway like platelets through an artery. I close my eyes. I feel dizzy.

Please, please, please, God. Just give me a plea deal I can live with, I pray in a hushed tone to the sprawl of Los Angeles below. *Please, please, please. I'll never fuck up again.* This is my sincere prayer. I'm willing to grovel to a God I don't believe in.

The door swings open and DA Carmen D. Villa marches out. I stare at her trying to catch her attention, but she ignores me. The clacking of her heels bounces hollowly off the walls. The 12-steppers say, if you pray for someone long enough, you'll stop hating them. *Well, not yet.* I don't hate her because she's doing her job. I hate her, because I know she knows I'm not a rapist, but she's willing to ignore that, because failing to get a sex conviction will be considered a loss in the DA's office.

Mark and Keri follow her out. Mark says to me, "Sorry, nothing good. We'll keep trying. I've got to go."

I'm stunned. Keri stands next to me. I stare as Mark walks off toward the elevator in his perfect wool suit and buttery, leather Bally shoes. That should be my suit, my shoes, my Jaguar. Like Mark, I've got the *it* factor that can make a great trial lawyer. I haven't developed it like he has, but I've got it. But, I'm losing it. I'm losing everything. I turn back to the window and stare out over Los Angeles. How can I be looking at something so beautiful and yet feel so horrible?

"So, Keri?"

She's pale again, not as bad as the day of my arrest, but it's not a good sign.

"Three years and two strikes," Keri says. "They won't budge off the sex conviction. They want Assault with Intent to Commit Rape and First Degree Burglary."

"What! What about Dr. Rothberg's report? What about Winston saying I didn't do anything sexual?" I ask, my voice rising significantly beyond decorum.

Keri tries to hush me by speaking softly, "Like Mark said, we just keep trying. You have to realize ... this case is specially assigned to the Sex Crimes Unit. If Villa doesn't get a sex crime conviction, it's not considered a win."

I lose it. "A win? That's what I am, a fucking win! What about the fact that *I'M NOT A GODDAMN MOTHERFUCKING RAPIST!*" I yell.

My voice bounces through the hallway. Everyone goes silent and turns and stares. A couple uniformed cops rush over toward us, and I feel a shot of adrenaline as I consider the idea that they might arrest me, and I may never be free again. Keri goes into lawyer-mode, puts her arm around me, and hurries me to the elevator bank, all while brushing the cops off. She gives me the look, like she's my mom, and I'm going to get a whipping when we get home.

It's so sunny and beautiful out. The traffic is even good driving into downtown Los Angeles. I'm traversing the towering overpass from the 105 to 110, an engineering marvel. It's like a giant Hot Wheels track a couple hundred yards above ground. Right now, I want to die. There is little keeping me from driving right off this giant ramp and into the sky. I could fly to my death like in *Thelma & Louise*. I think of the photos from the Flyer Motor Home products liability case I worked on when I was at Thomas & Colbert, the charred body of a man in the driver's seat of his quarter-million dollar RV. He was still belted in, even had his hands on the wheel.

I'm halfway back to Pasadena. I have to pull over. My breathing is tight, and I'm starting to get dizzy and hysterical simultaneously. I'm somewhere around USC. The windows are down so I can smoke. I don't *ever* smoke in my car, but there are no rules in my life anymore.

"… Keri McConnely with the Law Offices of Mark Ackerman… leave a message at the tone." How many times have I listened to this fucking message, and I still can't remember what buttons to press? "Keri," I say into her voice mail, "I know you have other criminals to save, so I'm sorry, but what the fuck am I doing killing myself every fucking day doing all these fucking meetings and rehab and drug testing if none of it means a goddamn thing? Clearly, I'm fucked. At least I could enjoy my last days before they chop my head off and send me to prison for the rest of my life."

Once I'm breathing normal, I get back on the freeway. I think of Las Vegas. I want to be by myself, drunk, wandering from casino to casino. I'd sleep and do it again and again, never seeing the day's light. When my money runs out, which would be soon, I'd head off to my first and last visit to the Grand Canyon. I wonder if I'll be cold while hurtling toward the canyon floor.

I need to continue on the 110 to get back to my office, but suddenly my car goes east on the 10 Freeway. My heart flushes adrenaline though my veins. I'm being taken to Francisquito Avenue, one of my favorite spots. Not twenty minutes later, I'm lying facedown on a padded table in a dimly lit room, naked. The little lamp with baby oil and my three twenty-dollar bills sit on an end table next to a chair where my clothes are draped. My skin is tight, and I tremble lightly. A tiny little Thai woman wearing clunky heels and a plaid miniskirt enters. The relief and intense pleasure is followed by disgust and guilt, as usual.

❖   ❖   ❖

I sit in the dark in my car parked on the curb. This is a liquor store that serves the dire. It's in North Pasadena where mostly poor black people live. It's dark out. I watch people come in and out, most are on foot. Most leave drinking out of a paper bag. They chug tall, cheap beers and pints. They smoke. It's the perfect combination, cigarettes and alcohol. I love cigarettes and alcohol. I can taste them right now.

My cell phone rings. It's been ringing since I left court, since I left the massage parlor. I hate that fucking noise. It's never anything good. No one calls me anymore to say anything good. It's Keri. She must have listened to my message, because she's called five times. My cell phone screen reads, *Do you want to take this call?* There is a *yes* and *no* button underneath. I press *no*. What could Keri have to say that wouldn't make me feel horrible? Nothing, nothing at all. The cell phone log reads, *14 Missed Calls.* 2 Will, 5 Keri, 1 Sallie Mae Student Loan, 2 Visa, 3 Vinny, and one with an Orange County area code that must be from opposing counsel on one of Ken's cases. I should call Keri, Will, and Vinny. I know I should, but I can't. I just can't.

A woman walks by in a rush to the liquor store. She's Mexican, dressed sexy, probably only thirty, but, even through the shadows and my tinted windows, I can see the outlines of a hard-living meth face. My cell phone rings again, that horrible ringing. It's Vinny. I press *no*. I'm smoking out the window. I like it here. I can get a bottle of Jack and a liter of Coke and a pack of cigarettes, take it all back to the office. Maybe I won't even get caught. The house manager at my sober living never tests me. The Lawyer's Assistance Program will, but fuck them. I'm probably going to be disbarred anyway.

I listen to Vinny's message. "Hey, Joseph. Vinny. Keri called me. She's really worried. So am I. You need to just call and let her and I know you're cool. I know court was rough— no way to sugarcoat it but uh ... isolating isn't going to help. So uh call me."

I press delete. I'm a dick. He's just trying to help me, but what am I supposed to say? "Thanks for all your help, but I just went to a massage parlor, and now I'm choosing a drunken spree followed by suicide."

My phone rings again. It's Todd, my sponsee. *Fuck.*

I let it ring and stare at the name on the screen. I don't know why, but I can't ignore it. I press *yes.*

"Hey, Todd, what's up?" I say as if nothing is wrong.

"Uh, hey man, I uh …," Todd's voice quivers, "I'm just …" He starts to crack and break. "I fucking can't take it anymore, Joseph! I went to visit, and they took all my shit out of my room, and nobody was there. I just went a little crazy."

"Slow down, buddy," I say, "Take a deep breath. You didn't relapse did you?" I ask.

"No, I just like … I trashed my sister's car, and then my dad said I had to leave and come back to rehab, or he was going to call the cops. The kids were in the car, my niece and nephew… totally crying. I would never hurt them. Why do they have to treat me like this?" Todd is sobbing.

Another call comes in. It's PRC's main number.

"Hold on for one second, Todd," I say. "Don't hang up, Okay? You promise?"

"Yeah, okay," he says.

"Hello?" I answer the other line.

"Joseph, it's Dr. Blume. I'm sorry to bother you, but Todd is really having a hard time. Can you come to the rehab and see him soon, real soon? He says he'll only talk to you. He says you're the only one that isn't getting paid to help him."

"Yeah, he's actually on the other line," I say. "But yeah I'll come right away."

"Oh. Okay. That's good. How are you?"

"I'm fine. I mean, you know, tough day, but I can get through it and start over tomorrow," I say, but I don't mean it.

"Good. We are all pulling for you here, Joseph, and I appreciate what you are doing for Todd," Dr. Blume says. He sounds relieved that I'm coming, and that makes me feel good. I'm not sure why, but Dr. Blume really thinks I can help Todd. He's the doctor who owns a rehab, who has known Todd since Todd was in diapers, but he thinks *I'm* the one who is qualified to help Todd.

I switch back to the other line, and I'm relieved that Todd hasn't hung up.

"Todd, I'll be over in five minutes."

I start my car and take a last longing look at the red and blue lights of the liquor store through the passenger window. This beautiful liquor store will be here tomorrow. I've been in it before for cigarettes. It has everything that a good hood liquor store should have: glass-doored coolers full of Mickey's, Schlitz, tall Buds; rows of vodka pints; cheap wine; all brands of whiskey; lottery tickets; rows of colorful cigarette packs; all the best cheap candy, and even a nice selection of porn. I pull off the curb and take a U-turn and head down to PRC.

I check in with the front desk. I have a PRC Alumni badge that I'm oddly proud of. Kib is off today. Florence comes around and gives me a huge bear hug. She leads me to Todd. He's sitting on the couch, watching TV in the group room. He's calm now. The Trazodone Dr. Blume gave him has kicked in. His hands are red, swollen, and bandaged. Todd's eyes are heavy-lidded, and he moves slowly and sloppily. He tells me the story of the visit with his parents. With exaggerated, sweeping, full-body motions, he demonstrates to me how he dragged his bike across the hood of his sister's Chevy Suburban while she was in it, because she wouldn't give him a ride back to PRC after his parents kicked him out, and after he punched out one of their pool-house windows, because they threw away all his belongings. He's too faded on Trazodone to care that I'm laughing. I sit next to him on the couch and tell him everything is going to be alright. He drifts in and out of sleep, while I watch the end of *Die Hard*.

FOURTEEN

I'm in LAX Court again, on the ninth floor. This time it's a different courtroom and a different judge. Mark clerked for this judge during law school. They both went to Yale. Keri and Mark think he might influence DA Villa to make me a better plea offer. He has a creviced, stony face with hanging jowls. He reminds me of a circuit court judge from the obligatory courtroom scene in every old Western movie.

I sit at the defense table, while Mark and Villa approach the judge's bench before my Trial Setting Hearing goes on the record. I can't hear what they are saying, except a couple short shrills followed by cackles from Villa, each followed by the judge glaring down at me. His eyes say, *you did what?!* I try to appear innocent yet remorseful, but it's not working. His eyes don't soften. I can't help but to think of a noose and dangling feet from a Western movie's public hanging scene. The judge's increasingly severe glare is surely incited by Villa repeating, *rape, erection, window,* and *choke hold* over and over.

I am able to make out one phrase clearly: *member of the Bar.* Villa says *Bar* in a high-pitched tone for emphasis. I imagine Villa says to the judge in a hushed tone, *Not only is he a violent, psychopathic, sexual predator—that has probably stalked your wife and daughter at some point—but he's given our hallowed profession a bad name—he's a member of the Bar!*

Whatever Mark is saying to the judge seems to be falling flat. But, the judge and Villa are in lockstep like old chums. Every time Villa says something, she looks back over her shoulder at me, like an older sister ratting me out to dad.

Mark and Villa turn and walk back to counsels' tables. Mark lets out a sigh as he sits down next to me. Although he's trying to mask it, his face reads disappointment. As far as I'm concerned, he might as well be yelling, *you're going to be ass-raped in prison for the rest of your life!* Villa, on the other hand, sports an alligator grin. She's as elated as an anger-fueled skeleton in heels can be.

We go on the record, and trial is set for a month out.

"This date is solid," the judge admonishes. "It is *going* to go on that date. I don't know if this case can settle," the judge continues, "but you are both here now, so this would be the time to do it."

We all rise formally as the judge leaves the bench.

I wait in the hall, while Mark and Villa discuss a plea bargain. This judge certainly isn't going to help my cause, but that doesn't change the fact that Winston testified at my prelim hearing that I didn't do or say anything sexual. That *has* to matter. I don't care if I have to go to jail, plead guilty to a felony, and even have my Bar license suspended. I just can't plead guilty to a sex crime, or I'll lose my Bar license permanently.

I'm still not a rapist, I mumble under my breath as I stand in the hallway through the glass wall of the towering court looking out over the Los Angeles sprawl.

God, please help me. Please. Please, God, please.

Not two minutes goes by before DA Villa and Mark swing open the courtroom doors. Mark walks toward me, and Villa trots to the elevator bank. She doesn't even look at me.

Yes, I'm still praying for you every night, I think as I watch her walk down the hall.

"Joseph, I'm sorry," Mark says, and then takes a deep breath. "Nothing's changed. Their best offer is two years prison, two strikes, both registerable sex convictions," Mark reports solemnly.

I close my eyes, and take a deep breath. I feel a bit dizzy as the black hollowness that accompanies my nightly, racing thoughts washes over me. I try to *pause before reacting* like they taught me in rehab.

Oh, my God. I can't believe it. Fuck. This is really happening. It's not getting better.

I can't hold it in. "Fuck her! I'm just a number to her, Mark! She doesn't care whether I did it or not, she just wants her conviction," I shout. "Let's go to trial. What choice do I have?"

Mark is embarrassed by the disturbance I've caused. He doesn't answer my question.

"I take the deal, and I go to prison for two fucking years, become a two-strike felon, a registered sex offender, and lose my Bar license? *What kind of deal is that?*"

"Joseph," Mark says, "take it easy."

"*Take it easy*, Mark? It might as well be the goddamn death penalty."

"Look, Joseph, I think Keri and I can get them down to less time," Mark says "but they are not coming off the sex crime conviction. It's not happening." Mark lets that set in for a moment. "It's not happening," he repeats and continues. "It's your choice, but you have to realize that if they try this case, they are going after all five charges. If you lose on all of them, you could easily do twenty years."

I turn away from Mark and gaze out over a sun-bleached Los Angeles. *Twenty years, twenty years, twenty years*. It's an absurd amount of time. I can't even fathom it. It might as well be two hundred years.

"And here is what you really need to think about," Mark warns me, "you have no defense against the Criminal Threats charge and ..."

I interrupt him. I don't want to hear it again. "I know. Keri told me. I do two years, no matter what. Even if I win on everything else. Two years ... no evidence to dispute the criminal threats. I said *shut up or I'll kill you*, and that's it. Two years."

I talk to Mark's reflection in the window.

"Nice choice, huh, Mark?"

There is a long pause between us.

"I'll try this case, Joseph. I will. If that's what you want. But you need to know what the risks are. I'm worried about what a jury is going to think, obviously. The facts aren't disputed. It's going to come down to the jury. But it's going to be hard to get the image of a six-foot-four, two hundred-pound, raging, drunk, naked guy breaking into their homes, or worse: their daughter's, wife's, girlfriend's, sis—"

"I get it Mark. I get it!" I lean into the window. Sweat and oil seal my forehead to the air-conditioned, cool glass. Los Angeles is still crawling around down there. It used to be the place I was going to conquer. Now it scares the hell out of me. *Twenty years ... twenty years*, it echoes through my brain.

"I'm not saying we can't win," Mark says. "I'm saying it's a *tough, tough* case, and the stakes are high."

Mark places his right hand on my shoulder and squeezes.

My legs feel weak at the thought of going away to prison for twenty years. My knees are going to give out. I'm dizzy, and I can hear my heart beating.

"Joseph ... Joseph," Mark says and jostles my shoulder.

I come back into the present moment. It's a horrible place.

"Yeah, sorry," I say, "I'm listening. Go ahead."

Mark tells me to think about it, and talk it over with Keri. I try to thank him, but he's gone before I can get it out.

"The kid said the same thing that he said in the police report," I say.

"Uh-huh," Dr. Kincaid responds without looking up at me. She's paging through my psych chart.

"It makes no sense," I say, deciding to fill the silence, especially since I'm paying five dollars a minute for this session. "If I'm going to rape a girl, why would I jump on her and start punching her? That doesn't make any sense. Why would I want to do that? Right?"

I wish I wouldn't have said that. I hate that I'm trying to convince her that I'm not a rapist.

"Actually," Dr. Kincaid says, finally looking up from my chart, "it's very common for rapists to batter their victims before raping them. Remember, it's a crime of power not sex."

Dr. Kincaid has that fake, overly sincere NPR voice, just like Dotty from the Other Bar, but I like that she's not shy about telling me exactly what she thinks. I'm required by the California Bar's Lawyer's Assistance Program to seek therapy once a week, and Keri thinks it's a good idea, too. Dr. Kincaid's office is in South Pasadena in a '70's office building with big, shady trees and dappled, natural light. It reminds me of Thomas & Colbert.

I wish I could go back in time to Thomas & Colbert before my DUI. God, I wish I could.

Kincaid's office is cozy. It's exactly what I would have expected of a pricey therapist's office, although I'd have told anyone that asked that I'd never set foot in a therapist's office. Therapy is for whiners. Now, I'm the whiner.

"Seriously? Rapists beat them up first?" I ask. I guess that makes sense, I think.

"It's very common," Dr. Kincaid responds dryly.

I'm pretty sure Dr. Kincaid thinks I'm a rapist, or, at the least, that I was going to commit a rape that night.

"Well, I don't like my rape victims beat up," I joke.

I shouldn't have said that. That was stupid. *Why did I say that?* I can't stand that she thinks I'm a rapist.

Dr. Kincaid chuckles ... at me, then redirects the conversation, "So what exactly did you do today?" she asks.

Her question catches me off-guard. I really want to tell her the truth. I can't rack up any more lies. I'm tired of secrets. I pause for a long moment. My pause affects Dr. Kincaid. She stops writing in my chart, leans forward, and places her crisscrossed fingers in her lap and gives me her full attention.

Fuck it. I might as well tell her.

"Well, I got up and went to a 12-step meeting, then to my office and uh ... that's right ... I prepared a demurrer to a complaint, filed it, and mail-served it, because our secretary was sick today. Before Will left, he gave me a bunch of cash, because one of our clients paid in cash. So, before I came here, I went to my favorite massage parlor over on Francisquito, and I fucked a prostitute. And, yes, I feel terrible about it. It's disgusting. Seriously."

Wow. That felt good.

I take a deep breath and wait for her response.

Dr. Kincaid is visually affected by my disclosure. Her face wrestles with itself as one expression is superseded by the next. Within a few seconds she cycles through shock, anger, and disgust. Her face says, *haven't you learned anything, you fucking idiot?*

"Do you think that is a problem?" Dr. Kincaid asks sharply and stares at me unblinkingly.

I can feel my face, ears, and neck heat up. I've never seen her worked up like this in our half dozen sessions.

"Yes," I say. "It's reckless, fully reckless. I know it. I've been killing myself with all this shit and the Bar and the court and rehab and work ... and nothing is getting better. In fact, it seems to be getting worse. I just needed some relief."

I feel a heaviness come over me, like what it must feel like right before I cry—if I could cry.

"*You need to stop doing it!* You need to treat it exactly the same as alcohol. Admit your powerlessness; let go, and let God take it away," Dr. Kincaid says tersely. "Can you imagine the ramifications if you were caught?"

I nod vigorously. I picture myself in my boxers, handcuffed outside a massage parlor.

"... as if you need another problem," she continues.

"I'll stop. I'm sure that is why I told you. Subconsciously, I wanted to hear someone tell me how stupid I'm being."

I leave Dr. Kincaid's office in South Pasadena and drive across town to Marina del Rey. Thank God for my little floating hovel, my hideaway from the world: a thirty-one-foot 1966 Columbia sailboat. Todd was going to lose it to the harbor master, because he hadn't paid the slip fees in months. I gave Todd money that he needed for his law school tuition, and I took over the slip fees and maintenance cost. I just stay here on weekends, hiding away from the world.

I sit on the raised teak decking at the stern, looking out over the water. The air is dark and thick and salty. The orange glow of my cigarette accents the starry white harbor lights in the background. There is something romantic and nostalgic about a harbor at night, so much so that sometimes I can sit out here in the chill and think about something other than the hurricane of problems that are the everyday activities of my existence. The boat gently rocks back and forth. The harbor is mostly still. My slip is in the last row of the thirty-five-feet-and-under boats, and the stern faces a row of giant yachts, next to a rock jetty that protects them from the mouth of the harbor that leads to open ocean. Usually, there is a party going on in one of the yachts, girls in heels and dresses, carefully traversing the wood docking. The music ebbs and flows with the air, sometimes faint and sometimes loud. Not tonight. It's just the ocean noises, the harbor lights, and the surrounding high-rises, hotels, and the wide-open, wild ocean. Not far away are pulsing bars and clubs. I can't see them or hear them, but I can feel their pull. There are the grinding beer bars of neighboring Venice Beach and the upscale hotel bars and clubs of Marina del Rey. I could walk to any one of a dozen of them. I could go have some drinks, get nice and loose, and seduce some pretty girl. At the end of the night, when it's time to go home, I'd ask if she'd like to come back to the harbor and see my sailboat. I'd say, *I know we just met, but I'm having so much fun with you.* The idea excites me and scares me like the dark ocean. For just a moment, I seriously consider it. It'd be easy, and getting laid would be much needed relief. There is no drug like new pussy. But then, thoughts of that late night, drunken club atmosphere, the desperation of it makes my stomach sink. It'd be no different from any one of a hundred bars and clubs I'd been to, from Manchester to Manhattan to Mazatlan to Moreno Valley. It's all the same club with all the same desperate characters, and it always ends in a pit of guilt and shame, no matter whether I get laid or not. In fact, it's even worse when I *do* get laid.

I'm not going anywhere. *I'm good.* I have my cigarettes and my coffee. I sit here in the damp sea air, rocking and smoking and sipping, thinking my thoughts, which are blanketed by a feeling of the surreal. *Twenty years* is still bouncing around in my skull. There is still a lack of acceptance of the fact that my life has come to this. How the fuck did I get here? I hear Dr. Kincaid's voice saying the word *powerless.* But what does it matter now? It's too late. Isn't it?

The moonlight creates a narrow stream of wiggling light on the water that starts at the moon and ends at the bow of the boat. Little pools of iridescent fuel float across the water. The Booze Cruise boat slides by in the mouth of the harbor on its way to sea. I can hear hints of its festivities, and I can see vague backlit silhouettes of intertwined couples, dancing and gazing out to sea from the mid- and top decks. They drink and smoke and kiss.

This is a beautiful place to be, sitting here on this sailboat. It's a place of privilege, but it doesn't mean anything to me because I'm just a visitor in this life now. I've snuck into the country club, knowing I'm going to get thrown out any minute. I'm a fraud. I'm pretending to be a lawyer with a yacht—yes, technically, it's a yacht, and yes, technically, I'm still a lawyer—gazing up at the stars. But, I'm not. I'm broken and cracked and chipping away in bigger and bigger chunks. Soon I'll be gone.

I light another cigarette and drag through it quickly. I go below deck. I'm too tired to masturbate, and it wouldn't be any good anyway. When I arrived today, I threw out all my video porn, this time *without* a promise that I'll never do it again. I just couldn't. It's too painful to break another promise to myself. Instead, I just did what the 12-steppers suggest:

I prayed that I don't do it today. Just for today: no porn, no alcohol, no prostitutes, no one-night stand, no bars, no clubs, and no suicide. I read another dozen pages of *Alcoholics Anonymous*. Then I read another twenty pages of *Moby Dick*. I'm wrapped in my dark green blanket with the lion in the jungle scene: the one Jack, from PRC, lent me before he hung himself. I pray. I have to pray. Maybe it's out of respect for Vinny, who is trying to save me, a dead man. I have to be able to say *yes* when he asks if I've been praying every night, and, anyway, it's become routine. I can't sleep without it. I pray for people I love, for people I despise, for people I wish I hadn't hurt. I recite the Program/Vinny-recommended stock prayers: Serenity Prayer, Set-Aside Prayer, other prayers:

God, your will, not mine, be done ... God ... whoever or whatever the fuck you are or aren't ... I offer myself to thee to do with me as thou wilt ... take away my difficulties that victory over them ... your will not mine.

I hear far-off laughter, and the water rocks me to sleep.

It's a four-level parking garage next to a high-rise on Wilshire Boulevard, a couple miles west of downtown LA. I'm here because I'll do whatever 12-steppers tell me, if it means I have a chance at life again. They keep telling me I'm going to get a life worth living. They say this with a sincere and unyielding confidence, despite all evidence to the contrary and none in support. There's a part of me that believes them. It's probably the stupid part. I'll do their steps, I told them, but I'm not telling my deepest and darkest secrets to anyone who doesn't have a legal obligation to keep his mouth shut, not even Vinny. I've been unwavering on this issue. And that's why I'm here to see Terry. Nobody can fuck with me about this, because I found a passage in the AA book that says that I can read my take-it-to-the-grave-list to anyone I choose. Terry is in the Program, and he's a priest. I heard him speak at a recovery meeting. He's been clean for twenty years, but he used to be a horrible lush. Now, he's the priest that deals with all the other addict priests. I'm not sure if he deals with priests whose primary addiction is sex, but I have a feeling he's the pope's go-to guy for all addicted priests in Los Angeles, no matter what they're into. He's like Tito and my lawyer, Mark, in that to meet him is to admire and respect him. He's just one of those men that people are drawn to.

The building is just like a regular office high-rise, with one major difference: instead of corporate-climbers in suits and skirts, it's full of Catholic priests and nuns—an entire skyscraper filled with them. Father Terry greets me, as if he has no idea he works in the world's most bizarre office building. He bypasses my hand that I've extended for a handshake and hugs me. I'm still not used to being hugged, especially by men, and my body stiffens. It does feel good, though. It feels really good. It feels like what I presume it is, unconditional love.

Father Terry's office is on a middle floor with a view south. We sit side by side on chairs at the non-working end of his desk.

I wonder what he does at his desk. Does he write memos? *Fellow employees, please do not use the copiers for personal use. Thank you for your cooperation –Management and God.*

"Well, you have forty-five minutes, Jeremy," Father Terry says. "We should get to it."

"It's *Joseph* ... your Father ... Your Honor. I mean ...," I stumble nervously.

"Terry. Just Terry is fine," he says. "Sorry, *Joseph*. Go ahead."

I open up my leather binder and pull out my legal pad.

"Just start right out?" I ask.

"Yes," he says. "This is about you sharing with another human being the wrongs you have done so that you can release them. We are only as sick as our secrets. You'll make amends to people you've harmed later, but now you are going to admit to me, me and God, your understanding of your wrongs."

That's the idea. I understood it before I walked in here, but I figured there'd be a little more pomp and circumstance. *Here goes nothing.* I take a deep breath, and I unload it all—page after page. Father Terry's expression doesn't change, no matter what I say. He just listens, as if I'm reading the instruction manual for a food processor. Finally, I read the last entry.

"That's it," I say.

"Good. Did you leave anything out?" Terry asks. "Is there anything you *just* can't tell me? You don't have to tell me what it is; just tell me if there is anything else."

"No. Not a thing. I just told you I had sex with four different prostitutes in one day, nearly killed someone, and broke into someone's apartment naked and attacked them. I thought I did a pretty good job, Father."

"Terry."

"Sorry, right," I say. "Just Terry."

"Jeremy I—"

"Joseph," I interrupt softly.

"Right, right, *Joseph*," Terry corrects himself. "Sorry, I get something in my head, and it gets stuck there. Anyway, I was saying, yes—that wasn't the worst I've ever heard—not by a long shot." Father Terry speaks with a warm kind smile.

"Now you are sure there is nothing else?" Father Terry asks. "There is nothing worse than keeping hold of secrets. You're an attorney. You know I have an obligation to keep anything you tell me confidential."

I think about it. He's right. I want to leave it all here. I don't care how embarrassing or horrible it is.

"I guess there is one thing," I say. "The DA says I'm a rapist, but I've told you what I remember of that night and what the facts are as I know them. I don't think I'm capable of rape, even in a drunken rage, but I guess I don't know for sure. I, obviously ... you know, am guilty of lust with all the prostitutes and porn and cheating ... but when I search my heart I don't think I could ever do that."

Father Terry closes his eyes and places his hands together at his chin, as if channeling a message. After a few beats, he opens his eyes. "I've heard your story, Joseph. It sounds to me like you went insane with alcohol. It's not uncommon. But it isn't for me to say. The only thing that matters here is that you were rigorously honest; that you turned all of your wrongs over to God and to another person. If you've done that, you're as free as a person can be." Father Terry, it seems, stares through my eyes and into my thoughts. "Have you done that here today? Have you been rigorously honest?"

"Yes. *Yes*, I have," I say excitedly. It comes to me as good news: Yes, I have. I've told him everything. I completely believe Father Terry when he says that I am free. There isn't a blink of doubt in his eyes.

"Now go home and pray and meditate," Terry instructs. "Thank God for this opportunity to start anew. It's your quickening."

Father Terry walks me out to the elevator. The doors close together, and his kind smiling face disappears behind them.

It's your quickening.

I alight at the ground floor and float past a group of nuns. The air I'm breathing is fuller. The oxygen is spreading through my brain. My mind is clear. I can see every detail, as if I have a new pair of glasses. I'm a little tingly. I feel like I've set down a thirty-pound dumbbell I didn't even know I'd been carrying. I don't wait until I get home to pray and meditate. I don't want to lose this feeling. I sit in the back seat of my car behind tinted windows. I close my eyes and breath and I say aloud: *Thank you God for this opportunity to start over.* I say it aloud, slowly, purposefully, over and over. It's your quickening. I think of the word *quicken.* I looked it up in the dictionary after watching *Highlander* many years ago, and I remember Preacher Dale, Beth's father, using it in his sermons. *God quickens us,* he used to say. *He gives us new life.* I really feel something. I don't know if or what God is, but there is something to unburdening one's self and believing in something. Right now I believe I might have a second chance. Somehow I believe that doing what I just did has opened the door to the possibility. Maybe this feeling will end tomorrow, and I'll be suicidal again. Maybe I'm so close to a nervous breakdown that my mind is using this to save itself. I don't care. I need this, and if I believe it, it's as true as anything else. So, I just keep my eyes closed in the back of my car in the parking garage of the Los Angeles Archdiocese's headquarters, repeating, *Thank you God for this opportunity to start over ... Thank you God for this opportunity to start over.*

FIFTEEN

Almost every night for nearly a year now, after my day is over, I come outside and sit in the dark and chain-smoke and envision what will happen at my trial. It's not hard to do. Trials are not as spontaneous as people think. It's not unlike directing a play. You know what the characters are going to say because they've already said it. Most cases don't go to trial because the ending is too obvious. I know exactly what the actors in my play are going to say. I just don't know what the audience is going to think. Will they clap or convict? Will I get sympathy or prison? Every time I get to the end of my trial—my script—the last page is missing. The rest I have scripted verbatim.

VERBATIM:

THE TRIAL OF JOSEPH NAUS BY,
AND IN THE BRAIN OF, JOSEPH NAUS:

I sit in the courtroom next to Keri and Mark at Counsel's table. Keri and Mark are whispering about a pre-trial motion, waiting for the judge to take the bench. I try to avoid eye contact with District Attorney Villa. She's so happy to be in trial. She's beaming. This is just the type of case a young DA wants: high profile, high stakes, going against Mark, one of the best criminal defense lawyers in the country.

Mark begins jury selection from the pool of about forty prospective jurors that are in the audience and jury box. A black female juror proudly tells Mark her brother is doing time at Stanislaus Prison for a rape he didn't commit.

Mark doesn't even bother asking her any more questions, because he knows Villa is going to use one of her peremptory challenges to get rid of her.

I scan the jurors in the box and the ones in the audience that may replace the jurors in the box, if they are dismissed for cause or preemptively. We have ten preemptive strikes. What am I looking for? Does it matter what they think of rape? Not really. It matters what they think about alcohol. Do they believe that someone can lose their mind, really lose their mind, when they drink?

"Please raise your hand if you have or have had any relatives that are alcoholics," Mark instructs the potential jurors. Two hands pop up, both Hispanic women, one in her forties and one in her twenties. Then another hand goes up slowly, a black man in his thirties. He's straitlaced. He dresses without any soul. I don't want him. Black guys who dress like that are trying not to be black. They are without compassion. He's contemptuous. I put an X next to "Chair 11" on Mark's jury selection diagram. Mark looks at me curiously. I circle the X. I know I'm right. He shrugs. I whisper in his ear, "Get rid of him." I box Four and Eight on the diagram with a pencil, "Let's keep them," I whisper. He nods in agreement. I know why. Mexicans don't see rape the same way white culture does, and alcoholism is hugely common in Mexican families. Jury selection is no time for political correctness. These people are going to decide whether I live or die.

The judge dismisses a man that works for the judge's son's computer software company, and a lady who says she'd have a hard time finding anybody guilty because the government is corrupt. She's right, and it's a shame she has to leave. DA Villa does us a favor and gets rid of Juror Eleven, the stiff black guy. He's replaced by another black guy, an older man wearing a blue mechanic's uniform. We score on that one. Then Villa uses her peremptory challenge to strike our younger Mexican girl, Juror Number Four. Mark gets rid of a middle-aged white woman real estate agent and an old law-and-order white guy who reminds me of my Grandpa. If he's anything like my Grandpa, he's probably wondering why we even have trials. If the police arrest you, you must be guilty.

Mark questions the three replacement jurors. One had a DUI. I don't know if this is good, bad, or indifferent. I'm just looking at him, trying to get a read on him. I noticed when he walked from the audience to the juror's box that he was wearing a cell phone on his belt. There is something very disturbing about someone who puts functionality so far above fashion, but Mark and Keri agree that we should keep him.

We have our jury. I'm happy about a couple of them. But I know it isn't enough to be sympathetic to me. A juror needs to be stubborn to deadlock a jury. The juror that won it for me on the civil case I tried in San Diego was a young proud black woman. I know she stood up to everyone in that jury room and refused to budge. I don't know if Juror Eight, my older Mexican woman, will hold out for me. I think my new Juror Eleven, the black mechanic, might. He looks like he's been around. He'll stick to his guns. I'm just not sure whether his guns will be pointed at me or not.

There is only one pre-trial motion that is hotly contested. Keri wrote a great motion in limine, but I know we are only going to get a partial victory. The jury is on recess while Mark and Villa address Judge Von Silkman.

"Seven character witnesses is a ridiculous amount," Villa argues. "It's an attempt to persuade the jury that Mr. Naus is a," she air quotes, "'good guy' and couldn't have possibly done this act which is undisputed. The People takes the position that no character witnesses should be allowed. There's no relevance. They can't speak to the issues of the case."

"I understand your position, Ms. Villa," Judge Von Silkman says and then turns to Mark. "Mr. Ackerman, isn't seven a bit excessive?"

I'm relieved by the judge's question. It means he's open to allowing at least some of my character witnesses to testify.

"I don't believe so, Your Honor. Mr. Naus is on trial for his freedom, for his profession, for his life. As you've stated, Your Honor, this is a highly unusual case. My learned colleague, Ms. Villa, says this is 'ridiculous' and 'irrelevant.' That is not the case. The Evidence Code allows character evidence that—"

"No need," Judge Von Silkman interrupts Mark. "Thank you. I'm going to allow three character witnesses, and I want their testimony to be succinct and on-point."

"Your Honor I—" Ms. Villa starts to argue.

"No need Ms. Villa. The People's position and objections are on the record, and I've made my decision."

The bailiff walks out the dozen-plus jurors that weren't selected and, after a short break, the trial officially begins.

Judge Von Silkman admonishes our newly selected jury: Don't talk about anything you hear or see to anyone. You are only to consider the evidence presented and nothing else. If I tell you that evidence or testimony is not to be considered, you must not consider the evidence. If you see anything on TV, the radio, in a newspaper, on the Internet, or anywhere else about the case, you should immediately stop watching or reading, and you mustn't consider it.

Keri, Mark, and I are all wearing earthy colors. We didn't arrange this, but I'm sure we all heard somewhere along the line in our law careers that some jury expert says that juries like warm colors. It makes sense, and it's kind of like Christianity, if you believe and you're wrong, so what? If you don't believe and you're wrong, you could end up in hell. And I am definitely facing the possibility of hell.

Villa, all in black, apparently didn't get the memo. Or, more likely, she got it, and she doesn't care. She knows there is nothing more important in trial advocacy than being yourself. Dressed in warm colors, she'd look like Satan in a sundress.

Villa walks to the front of the jury box for opening statement.

Here we go.

MS. VILLA: GOOD MORNING, LADIES AND GENTLEMEN OF THE JURY. MY NAME IS CARMEN D. VILLA. I AM A LOS ANGELES DEPUTY DISTRICT ATTORNEY, AND I REPRESENT THE PEOPLE OF THE STATE OF CALIFORNIA. MR. NAUS IS THAT MAN RIGHT THERE [INDICATING THE

DEFENDANT] BEING CHARGED WITH ASSAULT WITH IN-
TENT TO COMMIT RAPE, CRIMINAL THREATS, AND THREE
OTHER RELATED CRIMES, WHICH I WILL ADDRESS LAT-
ER. WHAT IS INTERESTING ABOUT THIS CASE IS THAT
THE FACTS ARE UNDISPUTED. THAT'S RIGHT, LADIES
AND GENTLEMEN. THE FACTS OF THIS CASE ARE UNDIS-
PUTED. YOU'RE GOING TO HEAR A LOT FROM MR. NAUS'S
ATTORNEYS AND WITNESSES ABOUT MR. NAUS BEING
DRUNK, ABOUT HIS BEING AN ALCOHOLIC. YOU ARE
GOING TO HEAR THAT MR. NAUS WAS IN A BLACKOUT,
THAT HE IS A LAWYER AND NEVER COULD DO SOMETHING
LIKE THIS. BUT, WHAT YOU AREN'T GOING TO HEAR IS
ANY ARGUMENTS DISPUTING THE FACTS OF THIS CASE.

*I know Mark is doing the right thing by not objecting, but I want him to
stand up and shoot her with a comically large gun he snuck in through security. Judges and juries hate it when opening statements are interrupted. Unless
Villa says something that could justify a mistrial, he is right to listen and not
react to anything she says.*

MS. VILLA: SO, HERE ARE THE UNDISPUTED FACTS.
ONE: MR. NAUS BROKE INTO MR. WINSTON JONES'S
APARTMENT THROUGH A SMALL BATHROOM WINDOW. HE
REMOVED THE SCREEN FROM THE SCREEN FRAME AND
CRAWLED INTO THE WINDOW. TWO: MR. NAUS TOOK OFF
ALL HIS CLOTHES AND ENTERED THE MAIN ROOM OF MR.
JONES'S APARTMENT. THREE: MR. NAUS HAD AN ERECT
PENIS. FOUR: MR. NAUS JUMPED ONTO MR. JONES WHILE
MR. JONES WAS ASLEEP IN HIS BED, AND MR. NAUS BE-
GAN CHOKING HIM AND HITTING HIM. FIVE: MR. JONES
AWOKE AND BEGAN DEFENDING HIMSELF, AND DURING
THAT STRUGGLE MR. NAUS TOLD HIM TO BE QUIET, TO

SHUT UP, AND AT LEAST ONCE SAID, "SHUT UP OR I'LL KILL YOU." SIX: MR. NAUS PUT MR. JONES IN A DEADLY CHOKE HOLD, BUT MR. JONES WAS ABLE TO BREAK FREE AND RUN OUT THE FRONT DOOR. MR. NAUS WENT OUT THE BATHROOM WINDOW AND TRIED TO GET AWAY. MR. JONES AND A NEIGHBOR PINNED HIM IN THE FRONT YARD ACROSS THE STREET UNTIL THE POLICE ARRIVED. DURING THAT TIME, MR. NAUS SAID, AMONG OTHER THINGS, "I THOUGHT THERE WAS A GIRL IN THERE," AND "I THOUGHT YOU WERE A GIRL."

Villa pauses and purposefully scans the eyes of both rows of jurors.

MS. VILLA: THAT'S IT, LADIES AND GENTLEMAN. THOSE ARE THE BASIC FACTS OF THE CASE, AND THOSE FACTS ARE ENOUGH TO CONVICT MR. NAUS OF FIRST DEGREE BURGLARY, TERRORIST THREATS, FALSE IMPRISONMENT, ATTEMPTED FORCIBLE RAPE, AND ASSAULT WITH INTENT TO COMMIT RAPE.

Villa discusses the elements of the crimes, tells the jury who will be testifying, and basically what they are going to say. She keeps it short. She saves the details for witness testimony and closing argument. It's exactly what I expected. It's textbook. It leaves the jurors wondering what possible defense I could have if I don't dispute those facts. It leaves them knowing that I am a monster.

Villa ends with, "I trust you will do the right thing and convict Mr. Naus on all counts."

I try to pretend that I'm not thinking of what it will be like to be sodomized in prison.

It's Mark's turn.

Mark walks over to the jury box. He's dapper but not too dapper, clean-cut but not sterile, Jewish in that strong Israeli way, handsome but not distractingly so. Maybe that is why he's so good. Like a perfect politician, there is nothing objectionable about Mark.

MR. ACKERMAN: MY NAME IS MARK ACKERMAN. I'M AN ATTORNEY, AND I REPRESENT JOSEPH NAUS.

I stand and then nod while looking directly at the jury as Mark previously instructed me to do.

MR. ACKERMAN [CONT.]: AND THAT IS KERI MCCO-NNELY SITTING NEXT TO JOSEPH, SHE'S ALSO AN AT-TORNEY, AND MY COLLEAGUE AND WILL BE HELPING ME.

Mark leans up against the edge of the jury box, as if he's about to have a casual conversation with his best friend.

MR. ACKERMAN: WE - - MYSELF, JOSEPH, AND KERI [PAUSE] WE KNOW YOU HAVE BUSY LIVES, AND THAT THIS IS THE LAST PLACE YOU PROBABLY WANT TO BE, AND WE APPRECIATE THAT YOU ARE TAKING THE TIME TO HEAR THIS CASE. WE KNOW IT'S NOT BY CHOICE, BUT WE APPRECIATE IT ANYWAY.

Some jurors nod, a couple chuckle.

MR. ACKERMAN: WE WILL TRY TO GET TO THE POINT, SO YOU CAN ALL GET ON WITH YOUR FAMILIES AND YOUR LIVES. YOU HEARD FROM MS. VILLA EARLIER. WHAT SHE SAID IS TRUE. JOSEPH DOES NOT DISPUTE THAT HE DID ALL THOSE THINGS THAT SHE TOLD YOU HE DID. HE CAN'T DISPUTE THEM. AS HE'LL TESTIFY THAT THE ONLY MEMORIES HE HAS OF THE INCIDENT

ARE VAGUE AND CLOUDY, AS IF HE WAS IN A DREAM. AND, AS HE'LL TELL YOU WHEN HE TAKES THE STAND, HE DOESN'T HAVE ANY REASON TO THINK MR. WINSTON JONES ISN'T TELLING THE TRUTH. MR. JONES WAS THE VICTIM OF A BIZARRE ACT OF INSANITY AND FOR THAT JOSEPH IS TERRIBLY REGRETFUL. LUCKILY, THE ONLY PERSON WHO WAS SERIOUSLY INJURED AS A RESULT OF JOSEPH'S INSANITY WAS JOSEPH. WITH THE EXCEPTION OF A COUPLE MINOR BRUISES, MR. JONES WAS LEFT UNSCATHED. JOSEPH, ON THE OTHER HAND, SUFFERED A SEVERE CONCUSSION AND HAD TO HAVE HIS SCALP STAPLED SHUT, AS A RESULT OF MR. JONES WHACKING HIM IN THE HEAD WITH A SKATEBOARD SEVERAL TIMES. JOSEPH WILL TELL YOU THAT HE DESERVED EVERY ONE OF THOSE WHACKS OVER THE HEAD, AND THEN SOME. JOSEPH WILL ALSO TELL YOU HE'S LUCKY TO BE ALIVE. IF MR. JONES WOULD HAVE KILLED JOSEPH THAT NIGHT, HE'D HAVE HAD EVERY RIGHT TO HAVE DONE SO.

Mark pauses to let it sink in.

MR. ACKERMAN: YOU KNOW [PAUSE] THERE IS ONE THING THAT MY LEARNED COLLEAGUE, MS. VILLA, DID SAY THAT WE WILL TAKE ISSUE WITH. SHE SAID, AND I QUOTE "THOSE FACTS ARE ENOUGH TO CONVICT MR. NAUS OF FIRST DEGREE BURGLARY, TERRORIST THREATS, FALSE IMPRISONMENT, ATTEMPTED FORCIBLE RAPE, AND ASSAULT WITH INTENT TO COMMIT RAPE."

NOT TRUE. SIMPLY NOT TRUE. JUST ADDRESSING THE ATTEMPTED RAPE CHARGE: IN ORDER TO CONVICT JOSEPH OF ASSAULT WITH INTENT TO COMMIT RAPE THE DA HAS TO PROVE BEYOND A REASONABLE DOUBT THAT

JOSEPH SPECIFICALLY INTENDED TO COMMIT A RAPE. NOW . . . RAPE IS BETWEEN A MAN AND WOMAN. A WOMAN CAN RAPE A MAN, AND A MAN CAN RAPE A WOMAN, BUT A MAN CANNOT RAPE A MAN, AND A WOMAN CANNOT RAPE A WOMAN. MR. JONES IS A MALE, AND JOSEPH IS A MALE, SO IT WAS IMPOSSIBLE FOR JOSEPH TO RAPE MR. JONES. LET ME SAY THAT AGAIN, SINCE JOSEPH IS A MALE AND MR. JONES IS A MALE, THE CRIME OF RAPE WAS A LEGAL AND FACTUAL IMPOSSIBILITY.

Mark pauses. The jury is intrigued.

MR. ACKERMAN: NOW JOSEPH ISN'T BEING CHARGED WITH RAPE. HE'S BEING CHARGED WITH ASSAULT WITH INTENT TO COMMIT RAPE. THE DISTRICT ATTORNEY'S THEORY IS THAT JOSEPH THOUGHT MR. JONES WAS A WOMAN, AND THEN WHEN HE DISCOVERED THAT MR. JONES WASN'T A WOMAN, HE CHANGED HIS MIND. THEY WANT YOU TO BELIEVE THAT A THIRTY-TWO-YEAR-OLD ATTORNEY WITH HIS OWN LAW PRACTICE, WITH NO CRIMINAL RECORD OTHER THAN A DUI, DECIDED AT TWO IN THE MORNING ON A WEEKDAY THAT HE WAS GOING TO CLIMB INTO A RANDOM PERSON'S APARTMENT, IN THE HOPES THAT THERE WOULD BE A WOMAN FOR HIM TO RAPE. JOSEPH HAD A SEVEN A.M. TEE TIME IN PASADENA TO PLAY GOLF WITH HIS LAW PARTNER AND ONE OF THEIR MOST IMPORTANT CLIENTS WHO JUST FLEW IN FROM SINGAPORE, AND YET HE JUST DECIDED HE WAS GOING TO RANDOMLY PICK AN APARTMENT, NOT TWO BLOCKS FROM HIS HOME, IN THE HOPES OF FINDING A SUITABLE FEMALE RAPE VICTIM.

NOW LET ME TELL YOU THE WHOLE STORY, NOT JUST

THE PARTS THAT ARE HELPFUL TO JOSEPH AND NOT THE
PARTS THAT ONLY SUPPORT WHAT THE DA BELIEVES . .
. [LONG PAUSE] BUT THE WHOLE STORY.

*Mark is attempting to distinguish himself from Villa, and he's doing a
good job. Now he's going to take the bullets out of her gun.*

MR. ACKERMAN: JOSEPH WAS NOT LIVING THE LIFE HE
WANTED TO BE LIVING. A YEAR AGO JULY, JOSEPH WAS
LIVING IN A CONDOMINIUM IN SANTA MONICA, A BLOCK
AWAY FROM MR. JONES'S APARTMENT. IT WAS TEN AT
NIGHT AND JOSEPH HAD TO MEET HIS LAW PARTNER AND
THEIR VERY IMPORTANT CLIENT, THE ONE I MENTIONED
BEFORE. HE'D JUST FLOWN IN FROM SINGAPORE. JO-
SEPH AND HIS LAW PARTNER WERE HANDLING A LARGE
CIVIL MATTER INVOLVING PROPERTY THAT THIS CLIENT
FROM SINGAPORE OWNED. JOSEPH WILL TESTIFY THAT
HE KNEW HE NEEDED TO GO TO BED, BUT HE STRUGGLED
AND STRUGGLED WITH HIS DESIRE TO DRINK ALCOHOL,
AND HE CONVINCED HIMSELF TO GO HAVE A QUICK DRINK
AT A LOCAL BAR, THE LIQUID KITTY, A BAR JOSEPH
FREQUENTED QUITE REGULARLY, SOME WOULD SAY, AL-
COHOLICALLY. HE KNEW HE SHOULDN'T BE DRINKING AT
ALL. HE WAS ON PROBATION FOR A DUI INVOLVING AN
INCIDENT WHERE HE ROLLED HIS CAR OFF THE SIDE
OF THE FREEWAY, AND HIS ALCOHOL LEVEL WAS OVER
THREE TIMES THE LEGAL LIMIT. THAT HAPPENED ABOUT
A YEAR PRIOR TO THIS INCIDENT. IN FACT, JOSEPH
WAS SCHEDULED TO START DRUNK DRIVING SCHOOL AND
MANDATORY AA MEETINGS IN LESS THAN A WEEK FROM
THE INCIDENT THAT BRINGS US HERE TODAY.

YOU ALREADY KNOW WHAT DECISION JOSEPH MADE.

HE WENT TO THE BAR. HE DIDN'T HAVE ONE OR TWO DRINKS. HE HAD ABOUT A DOZEN WHISKEY DRINKS IN ABOUT THREE HOURS. THIS WAS NOT UNCOMMON. HE HAD BEEN BINGE DRINKING OFTEN. JOSEPH'S DRINKING WAS OUT OF CONTROL. HE BLACKED OUT, WHICH AS YOU'LL HEAR FROM AN EXPERT ON THE SUBJECT, MEANS THAT HE DOESN'T HAVE A MEMORY OF THE INCIDENT, BE-CAUSE THE BRAIN BASICALLY STOPS RECORDING DUE TO THE EFFECTS OF ALCOHOL. THAT SAME EXPERT WITNESS WILL TESTIFY THAT, BASED ON THE EVIDENCE, HE ESTIMATES THAT JOSEPH'S BLOOD ALCOHOL LEVEL WAS PROBABLY BETWEEN .30 AND .40.

Apparently familiar with the relevance of the numbers, one of the jurors gasps. Several make wow faces. A couple remain unfazed.

MR. ACKERMAN: YES, POINT-THREE-ZERO TO POINT-FOUR-ZERO. THIS IS SO HIGH THAT MANY PEOPLE WOULD DIE IF THEY REACHED THE SAME BLOOD ALCOHOL LEV-EL. BINGE DRINKING WASN'T JOSEPH'S ONLY NASTY HABIT. JOSEPH HAD BEEN GOING TO ASIAN MASSAGE PARLORS AND PAYING PROSTITUTES TO PERFORM SEXUAL ACTS FOR A LONG TIME. HE WILL TESTIFY THAT HE'D BEEN DOING THIS OFF AND ON SINCE HE WAS EIGHTEEN. HE WILL TESTIFY THAT THERE WERE THREE MASSAGE PARLORS CLOSE TO HIS CONDO, AND HE HAD BEEN TO THE CLOSEST ONE SEVERAL TIMES, SINCE HE MOVED TO SANTA MONICA ABOUT A YEAR PRIOR TO THAT NIGHT. JOSEPH'S NASTY HABITS, OR, IF YOU WILL, ADDIC-TIONS, COLLIDED THAT NIGHT.

IN A CLASSIC ALCOHOLIC BLACKOUT, JOSEPH WALKED SEVERAL BLOCKS FROM THE LIQUID KITTY DOWN PICO

BACK TO THE 34TH STREET WHERE HE LIVED. HE DIDN'T
GO HOME. HE WENT TO THE ATM MACHINE RIGHT ACROSS
FROM THE MASSAGE PARLOR ON 36TH AND PICO. IT WAS
PAST TWO IN THE MORNING. JOSEPH WITHDREW EXACTLY
ONE HUNDRED DOLLARS. HE WILL TESTIFY THAT THIS
IS EXACTLY HOW MUCH IT COSTS TO GO THE MASSAGE
PARLOR. FORTY TO GET IN AND SIXTY TO TIP THE
MASSEUSE FOR SEXUAL FAVORS. HE'D DONE IT DOZENS
AND DOZENS OF TIMES BEFORE AT VARIOUS MASSAGE
PARLORS, INCLUDING THIS ONE.

JOSEPH WILL TESTIFY THAT IN THE DOZENS OF TIMES
HE HAS BEEN TO A MASSAGE PARLOR, HE HAS NEVER
BEEN TO A MASSAGE PARLOR AT NIGHT, AND HE KNOWS
QUITE WELL THAT NO MASSAGE PARLOR WOULD BE OPEN
PAST SEVEN OR EIGHT, LET ALONE PAST MIDNIGHT.
HE HAS NO RECOLLECTION OF GOING TO THE ATM OR
THE MASSAGE PARLOR OR LEAVING THE LIQUID KITTY.
HE HAS NO IDEA WHY HE WOULD THINK THAT HE COULD
GO TO THE MASSAGE PARLOR, SINCE HE KNEW THAT IT
WOULD BE CLOSED AND THERE WOULD BE NO ONE THERE.
HIS ONLY EXPLANATION IS THAT HE MUST HAVE BEEN
OUT OF HIS MIND FROM THE EFFECTS OF ALCOHOL.

*Mark walks over to defense counsel's table where Keri and I are sitting.
Keri hands him a large whiteboard, with a simple schematic drawing on the
front in blue.*

MR. ACKERMAN: YOUR HONOR, COUNSEL HAS STIP-
ULATED TO THE ADMISSIBILITY OF THIS EXHIBIT.
WE'LL LAY THE FOUNDATION LATER. IT IS MARKED AS
DEFENDANT'S ONE.

MS. VILLA: NO OBJECTIONS.

THE COURT: GO AHEAD.

Mark sets the Exhibit on an easel in front of the jury.

MR. ACKERMAN: THIS DRAWING IS A TO-SCALE DIA-
GRAM OF THE BUILDING, IN WHICH THE ASIAN MASSAGE
PARLOR AND MR. WINSTON JONES'S APARTMENT ARE LO-
CATED.

He points to an X on the corner of the U-shaped diagram and then to an-
other X up and to the right of it.

MR. ACKERMAN: YOU'LL SEE PHOTOGRAPHS LATER ON.
THIS IS JUST TO GIVE YOU AN IDEA. IT'S AN OLD
MOTEL BUILDING, AND IT STILL LOOKS LIKE A MOTEL,
BUT THE OLD MOTEL ROOMS HAVE BEEN TURNED INTO
SMALL APARTMENTS, AND THE ASIAN MASSAGE PARLOR
RENTS OUT THE SPACE THAT USED TO BE THE MOTEL
OFFICE.
THE EVIDENCE WILL REVEAL THAT JOSEPH, DRUNK
OUT OF HIS MIND AND WITH A HUNDRED DOLLARS IN
HIS POCKET, WENT TO THE FRONT DOOR OF THE MASSAGE
PARLOR AND, IN HIS DRUNKEN FUGUE STATE, KNOCKED
SEVERAL TIMES LOUDLY, STUMBLED AROUND, AND MADE
SOME NOISE, WAKING A FEW PEOPLE UP. HE TRIED SOME
OTHER DOORS AROUND THE MASSAGE PARLOR. HE WENT
AROUND TO THE BACK OF THE BUILDING AND CLIMBED
INTO MR. JONES'S WINDOW. IT IS PRETTY OBVIOUS
THAT JOSEPH INTENDED TO ENTER THE ASIAN MASSAGE
PARLOR. MR. JONES'S WINDOW WAS RIGHT NEXT TO
THE MASSAGE PARLOR'S WINDOW AND FROM THE BACK,
ESPECIALLY DRUNK AND IN THE DARK, IT WOULD BE

VERY EASY TO MISTAKE THE TWO. HAD HE GONE INTO THE MASSAGE PARLOR, HE WOULD HAVE FOUND AN EMP-TY BUILDING, AND WE WOULDN'T BE HERE RIGHT NOW. BUT HE DIDN'T. HE MISTAKENLY ENTERED MR. JONES'S APARTMENT.

NOW, MR. JONES IS A SELF-PROCLAIMED NEAT FREAK, AND JOSEPH ENTERED A DARK BATHROOM . . . HE'LL TESTIFY THAT IT LOOKS JUST LIKE THE BATHROOMS OF ONE OF THE MANY MASSAGE PARLORS HE'S BEEN IN, INCLUDING THE ONE NEXT DOOR TO MR. JONES'S APARTMENT. THERE WAS NOTHING SITTING OUT. MR. JONES IS A MINIMALIST. SO, AGAIN IN THE DARK AND INTOXICATED TO AN INCREDIBLE LEVEL, IT WOULD HAVE BEEN EASY FOR JOSEPH TO THINK HE WAS IN THE MASSAGE PARLOR.

SO WHAT DOES THIS MEAN? JOSEPH INTENDED TO CRAWL INTO THE WINDOW OF A MASSAGE PARLOR AND NOT MR. JONES'S APARTMENT. IT MEANS THAT EVEN WHEN HE WAS IN THE APARTMENT BATHROOM, HE STILL THOUGHT HE WAS IN THE MASSAGE PARLOR. IT MEANS HE WAS THERE TO DO WHAT HE DID AT MASSAGE PARLORS: PAY A WOMAN TO HAVE SEX WITH HIM. THAT IS WHY HE GOT THE HUNDRED DOLLARS OUT OF THE ATM MACHINE. THAT IS WHY HE WAS KNOCKING AT THE FRONT DOOR OF THE MASSAGE PARLOR. THAT IS WHY HE WAS MAKING A RACKET OUTSIDE THE FRONT OF THE MASSAGE PARLOR. THESE ARE NOT THE ACTIONS OF A MAN WHO IS TRY-ING TO SNEAK INTO A WOMAN'S APARTMENT TO COMMIT A RAPE.

OF COURSE, NONE OF IT MAKES SENSE. THE WHOLE INCIDENT IS CRAZY. THERE IS NO WAY TO EXPLAIN THE ACTIONS OF JOSEPH THAT NIGHT WITHOUT CON-

CLUDING THAT HE WAS INSANELY INTOXICATED AND IN SOME KIND OF DREAM STATE. I CAN'T TELL YOU WHAT HE WAS THINKING, AND HE CAN'T TELL YOU WHAT HE WAS THINKING. BUT, THE EVIDENCE REVEALS THAT HE DIDN'T TAKE THE ACTIONS OF A RAPIST. HE TOOK THE ACTIONS OF A CRAZED DRUNK, WHO WAS DREAMING THAT HE WAS GOING TO AN ILLICIT MASSAGE PARLOR. WAS HE INTENDING TO HAVE SEX THAT NIGHT? YES, IT APPEARS SO. THAT IS WHY HE GOT THE HUNDRED DOLLARS OUT OF THE ATM. WAS HE INTENDING TO COMMIT A RAPE? NO, THAT IS NOT CONSISTENT WITH THE EVIDENCE.

JOSEPH WAS AN OUT OF CONTROL DRUNK THAT WAS LIVING A LIFE INCONSISTENT WITH HIS OWN MORALS. HE DRANK ALCOHOLICALLY. HE'D ALREADY HAD A SERIOUS DRUNK DRIVING ACCIDENT, IN WHICH HIS FRIEND, WHO WAS A PASSENGER, SUSTAINED SOME MINOR INJURIES, SO HE KNEW THAT IF HE CONTINUED TO DRINK, HE WOULD BE A DANGER TO HIMSELF AND OTHERS. HE ALSO HAD A LONG-TERM SERIOUS PROSTITUTION HABIT. HE SHOULD HAVE CHANGED HIS BEHAVIOR, AND IF HE COULDN'T DO IT ON HIS OWN, HE SHOULD HAVE SOUGHT HELP. HE'S A MEMBER OF THE BAR, FOR GOD'S SAKE. HE SHOULD BE PUNISHED FOR HIS ACTIONS. [PAUSE]

BUT, LADIES AND GENTLEMAN OF THE JURY, HE SHOULD ONLY BE PUNISHED FOR HIS ACTIONS, NOT FOR THE THOUGHTS THAT THE DA THINKS HE HAD. AFTER YOU HEAR ALL THE EVIDENCE, YOU'LL SEE THAT JOSEPH PROBABLY DIDN'T HAVE ANY RATIONAL THOUGHTS, LET ALONE THE SPECIFIC INTENT TO COMMIT RAPE. HE WAS IN WHAT EXPERTS CALL A "FUGUE STATE."

AND IN ORDER TO CONVICT HIM OF ATTEMPTED RAPE

YOU HAVE TO BELIEVE BEYOND A REASONABLE DOUBT THAT JOSEPH ENTERED INTO MR. JONES'S APARTMENT THAT NIGHT WITH THE SPECIFIC INTENT OF COMMITTING A RAPE. THE DA WANTS YOU TO BELIEVE THAT JOSEPH IS A NIGHT-STALKING, VIOLENT RAPIST. BUT THAT DOESN'T MAKE SENSE, AND THE EVIDENCE DOESN'T SUPPORT IT.

WE HAVE NOTHING TO HIDE, AND WE ARE GOING TO TELL YOU THE WHOLE STORY, NOT JUST THE PIECES THAT WORK FOR JOSEPH. THE DA TOLD YOU SOME OF THE FACTS OF WHAT HAPPENED THAT NIGHT, BUT SHE LEFT OUT A LOT OF OTHER FACTS. SHE TOLD YOU THAT MR. JONES SAID THAT JOSEPH SAID HE "THOUGHT THERE WAS A GIRL IN THE APARTMENT." BUT SHE DIDN'T TELL YOU THAT MR. JONES ALSO SAID THAT MR. NAUS SAID, "THIS WOULD NEVER HAPPEN IN HAWAII," A PLACE JOSEPH HAS NEVER BEEN. AND SHE DIDN'T TELL YOU THAT MR. JONES SAID THAT JOSEPH REFERRED TO MR. JONES AND HIS FRIEND, WHILE THEY CONFRONTED JOSEPH IN THE FRONT YARD, AS "BROTHERS" AND MADE SEVERAL REFERENCES TO THEM AS IF THEY WERE IN A "FRATERNITY" TOGETHER. JOSEPH HAS NEVER BEEN IN A FRATERNITY. AND DISTRICT ATTORNEY VILLA ALSO DIDN'T TELL YOU THAT JOSEPH RAMBLED ON ABOUT A "VOLKSWAGEN," A TYPE OF CAR JOSEPH HAS NEVER OWNED AND THAT HAS ABSOLUTELY ZERO RELEVANCE TO ANYTHING THAT WAS HAPPENING. THESE ARE ALL THINGS MR. JONES SAYS JOSEPH SAID. JOSEPH HAS ONLY A SPOTTY, DREAM-LIKE RECALL OF THE ENTIRE EVENT. HE DOESN'T REMEMBER ANYTHING THAT WAS SAID. IN FACT, JOSEPH THOUGHT THAT MR. JONES AND HIS FRIEND WERE ASIANS, PRESUMABLY BECAUSE IN

HIS DREAM-LIKE FUGUE STATE, HE THOUGHT HE WAS IN A MASSAGE PARLOR AND THOUGHT MR. JONES WAS CONNECTED TO THE MASSAGE PARLOR.

AS AMERICANS YOU HAVE ALL HEARD ABOUT A DEFENDANT CHOOSING NOT TO TESTIFY IN HIS OWN CASE, TAKING THE FIFTH. IT IS PART OF OUR RIGHTS UNDER THE UNITED STATES CONSTITUTION. BUT JOSEPH ISN'T GOING TO DO THAT. HE WANTS YOU TO SEE HIM TESTIFY. HE WANTS YOU TO SEE HIM SPEAK, SEE HIS EYES, HEAR WHAT HE HAS TO SAY, SO YOU CAN MAKE THE DETERMINATION YOURSELVES OF WHETHER HE'S TELLING THE TRUTH. YOU WILL MAKE YOUR OWN DETERMINATION OF WHETHER JOSEPH IS A NIGHT-STALKING, VIOLENT RAPIST OR WHETHER HE WAS IN AN ALCOHOL-INDUCED FUGUE STATE THAT NIGHT.

JOSEPH ISN'T HERE TAKING UP YOUR VALUABLE TIME BECAUSE HE'S UNWILLING TO ACCEPT RESPONSIBILITY FOR THE CONSEQUENCES OF HIS ACTIONS. HE HAS, IN FACT, ACCEPTED RESPONSIBILITY FOR THOSE ACTIONS. HE'S HERE BECAUSE THE DA IS GOING MUCH FARTHER THAN THAT. HE'S HERE BECAUSE THE DA INSISTS THAT JOSEPH IS A RAPIST. YOU ARE GOING TO SEE AND HEAR THE EVIDENCE, HEAR FROM EXPERTS AND PEOPLE WHO HAVE KNOWN JOSEPH INTIMATELY FOR MANY YEARS, AND WHEN YOU DO, YOU'LL SEE THAT THE EVIDENCE WILL NOT SUPPORT THE DA'S CASE.

THANK YOU FOR YOUR TIME.

Mark does a good job attacking the DA and setting us up as the side that is going to tell them the whole truth, and also setting up a dichotomy decision for the jury: crazed alcoholic in a blackout or night-stalking rapist. Every piece of testimony from here on out will be steered toward making the jury believe that that is the only issue and that the obvious choice is that I am a blackout alcoholic, not a rapist.

CROSS-EXAMINATION OF DEFENDANT, JOSEPH NAUS:

MS. VILLA: DO YOU THINK YOU WENT TO THE ATM TO GET MONEY TO HIRE A PROSTITUTE AT THE MASSAGE PARLOR?

DEFENDANT: I DON'T KNOW WHAT I WAS THINKING, BUT IF I HAD TO GUESS WHAT THE HUNDRED DOLLARS WAS FOR, I'D SAY THAT IT WAS FOR THAT PURPOSE, YES.

MS. VILLA: IF YOU COULD ANSWER MY YES OR NO QUESTIONS WITH A YES OR NO, I'D APPRECIATE IT.

DEFENDANT: OF COURSE, WHEN I CAN.

MS. VILLA: AND DID YOU HIRE PROSTITUTES OFTEN?

DEFENDANT: YES, MORE SO WHEN I DIDN'T HAVE A GIRLFRIEND.

MS. VILLA: WERE YOU SOBER WHEN YOU DID THIS?

DEFENDANT: ALWAYS, EXCEPT IN VEGAS AND AMSTER-DAM.

This draws a couple wide eyes and awkward light laughter from the jury box.

MS. VILLA: SO, COMPLETELY SOBER YOU SOMETIMES HAVE NO PROBLEM BREAKING THE LAW IN REGARDS TO SEX? IS THAT CORRECT?

DEFENDANT: I GUESS THAT'S CORRECT. I DID GO TO MASSAGE PARLORS AND PAY TO HAVE SEX, WHEN I WAS NOT IN A RELATIONSHIP. I'M NOT PROUD OF IT, BUT I DID DO THAT.

MS. VILLA: SO ON THE NIGHT IN QUESTION, YOU

WENT AND GOT MONEY FROM THE ATM SPECIFICALLY FOR THE PURPOSE OF HIRING A PROSTITUTE, IS THAT CORRECT?

DEFENDANT: I'M NOT SURE WHAT MY STATE OF MIND WAS. I WAS OBVIOUSLY NOT THINKING STRAIGHT.

MS. VILLA: WELL, IF YOU HAD TO ESTIMATE WHAT YOU WERE THINKING?

DEFENDANT: I'D ESTIMATE THAT I WAS IN SOME TYPE OF FUGUE STATE THINKING I WAS GOING TO THE MASSAGE PARLOR TO HAVE SEX.

MS. VILLA: OK, FINE. AND YOU ACTUALLY DID GO TO THE MASSAGE PARLOR AFTER THAT, CORRECT?

DEFENDANT: I DON'T RECALL, BUT I KNOW FROM MR. JONES'S TESTIMONY AND THE POLICE REPORT THAT I WAS AT THE MASSAGE PARLOR.

MS. VILLA: DID YOU HAVE ANY TROUBLE REMEMBERING YOUR PIN AT THE ATM?

DEFENDANT: I DON'T REMEMBER, BUT I DON'T THINK SO, BECAUSE I GOT THE MONEY. ACTUALLY, I DON'T KNOW. MAYBE IT TOOK ME A WHILE. I DON'T REMEMBER BEING AT THE ATM AT ALL.

MS. VILLA: AND YOU WERE NOT SO CRAZED THAT YOU COULDN'T FIGURE OUT HOW TO REMOVE THE SCREEN FROM MR. JONES'S WINDOW, CORRECT?

DEFENDANT: I DON'T RECALL, BUT I BELIEVE THAT IS TRUE BASED ON THE POLICE REPORT.

MS. VILLA: IF IT IS REASONABLE TO ASSUME THAT YOUR PURPOSE OF GOING TO THE ATM MACHINE AND WITHDRAWING MONEY AND THEN GOING TO THE MASSAGE PARLOR TO HIRE A PROSTITUTE WAS TO HAVE SEX, ISN'T IT ALSO A REASONABLE ASSUMPTION THAT ONCE YOU REALIZED THE MASSAGE PARLOR WAS CLOSED YOU

DECIDED TO GO INTO IT ANYWAY AND GET WHAT YOU
CAME FOR?

I wait a beat for Mark to object, but then I realize it's better just to answer.

DEFENDANT: I DON'T KNOW WHAT MY THINKING WAS.
I MEAN, I'VE NEVER BEEN TO A MASSAGE PARLOR AT
NIGHT AND I'VE NEVER BEEN TO ONE DURING THE DAY
AND HAD IT BEEN CLOSED. IF I HAD I . . .

MS. VILLA: OBJECTION. NON-RESPONSIVE. I'D ASK
THAT THE COURT ADMONISH THE WITNESS TO ANSWER
YES OR NO QUESTIONS WITH A YES OR NO ANSWER.

THE COURT: OVERRULED. YOU ASKED THE QUESTION
ABOUT HIS REASONABLE ASSUMPTION. IT IS RESPON-
SIVE. YOU MAY CONTINUE MR. NAUS.

MR. NAUS [CONT.]: I WAS SAYING THAT HAD I GONE
TO A MASSAGE PARLOR SOBER AND IT WAS CLOSED, THE
LAST THING IN THE WORLD I WOULD THINK ABOUT DOING
WAS CLIMBING IN THE WINDOW.

MS. VILLA: WELL, MR. JONES DIDN'T TESTIFY THAT
YOU WOKE HIM UP AND ASKED HIM IF YOU COULD PAY
FOR SEX, IT WAS THAT YOU JUMPED ON TOP OF HIM
NAKED, WITH AN ERECTION, AND ATTACKED HIM, SO
ISN'T IT A REASONABLE ASSUMPTION THAT YOU IN-
TENDED TO USE FORCE TO GET WHAT YOU CAME FOR?

MR. ACKERMAN: OBJECTION YOUR HONOR . . .

"Jesus Christ, Joseph!" Peter says. "You've been out here smoking for
over an hour. You're going all nuts on that pack of cigs."

Peter startles me into the present from my daily recounting of my
trial in my head.

Peter is six-foot-five, 260 pounds, and tattooed from head to toe, so he can be startling. It's 1:30 a.m. I'm in the little chic backyard of his home in Franklin Hills, about five miles from downtown Los Angeles. I met Peter through Bob from rehab, and we've been inseparable since. He said we should surf together. I gave him my number, and I figured he'd never call. But a couple days later, I was sound asleep in my boat in Marina del Rey. The sun wasn't even up, and Peter called me on my cell phone, and he was waiting outside the dock. I tried to get out of it, but he brought an extra board and wetsuit. Next thing I knew, we were surfing El Porto together. Ever since then, we've surfed together, worked out together, and gone to 12-step meetings together. Peter was in a famous punk band but is now a college professor with a PhD in English from Columbia. He's also a recovering junkie and, more recently, a recovering crackhead.

"This is what I always do," I tell Peter. "I come out here and fantasize about the trial in my head—over and over. I know everything that is going to happen, down to how the judge is going to rule on our pre-trial character evidence motion. I could try this case myself."

"Yeah, that's a good idea," Peter says sarcastically. "What's that ... a fool for a client? A client is a fool?" Peter asks as he sits down in the muted copper-colored patio chair and lights up one of my cigarettes.

We sit in silence for a minute, and then a monstrous raccoon appears and straddles the retaining wall eight feet away.

"Oh yeah ...," Peter whispers through his teeth. "He's back."

The raccoon peers at us unblinking while he makes his way toward Peter's koi pond.

"He's going to go *commando*," Peter whispers.

The big raccoon reaches the edge of the pond. Peter carefully lights up another cigarette. There hasn't been a koi fish in that pond since this raccoon slashed and ate the last two, a solid orange one and a white one with orange specks, nearly a week ago. Suddenly, the raccoon smacks the plastic water pump across the pond with his little matte black paw while he stares at us threateningly. The water pump topples over and comes to rest akimbo atop the pond's river-rock edging, sputtering and spurting like it's suffocating. The raccoon coolly retreats to the wall, all the while keeping his eyes trained on us. He stops at the wall, still staring at us menacingly and then disappears with one quick hop.

"That was awesome!" I revel.

"Straight gangster," Peter declares and walks over and fixes the pump and replaces the rocks.

"Don't think we aren't paddling out dawn patrol tomorrow to surf Dos Banos or Malibu Surfrider, just 'cause you're chain-smoking a whole pack of cigarettes and daydreaming about your fucked-up life again."

I chuckle. "Shit ... *Jesus*. Fucking crazy life, right? Sometimes I still can't believe I'm not dreaming ... so, what's the surf supposed to be like?"

"Man vs. nature ... seriously," Peter says.

Man vs. nature is one of Peter's favorite phrases. It means it's going to be stormy and the waves are going to be choppy and big. He sneaks the phrase into non-surf related conversation whenever possible. Same with *prison rules*, which means that the surf spot is crowded, and surfers aren't following the surfers' code of conduct, but instead, just dropping in on waves no matter whether they are in position or not. In a non-surf context, *prison rules* can mean anything from *harshness* to *aggression*, or a response to *How was the traffic? Dude, the 101 North: straight prison rules.* He also likes to quote lines from *Apocalypse Now* and *Full Metal Jacket* in everyday conversation, which I've begun doing, too, because it's contagious.

Peter lights up another cigarette and takes a deep drag.

"So when you go through the trial in your head how does it end?" Peter asks.

I was hoping he wouldn't ask.

"That raccoon is relentless," I say.

"No doubt," Peter responds.

Peter smothers out his third cigarette and gathers himself. "Dawn Patrol, brotha-man. I'll be waking you up shortly, and it's your turn to drive."

"Good-night, Peter," I say.

I put my feet on the table and stare up at the stars. There aren't many to see tonight. It's getting damp, and the koi pond pump gurgles quietly.

SIXTEEN

"I pray, I meditate, I go to a meeting, I talk to a newcomer, and I call my sponsor ... every *fucking* day," Janine A. announces to about forty recovering addicts in a room that comfortably holds twenty-five in the back of the Café Tropical.

"That's how I stay clean," she continues. "Thank God I hit a bottom where I didn't even think about whether it was too much work to stay clean. That's how I did it when I was using. I didn't wake up one day and say, you know, I think today I won't get high. It's too much of a hassle to call my dealer. Shit! I shot dope or smoked crack every fucking day and twice on Christmas. I did whatever it took, no matter if I had to go to jail, beg, I even sold my ass, to get my dope. I did whatever it took. That's what I do in here, whatever it takes to stay clean. *Whatever it takes.* So for you newcomers: look ... you better get busy in here, because while you're resting on your laurels thinking because you are clean for a minute, it's all good, your disease, your addiction is in the corner doing push-ups. That ain't no—"

Janine A. is interrupted by the ringing of an egg timer. It stops after several seconds, and she continues.

"Okay, my time is up, and I want to thank the secretary of this meeting, Lois W., for asking me to share. And remember, *you do your part and God will do the rest.* If we're wrong, we'll refund your misery. I'm Janine, and I'm an addict."

The packed little room jumps and claps and hoots, me included. I believe everything she said. This girl has a powerful energy about her. I don't know if it's God, but she's connected to something. Tattoos crawl from her wrists up her arms and halfway up her long neck. I wonder how she can get a job with tattoos on her neck. I know what she'd say if I asked her, because I've heard it nearly every meeting I've been to, more than one a day for over a year now. She'd say her job is to stay clean and to help another addict get clean and that the rest is up to God. That's what all the 12-steppers say.

Everyone joins hands and prays out with the Serenity Prayer.

I flow with the room out to the sidewalk and corner Janine's boyfriend. "Can I talk to you for a second?" I ask him. He looks like the male version of Janine A., tatted-up, tan and ripped. He wears slim Levi's with a chain wallet and a skin-tight, worn T-shirt. His kind eyes belie his getup.

"Yeah, man," he says, "What's up? I'm Charley." He extends his hand. I awkwardly attempt to shake his hand thumb-up, and he's giving me the much cooler thumb-back. We both try to correct and then re-correct until we get a semblance of a shake, then we both laugh in recognition of the awkwardness.

"I'm Joseph," I say. "Uhm ... I've heard you share at a different meeting. My sponsor from another program recommended I talk to someone that's been to ...," I look to make sure no one is listening, "*prison,* because it looks like I may be going there, and I need to know whether to take this deal or whether to roll the dice at trial."

In any other context this would be terribly awkward.

"I'm sorry to hear that, man. What are you looking at?" Charley asks.

He nods to Janine A., who is floating in the background, and then I follow him into the café. We sit at a small wood table.

"The offer is a ninety-day evaluation with a two-year lid. You know what that means?"

"Oh, yeah," he smirks and nods.

"Yeah, and uhm ... so I take the ninety-day evaluation with the two-year lid depending on whether the judge wants to let me go or not after the ninety-days, or I roll the dice at trial and get two years at the very minimum and possibly twenty years if I'm convicted on all the other charges."

"Wait. Two years minimum?" he asks surprised. "You get two years if you *win* at trial and *twenty* if you lose?"

"Yeah, it's a long story, but basically one of the charges I have no defense against, and there is virtually zero chance of not getting convicted on that one … criminal threats."

"Fuck. *Criminal threats*, terrorist threats, it's such a bullshit count," Charley responds, as if he has some personal experience. "Well, sounds like a no-brainer. Why wouldn't you take the deal if you are looking at twenty?"

I pause. I have a feeling that not only is it okay to tell him but that I should tell him. I go with it. I tell him the story in brief, and I tell him about the sex charges.

Charley takes it all in for a moment.

"*Fuckin' A.,*" he says. "That's a tough one. You need …"

Janine walks up and presses her hip up against Charley's cheek. He wraps his arm around her waist.

Charley introduces us.

I shake her hand.

"You were amazing," I say. "Thanks for your share." I realize I said that with way too much enthusiasm.

"Thank you," she responds. "I'm just trying to be a channel for God."

I can't believe she says that so matter-of-factly. I think she actually may be a channel for God, whatever that means.

"Are you in the Program?" Janine asks.

"The other—I mean—another program," I answer.

"Well, then you are in this one, too. You know what we say: Alcohol is a drug. *Period.*"

"You ain't kidding," Charley says. "Babe, give us a couple minutes, and then we'll get out of here." Janine smiles at me and kisses the crown of Charley's head and walks off.

"She's amazing," I tell Charley. "I mean . . . she's like ... like really, really tapped in. She makes me want to believe in God. You know?"

"She is. She's *all God*, all the time," he says, as if he's a little tired of the subject. "So, look. This is your decision, and your sponsor is right when he tells you to talk to people to get info to make this decision. You've talked to your lawyer, your sponsor, and other people. I'm just one of those people, but I've been there. You're going to Chino for the ninety, but you may go somewhere worse if you do *real* time. Like Calipatria, Folsom, or fucking Corcoran. *Chino ain't no joke.* It's like County. You'll be in Central Processing. Shit is *fucking crazy* in there. Everyone is going somewhere else for a long time, so they don't give a fuck."

"I just want to know if I can survive," I interject.

Charley takes a swig of coffee and stares up at the ceiling as if the answer is up there.

"Yeah. Of course. Here is the thing. In order to survive a long stint, you'll have to change. I mean ...," Charley struggles to find the words to say what he means. His face twists up as if remembering something scary. "You'll have to do things and become *so* fucking like ... hard, *hard*, you know ... that it's tough to get back to you. You feel me?"

"Kind of. Not exactly?" I respond.

"Look, you *can* survive. You're a big, white guy. You'll saddle up with the Woods. That means white guys. Maybe even have to hang with the Nazis. But what does survive *mean*? You physically *survive*, but emotionally and mentally, it'll scar you. It's like going to war or something."

"You mean like getting stabbed or prison raped or something?" I ask.

"You probably won't ..." Charley stops when he sees my eyes bulge in response to the word *probably*.

"You aren't going to get raped or stabbed, unless you are fucking around. You know, getting involved in race-shit or drugs. But you can't be in there for five years ... shit, *two years* ... without getting caught up in *something*. You'll eventually do something, because otherwise you are just not living, and you'll go crazy, and you'll be willing to risk something just to be living, and then you get in a situation. Some bullshit drama, and bullshit drama can get you killed or punked-out. I'm too ugly to get punked out, but you're kind of pretty ..."

I'm terrified. I feel sick.

"Shit happens in there," Charley continues. He pulls up his shirt and runs his index finger across an eight-inch, raised scar that intersects his striated, abdominal muscles. His cell phone vibrates on the table. He picks it up and turns around. Janine is a few tables back calling. His back is to her, but I'm looking at her calling him. She winks at me as if we are in on a prank.

"I got to go," Charley says. "Look, man, if it's me, I'm doing *whatever it fucking takes* to be anywhere but in prison. Pleading to a sex crime— that's some fucked up shit. *Really fucked up. You'll be a registered sex offender for life.* Jesus Christ. It's fucked up. But doing a stint in prison, especially a guy that looks like you—used to be a fucking lawyer, on a *sex case*—that's even more fucked up, be-lieve that, brother. I mean, that's a fucking ride you don't want to get on."

He stands up and drains the last of his little Cuban coffee. I try to stand with him but my legs won't let me.

"Oh, one more thing: If you take the ninety-day eval deal, when you go in to Chino, whatever happens, you make up a story about being in protective custody. You don't tell nobody you are in on a sex crime. *Nobody.* You'll be in protective custody, PC'd-up for sure. You are a lawyer. Should be easy to make something up." He squeezes my shoulders together. "Don't you ever admit to having an R on your jacket ..."

"An R?" I ask.

"You know," Charley explains, "R, R for rape ... being in for a sex crime. Don't matter whether it's stat rape or what, you're a child molester as far as they are concerned. You tell them you are PC because you're an attorney. Don't ever back off that."

I nod and swallow hard. I must look pathetic because Charley comes around the table and lifts me up and gives a big hug.

"You stay strong. Just like Janine said, chop wood, carry water and let God take care of the rest. It's gonna be hard, but you be a'ight."

Nearly every night for the last two months I've followed the same routine. I go to a recovery meeting in Silverlake, and then I stop by the 7-Eleven on Hyperion for Marlboro Red 100s and a giant coffee with vanilla creamer and sugar. It's the best I can do. As every night before, Hal stands out front of the 7-Eleven. He doesn't have to pitch to me. I give him money every night. He's a huge, bearded, homeless guy. We talk for a couple minutes after I come out and hand over a dollar and some change. I'm completely honest with Hal, kind of like I was with Dr. Kincaid, but I can't afford her anymore. All she did was repeat the things I hear every day in recovery meetings anyway. I *am* grateful she confronted me about going to massage parlors. I haven't been to one in three months now. She was right. I had to treat it like alcohol. I get cravings occasionally, especially when I'm driving, but I pray or meditate or go to a meeting and it goes away. So far, so good.

Hal is appealing a denied disability claim, and that is all he wants to talk about. After I hand him his change, he mumbles *thanks*, a little softer if there are no bills involved. Things have evolved between Hal and me. Now, I actually have enough time to smoke an entire cigarette while we talk. He seamlessly talks to me, while begging for money from customers as they enter and exit the store. His little trick is that, when someone says, *No, I don't have any change,* he responds, *So, can I have your change after you buy something?* I'm always surprised at how well this works. It worked on me. It's like he's catching them in their little lie, and they aren't willing to admit that they were making an excuse. So, on their way out, he acts as if to say, *But I thought we had a deal that I was going to get your change? You promised.*

"How's things?" I ask Hal, while trying to find a place to set my coffee other than the ground. Hal holds it for me while I light my cigarette.

"Fucking disability pricks. Lawyer won't call me back. Press all these fucking buttons. Press one, press two. Leave a message that no one ever hears. America. I'm disabled, and they won't give me what's due. You do disability? No, you already told me. You do criminal. No, no, no. First hearing. I didn't have a lawyer, railroaded."

"I don't do criminal," I say. "I am a criminal, Hal, remember?"

"Yeah," Hal interrupts. "I live with three other guys and have to do this to make money. This appeal is going to change all..." Hal steps away and walks to the door with his hat out toward a customer exiting. He walks back, as he inspects the coins in his hat and continues, "I live with other people. It's terrible. The appeal is going to change all that. They can't deny me the right. I'm disabled."

I cut in, "I think I may have to go to prison for at least three months, maybe a couple years. And, I take the plea bargain, either way, when I come out I'll be a registered sex offender for life. Monday, the Bar finally sent me a letter saying I am officially disbarred as of tomorrow. I spent a lot of time and money on that law degree and passing the Bar ... You been to jail, Hal?"

"Nah, nope, not me. Do you do disability appeals? I was denied. My claim was denied, but I didn't have a lawyer. Should have had a lawyer. I am disabled mentally. Can't work."

"Alright, Hal. Well, I might not see you again if I decide to ... *go to prison.* Good luck with that disability appeal."

"Okay. Thanks. I'm gonna get a lawyer for the appeal. Can you spare some change?"

I figure why bother explaining that I already gave him money. I open my wallet and give him another couple dollars. "Here you go." I open my car and look at Hal in the glow of the 7-Eleven window. He smiles at me.

"Joseph!" he yells, "Don't drop the soap!"

I drive down Sunset back to my apartment in Silverlake. I rented it after Peter's wife moved back into their house after another stint in rehab. For a moment, long enough to sign a month-to-month lease, I'd convinced myself that if I just kept doing what I was doing and living clean, everything would work out, and I wouldn't have to go to jail or prison.

I keep thinking: *Don't drop the soap. Don't drop the soap.* I wonder if I'll be raped in prison. I can't believe I'm thinking this. I can't believe anything. I can't believe this is me, that I just lost my Bar license, that I don't get to drink anymore, that I don't get to fuck prostitutes anymore, that I'm likely going to prison. Wait a second. *Likely?* You aren't *likely* going to prison, Joseph. You *are* going to prison. It's just a matter of how long: three months, two years, or twenty years.

Don't drop the soap. Yes, losing my Bar license, losing all my money, losing my business, going through two years of hell, spending time in jail and prison, becoming a two-strike felon, and having to register as a sex offender for the rest of my life is plenty in exchange for my misdeeds. I think being prison-raped might be a little much.

I drive down Sunset, getting caught at every light, operating in a trance. Then, with absolute certainty, as if from the mouth of God, it comes to me: *I'm taking the deal.* I simply can't allow for the possibility that a jury will find me guilty and put me away for two decades. It's just too high a risk. I've already talked it over with Vinny, Keri, and Mark so many times, and there is nothing left to talk about. It's done. I'm taking the deal. I'm going to prison. I'm at the stop light at Benton on Sunset in Silverlake. The giant podiatry office *happy foot-sad foot* sign slowly turns in the sky. I stare at it as it slowly rotates from the *sad foot* to the *happy foot* and back to the *sad foot* until the driver behind me honks.

❖   ❖   ❖

Caroline is waiting for me at my apartment. She sits on the stoop in front of my apartment smoking.

"Darling!" she shouts.

Normally, I'd tell her to be quiet. It is 11:30 at night. Tonight I don't care. Wake everybody up. *Fuck 'em.* We go to the backyard and talk. Caroline still drinks, copiously. She's brought a couple bottles of wine. After a bit of a panic, she finds a corkscrew and uncorks her first bottle.

"You don't mind?" she asks even though she doesn't care if I mind because nothing could stop her from drinking both of these bottles tonight. We smoke. She drinks. Neither of us wants to talk about the present so we talk about the good times in the past. We jump from island to island, carefully avoiding the sea of pain in between. It's hard. There isn't much there. Even the good days usually ended, at best, in some drunken stupor. There wasn't much purity in our history. I wonder if things had been different would I have given her another chance. By the time she opens the second bottle, she's forgotten I don't drink. That makes it easier to talk her out of the necessity of my going out for another bottle, since she won't have to share this one. Her mouth tastes deliciously of wine and cigarettes. I dip my finger in her glass and rub it on her. I taste her while she sits on a chair smoking. There is just a hint of red wine. She squirms deliciously.

After a couple proper good-byes, I watch her drive off in her sugar daddy's Mercedes SUV. I know it's not possible, but I wish we could have another chance at saving each other.

I wake up late and head out to Marina del Rey to say good-bye to my blue sailboat. I know the proper thing to do is to sail it out a mile with my surfboard on deck, sink it, and paddle back. But, I have no idea how to sail it, and the motor is shot, thanks to Todd's tweeker tinkering, so it'll sit here until the harbormaster auctions it off. There is nothing on the boat to salvage, except my half-read copy of *Moby Dick.* There was a fine collection of porn DVDs that I used to watch on the cabin's TV, but I made them walk the plank, after my last session with Dr. Kincaid on going to massage parlors.

Larisa's car, her dad's old white BMW, is parked in my spot next to the dock gate. She steps out of her car and walks around when she sees me pull up. She playfully bumps her hips once to the right and then into the left, showing off her little jean skirt that I bought her a couple years ago.

"You like?" she asks.

"You know I do."

She jumps onto me and wraps her legs around my hips. She kisses me, and I try not to fall and drop my giant Starbucks' coffee. She's so playful and vivacious. She loves to be handled. Everything about her is thick and strong, from her lips to her feet.

"Speck!" I shout her nickname playfully.

"My poor little Joseph," she says, "I can't believe this is happening. I thought Keri would work it out—or something." Larisa pouts her lips.

"I know, I know," I respond. "Keri and Mark did their best. It's the best deal I could get."

I set her down and walk her across the dock to the boat. We hold hands. I wonder how I could have been so cruel to her. She can be so lovely. The cabin is hot and dark. We make love like we're wrestling. I get on top of her, and then she regains control and pins me down. I regain position. There is always tension in our sex. After nearly an hour bouncing around the cabin, her skin is slick with sweat. She's white and taut. The orange light through the red cabin curtains soften the flexed striations in her upper back and the deep spinal gully just above her ass. Larisa clenches up on me like a vice. She's so strong. I retaliate. We collapse.

"Goddamn, Larisa," I say, exhausted.

I sit up on the cabin's bed. Larisa slides her head onto my lap.

I push a sweaty swath of hair off her forehead. I think, if I'd just stayed with her and been a man and gotten some help, gotten my shit together, I wouldn't be going to prison, and she would still look at me like she was madly in love with me.

Larisa snuggles in to me tighter; she peers up at me with those big, dark blue eyes.

❖   ❖   ❖

I walk up the stairs to the office. I always come in from the back, but today I missed the off-ramp, daydreaming about a modern, Joseph-centered version of *Cool Hand Luke*. The result is that I have to pass by the front of the building to get to the back parking lot, and I see our sign—blue lettering on white—*Law Offices of Yi & Naus*. We rented this space from the father of a guy I went to rehab with, a nice old man who loves to tell stories about when he and his wife first moved to Malibu. After the office remodeling was complete—adding a wall for the waiting room and moving another wall to lengthen the conference room—he handed me two keys, one for Will and one for me. He told me not to let his son in the office. *I love my son*, he said, *but the drinking and the drugs ... once it starts, he's not to be trusted.*

Our suite number is 108. Will insisted the original number be changed to end in eight, because eight is a lucky number in Chinese numerology.

The door is locked. I'm not surprised Will isn't here on my last day. I wouldn't want to be here either. He probably gave our secretary the day off, too. And Todd, who I hired against my better judgment, only shows up sporadically. So, it's just me today. I do wish Will's Boxers, Athena and Zeus, were here, so I could play with them in my office one last time. The entryway is full of the decorative, Chinese, ornate furniture Will's parents bought us when we moved in. I wonder if Will, like Caroline and Larisa, thought this day wouldn't come, that Keri and

Mark would save me. Probably not, for Will, to his credit as a lawyer, is a pragmatist.

I love this copy machine. We bought it from a guy in Arizona that purchased post-lease copiers from hospitals. We own it outright. We were about to pull the trigger on a new one that would have cost us four hundred dollars a month, but then we found this one, and the guy delivered it to us for twelve hundred dollars. It does everything: collate, color copies, staple, and print from our network. It even prints envelopes and labels. I remember when the guy got here to deliver it. He said he didn't know we were upstairs, even though we told him a dozen times. He dropped it off and left. We didn't know what to do. We were going to rent a stairs dolly, something I didn't even know existed, and then we decided to hire two day laborers from the parking lot of Home Depot. It took the four of us to get that beast up to the office, one stair at a time. Every time I used this copy machine I think, *we made it.* This is the type of copy machine real lawyers with real law offices have.

The closet in the entry has our phone system. We bought a full phone system with five lines, plus a fax line. It's deluxe, and we own it outright. One of Will's friend's dad worked for AT&T and did our system on the side. I couldn't believe how much of an ordeal it was, but once it was done, we had a serious system. The closet also houses our computer network. Will is a one-man IT department. He had everything on a system. We could even access all our computer files off-site with a laptop.

I found the conference room table at a used office furniture store. It wasn't anything like the mahogany monstrosities that Tito had or that we had at Thomas & Colbert, but it did the trick. I found a deal on eight black leather chairs at an office furniture store. We also have a nice teleconference unit that sits in the middle of the table. The white and black toy robot my mom bought me the Christmas after I was arrested sits on the table next to its matching remote. If Athena and Zeus were here, I'd shut the door and put the robot on the ground and play with them until Will made me stop, like I used to do when I couldn't handle doing anything productive. The robot would walk, and they'd go nuts, scrambling around it. I'd stop it. Then they'd get up the nerve to approach it, carefully sniffing it. Then, right when one, usually Zeus, got its nose right close, I'd press the button and activate the robot's arm. They'd bark and bark, back off, and swarm again. I'd hush them and then start all over again until Will came in and broke it up.

I shut the door on the conference room I'll probably never see again. My office is clear. I put away all the files last time I was in. It's weird. Law practice never ends, and yet mine is ending. Everything I needed to take to storage is in boxes next to the wall. My Pepperdine Law diploma, with the colorful drawing of the campus overlooking the Pacific, rests sideways against the cabinet, so the line where the sea and sky come together is vertical. There is my California Bar License with the Supreme Court of California emblem, my name in Old English, my plaque from Cal State, the Annual Campbell Writing Competition on Law and Morality, and then my favorite, the little dark wood plaque from Pepperdine, given when Keri and I won the Dalsimer Moot Court Competition. It's scratched across the first letter of my name, because I'd carried Keri's plaque around facing mine and the tiny little screws that hold the plate to the wood on her plaque scratched mine. Hers went unblemished. *If it's a metaphor*, I contemplate for a moment, *it's a little too on the nose.*

These plaques are the same ones I hung on the wall of my office at Lanny's, Thomas & Colbert, VSB, and now Yi & Naus. I sit at my desk and read the letter from the Bar one more time. *As of February 20, you are no longer permitted to practice law in the State of California. Your license to practice law in the State of California is suspended.*

Will and I have already notified the important clients and sent out the mandatory letters notifying all our clients that I was no longer with the firm and that Will would be handling all their matters. Technically, it wasn't necessary, because everyone was under retainer with Yi & Naus, not me or Will personally, but we did it out of an abundance of caution. I wrote a joke letter that I decided not to show Will that I think at least a couple of my clients would have appreciated: *Due to an unsuccessful rape, burglary, murder, assault, and successful prosecution of the aforesaid "alleged" crimes, your attorney, Mr. Joseph Naus, will be attending Chino Men's Prison for an unspecified time period. Therefore, and due to the State Bar's surprisingly strong opinion on such matters, Mr. Naus will not be available to handle your cases for—forever. Furthermore, Mr. Naus will now and forever more be a registered sex offender, so you, your family, and anyone else you know or might know in the future would be well advised to disassociate with him . . . forever. We cannot overemphasize the word "forever" in this correspondence. Sincerely, your attorneys, Yi & Naus.*

It only takes two trips to my car to carry out what is left of my career, a couple banker's boxes and a few plaques. I find myself standing in the hall, face to face with the suite number on our door: 108. Reyes Mortgage Broker's office across the hall is buzzing with business. I hold an envelope containing my office keys. I slide it under the door. That makes it official. It's no longer my office. I'm not a lawyer anymore, and I'll probably never be a lawyer again.

I have that heavy feeling in my chest, like I'm going to cry, and if I don't I'm going to explode, but I know I can't cry. *I never cry.*

My car heads south to the 10 Freeway when it should be going north to the 210 Freeway. This means I'm going to Francisquito Avenue.

The big, green, freeway sign reads, *Francisquito 3 Miles.*

In my mind I hear Dr. Kincaid.

I thought I could stop for good, but now I don't know because my car is in control.

For a moment I think I'll find the strength to drive right past the off-ramp, but then I think of the letter from the State Bar, of sliding my key to *my* law firm under the door, of the fact that I'll probably never practice law again. My car exits Francisquito Avenue. I'm watching me as I drive past the Taco Bell, past the long cinder block wall with the graffiti, into the drug store parking lot. People walk in and out of the automatic doors. I have to stop. I can feel my heart beat, and my breathing is quick as I walk into the drug store to use the ATM. I can already smell the baby oil. April or maybe Sunny will dim the lights and go get a condom. I've withdrawn a hundred dollars like this so many times before. I sit in my car with my hundred dollars, and I can see the red and blue neon sign, *Oriental Massage* in my rearview mirror. *Don't start the car. Figure out a way not to do this. Please, God, help me.*

I close my eyes and take deep breaths. The ring of my phone startles me. I hate the sound of my phone. It's Will.

"Hey, man," he says, "you leave yet?"

"Yeah," I answer.

"You okay?" Will asks.

"I'm okay," I say. "You know ... I put the key back in an envelope ... just under the door." I speak slowly and carefully, as I watch a man in my rearview mirror walk into the front door of the massage parlor. Cars cross the street and block my view intermittently, but I know that walk. That's me. That guy just wants to get in the door as inconspicuously as possible so he can get his fix and get out of there.

"You sound distracted," Will says.

"You know, I'm good, relatively speaking ..." I start the car and back out quickly. "Hold on," I tell Will. I set the phone down so I can turn right on Francisquito and flip a U-turn to head back north. I pick up the phone and look at the tinted glass front of the massage parlor. "Sorry, had to pull a traffic maneuver. I'm glad you called, man."

"Where you at?" Will asks.

"Near the 10, headed back to Silverlake. I'll be staying with different people until I go in, but I'll have my cell right up until they slap the cuffs on."

"Alrighty champ ... I uh ... I ..."

"Thanks for calling, dude." I interrupt. I feel emotion coming up through my throat and into my head. I clamp down tight, choke it out. Will doesn't need to deal with this. No need to make Will think of something to say to his prison-bound law partner. There is nothing left to say. He did all his talking by standing by me over the last eighteen months since my arrest.

"I'll be talking to you, Will. Take care of my clients, man." I hang up. I'm back on the freeway, Francisquito Avenue behind me.

❖   ❖   ❖

I'm in jeans and a white T-shirt. Keri told me to wear clothes I can abandon. It feels wrong being in a courthouse dressed like this. The law hates me, but I still respect it. We are stuffed in the elevator with the stiff DAs and thick cops and ponytailed defense attorneys in brassy outlet suits. They don't talk freely as usual. Without my suit to fool them, they know I'm a criminal.

"Good luck, Mr. Naus. I don't envy you," Judge Von Silkman says. "Where you are going—it's a *horrible* place. Good luck. May God be with you." The judge's demeanor is as solemn as his words. I stand, and the bailiff leads me to the door to the rat matrix. I stand facing the door as he pats me down. I look back over my shoulder at Keri while the bailiff cuffs me. She has her lawyer mask on. Her eyes are vacant, like when she told me I was charged with attempted murder when I was first arrested. I wait for her to mouth something. She just stares at me and anxiously chews her bottom lip, while gathering papers into her attaché case. There is nothing to say. I smile at her. The bailiff handcuffs me and takes me away.

This is really happening.

SEVENTEEN

The bailiff opens the cell door, closes it behind me, and uncuffs me through a slot welded into the horizontal bars. The two men in the cell go silent and eye me. I sit across from them on a built-in steel bench. I look away. My hair is cut short, and I'm wearing my tortoise-shell glasses. In preparation for my stay, Peter and I have been surfing nearly every day and lifting heavy and hard for the last six months, so I'm as big and thick as I've ever been, about 220 pounds, all muscle. My appearance is part of my survival plan. I want any would-be attackers to look at my bespectacled face and see that I am a geeky anomaly and pose no threat. Then, in case they are still thinking about it, I want them to look at my body and decide to move on and find an easier target.

In here, I'm going the way of Kwai Chang Caine of TV's "Kung Fu", Channel Five. I know this is naïve, but it's all I got. *My favorite.* My mom was usually dead asleep on the green, plastic, foldout couch in the Alley apartment, while I watched the opening credits for the hundredth time. It's a montage of Caine, the main character, an ass-kicking, pacifist, Chinese monk, training in martial arts from childhood through young adulthood. At the end of the montage, Caine snatches the pebble from the hand of his master, meaning it's time for him to take his kung fu skills into the Old West to look for his long lost brother. Before he leaves, he picks up a cauldron of hot coals with his inner forearms, branding himself with Shaolin dragon symbols. Caine's a bad ass, but he never fights unless he has to. In here, I'm Caine, although I hope I can avoid fighting better than Caine does, because he beats up a few racist cowboys every episode.

"What are you in for?" one of the prisoners asks.

My ears heat up like the guts of a toaster. I wonder if it was a good idea to call Charley from Narcotics Anonymous, after we spoke at Café Tropical that day. Everything he said scared the hell out of me. "I don't care how badass you are," he said, "you can't beat down six Mexicans with shanks." *Six Mexicans with Shanks.* I told Peter what Charley said. Peter said that would be a great name for a punk band.

What are you in for? The voice's owner is a portly, white man with long, thick sideburns. He's not dressed as if he turned himself in. He wears jean shorts and man-sandals.

My thoughts are coming in like Chinese throwing stars. External time has slowed. It's strange. I'm having full conversations with myself in the space between a question and answer.

"Assault and Terrorist Threats," I respond deadpan.

I decided to answer this question with *Assault and Terrorist Threats* a couple weeks ago. Keri told me that Criminal Threats used to be called Terrorist Threats pre-9/11. It sounds scarier. Better to be a domestic terrorist than a rapist. That's what I am, a terrorist. I'm here because I terrorized someone. I picture myself with a bomb vest running into a liquor store. *I'm going to need a bottle of Jack Daniels, a liter of Coke, Marlboro Red 100s, all your porn, uh ... some matches ... and some ice ... yeah ice, good ice, the kind with the nice little square cubes, or I'm blowing this whole place up!*

"Then why you PC?" the other inmate asks.

He's a wiry, short man with long, dark, scraggly hair and dark skin. He wears the standard, safety-orange, LA County Jail prisoner's uniform.

"Because I'm a lawyer," I respond so quickly I clip the end of his question. I don't want to sound argumentative, so I clarify. "My lawyer said my time would be easier if I'm put in protective custody, and I technically qualify for it, because I've handled a few criminal cases."

The wiry guy that just asked me the question stands up, and shakes the bars and shouts, "This motherfucker is about to pop off, big time!" He has a teardrop tattoo under his left eye.

The portly man with the man-sandals gets up and sits next to me.

"So you're a lawyer," he asks softly, not to interrupt the other inmate who is now quite agitated. "I'm Leonard," he says. He's hairy, pale, and somehow doughy and skinny at the same time.

"I'm Joseph. I was a lawyer for several years until ..."

"So you know the law, right?" Leonard interrupts excitedly.

"Kind of," I answer hesitantly. "Actually, not really. I mostly did civil, real estate, and PI, and things like that."

"Fucking riot is going down!" the apparently-crazy inmate with the teardrop tattoo yells out the bars and turns to Leonard and me and screeches, "It's going down! I'm high-powered. These *motherfuckers* don't know the shit I know. You know Dee, 18th Street and Serranos. I'm brokering a deal, but if I can't get them to come together ... You got to pick a side, *man!*"

Leonard nods in response. I follow his lead and nod slightly.

"You in?" Teardrop asks Leonard menacingly.

Leonard nods with appeasing enthusiasm.

"My old lady is out on the streets taking care of my shit," Teardrop says. "I got businesses and cars. She could just bring cash and bail me out, but I'm fighting this shit from the inside out ... *the inside out man.*"

Leonard and I feign interest. Teardrop must be satisfied that we understand the severity of the situation, because he goes back to the bench and lies down.

"So listen to this," Leonard continues quietly, "I'm just walking down the street in the alley off Montana Avenue, nice neighborhood, *right?*, and these girls are taking off their clothes changing, and I can see them over the gate from the alley."

I nod. It feels like the many times I've been cornered at a party by someone who goes wide-eyed when they find out I'm an attorney. They think I'm going to tell them how to fight their parking ticket, after a twenty-minute diatribe on how the parking sign was too confusing.

"One of the girls has white panties on and ... so a neighbor saw me, and then came out and yelled at me something about Neighborhood Watch. There are signs, you know, Neighborhood Watch signs, but I'm not breaking any law, right? I'm on public property. If they want to be naked with their blinds open, what do they expect? Not against the law, right?"

"I guess not," I shrug.

I think about a case, maybe I read it when I was in law school, where a guy was in trouble for being naked in his house with the curtains open. I can't remember the legal issue.

"I walk around that area because it's not far from my house," Leonard repeats.

"Oh, you were just taking a walk?" I say.

"Yeah, well, actually, I drive my van over there and then walk around."

I forget myself for a second and almost laugh. *He's got a rape van. Classic.*

"Oh, okay," I respond.

"I look. Wouldn't you? These beautiful naked girls. They *want* to be seen. So the guy calls the cops and tells them I'm trespassing, but I'm not trespassing. I'm on public property, right?"

"Right, yeah, yeah, of course," I respond. "So what happened?"

"Nothing they could do," he says proudly, "because I wasn't trespassing, but the cops called my parole officer, and he did a search of my apartment."

"And?" I ask.

"Nothing. I didn't have nothing. Except I had some nudist camp magazines. You know the one's you get? They're all about nature and camping and stuff, and there are some pictures of—*you know*—families, and some of the families have kids. So what, right? I didn't even look at them. I just had them. You know those camping magazines?" Leonard looks at me for an answer.

"I uh ... I don't camp, not into camping, not really, mostly vacation in—"

"Well, they are common," he says a tad defensively.

"You guys *down for yours* if the fucking shit pops off?" Teardrop yells at us.

"Yeah, for sure," Leonard says to appease him. I nod along.

The bailiff brings in a skinny, moustached, white man with khaki shorts and bright white tennis shoes. He's outraged and is shotgunning his story at us before the bailiff can get the cuffs off. Nick holds nothing back. He's from Phoenix, married, has a baby daughter, works in computer software sales—*real good commissions*, he tells us. For the last several months, he's been e-mailing and instant-messaging a Mexican mom who is interested in having her two daughters, eight and ten, *taught the ropes*. I'm shocked he's telling us this, completely without shame. He says the e-mails have been going back and forth for several months. They write about what and how he will teach the woman's daughters and the *expenses* he will *cover*. Finally, it was agreed that she would meet him at a Starbucks in Culver City, then take him to her house and *introduce* him to her girls. He takes the day off from work, drives from Phoenix to LA to meet her at 8:00 a.m. He gets to the Starbucks. She meets him. She's an undercover cop. She gives the signal, after he says enough incriminating shit, and cops swarm Starbucks and arrest him. They search his car.

"All they found was some dildos, lube, videos ... condoms, some straps. Nothing illegal! This is bullshit!" he says and raises his voice for show, as if the bailiff is going to hear him and relay the warning to the judge. "I have to get back to work. If I lose my job they are looking at a lawsuit *big time*."

He has no idea how fucked he is, I think.

"They got no grounds to arrest." he continues, "They didn't find any-thing in my car that was illegal. The judge will have to let me go. How can I be convicted of committing a crime that was impossible? There were no girls! They don't exist. I can't get busted for having sex with girls that aren't there."

"He's a lawyer," Leonard says, points to me, and asks, "What do you think?"

Ken turns to me with bulging eyes.

Great.

"I don't know, man. Wish I could help, but not my specialty," I re-spond semi-apologetically.

I want to tell him he should have been indicted on pedophilia-re-lated charges on his moustache alone, but I shrug my shoulders and feign ignorance. Truth is, I know Nick is going down. One of the cases I reviewed in helping Keri prepare my motion—where we argued impos-sibility as a defense to attempted rape—was the *exact* same facts as what Nick just described. Ruling: Factual impossibility is not a defense to an attempt crime. The sting operation in the case I read even occurred at a Starbucks in LA. I'd bet a chunk of change Nick was arrested in a con-tinuation of the same sting operation, probably the same cops.

Busted for attempted molestation at a Starbucks. Damn.

Starbucks. Starbucks. It's only been two hours since my last large, dark roast, drip coffee with half & half, a cigarette, several actually, and four packets of sugar. I'm probably going to have some intense caffeine head-aches coupled with nicotine withdrawal over the next week. I may get some coffee in here, but it won't be enough. It'll be like when I used to go to dinner parties and was offered wine with dinner. I'd rather not drink at all than drink one glass of wine. More than once I remember being asked, "Oh, you don't drink?" *Give me that fucking bottle, I'll show you who doesn't drink.*

I'm going to be without cigarettes and coffee for three months! I hadn't even thought of this. I feel a little wave of panic roll through my stomach. I haven't been without coffee and cigarettes in ten years.

A couple quieter hours go by in our holding cell. We listen to the hollow, violent sounds emanating from the other cells.

Finally, movement: Leonard and I are shackled together and led by a bailiff through the cement, windowless corridors of the LAX Courthouse. Other than the memory that I entered the LAX Courthouse a few hours ago, there is no evidence I am here now. Civility, natural light, and humanness have all been eliminated. The bailiffs order us into a brushed, stainless steel elevator facing the rear. We descend below ground and land in a large, hollow room, filled with the noise of running buses, and hoots and hollers from the regular inmates, mostly blacks and Mexicans. There are nearly a hundred inmates. Leonard and I and Nick and Teardrop are PC, so we're shackled together, sequestered, and made to face the wall away from the other inmates, but I haven't quite caught on and stand facing out, looking over the sea of orange-uniformed inmates. It's raucous and bizarre, and I'm awestruck. Leonard yanks our arm shackles to get my attention.

He whispers, "Face the wall, man." He's a beat too late. One of the hulking deputies catches me unknowing. He steps toward me and yells with palpable malice.

"Get your fucking nose against the wall!"

I can feel my solar plexus against my spine, and all my nerves reach outward, as the guard marches toward me. He wears black Easton baseball gloves, which seem to be moving toward me faster than he is. I know better than to look him in the eye. All I can see is his massive, khaki-uniformed figure and those black baseball gloves. I try to move into the requisite position before he reaches me. My nose is touching the wall, when he places one hand on my shackled wrists and the other on the back of my head. For a moment, he seems to be contemplating the idea of crushing my nose against the cinder-block wall but then thinks better and shoves my wrists forward against my lower back, forcing my whole body against the wall, so that that I have to turn my head sideways. My left cheek is flat against the wall, and I'm looking at Leonard. My cuffs *click-click* tighter. I feel sharp pain shooting from the knobby bones in my wrists to the tops of my forearms. I hold my breath.

"Pay ... *the fuck* ... attention," the deputy says angrily.

My hands tingle and begin to numb.

Several silver buses with barred, tinted windows and green, Los Angeles Sheriff's logos idle in the dark underground parking garages, just outside the landing area. The cement is glossy, and the air smells of diesel fuel. Leonard and I, followed by Nick and Teardrop are led onto the bus first and directed to sit in the front, caged section. My left arm is pulled tightly behind my back. My hands are numbing rapidly. Inmates board the bus and pass us single file. Some are emboldened and yappy, most seem comfortable. They all look at us. I can feel their stares. I try to ignore them.

"They put us at the front of the bus 'cause we're PC," Leonard whispers. "They are flagging you. They don't care if you are in for stat rape, or because you are testifying in some big case. They'll assume you're a snitch or a chester."

Leonard bends down between the seats, so his cheeks are lodged between his knees.

"You have to make sure the pigs don't put you in general pop. Don't be shy about it," Leonard says. "You just go up to them and say, *I'm PC. Please don't put me in there. I'm afraid for my life.* And make sure you look at their badge and say their name so they know you know their name. Say, *Officer Whatever-his-name-is, I'm PC. Please don't put me in there. I'm afraid for my life.* Say that exactly ... Don't piss a guard off, either. They think we're pieces of shit already. They have more respect for someone who just murdered a family. If you get some pig that doesn't like you, he'll set you up and leave you in some cell with a bunch of niggers or spicks, whose biggest thrill in life is fucking up some PC. If that happens and one of them recognizes you from the bus or intake, you're fucked."

Inmates are still filing by, separated from us by thick chicken wire caging. Leonard turns his head toward mine. We are so close I can feel the heat of his breath in my ear. "I'm serious about this shit, man," he tells me, "Believe me, *I know.*"

The air brakes release, then hiss, then the bus's reverse warning beeps. We emerge from the dark, subterranean parking lot into a bright, hot Los Angeles. Men and women in suits with briefcases shuffle quickly down the sidewalk. I'm glad the windows are darkly tinted so no one can see us. It's ten miles north on the 110, across downtown to Twin Towers. The people on the streets are now *civilians* to me.

I remember from my arrest: Central Processing is Twin Towers' hellish initiation process, and here I am again. It's been nearly two years. I recall it being easier, maybe because I was suicidal. Now, I want to live. I want to make it through this, and see if the 12-steppers are right when they say I can have another chance at a meaningful life.

We go from one concrete dank room to the next. Sit on a steel bench; sometimes for five minutes, sometimes for three hours. Disrobe. Line up. Shut up. Handcuffs on, handcuffs off. From the control of one set of khaki-clad deputies to the next. Some are just trying to get through their days without incident, usually the older ones. Some, the ones fresh from the academy, doing their time until they are released to the streets, are looking for an ass to beat, a sacrifice for the fact that they have to work here for two years before they get to move on to where they really want to be.

The most recent set of cuffs isn't too tight, but I still can't feel the top of my right hand, due to what the deputy with black batting gloves did at LAX. I wonder if it's permanent nerve damage, like the spot below my ear where the airbag hit me in my DUI accident. I'm exhausted. Only the homeless types who are getting a respite from the streets sleep. I have no idea what time it is. There are no views to the outside and no clocks. I don't dare ask a deputy what time it is. We march again, hand-cuffs off. The memories of my first trip through here are starting to meld with where I've been this time. The cells and halls and open areas are becoming fungible. I'm starting to see flashes in my periphery from sleep deprivation. I'm sure it has been at least a full day since Keri and I sat before the judge. I'm sitting with two dozen inmates. We've been going through the maze together for so long. We are sitting on a long, steel bench in our underwear now. It's cold, and I can no longer keep my teeth from chattering. A stubby, mullet-haired, white guy is freak-ing out. He can't contain his discomfort and yells, *fuck!* The deputies sit at desks with computers, in front of us, waiting for something, maybe the next stage of the process to clear. The stubby guy asks the deputies if he can get up. They seem to know him. First, he gets up to go to the bathroom, then to stretch, then to speak to the deputies. He gets up for the fourth time and struts down the line toward his destination. He is agitated and tries to catch, so he can fuck with them. A Mexican kid obliges.

"What the fuck are you looking at?" Stubby asks the Mexican kid.

I hear a dense thump. I glance over and see the Mexican kid leaning down, holding his face. Blood drizzles out from between his fingers and plops onto the shiny cement.

"*Pinchie* motha-fucka!" the Mexican kid says and sneers.

Stubby catches my glance, and I quickly look away.

The deputies are seated within clear view and a car's length away from the incident.

"What's going on?" the bigger one asks Stubby like a dad yelling to his-nine-year-old from the living room after too long a silence in the bedroom.

"Nothing, boss. Everything is good, boss," Stubby replies.

Stubby does this little act twice more, over the next hour, each time his strut is more confident than the last. The deputies are yucking it up, pretending not to notice. Our row is on high alert each time Stubby gets up. Leonard, seated five inmates down from me, was the last victim. He put up a fight, and the deputies stood up and told him and Stubby to sit down. I'm so tired. I know that my chance at safety in here is to stay off the radar, but I want Stubby to try and hit me, so I can crush him. My mind is hazy, and I begin to recollect a hot day at a boxing gym in El Monte next to the ring.

Lorenzo Rodriquez has me locked up and is showing several other fighters a technique. He jerks me backward, forward, right, left, kicks me half-speed, knees me. "Control the head," Lorenzo says, "and you control the body." Lorenzo kicked me in the thigh one time during a sparring session. He wanted to convince me that I *could* improve my leg kick, and he instantly made me a believer. It was like being hit with a wood bat at full speed.

Stubby is *mentally ill, spiritually ill*, I think. Ignore him. Despite all the things I've learned from the 12-steppers, my ego is still trying to get me killed. *Kwai Chang Caine. Kung Fu. Peaceful Warrior.*

"Fuck!" Stubby shouts. "I can't feel my *fucking* ass—I've been sitting here so long. Officers, are we going to move soon?"

"Shut up," a deputy barks at him.

"Can I get a drink of water?" Stubby asks.

"Go ahead."

Stubby stands and the tension rises. He's staring right at me. I look to the deputies, and this time, they are watching it happen. I straighten up. I turn toward Stubby, and he is ten feet away. I stare back. I don't want trouble, but I'm allowed to defend myself. *Isn't it enough that I have to sit on this freezing bench in my underwear for hours, but I have to put up with this idiot for the sake of these asshole deputies' entertainment?* I've got my feet planted behind the bench so I can spring up. Stubby is right over me. He purposefully kicks my ankle.

"You kick me, motherfucker?" he snarls at me.

I stand.

"Get the fuck over here," a deputy snaps at him.

I sit back down.

The deputies rise from their office chairs, and the big black one orders Stubby to lie on his stomach, with his hands behind his back and his feet crossed. He straddles Stubby's back and orders him to lift his hands into the air above his back, palms up. He cuffs him and lifts him off the ground by the cuffs. Stubby is suspended in the air like a fat spider. He squeals with pain. The deputy dangles him and then drops him on his face. The percussion of his chin and teeth striking the cement bounces through the hall. The deputy orders him up. Stubby slowly gathers himself. His previously wild and arrogant eyes are now barely lit. His mouth is bloodied. He gasps for air.

The deputy takes him into a holding cell. I hear the toilet flush, followed by several thuds, and then moaning. *Flush, thud, moan, thud, moan, thud.*

A few minutes later, we are given our white boxers, white T-shirts, black slip-on shoes with white soles, royal blue hard cotton pants, and shirts that are shaped and fitted like a modern nurse's top. Stubby limps to the back of the line guarding his right ribs. The labyrinth of arteries that connect the organs and limbs of Twin Towers is demarcated by solid-colored lines. The blue vein goes to the heart, the red to the brain, the green to the leg. Two new deputies walk behind us as we follow the white line up, down, and around cement hallways, with cells and chicken-wired glass and dirty, white-painted steel. A few hours and steel benches later, we arrive in the medical clearing unit and are ordered to sit on the floor in front of the steel benches, which are already full of inmates waiting to be called in.

In the middle of the vast unit is a fully enclosed, raised control center the size of a small office. In the control center from behind tinted glass, the deputies view 270 degrees of the forty-foot-wide staging area, beyond which are six pods. Like human ant farms, each pod has a glass face that rises two stories and is sixty feet wide. Each pod has a glass door, which can only be unlocked from a buzzer at the control center.

The staging area has the feel, lighting, and furnishings of an oversized racquetball court. Each of the six identical pods houses about seventy inmates. The affixed, bright steel benches that run near the front of the glass-walled pods are full of inmates, waiting to be called into the medical area, which is out of sight through a doorway behind the control center. The deputies order us to sit on the floor off to the side of the benches, facing away from the pods and toward the control center. I can feel the inmates' eyes from behind the glass as they size me up. We are within a body length of the glass wall in the pod closest to the entryway to the Medical Unit, and some of the rowdier inmates tap on the glass to get our attention. One focuses on me. This reawakens my anxiety, irritation, anger, and abject fear, all of which had been somewhat numbed by exhaustion since my near miss with Stubby, somewhere between two and four hours ago. My new suitor taps continually on the glass. He might as well be tapping on the back of my head.

"Hey you, with the glasses ... hey, man, c'mon. I know you hear me. Hey, *white* boy."

The black voice pauses for a second, but like a fly caught in the house, I know it's coming back.

Now with anger, I hear, "You better turn your fucking ass around *white boy ...*"

I don't respond.

"Oh, I see how we're going to play it ..."

This is the inevitable dilemma. Turn around, and I'm in his world. He'll tell me to get him an extra sandwich or a blanket or to get the attention of a deputy. Whatever it is, it's something I'll have to stick my neck out to do. If I acquiesce, I risk getting caught by the deputies and getting whatever they are in the mood for, maybe a beating like Stubby took. If I do what he wants, I become a mark for other inmates. If I ignore him, he might attack me.

I get a quick look at him. He's bigger than Stubby, but he's still just a punk. I can take him. *Shut up, ego.* Don't respond. I pretend to be

282 | JOSEPH W. NAUS

hunched over asleep. He bugs me incessantly like the poor kids in Baja Mexico selling Chiclets.

"Man, c'mon, *nigga.* Just get the deputy for me so I can ask him for my lunch ... I didn't get my lunch 'cause I was in the infirmary."

This is out of the question. The deputies have proven unpredictable. I don't want to be beaten or *accidentally* placed in general population. I'm exhausted. I nod off and then twitch awake. I wonder if the medical staff has a record of the last time I was here, when I was suicidal. I think I was in this room before, but I'm not sure. It all looks the same.

"C'mon, man. Get the deputy for me, nigga. I'm hungry."

I fantasize: *Giant Black Officer, yes, you Sir, the one I just watched brutalize an inmate under your care in violation of your oath, Section 1983 of 42nd Title of the United States Codes Annotated and the Unruh Act of the California Civil Code ... and I know you are busy ... as I've watched you lounge around for the last six hours. I just want to relay the message for this gentleman whom apparently didn't get his lunch due to some administrative error. Perhaps you could rectify this situation?*

Mr. Naus, he'll undoubtedly respond, *Thank you so much for bringing this to my attention. I do apologize. Sometimes our chefs and waiters fall short of expectations, but I do so appreciate your concern. In fact, why don't you go around to all our fine guests and make a list of anyone who is displeased with their dining experience, and I'll be sure to ...*

"Motha Fucker!" my suitor yells in frustration, and then pounds the glass hard. "Gonna sit there and ignore a nigga like I ain't even exist. You better hope they don't put your glasses-wearin', Harry Potter-lookin' ass up in this motherfucker."

This feels less and less like a real experience. Fatigue is coating all my perceptions milky and surreal. A delay has developed between my hearing and my processing of what the words I hear mean. I wonder if it's been a full day since Keri turned me in.

My name and number are announced over the loudspeaker, along with those of several other inmates. *887 Naus!* We are ordered to extract from a six-foot pile what the deputy over the loudspeaker refers to as a *mattress*, which is a blue, plastic-covered pad, unfit for the cheapest patio furniture. A thick, blue blanket and a sheet, the edges of which have been torn off into strips so many times it is reduced to an anorexic's sari, is handed to us by a trio of inmate trustees. This is our bedding. I guess they are out of pillows.

Our haggard bunch is lined up in front of the dorm from wherein my admirer resides. He is waiting for me, menacingly chatting up several inmates, who have gathered for our reception.

"Yeah, that motherfucker *right there*," he says to another inmate and points at me.

The door buzzes, and the inmate leading our line opens it. Most of the inmates are sleeping in steel bunk beds, some on the floor. There isn't a single unoccupied spot. The door shuts behind us, and the six of us stand there scoping out our options. I'm apparently the only one who doesn't know how to act in this scenario, because everyone else scans the situation and makes a decision. A couple of the Mexican gang-bangers are received by friends. They sport shaved heads, *something-18* tattooed in Old English on their forearms; they're warmly greeted with *homey*-this and *esse*-that. Within a few seconds, I'm still standing at the front of the door, and everyone else has scattered. Directly in front of me, sitting on the stairs at my eye level, is a thuggish black guy with cornrows, my suitor.

"White boy. Kinda hard ignoring me now, ain't it?" he asks.

I have no words or actions that seem any better than just standing there, mouth slightly agape, waiting for the next event. It occurs to me that I can turn around and press the speaker button next to the door and say something like, *I think this guy is about to terrorize me ... can I get a little help?* I choose to do nothing.

"I'm gonna need to have a word with you, white boy."

Now I'm awake. The adrenaline rushes in. I clench my jaw to stop the chatter of my teeth. He looks just like Harvey from David's gym, but scrawnier. His hands are rolled up in the front of his shirt, revealing his stomach and the bottom edges of a banner tattoo. I think to myself, *clench your teeth so he won't break your jaw.*

"Look, I just want to go to sleep," I say. I hear myself speak. I sound terrified. He stands up and puts his arm over my shoulder, as if he is going to lead me toward the back of the pod.

"Come on over here with me."

I step back a half step, moving out from under his arm as casually as I can.

"No. That's alright," I say. "I'm cool. Thanks. I'm going to get some sleep."

"No, it *ain't* cool, motherfucker," he says through clenched teeth, which exaggerates his jawbone and lips.

"Do you have a weapon?" I ask. I toss my bedding to the side. *I can't believe I just said that, but fuck it, why not?*

"Oh, shit! Eh, homey, he wants to know if I got a weapon," he says as if he's talking to a friend that is standing to our side, but there is no one there. He looks off to the distance and then glares at me. "*A weapon? I don't need nothin' to fuck you up.*"

"A homey!" he says louder and keeps one eye on me as he looks off to the side.

I don't know if he's crazy, or this whole talking-to-someone-who-isn't-there is some weird, jail-gangster shit.

Let me be ... a channel of peace. I must have said that prayer a thousand times over the last eighteen months—in my head and out loud in recovery meetings. The 12-steppers love that prayer. I wrote it out once. I always picture a ray of light shining out of my eyes like some mutant superhero.

"Hey, man," I say to him softly, "I thought one of those cops would beat the hell out of me, if I said anything to him about your lunch. I just saw him beat this guy down for no reason at all."

"Yeah?" he asks.

"Can you show me where I can lay down?" I ask him, "I'm exhausted."

He stares at me for a second, looks off to his imaginary homey, then back at me. His face softens.

"Yeah, motherfucker," he says. "Next time, help uh brotha out. Grab yo shit, nigga. Call me Pookie."

I follow Pookie and lay down my mattress. It's close to the window. Then the intercom sounds, "Naus 8-8-7. Naus. Cell 33. Naus Cell 33."

"Oh, you PC'd up *motherfucka*. Get yo' shit," Pookie says and points up the stairs. "Up there, nigga."

"Naus. 887 Naus. Cell 33, *now*," the voice over the intercom repeats.

I walk up the stairs. I stand next to the cell door. Cell 33 is empty. The door buzzes unlocked. It's like all the others, but it has a vent that is blasting cold air, as if the entire jail's air conditioning is being directed to this one vent. There is no way to reach the vent, because the bunk, stool, and bench are all built into the walls; but, someone before me had attempted to silence it, by throwing wet toilet paper balls between the louvers. This has decreased the size of the vent, creating even more pressure, like one of those custom mufflers installed on lowered Japanese cars. It's as loud as a hair dryer, and the cold air is swooshing strong enough to blow my hair back. There's a slit window in the three-foot-thick, concrete wall opposite the vent, not quite wide enough to fit my head in. The view is of the fifteen-foot wall surrounding the jail topped with razor ribbon, and beyond is a vast municipal bus boneyard. Beyond that, I can see an occasional civilian crossing a sparsely driven intersection in the northern downtown LA commercial area. It's dawn. The omnipresent, overhead fluorescent lighting blares down. I think about sleeping on the top bunk, so that if anyone enters my cell I'll have some type of protection from attack, but I change my mind, as the bottom bunk is somewhat protected from the onslaught of bad light and cold air.

I ball up the sparse sheet and use it as a pillow, keep my clothes on to stay as warm as possible, and pull the blanket over my head. I am too exhausted for racing thoughts. Names and numbers are intermittently called throughout the morning, afternoon and night, and I wonder if I'll wake if they call my name. I doubt it.

I awake to the banging on the cell door window. It's an inmate trustee passing out breakfast: an apple, a peculiar packet of peanut butter, a juice drink, milk, and cornflakes. I try to wave him off, but he insists that I stand by my cell door, dressed and ready. All the inmates not in cells are lined two-by-two on the stairs, and the deputies are threatening to withhold *feeding* if everyone doesn't line up properly. Apparently, I am the hold up. The couple dozen inmates on the stairs are glaring over at my cell, whilst the inmate trustee is beckoning me to stand by the cell door window, as if he'd been trying to get me to do so for some time, which is entirely possible. I just want to sleep and am beginning to wonder if sleep deprivation is part of jail management curricula. Apparently, the cell lights had actually been dimmed when I first came into the cell, because they are now even brighter. Not five minutes after my cell door is buzzed open so I can take the breakfast I don't want, a list of names is called out. I hadn't noticed it when I entered the cell, but there is an intercom speaker and button on the wall next to the cell door. It serves as a direct connection between me and control center. It speaks to me.

"Naus, 887. Naus, 887."

I don't know how to react to this. After a few moments, I decide to press the button and speak to the stainless steel intercom.

"Officer, my name was called. This is Naus ... uh, 887."

A minute goes by before the voice comes back.

"Don't press the button, *dumbass*. Just get ready for unlock."

Back to the steel benches. We straddle the benches forced so close together that it is physically taxing to stay awake and not lean on the inmate in front of me. My ass no longer hurts because it's numb. Several inmates on my bench are called into the medical unit, and when they come back out, they are let back into the dorm and replaced on the bench by another inmate. I long to return to my horrible cell, but I sit for a couple hours. Finally, we are sent back to our pod just before dinner. My legs are locked up at the thighs. My back is so stiff I walk in the shape of a question mark. I hear the murmurs that the rule is that at dinner everyone has to be in their assigned dorm. Soon after dinner, the entire pod is placed on lockdown.

Thank God for lockdown. Nothing happens. I sleep despite the light, the blasting air, the buzzing, the echoing and slamming of cell doors, and violent yelling. I sleep an entire day. I don't even wake to eat.

My name is called in the middle of the night. Just mine. I am told to follow a yellow stripe. No guards, no handcuffs, no other inmates. Just me and a stripe winding through the cold labyrinth, occasionally passing a tinted glass booth with the green glow of a computer screen and the silhouette of a deputy or two. They don't look my way. It apparently isn't odd that I am following the stripe unattended. I don't know where I am going, and I don't want to go there. Maybe I can just follow stripes until they end and then pick other colors. The officers will ignore me. I'll live in Twin Towers purgatory.

The stripe ends in a room with a stairway that lead up to offices, and the room looks onto a pod configured exactly as the medical unit area I had come from. An inmate trustee is watching television with his feet up and reacts to me with as little interest as if he's a desk clerk at a road motel. He hands me a bedroll and tells me to sit on the stairs and wait. It's cold and hollow in here, just like everywhere else in this dastardly glass, cement, and steel compound. I'm rested. I'm scared. I just want to get where I'm going, but I'm not even in the right institution yet. I have to survive Twin Towers just to get a chance to survive Chino.

I am buzzed in to the staging area by the intercom voice from the deputy behind the tinted glass in the control room. Then I am buzzed into one of the six pods. The television mounted high in the corner is off, and only the night lighting is on. There are several inmates sleeping on the ground, so I figure all the bunks must be taken. As I lay my mat out, I am approached by a skinny guy with long black hair. He has a witch's crooked nose and a mole to match.

"Horse Face," he introduces himself and extends his hand out to me.

"Joseph," I whisper and shake his hand.

"There's an open bunk right over there," he says.

He indicates a bunk toward the back of the ground floor behind a kiosk with four pay phones. I want to sleep on a bunk instead of being totally exposed, but I am leery of the idea of taking a bunk, when others have apparently chosen not to. I also don't want to wake anyone up talking to Horse Face. So, as quietly as I can, I mount the bunk.

I pray silently. I sleep.

EIGHTEEN

I wake. It's dark, it's quiet, but I'm not alone. I'm still here in this place. I reach for my glasses, which I've tucked in to the edge of the steel bed frame. I can't feel them. A shot of terror penetrates me, but then I feel the plastic arm of glasses. *Thank God.* I leave them be. I don't want to see. It's never completely dark here. The night-lights are on. I feel the residue of a dream.

I dreamt of the 2001 Thomas & Colbert retreat. *That's right.* What happened, what I did, it should have been a sign I had a problem, not a badge of honor. All the attorneys, the associates, and the partners were in the bar on the third mezzanine level of the Grand Marriot in Palm Desert, overlooking the garish lobby of the massive hotel. A mini, man-made river emptied into the hotel lobby through a three-story wall of glass. Gondolas floated in and out taking guests around the resort. There was a baseball game on TV at the bar. The drinks were free and flowing, as usual. We were there for two days of nothing but golf and massages, dinners and drinking.

I was drinking but trying not to get too hammered. Everyone was standing around having a good time. Someone, one of the partners, maybe Jack Clinton, started talking about the gondolas and the little river. It was a *goddamn* unbelievable sight. The engineering of it all was staggering. And then one of the other partners says, wouldn't it be a hoot if someone dove in there and swam across? It's about the length of an Olympic-sized swimming pool, but that's not what'd make it crazy. It's the outrageousness of it. This is a nice resort hotel. Everyone in this gigantic lobby will stop and gawk. Then a hundred bucks started to get thrown around. Would you do it for a Ben Franklin? It was an offer not meant to be accepted. I was several drinks in, still completely okay, but a little daring. *I'll do it,* I heard myself say. A couple of the more conservative partners looked concerned. Sawyer, the newest partner, she had that look, like, *you can't be serious.* But the rally was on. I took off my shirt and tie, stripped down to my boxers and white-ribbed tank top and pranced down the stairs. Everyone gathered at the edge of the bar and down onto the dock. I dove in. The hotel employee in the cheesy outfit operating the gondola was shocked and didn't know what to do. The water was cool, and I swam through quickly; a bit of embarrassment cut my buzz as people gathered from the lobby, and eyes and voices congregated to watch the spectacle that was me. Jack met me at the water's edge, as if I'd just won Olympic freestyle gold. He had my clothes, and he dramatically presented me with a hundred-dollar bill. He raised it up to the lawyers looking over the mezzanine balcony. I climbed out on to the fake rocks and held up the hundred-dollar bill up toward the bar. There were cheers and claps.

I close my eyes. I see Matt, one of the partners at Thomas & Colbert, his massive front teeth and nose, even bigger than my own. He was on the board of directors of the Mission Inn. He used to take the young lawyers to the Mission Inn's fancy steak house. The police report says I used my Mission Inn Hotel card key to separate the screening from the screen frame, before I entered Winston's apartment. I had it because Will and I represented Flyer Motor Homes, and they had a corporate account there, because their national corporate headquarters is in Riverside, not too far from the Mission Inn. I got that card key the night I stayed at the Mission Inn. I stayed there so I could be close to the Riverside Courthouse the day before I settled my DUI. I kept it because I loved the Mission Inn. So many memories: riding around there when I was a kid on my red Schwinn, stealing figurines for my mom from the gift shop, long before investors decided to bring the Mission Inn back to its glory days, when U.S. Presidents honeymooned there. *Fucking Matt,* I think. He'd be surprised if he knew I was here in jail, or maybe he wouldn't. Maybe he knew I had a problem.

The intercom booms and crackles something about "roll call." The dreaded, blaring fluorescent lights. So unkind. My fellow criminals are agitated, pissing, groggy, facing another day. I spot Leonard, the innocent voyeur, and follow him to the steps that lead to the second tier. The pod is like a giant glass-fronted loft. Leonard explains morning roll call to me, as we sit hip-to-hip on the steps leading up to the second tier. There are nearly sixty of us. The steps are full, two inmates each, and then the line singles out along the railing of the loft overlooking the spider benches.

"*Motherfucker.* White boy!" a little roach of a man yells. I look down over the railing. The roach is tossing my bedding and yelling about *me. I'm* the white boy. I'm the *motherfucking stupid ass white boy.* My pulse races.

"What should I do?" I ask Leonard.

"He's disrespecting you," Leonard answers. "You have a right to that bunk."

Sage advice from a guy who's trying to sell me on the commonality of faux-family-nudist-camping-pedophilia magazines. I decide to ignore the situation until roll call is over.

A deputy opens the glass door directly in front of the stairs. He is flanked by three trustees with orange and brown, plastic, cafeteria food carts. The deputy calls a name, and then the inmate calls his name back along with the last three digits of his number, then shows the deputy his inmate wristband. The inmate is given breakfast by the trustees and then sits on one of the spider benches. I'm not good at stuff like this, but I can do it. It's alphabetical, so I have some time.

"Naus 887".

"Naus 887," I holler back.

I walk down the stairs. The deputy takes a long look at my wristband. I walk back to the spider benches and sit across from Horse Face. I look at him, smile wryly, and think better about his recommendation of bunks last night. He looks like something out of *Grimm's Fairy Tales*. There is no confusion why he is called Horse Face. I feel someone behind me. It's the roach that just tossed up my bed.

"Get the fuck up. You done," he says to Horse Face and turns to a beast of a black man that stands with him. "Am I right, *nigger?*"

"You, too, motherfucker," the beast says to a little Mexican guy next to Horse Face, in the deepest tone of voice I've ever heard. Horse Face and the Mexican disappear, and I'm sitting across from Roach and this beast.

"Naus. What kind a name is that? Sound like Nazi. You don't like niggers?" Roach asks.

He's blue-black with mincemeat acne scars in his cheeks. His eyes are yellow and fast. He keeps talking, and I'm trying to listen, and I'm trying not to look at the eyes of the beast sitting next to him.

"You *hearin'* this shit?" the beast asks me.

I look at him. I try not to act shocked, but he's shocking. His head is cartoonishly huge and pear-shaped. He has a steroid jaw, and each giant tooth stands alone, separated by gum growth. Nostrils like a bull. Big black droopy eyes. His hair is rolled into buns that on first glance appear to be horns. His necklaced gang tattoos are unreadable through his chalky black skin. He has a teardrop under his left eye. The tattoo on his massive forearm reads his name in block letters, ROMAN.

"I'm listening," I respond. "Sorry, didn't know. I got here late last night. I just went into a bed that was open. I'll move my stuff."

"You think that's it," Roach says.

I ignore him and eat the rest of my sad, small apple. Roman gets up. He's six feet, no fewer than 270 pounds. He has a prison body, all the show-muscles overdeveloped. His biceps, traps, pecs, all hang like meat on a hook. He lifts his shirt and scratches his belly. A long, furrowed, smooth scar bisects his abdominals.

"Whatch-you in here for, white boy?"

I stand up and reach my hand across the table and introduce myself as if we are in a business meeting. Roman is amused but plays along and shakes my hand and tells me his name. His hands are thick and rough. He has grotesque, yellowing nails, thick as quarters. I do the same with Roach, who introduces himself as Trap. I tell them my modified story.

"You a bitch-ass liar. You ain't no fucking lawyer. You probably a child-molesting *motherfucker*," Roach says, and looks over at Roman, "Yeah, he like little boys, don't he?"

"I'm not a child molester," I say. "I'm a disbarred attorney. I went to Pepperdine Law School. I had an office in Pasadena. I'm in here for an assault I committed when I was blacked-out drunk. Part of my plea deal was that I go into protective custody."

"You ain't no lawyer," Roman says. "But Trap here, he is what we call a jailhouse lawyer. Motherfucker's a straight up, Johnnie-Mother-Fucking-Cochran. He goin' to tell me if your ass is a-lyin'."

"Roman is in here on a burg," Trap says. "But they done fucked up and questioned him after he done told them he wanted a lawyer, so we gonna get that shit throw out. Whatch you know about that, *lawyer boy?*"

"Burglary," I begin, "California Penal Code Section 459. California's burglary definition is, for the most part, the same as the common law definition, the breaking and entering of the dwelling of another with the intent to commit a felony therein. Where it differs, I believe is that it doesn't have to be a dwelling, and I believe they can get you for some misdemeanors. But that isn't the issue here. You are looking at a Fourth and Fifth Amendment issue, applicable to the states, of course, through the Fourteenth Amendment. Unfortunately, I practiced primarily civil law. All I remember about *Miranda* and search and seizure and all that shit is that the cops usually found a way to use the fruit of the poisonous tree. The rest I forgot after I took the Bar."

That was actually kind of fun. By the look on Roman and Trap's faces, they're convinced I am a lawyer.

"A'yight then, nigger. You straight," Roman says. "We may be calling on you for your expertise. The DA be tryin' to hang an OG nigger, three strikes and shit."

I nod.

"This cracker done toll you he ain't know shit about no criminal law. We don't need him. *I'm* yo' nigga," Trap says to Roman.

"Shut the fuck up," Roman says in a cruel tone, his voice so deep I can feel it in my stomach. "I know you *down*, nigga. White boy might be able to help with the paper work and shit. They always be bouncin' a motherfucker's papers for bullshit." Roman looks away from Trap and at me. "You want some spades nigga?"

"No thank you," I respond quickly.

I get up and put my tray in the bin and collect my bedding from the floor. I love spades. This kid and I were a champion spades team in rehab. Even the prison guys couldn't beat us, except when the kid would nod out after he'd taken his Seroquel. Great way to pass the time. Sometimes we played for cigarettes. But I'm not playing any games in here. Anything that can lead to getting me hurt: gambling, trading, commissary. No fucking around. *Better to be bored than dead,* that's what Charley from Narcotics Anonymous told me.

There is one empty bunk upstairs. It is adjacent to Leonard's bunk. Oddly, I'm happy to see Leonard. I guess he's the devil I know. It's like the time I visited the Alley after I got my job at Thomas & Colbert. I wanted to drive through it triumphantly and say, *Fuck you, Alley. Look at me now. I'm a lawyer. I made it despite you. You can't scare me now.* But the Alley's familiarity was actually comforting, and I left confused.

I fit my blue sliver of a mattress into the metal grating of the industrial bunk bed. Leonard climbs down from his bunk where he is reading and pulls another blue mattress out and hands it to me without saying anything. I thank him and make my bed and lie down, close my eyes, still half thinking of the Alley.

"Are you new?"

I hear a child's voice and open my eyes. Its owner is hanging his head down from the top bunk. I see his unusually big head upside-down. He climbs down and sits at the foot of my bed.

"I'm Steven," the boy says. "You are new. I saw that angry man throw your stuff. He's cranky. He's always causing trouble. You'll like it up here better. I was down there. I didn't like it. It's better up here. The Reverend holds prayers every night, and a lot of us participate."

"I'm Joseph," I say. "Good to meet you."

"Rev," he shouts to an old, gray-haired black man who is playing cards on his bunk with a frumpy man. "Rev, this is Joseph. He might join us in prayer service."

"Alright, Steven. God bless you. Nice to meet you, Joseph," the Reverend says and nods his head at me. He then introduces me to the frumpy man, Michael. Michael is what a sketch artist would draw if you asked him to draw a picture of a pedophile. He asks me what my story is. I politely defer response and tell him that I'm exhausted and am going to try and sleep.

"You are going to sleep?" Steven asks with a tone of disappointment.

"I'm exhausted," I say.

"I've got three *Harry Potter* books. My mom is mailing another one. It should be here today. You can read one, but only if you promise to return it, okay?"

I needn't hear another word from Steven to have a pretty good idea why he's here. He's mildly retarded. He's not a mental infant, just a mental child. He's too old to be treated like a juvenile, so he's fallen between the cracks of the legal system. His parents are exhausted. He can't make a living, so it looks like he's going to live with them for the rest of forever. Maybe he has one of those part-time jobs they give mentally handicapped people, bagging groceries or collecting carts at the grocery store. His parents try to get him out of the house to get a respite and to get him socialized. They send him to a church group some nights. Next thing you know, Billy the eight-year-old is complaining, because Steven touched his wiener while they were wrestling in the rec room, and then Sally says Steven stuck his finger in her cooch while they played doctor. Steven gets in trouble and doesn't understand why everyone's so pissed. He's just doing what a kid does at that mental age. Maybe a social worker gets involved. People understand the situation. He's a kid in a man's body. He's monitored, does some therapy. Things die down. A year later, he does it again. This time, they aren't so forgiving, they say he should know better. Parents are throwing words around like *molestation*. He hits puberty but has no ability to control his urges. It happens again. Maybe this time, it's a little more forceful. Maybe he tries to stick his dick in Sally. The judge isn't having it this time. *He has to learn*, the judge says. If he's legally incompetent, the Corrections Department will label him as such. Next thing Steven knows, he's in here with grown-ass men, creepy and scary, violent criminals, but he's still acting like he's at summer camp talking about Harry Potter, because he's still a mental ten-year-old.

"You awake?" Steven asks.

"Uh-huh."

Steven scrambles down to my bunk and sits at the foot. His eyes are excited and wide open.

"Glen left yesterday. He was my friend. He was in here for three months. He helped me and told me what to do. He even read *Half-Blood Prince*. He called me Hogwart," Steven says and giggles.

"Wow," I respond.

Steven looks up at me with more puppy-dog intensity than I can handle on my best day. "Will you be my friend like Glen was?"

This is where you say, *yes, the kitten is cute, but I can't deal with a litter box and fleas. Sorry. So sorry.* But then I think of Vinny hammering it into me: Service, service, service. Service at work, service in the rooms, service to yourself, service to God. Your life is for service. That's how we stay sober. That's how we stay sane. *Vinny, man, I can't help this fucking kid. I have to figure out how to survive myself.* I think of Melody at Pepperdine. Tall, thin with flowing, long, modern hippie-hair, totally out of place at the most conservative law school in the country. She was this ultrasweet, ultraliberal, part-time professor of Special Education Law. I worked with her in a program she set up at Pepperdine, in which we were supposed to advocate for families with disabled kids. I was supposed to show up at a school with this kid's family. I called the night before the hearing and left a message telling Melody I didn't feel prepared, that I wasn't going, because I didn't know what I was doing. It was cowardly. It was bullshit. I knew the deal. It didn't matter whether I knew the law perfectly. Melody had told us that. She said, if we showed up and did our best, it would always be better than the family not having any support. I tried to play it like it was unprofessional to show up not being a master of the law and procedure, but I was just being a cowardly, selfish prick.

Steven and his dark brown, puppy-dog eyes wait for an answer.

"Of course ... I'll be your friend," I say. "I've never been here before, so I can't tell you what Glen could. You'll probably need to tell *me* what's going on."

The Rev looks over at us over his half-glasses. "Steven's a good boy. He just don't always be listening so good. Ain't that right, Steven?"

Steven tilts his head like a confused dog and refocuses his attention on his conversation with me. He's chomping at the bit to tell me his story and launches into it without introduction. He first got in trouble for playing too *touchy* with his little sister. Then he had to go stay in a group home, and they weren't nice. He got in trouble there for *touching where he shouldn't be touching.* He comes back home, and his mom gets him a volunteer job at a horse ranch. That's where the details get sketchy.

Something about Donny and his *thingy* and *mouth* and *he wanted to do it too* and *we were just playing*.

"I didn't mean to do anything wrong," Steven says. He begins to cry like an English siren. His anime saucer-eyes fill with tears. Steven soaks them up with the short sleeves of his undershirt. His underarms smell of baby powder. He doesn't have the words for it, but it sounds like he's going to Chino for a ninety-day evaluation like me. Moments later, he's stopped crying, and he's laughing, recounting a knock-knock joke the Rev told him.

Leonard and the Rev say it could be two days or it could be a month before we catch a *chain* to Chino. Luckily, books float around the tier. I get hold of *Last of the Mohicans* and a dictionary. I read it and write down every word I don't know or that I'm a little sketchy on. I'm surprised at how many there are. *Limpid—adj. marked by transparency, clear and simple in style, limpid waters, perfect for baptism.* I should know that. I do the same with *The Screwtape Letters*. Steven insists daily that I read some Harry Potter. It has been several days, and I keep deferring. I will, I will, as soon as I'm finished with this book—and then this book. I get a hold of *Uncle Tom's Cabin* in the nick of time.

Roman comes up from time to time and asks me questions about his case, and when he does, the whole second tier goes on high alert. He's the school bully, visiting with his ever-present sidekick Trap. It usually has to do with some procedural issues that I can answer quickly. Once it was the form of an affidavit, then at breakfast, it was how to do a proof of service, then something about the formatting of the pleading paper. I keep it quick and polite. Roman keeps trying to draw me in. Do I want to play cards? Do I want to trade my meds? You need a little *something-something?* Roman asks and points out this skinny Mexican lady-boy who ties his T-shirt above his navel and walks around with his ass stuck out. I politely decline. Roman and the other gangbangers, including a muscle-swollen Mexican who is the leader of the Mexican gangbangers, have a little compound in the back of the first tier. They move their bunks in a half-circle and hang sheets to block the deputies' view.

It's been a week. Every day in here is another day added to my sentence. Whether I spend one day or a hundred days here, I'm spending at least ninety days in Chino. Rumblings are that we'll be catching a chain to Chino any time now. It's after dinner but before the Rev's Bible Prayers. It's getting tense in here. We've got a new guy, a toughie white guy, a *Wood*. He belongs downstairs, but he's up here, and he likes drama, and he likes to use the word, *nigger*. Loves it. He joined me uninvited in my daily calisthenics workouts, so now he talks to me. He's collecting *Woods*. Several guys have come up from the first tier. *Wood*— this and *Wood*—that. The *Woods* gotta stick together, so the niggers and the spics can't *getatchew*. Now I have this idiot talking to me, and Roman is watching this develop, and they've had words. I just want them both to get the fuck away from me.

I'm lying in my bunk and I hear, "Joseph. Joseph. I need some paper." It's Roman shouting at me from downstairs.

His bass voice makes me clench. I've been trying to keep our relationship something short of *punk-or* and *punk-ee*. I don't know what to do. I just keep reading. The Rev and Leonard tell me to give him some paper. They don't want him up here. King Wood says way too loudly, "You're the nigger's nigger."

I pull some of my letter paper, place it in a book, walk over to the railing, and drop it to the ground. The sound is louder than I anticipated.

"There you go, Roman," I say.

There's no response. I watch until I see the crown of a black man's head, one of Roman's crew. He picks up the paper and looks up at me coldly.

"It's like that?" I hear Roman ask. I presume his anger is due to the fact that I didn't come down and give him the paper personally. But, pissing Roman off a little is better than venturing into his little enclave. I don't want any part of whatever evil shit is going on back there. At the very least, they are selling meds. Leonard has already told me he is tonguing his Lexapro when he can and trading it for coffee and stamps. The Lexapro crushes up into a white powder and when snorted has an effect similar to meth, Leonard tells me.

A half-hour later, Roman saunters upstairs with one *vato* and a couple black guys, all about business. Leonard pretends to sleep, and the Reverend picks up his Bible. The Woods in the corner go on full alert. I try to keep reading, but I'm just staring at the page. Roman and a thick Mexican, flanked by two black guys, walk up to our bunk.

"Thanks for the paper, lawyer-man. I'mma need some real help with some shit tomorrow," Roman says.

I look up from my book. The sight of his monstrous face is still shocking. If I cast him in a movie as the bad guy, the critics would say I was overdoing it. His three cohorts are just plain old, scary, jailhouse thugs.

"Glad to help," I respond.

"Hey Steven," Roman says.

"Hi Roman," Steven answers, "I got another Harry Potter book today."

"Steven, why don't you come down and play some cards with us? We have fun down there." Roman looks to his cohorts for confirmation, "Don't we?"

One of them chimes in, "For *reals*, Steven, we be playing cards and having a good time like hide-and-seek and shit."

"A'yight, Steven!" Roman teases. "We gonna have a little powwow with these gentlemen over here, and then you can come down and play cards with us."

Roman and his crew walk over to the Woods. We can't hear much of what they are saying. Out of my periphery I see that Roman is using his forearm to pin King Wood's neck to the wall.

"Steven," I whisper. "You can't go down there with them. Those guys are trouble. Do you understand? Don't go down there." Steven is listening but staring at the confrontation. "Stop staring over there!" I say, finally getting his attention. "Come on, grab your Bible."

I pull Steven over to the Reverend's bunk.

"Reverend, we need to do Bible Prayers a bit early tonight, okay?" I motion my head over toward the confrontation. The Reverend is on the same page and immediately starts in on the ceremony.

"Let Steven start out, okay?" I ask.

Leonard climbs down from his bunk and goes downstairs and watches TV, like he always does when the Reverend does Bible Prayer at night. Six of us gather around.

"Steven, child, start us off with the Lord's Prayer," the Rev says.

"Our Father Who art in heaven, hallowed be thy name ..." Steven knows it by heart. He says it with the innocence of a child that doesn't know injustice, or more likely doesn't understand the cards he's been dealt. I wonder if he's ever questioned God. Did he wonder why God put him here?

During the prayer, all of us, except Steven who is proudly reciting the prayer, turn to the sound of the escalating confrontation. The thick Mexican has pushed a skinny Wood off the railing of a bunk. We all turn back, intentionally ignoring it, as Steven wraps up.

"... the power and the glory forever and ever. Amen." Our group mumbles *amen* cautiously.

Finally, the deputies take notice from the control center, and the loudspeaker crackles.

"Inmates on the second tier. Everyone to their rack immediately. If your rack is not on the second tier, clear out right fucking now."

The Reverend is preaching that one of our congregants, a young black-Asian, has to have faith that justice will be done and that the rape charges against him will be dropped. Yesterday I overheard him and the Rev talking about the nitty-gritty of a police investigator's rape kit—*so if you wear a rubber, they can't prove it was you, right?*

Roman saunters over on his way downstairs and stands above us.

"C'mon, Steven, let's go down and play," Roman says, interrupting the Rev.

Steven must have understood me, because he looks scared. He's not saying anything just staring between me and the Rev.

"Hey, brother," the Rev says, "Steven is participating in a sacred church service. *Wherever two or more are gathered in his name, there shall He be, sayeth the Lord.* This may not look like a church but ... do you and your friends want to join us?"

"Nigga, *please.* God ain't helping y'all. Steven's coming downstairs to play. He can be prayin' later." Roman grabs Steven's arm and begins to pull him up. Steven instantly shrills like an infant ripped from his mother. Roman let's go of Steven's arm. We all gather around Steven and console him. Roman goes back downstairs.

I wake up in the middle of the night. Steven is shaking me. He says they want me. They've been calling my name. I hop up. Everyone is still asleep. I pull on my stiff, orange uniform and rush downstairs. Trap and another inmate are waiting at the door. I'm finally going to Chino. I'm not ready for another transition. They're the worst, but I have to be. The sooner I get there, the sooner the ninety days starts ticking.

Trap and the other guy, a Mexican who barely speaks English named Miguel, seem to know the protocol for transfers. It's so strange the way they just let us go to follow the painted lines. I follow along. Trap is an old pro. He has a legal binder with him and walks with purpose. He teases Miguel over and over. "Are you a Mexi-*can?* or a Mexi-*can't?*" Trap says it over and over, "Mexi-*can,* Mexi-*can't.*" He laughs uproariously. Miguel rolls his eyes and shakes his head. "Nigger," Trap relents, "I'm just fucking wit' you. You'ze a Mexi-*can.* You be all over some mother-fucking Home Depot when you get out of here, huh, Negro? Don't be lyin'. I seen you outside Home Depot."

We cross a line in the concrete, where the new jail meets the old jail and join a stream of inmates. Everyone knows where they are going but me. I stick close to Trap. We bottleneck at two turnstiles. It's like a checkout line, one deputy for each register. Each deputy wears rubber gloves, grabs each inmate's wrist, and scans the UPC code on our wristbands with a handheld scanner. The scanner beeps just like in the grocery store. It's loud and roaring in here, sound bounces all over. It has the energy of a school field trip. I keep waiting for a deputy to tell me where to go, but it doesn't happen. There are no deputies past the checkout line, so I follow Trap.

"Trap, where do we go?" I ask hesitantly.

"I'm going to Inglewood. I don't know where you be goin'." He keeps walking. I follow him down a hall with cell after cell of excited, orange-clad inmates to my left. To the right are doors to the buses. Two deputies are shackling a line of men. Miguel enters a one-way revolving gate into a cell.

"I'm going to Chino," I holler at Trap. He stops and turns.

"Nigga, you ain't goin' to *mutha-fuckin' Chino*. This here court call. Where your court?"

Inmates rush past us. A deputy comes up behind, sweeping everyone clear with his official voice. I can't hear what he's yelling.

"I don't have to go to court. I'm supposed to go to Chino."

"This is court-call and your ass goin' to court. This ain't no chain."

The deputy catches up to us.

"Officer, I don't know where to go," I say. "I'm supposed to—"

"Get out of my face, and get into a cell, inmate!" the deputy shouts. His eyes are even more vicious than his voice.

"I'm supposed to go to Chino," I respond desperately.

"This is court-call. Get in your cell!" The deputy yells at me dismissively and continues clearing the hall.

"Where did you go to court?" Trap asks.

"LAX," I say, exasperated.

"Follow me, nigga," Trap orders.

I follow. We reach a packed cell. He points.

"Is this PC?" I say into his ear.

"Ain't no *PC* down here."

The same deputy comes back hollering. "I told you to get in your cells!" he yells at us with real venom. I have to make a decision before the deputy reaches me.

Trap walks off. I put on my game face, and reluctantly push through the revolving gate into the cell. There is nowhere to sit, so I make my way to an empty spot on the wall and try not to reveal how fucking scared I am. This is a mean crowd. No Harry Potters here.

"Joseph!"

I hear the shout from outside the cell. It's Trap.

"Joseph!" he repeats.

"Yeah?" I look at Trap. All the inmates look at me.

"You can't be in there," Trap says with a grin. "I told you, we gotta be with the PCs. You got an R on your jacket. You can't be in there."

Oh shit. I've been duped. My face heats up and turns red. I close my eyes, and try to pretend Trap isn't talking to me. I can feel the energy in the cell shift. The Wood that was standing next to me slides down the wall away from me. I open my eyes, and keep my head down. Legs and bodies are moving toward me.

"Eh, esse."

I look up and see a young Mexican gangbanger. He's shirtless, tatted up, has a shiny, shaved head with a Roman numeral inked on top. He has four homies in tow.

"Esse, I think you might be lost, Homie. Carnal," he turns to his boys, "shouldn't he be in the cell down there where they keep the faggot child molesters?"

"*Fuckin-A, si, Esse.*"

He's standing in my face. I want to push him away. I need to be cool. I need to de-escalate this.

"Yes. I seem to be in the wrong cell," I say. "My protective custody status is due to me being an attorney." I try the geeky anomaly approach.

I wonder if I shouldn't start screaming and going nuts. Am I not making a big enough deal of this? Am I too scared? It's so loud. I don't know if anyone would hear me if I did scream.

"Is that so, Esse?" he starts, "Cuz I know *puto* Trap, and that nigger is PC because he's a *pinche puto* fuckin' *rapist.* So if you with him, you a *chester.*

My pores open like missile silos, and my face and ears and neck burn. *Fuck. He knows. Deny, deny, deny.*

"I'm PC because I'm an attorney. That guy knows my name, because he's in the next dorm, and we were released out of the same pod, and I didn't know where to go. I told him my name, and he told me to come in here. Obviously, he was fucking around."

"He looks like a *chester,* holmes," one of the other vatos taunts. The main one is still in my face, close enough to kiss.

"That's right, Esse, and he's a fucking *pinche* liar."

I start to panic. I try to move away, but they close in on all sides.

"You are going to get fucked, *pinche* white boy," I hear. The vato in front of me steps back and punches me in the stomach.

I'm shocked, and I'm scared, but I'm not hurt. He telegraphed his punch. I couldn't help but flex and blow out at impact. I pretend it hurts.

"Alright, alright," I say.

"Alright *what,* homey? What you gonna *do,* esse?" He stands back ready to hit me again. I look up, and the entire cell, a full classroom of inmates are crowding around watching. He hits me again, this time in the ribs. I make no effort to block it. I fold in. It hurts, but he doesn't know how to punch, all arms and no body—thank God—so he doesn't do any damage. Everything is real quiet and slow, like when I was sliding sideways in my car during my DUI accident, watching my smashed windshield cut through the foliage.

Vato throws a right cross at my face. I parry it. He has his thumbs out, and he's doing that ridiculous Mexican fighting stance: hands just in front of his crotch, thumbs pointing at each other, weight on his back foot, his whole upper body behind his hips. His homies are containing me but leaving the fighting to vato. Vato is having fun. He thinks I'm just a scared punching bag. I put my hands up and come up off the wall. He throws another sweeping punch. I bob and thrust my hands as hard as I can against his bare chest. It throws him all the way across the cell against the opposite wall. I do the same to the homie to my right with the same result. He falls over the toilet. I dive through the crowd of inmates toward the bars.

"Guards! Guards!" I scream at the top of my lungs. Inmates in neighboring cells go wild and start shaking the bars. One of the vatos punches me in the back of the head and another grabs my neck. All four of them pounce. I throw a left hook and miss and then follow it with an overhand right that lands hard. He goes down. He's out cold. The others are trying to drag me away from the bars. I scream for help.

"Man down! Man down!" I hear someone yell. Now the vatos have me down. One is trying to get me in a headlock. I'm sprawled out trying to get free.

"*Callate* motherfucker," one of them says and tries to cover my mouth.

"Guard! Guard!" I scream.

Finally a deputy comes.

"What the fuck is going on?" he says.

The vatos scatter to the back of the cell, and I scramble to my feet. "Officer, I'm in the wrong cell. I'm PC. I've been attacked. I'm …" I look at his badge but I can't make out the letters. I go to my knees for my glasses. They are bent but not crushed.

"What is your name?" he asks.

"Naus. 887."

He shouts my name and number out to another deputy. A shout returns: "He's not on the list."

"Where are you housed?"

"I'm a PC 290, sex registrant," I say hushed. "Please, I'm afraid for my life. Please let me out of this cell."

He smirks at me and walks off.

"Officer, please! Officer!" I yell desperately.

I turn around with my back to the bars. This time I'm going to put my glasses in my pocket, and I'm going to smash one of these vatos. I have nothing to lose. None of them know how to fight. *Fuck it.* They'll win, but I'm going to get some good shots in. The one I landed the over-hand right on is now slumped against the wall semiconscious. I wonder if I broke his nose or jaw. The big one, the one I pushed first, he's talking to his homies looking at me, waiting to make sure the deputy is gone.

The rest of the crowded cell has cleared away from me.

The vatos move toward me.

"Leave that boy alone," an old, black inmate tells the vatos. "He ain't done nothin' to y'all. I'm tired of this shit!"

"Fuck that *pinche* white boy!" a vato shouts at the old man. "He's a fucking chester."

Two deputies appear and start barking orders. They call everyone off a list two-by-two. They put them in shackles and leg irons. In the end, everyone is gone but me and the old black man. I thank the old black man, but he ignores me and curls up and goes to sleep on the bench. I hear the diesel engines of the buses heave and fade off as they head to court. It's quiet. A deputy takes me to another cell. He doesn't even handcuff me. With the exception of a couple inmates that come in and right back out, I'm in the cell by myself all day. I can't stop thinking about that vato. He was just playing a role. If he'd had a shank, maybe I'd be dead, or maybe that was just horseplay to them.

Goddamn, I'm not even at Chino yet.

I have that feeling again. I'm not even that mad. It's just the way it is. It's that powerlessness the 12-steppers always talk about. In a strange way, it feels so good to hit the bottom, like when I was in rehab and couldn't do anything but play ping-pong and smoke cigarettes, or like when I'd surf and go over the falls and get pinned under a churning wave and all I could do was relax and hold my breath and wait for gravity to pull me back up. It's easy to let go when there's no choice, when there's nothing left to hold on to. I'd have fought the vatos, but they'd have eventually won. Maybe they'd have just kicked the shit out of me. Maybe they'd have killed me. Maybe they'd have raped me.

I'm not giving up, not at all. In fact, in powerlessness, there is more power to fight. I know now that I've never had much power over the results of anything; but that night, the night it all came crashing down, in that strange dark room with a man I'd never met, I gave up most of what little power I did have. I hit a glorious bottom. When the immediate fear and pain burned off a bit, and I landed in rehab, I felt it: this strange freedom. I can't control when the wave will stop churning, or what the judge will do, or the vatos, or what my mom and dad did or didn't do when I was a kid. All I can control is me. There is nothing in here to chase. I just have to be here alone with no addiction to hide in. If it doesn't kill me, this may be the perfect rehab.

I'm back in the sex pod, and all the inmates are posted in roll call formation. We are naked except our white, county-issued boxers. All the laundry lies in tremendous piles, one for each: white tube socks, white shirts and towels and orange V-necks and orange pants. I sit on the stairs waiting. Steven sits next to me. He's playing with his nails. His hands are overgrown child's hands. I bury my head between my knees and gaze down to Roman and Trap, sitting at the spider tables. Trap's entire frail body is pockmarked. Roman leans back onto the table, watching the inmate trustees gather the giant piles of laundry. He has one of those hard, bulging bellies like an off-season body builder.

The trustees hand out clean clothes during lunch roll call. I put on my new clothes and eat the standard lunch: peanut butter packet, an apple, a carton of milk and two slices of white bread. Steven and I sit at the spider bench closest to the stairs.

"Where did you go, Joseph?" Stephen asks. Horse Face is sitting across from us.

"Disneyland?" Horse Face jokes.

"How did you know?" I kid.

"A hunch," Horse Face responds. "You just look so happy, like you've been to the most magical place on earth."

"You didn't really go to Disneyland," Steven says. "Did you?"

Roman, Trap, and another black guy walk up behind us. I see their reflection in the dorm's glass wall. Roman grabs Steven's milk carton.

"Roman, I want that," Steven says.

Roman reaches for my milk. I put my hand over it, and he pulls away and shifts his focus to Steven.

"You owe me, motherfucker," Roman barks at Steven. "You owe me ten motherfucking soups and three shots of coffee."

"No, you said we were just playing, Roman. That isn't fair," Steven says.

"Turn the fuck around," Roman orders Steven. "You shouldn't be *playin'* if you can't be *payin'*, nigga."

Trap turns to me. I can tell he's just dying to tell the story about how he almost got me killed.

"Nigga," he says to Roman, "I told you, this motherfucker so stupid. He went in the cage for Central with all them vatos, and I put his ass out on front street—full-blown front street. If he a lawyer, he a dumb-ass lawyer."

"Nigga, you cold," Roman says and chuckles.

"I'm two cells down waiting for my ride to Inglewood," Trap continues, "I hear this nigga here yellin' like a straight bitch. *Help! Help! Officer!*" Trap flails his arms mocking me. "Oh please, save me! I'm PC. Help! Help!" Trap is doubled over in laughter imitating me. "Oh please, God, help me! Help me!"

King Wood is on the stairs watching the whole thing. "How about leaving those Woods alone," he says to Roman.

Steven and I get up and leave. We walk right past King Wood. Roman glares at King Wood while shouting at Steven, "I'mma get mine, by lunch tomorrow, or it's your ass."

I lie in my bunk, thinking. Steven pouts, then cries, then sleeps. Trap's reenactment was actually kind of hilarious—the way he flailed his arms. It wouldn't be nearly as funny if the vatos had shanked me. I should want to kill that little roach, Trap. I heard somebody say at one of the recovery meetings, something like: *if you are out for revenge, dig two graves first.* Maybe that's why I'm not too mad. Or maybe it's because I realize Trap is just being Trap.

"Naus 887, prepare for unlock," the intercom sounds.

Finally, I'm going to Chino, I think. It has been over a week. I'm buzzed out of the pod door into the waiting area by the trustees. A deputy comes out of the control room. He cuffs me and leads me into the visiting area. There is a single row of several booths with floor-mounted stools. Each is separated by Plexiglas, and there is a receiver on each side of the glass. I guess I'm not going to Chino. It's either Vinny or Keri. I told them not to visit me, but I can't begrudge them. The deputy unlocks my cuffs from my left wrist and clamps it onto the leg of the stool. He shuts the door behind him. I wait. A half-hour goes by, and I wonder if this is another mix-up like yesterday. Then, I hear a buzz, and on the other side of the glass an old, black lady waddles in leaning on a wooden cane. A small black hat is attached to her hair, and she wears gray nurse's shoes. The intercom tells her to sit at booth five, two past me. The door on my side buzzes. Roman enters. No deputy. No cuffs. He walks past me with barely a nod and sits at the booth.

I hear his deep hushed voice.

"Nana, thanks for coming ... Nah, Grandma, it ain't like that ... tell her I'll be out soon ... nah ... I can't make no money in here ... I don't know what to tell her ... tell him he's the man ... I'm sorry ... No, no, yeah, of course ... I'll beat it ... I love you."

The receiver clicks, and she waddles back past. The door buzzes.

Roman walks up and leans against the wall behind me. I'm trying to act casual, but my face and ears are radiating. I'm cuffed to this stool. He can do anything he wants to me.

"Who here to see you, lawyer-man?" he asks. He seems almost contemplative.

"I don't know. Maybe my friend or maybe my lawyer."

The door buzzes. Keri walks in. She jerks her head back at the sight of Roman. He has a face that a jury couldn't *not* convict. She's wearing a black pantsuit and heels.

"Damn, that is one fine *fat ass*," Roman says to me.

I pretend I don't hear him.

The door on our side unlocks and a deputy appears.

"C'mon, Roman."

Roman ogles Keri. Keri averts her eyes.

"Who that fine bitch?" Roman asks me as he slowly moves to the door toward the deputy.

I don't answer. I pick up the receiver. "Don't ask," I say to Keri, "just one of the fine gentlemen in my new community."

"You wouldn't believe what I had to do to get in here," Keri says, "Twin Towers is run by idiots."

Keri likes to complain about *the man*. We have that in common. Keri doesn't know anything about yesterday, and I don't tell her. She asks whether I've had any trouble. Smooth sailing, I reply. Everything is fine. No HBO though. Keri smiles. She knows I'm scared.

She's spoken to Vinny, my mom, filled them in. Good. I've had all my mail forwarded to her house. She starts listing the senders: IRS,

Franchise Tax Board, State Bar, DMV, St. John's Medical Center, Ford Motor Credit.

"*La, la, la, la, la, la, la,*" I chant in response.

Keri taught me this technique not long after we first met, and I've been using it ever since. She does it all the time. It works best when you put your hand over your ears, but my left hand is handcuffed, and my right hand is holding the receiver, so this is the best I can do. Just pay the bills on the list I gave you, I tell her. The rest will have to wait. Keri says something witty and walks out. She's not the sentimental type.

I wait and I wait and I wait. I'm pretty sure they've forgotten about me. Probably a shift change. *Fuck it.* I lay my head down on the stainless steel table. My ass is killing me, but, for now, I'm safer in here than in the dorm. I doze off.

❖   ❖   ❖

A buzz. I pop up startled. A string of saliva connects the corner of my mouth to a little pool on my shirtsleeve. It deepens the orange. The door buzzes twice. Five minutes later a deputy arrives, this one a particularly stocky, badass.

"Didn't you hear the fucking door buzz," he asks?

I rattle my cuffs. "I'm cuffed."

"Who the fuck cuffed you and left you in here?"

There is nothing I can think to say that wouldn't sound smart-assed, so I have to pause before answering. "I don't know which officer, Officer."

He uncuffs me and sends me back to the dorm. It's quiet. Everyone is watching TV or playing cards. I go upstairs to my bunk. I'm careful about when to take a shower, but this seems like a good time. I quickly get in and out.

I go back to my bunk. Steven isn't in his bunk. In fact, I don't think he was in his bunk when I got my stuff to shower. I look around. I look down over the railing down on the spider benches. I ask the Rev. He doesn't know. I ask Leonard.

"I don't know, man," Leonard says reluctantly. "I think he might be downstairs."

"I just looked," I say, "I didn't see him."

"You can't take care of that retard," Leonard says. "You need to watch yourself. You're going to get hurt, fucking with those ... *gangbangers.*"

Niggers is what he wanted to say. He held back because of the Rev. You hear that word so much in here, it's hard not to say it like it's a pronoun, but Leonard says it in the most toxic way possible.

"Yeah, I know. Okay. But where is he?"

Leonard sighs. "I'm not involved," he says, "but Roman came up, said Steven's time was up. I wasn't about to get involved. I feel sorry for that retard, too, but you know ..."

I lie down and pull the pillow tightly over the back of my head and around my ears. I can smell the sickly sweet detergent from the freshly mopped tile. The irritating high notes of Mexican TV invade my head. I'm wide-awake. I squeeze tighter. I can't go downstairs. I can barely tend to myself. After a while, I loosen up and fade into a meditative daydream. I try to think of bobbing on a longboard at Latigo Bay, Malibu with a warm Santa Ana offshore wind. Peter and I have the whole bay to ourselves. We take turns dropping in on five-foot sliders all the way across the bay. In the 12-step meditation meetings, they say be specific about it. Try to smell it, feel it. I splash some water. I taste the salt. I can feel it.

The bed jerks with the familiar movement of Steven climbing up onto his bunk. I come back from Malibu and listen to him cry into his pillow. The Rev climbs up a couple steps and looks on. He tries to console him.

"I don't want to be here!" Steven cries out. "He hurt me! He hurt me! I didn't do anything! *Ahh-uhh-uhh!* I hate it here! I want to go home! Why did he have to do that to me!" Steven cries and cries. I pull the sheet and blanket over my head and pull the pillow tightly over my ears. It only muffles Steven's moaning.

PART III

The 60 Freeway cuts through the largely industrial blue-collar cities of East Los Angeles: Commerce, Industry, El Monte, Hacienda Heights. It's an ugly freeway. There are patches without uniform sound walls, and through chain-link, I see Mexican kids at play and sagging clotheslines, both in dry dirt. Weedy grass grows up and into abandoned shopping carts and rusted-out barbecues. An old brown-on-yellow Winchell's Donuts sign, altered to read *Wi ll's*, imposes itself from high above. I'm one of eight inmates on this Los Angeles County Sheriff's bus. My return to the Inland Empire, or *the I.E.* as it's called, twenty miles east from here, feels ignoble. I'm shackled to a fellow sex criminal, a long-haired, generic white guy, about my age, who looks like a surfer. *What's up, dude? Nothin', dude, small-but-glassy peaky rights. See you in the lineup.* I wonder what he's here for. I can't picture it. I usually can, because most of these guys fit the creep profile. He stares into the dark, vinyl back of the seat in front of us, and I stare out at the freeway. I don't like leaving Los Angeles. It took me so long to get away from the IE, and I seem to keep going back. This is the worst return yet.

My mom was raised in Glen Avon, right off the 60, not far from Chino. On weekends, when my mom and I lived in the Alley, Grandpa would pick me up, and he'd drive us up the 60 in his little truck. We'd exit where the life-sized dinosaur sculptures stood: a T. Rex, a Stegosaurus, and one of the lesser-known dinos, the one with the spikes that form a mohawk. We'd hike up through the dusty, yellow mountain to a point and look down on the 60. From up there, the cars looked like

Hot Wheels, barely moving, east and west, one meandering here, then maybe another; there was never any real traffic, not like now. Grandpa and I would follow a utility road and switchback up to the Stringfellow Acid Pits. It was nothing to see, just a big fenced-off pit of blackness.

The bus pulls off the freeway. My stomach hurts, but I'm enjoying the radio all the same. Even this standard pop-rock radio, Foreigner or Styx or one of those '80's ballad rock bands, is a rare treat. There is no music in jail. I miss it. I didn't even realize I missed it until now. The bus maneuvers awkwardly through town—one of those dreadful towns I do my best to avoid, maybe Downey or Lakewood. Where we're going, I don't know, because we aren't even halfway to Chino. Pedestrians, mostly Hispanic woman with kids, peer up at the imposing metallic bus with its California golden bear badge logo, and a huge banner written across its entire length: *Los Angeles County Sheriff's Department.* They can't see past the barred, dark windows, but they know who's inside. It must make them think. It used to make me think. I'd wonder how many were on board, where they were going, what they'd done to get there. I'd think of how horrible it must be sitting on that bus. I'd wonder what one little thing could have changed to alter their course. But I knew better than that. After working with group-home kids, I knew it was a whole life that got them there, not just one crime. Hell, it was usually their parents' fucked-up lives before they were even born that got them there. Nearly all those kids I worked with in group homes were going to take a ride on a bus like this, sooner rather than later for most.

The driver parks the bus in the rear of a Taco Bell. This must be a common spot for deputies on transport duty, due to its unusually large parking lot. Funny, that is one good thing about going east from LA: more parking. There is parking for *all* in the IE; presumably because no-body wants to be here. The deputy riding shotgun goes inside to get his and the driver's lunches. The driver stays with the idling bus. A thick, chicken wire cage separates the driver from us. Luckily, it doesn't block the music. Otherwise, I couldn't hear Jon Bon Jovi.

The deputies inhale their *gorditas*, and we're back on the freeway. Chino steadily reels us in via the 60. I *have* to believe that it *can't* be that bad. *It just can't be.* They wouldn't put someone like me into one of those prisons I've seen on MSNBC, the kind with blurred-out faces, unyielding metal-on-metal factory noises, and men with gang tattoos. I was picturing something open, with a yard and a spirited game of pick-up basketball, a flat-screen TV, pool table, and football, maybe even an old pinball machine. Basically, I was envisioning a hybrid of the Riverside Boy's Club and my rehab. I know it doesn't make sense, but I was thinking this, even before I decided to take the plea bargain *and even after* I'd talked to Charley from Narcotics Anonymous. Charley made it dramatically clear that Chino Prison was a violent and terrible place. But, I just can't believe it. Surely they'll put me in a part of the prison where they house the *he-really-shouldn't-be-here* types.

I look out the window and watch Los Angeles blur by to the west, and for a moment, I'm not *thinking* about anything. I'm *feeling*. This is dangerous territory. As I've done since the day of my arrest, I try to avoid *feelings*. If I start *feeling*, I don't know what will happen. Maybe I might start crying. I'm scared. That's for sure. This isn't a movie. This is my life. And I'm on my way to prison. It's like I'm floating in the open sea, kicking my legs to stay afloat, trying to think happy thoughts, but all the while knowing deep down that it's just a matter of time before a great white shark eats me alive.

Stop it! I must stop this right now. I can *think about how I feel* later, when—*if*—I survive this.

Think trivial. Think funny. Okay, okay ... funny ... funny. I'm on my way to prison, and I have a degree in criminal justice. Now that's funny.

"What?" my shackle-mate asks.

His voice startles me out of my daydream and into the present. "Nothing ... uhm, just thinking," I murmur, just as surprised as he that I was speaking aloud.

I feel the bus gear down as we pull onto the prison grounds. If not for razor ribbon atop two rows of curiously tall fencing, the scene is bucolic—more like a sprawling dairy farm than one of the country's most dangerous prisons. The squatty sign reads: *California Institute for Men* and is the type associated with golf course communities or small private universities. We stop near a plain, single-story office building and wait. Ten minutes later, a prison guard walks out, ushering two young white prisoners. They are in bright orange uniforms and look barely old enough for junior prom. The guard wears a military-green uniform. His pants are tucked into black combat boots. The skinny, shaved-head boys are not cuffed, which makes me nervous. They board and are abuzz with the excitement of wherever they just came from. If I hadn't seen them I'd think they were as black as Biggie. They talk like they grew up in Compton. Every sentence starts out with *Damn!* Or *Nigga, please!* We sex offenders are all Presbyterian-church-silent, intently listening to them while pretending not to. We are on the way to a funeral, most likely *our own*, and they are on a school field trip. One asks, *Where y'all niggers be comin' from?* I know this isn't like any place I've ever been, because white-as-Iowa white boys are blurting out the N-word as if it's a pronoun. I pretend I don't hear the question. Leonard, seated two rows up, tells them we came from Twin Towers. They ask, *Where in Twin Towers?* Leonard makes something up about fourth-floor mainline. One responds, *Twin Towers, be off the hiz-ook, nigga!* We reach their destination, and they bound off the bus. One hollers back, *Good luck, bitch-ass fishes.*

Good luck, indeed.

We drive past convicts, the types with thick moustaches and dense bodies, walking around an open grassy area. One wears a pre-Walkman headphone radio. A couple of others are picking up trash. One does push-ups like a piston in the grass. Another is reading a Bible at a picnic table. *This doesn't look so bad.* The bus stops, and its air brakes hiss and sigh. Our four twosomes shackle-walk down the bus aisle, down the steps onto the asphalt, and into a drab office building. A deputy nonchalantly removes our shackles and leg irons. We are placed in a small holding cell facing a high counter, where two correctional officers answer phones, banter about how poor the coffee is, and converse with our transporters as they noisily gather shackles and cuffs. A cheeky radio commercial for auto insurance plays in the background; there's the voice of a dry-witted lizard with an Australian twang that even in these circumstances makes me grin—a moment's escape from anxiety that's surging in my chest and stomach. This cell smells of shit, urine, bleach, and just a hint of burnt coffee. The desk officers keep talking. It's good—reminds me of normalcy. They are at work, doing their job, and enjoying the camaraderie. I think: things used to be like that for me. I used to enjoy talking to people at work.

A fellow inmate asks when these fucking *COs* are going to do their job and check us in. If he heard it, the head CO, the one the others call, *Sarge*, ignores the comment. He's all about business. There is also a female CO with her hair tucked into a green baseball hat with CDC written across it. Sarge slides out several manila folders onto the counter like he's dealing a hand of blackjack from a giant deck of cards, then calls out the names. Everyone's name is called except mine. Now I'm alone in the cell. I wonder if I'll see poor Steven again. A half hour later, my name is finally called. A CO orders me to strip naked. I do. I flash to eighth-grade gym, the first time I had to get naked in front of other boys. It was cold then, relegating me to a couple grapes and a golf pencil. I was horrified that every other eighth grader was going to have a penis like my dad's or the one's I'd see in porn mags. I can't believe I'm thinking about this. It's warm in here, so my cock and balls are full, loose, and hanging. So that's good, for whatever reason I can't deal with right now: low self-esteem, ego, self-obsession, some Freudian shit, *whatever*. But what if I get hard? *That'd be horrible.* Sometimes nakedness in-and-of-itself makes me hard. *Don't get hard.* I follow the CO about thirty paces, and shower at a stainless steel kiosk with multiple heads like the ones at public beaches. He tells me to bend over and pull up my nutsack. I think: *this seems particularly crude.* He tells me to spread my ass cheeks and cough. I do. I think: I heard about this in an Ice Cube song. The CO visually checks my asshole with a flashlight—for drugs and weapons, I presume.

An image of Halloween flickers into my mind—it must be the CO's flashlight. I laugh nervously. It's so humiliating. The CO must have heard me laugh, but he doesn't react. Maybe it's not unusual. Maybe standing naked, having your ass searched by a man in a green military uniform commonly induces laughter.

An inmate trustee wearing solid blue gives me a set of orange prison clothes. *CDC* in black block letters is stenciled down the right leg. The prison shoes are cheap slip-ons like Chinese people wear in old kung fu movies. The trustee can't find a size 13, so the CO has him give me back the ones I came in with from Twin Towers, which are much more substantial, like knock-off Vans slip-ons. I think of second grade when I used a black marker to draw a checkerboard pattern on the foxing of the knock-off Vans my Grandpa bought me at Kmart. I was humiliated at recess the next day, when one of the rich kids at recess pointed out to seemingly everyone in the entire school that I was wearing Kmart shoes and not custom Vans.

I'm taken out the back door of the intake area and placed into a small holding cell in a giant, echoing hall. It's only twenty feet from the cage I just left, but it is a different place altogether. I can feel the change in mood and emotional temperature. I've crossed through a thick metal door from central intake into the *prison* part of the prison. There is no outside world here. No more Sarge and coffee talk. That was boot camp. This is the war zone. That was purgatory. This is hell. The hall is tall and long and shaped like an airplane hangar. It's two hundred yards deep and three stories high. There are industrial windows at the top of the walls. Thick, grayish chicken-wire cordons off equal sections of the hall, like firebreaks for humans. The floor is concrete, painted a glossy brownish-orange. I hear a low steady din of something huge and ferocious in the distance, and although I want no part of it, I know it's in my future. Through the first chicken-wire wall, I can see a guard with a group of several orange-clad inmates. They stop inside a white line that runs on the floor parallel to the east wall for as far as I can see. Shoulder-to-shoulder, hands clasped behind their backs, they stand with their noses to the wall. The CO opens a door causing the sound to rise dramatically; details come through: tinny, banging metal, a roar of men's voices, high and low, a glimpse of tatted, shirtless men. The door shuts behind the inmates, and the volume and its clarity recedes.

There are two men in this holding cell with me. They speak gang-Spanglish. I know enough to know they're talking about me, but not enough to know exactly what they're saying. I look straight ahead. They stop talking, and the shorter one gets up and stands in front of me. I study my shoes intently and wonder whether I'm going to have to fight them.

"Hey holmes, Wood, where you from, *eh?*" He raises his chin a notch as if inserting commas: "*Hey holmes,*" one uptick, "*Wood,*" another uptick, "*Where you from?*" another tick, "*Eh?*" two upticks. By the end, his chin is skyward, and I can only see his neck tattoo, *Shorty*. His head comes back down. I look at him intentionally wide-eyed. *MS 13* is tatted on his forearm. His brooding eyes are just slightly more curious than vicious.

"Los Angeles County Jail, Twin Towers. I don't know exactly where, you know ... I was only there for eleven days."

"Where you from, *holmes?*" Shorty repeats slowly. This time he stores all the upticks for *holmes?* As if he thinks I didn't hear him the first time, because English is my second language.

I get it. I listen to gangster rap. He wants to know what set I'm claimin'. Crenshaw Mafia? Inglewood Crips?

"Oh, uh, Santa Monica and then, *uhm*, Pasadena ... oddly both in Los Angeles County but not part of Los Angeles City as they are separate cities ...," I answer.

He looks dumbfounded, so I expound a bit. "You know—uhm ... they're incorporated separately from LA proper. Uhm ... you probably didn't want to uh—anyway, I mean ... I lived in Santa Monica, but my office was in Pasadena."

Awkward, naïve, geeky: That should do the trick.

"He said *his office*, holmes," Shorty says. At that, they laugh, full-belly laughs. "His *fucking* office! No *fucking* way holmes!" Shorty takes a moment to compose himself. "*Whatchyou* in here for—ripping someone off? like with your *com-pute-or* or some shit?" he says mockingly. Shorty turns to his homey, "like in that movie, eh? You know, *esse, that fucking movie*. The one with the fucking guy that talks all fucking ..."

"You mean that fucking movie where he's all like ..." homey says and twists his body like he's doing a superslow-motion limbo. ". . . you know . . . the uh, the fuckin' ... the fucking *Matrix!*"

"*The fuckin' Matrix?* You're a fucking retard, *esse!* The *fucking Matrix?*" Shorty repeats indignantly. "What the fuck is *The Matrix* got to do with stealin' shit with your *pinche* com-pute-or, dumbass? *Yeah, he's like Neo and shit.* You're a dumbass, holmes."

"Nah, fuck you," homey retaliates lightly. "I don't know. *Shit.* I just thought ...*you know ...* white boy, all fuckin' trippin' and shit like a whole 'nother world and shit, right? They got fuckin' com-pute-ors in that movie, *esse*. Why you got to be all up in my shit, holmes?"

Shorty doesn't respond immediately but thinks demonstratively.

"Eh holmes, check it out, check it out," Shorty says to homey while pointing at me. "He *is* in the *fuckin'* matrix, homey ..." Shorty gives us both a moment to reflect on this gem of a revelation.

"This motherfucker took the *blue pill* and shit. You know? Like ... where the fuck am I holmes?" Shorty turns to me. "You're in the motherfucking matrix, holmes!"

They laugh and intermittently misquote *The Matrix* for several minutes. I chuckle along. I breathe. I'm relieved. Call it *The Matrix* or whatever, I'm in the *anomaly zone*, where I belong. In the *anomaly zone*, so I'm something to laugh at, not something to kill.

"So why you up in here, holmes?" Shorty asks me. He turns serious and hops back on his pre-*Matrix* train of thought. His dangerous upticking chin has returned.

"I committed a felony assault during an alcohol-induced blackout," I read aloud from my mental script.

"No way, *esse*. For *reals?* You got all *loco* up on some *pinche* motha fucker, huh?" Shorty pauses in thought and then takes up a playful *cholo* boxing stance: upper body leaning far back, chin up, elbows in, knuckles up, thumb out.

I think, *Boxing for Idiots.* It reminds me of all the *vatos* that came in to David's kickboxing gym.

"Yep, that's what I'm here for."

"No shit, eh?" homey says as Shorty shadow boxes. "Fu-uu*uck.* Your first time, eh?"

I nod.

"You better hope they don't put your ass in the gym, *esse*. It's *loco* in there, eh. You gonna be putting in work for the Woods, holmes," Shorty says and turns to homey as if he just remembered something important. "*Esse*, check it out. He looks like my *pinche abogado* ... no way, holmes ...*ser-i-ous* ... with the glasses and shit ... check it out, holmes." Shorty inspects me from several angles as I pose awkwardly. "Punk-ass-lawyer-bitch-motherfucker didn't do shit for me except suck the DA's dick. Fuckin' faggot *maricon*."

With that, I look back to my shoes. Thankfully, Shorty and homey are done with me. They go back to gangster-Spanglish as if I was never there.

I spend the next two hours trying not to think of classic prison movie scenarios: the prison rape, the prison shank, the prison riot, the prison fight to the death. For each of these, I have a game plan: *Shut up, and don't get involved ... in anything.* Finally, a CO comes for me. We march down the hall. He reminds me of the news footage of American soldiers in Iraq during Desert Storm—geared out from head to toe among haphazardly outfitted, eagerly surrendering Iraqi soldiers. This soldier wears black wraparound sunglasses; he has a black-padded, nylon suspender-system, which holds a Velcro handcuff case and two black tear gas canisters, like oversized grenades, and a graphite black baton. His military-green pants are tucked into high-tech, black leather boots. I'm his captive, intimidated by his gear-enhanced presence. A line of inmates walks single file toward us. Their soldier has them stop and turn to the wall as we pass, *nose to the wall!* I look straight ahead, listening, watching; the tension, fear, and restrained violence are as solid as the concrete we're walking on. Our marching soles squeak on the shiny concrete in near unison. I clench my jaw to quell my chattering teeth.

The CO leads me through a heavy steel door and into a vestibule. There are guards in an old glassed-in control room. A white-faced, relic of a wall clock with black hands is mounted above the glass. The clamor is enormous and harrowing. Banging and screaming and rattling and talking and slamming, all join in one horrible deafening cacophony. *How can it be this loud?* I can't see where the clamor originates. The CO doesn't say anything. He just leaves me here, standing, backstage to hell. I wait while he goes into the control room. His comrades look over at me, one looks onto a clipboard. Soldier comes back out.

"Naus, second tier," he says sternly.

I don't move. I don't know what that means to me.

"Naus, go!" he points angrily.

I take a deep breath, roll my shoulders back, and stand up straight. I walk in the direction indicated. I go to the roar. On the right is an empty cafeteria. Then, the walkway opens up, and I come out into the cellblock. I don't so much see it as it *hits* me. *Oh my fucking God!* It's nothing short of awesome: a wall of orange-clad inmates pulsating out from behind bars. The violence and tension hang in the air like steam. This wall of pain is alive. It's the balcony section of a giant opera house,

with screaming convicts instead of debonair socialites, steel and concrete instead of ornate woodwork. Where I stand is open four stories
high. On the right is a wall that turns to dirty, square, window blocks all
the way up some fifty feet. On my left are three tiers of cells, each with
two inmates, thirty or so on each tier. The second and third tiers have a
catwalk with steel rails. The walls are painted beige, and the railings yellow. The paint is chipped away, dirty, revealing the raw steel beneath.

Like nothing I've ever seen, there is a constant motion of torn strips
of white sheets, tied into long ropes looping hundreds of feet from tier
to tier and cell to cell. Black prison shoes and tightly wound balls of
orange prison uniform are tethered to the ends of the lines for weight.
The muscled and tatted arms of inmates reach through cell bars, ma-
nipulating at least a dozen of these lines. Some are being reeled in, and
some are being cast, caught, and passed. I wonder how I'll get to my cell
without being ensnared in this giant, shifting spider web.

An electronic buzz precedes the slide and slam of a cell door being automatically opened. I see the opening. I walk up the steel-grated
stairs. Shadowed faces take form. It's so loud I can't hear the noise of
my footsteps. Hands reach out from the cells toward me, words being
hurled: *fish, pinche, puto, faggot, Wood, ass, hey, nigger.* I ignore it all and
keep looking toward my destination, the open cell in the middle of the
second tier. A triangular folded-up piece of paper hits me in the chest
and bounces to the ground. I keep walking.

"Gimme that! *Holmes,* eh … gimme that shit."

I pick it up, and hand it to the arm's hand. The Mexican connected to
the arm presses his face up to the bars.

"Holmes, eh man, c'mon man, take it to O.G., just one cell past yours."

I take it.

I reach my cell. There is a linebacker-bodied white guy slouched per-
pendicularly across the bottom of two bunks.

"I'm supposed to give this to O.G.," I report, trying not to appear as
shaken as I am.

He grabs the paper from me as I walk in, and in one move reaches around to the cell next door. The cell door loudly slides back into place. "O.G., kite for you. New celly delivered it." He looks at me to finish. "Joseph."

"Joseph," he repeats.

"Thank you, Joseph," I hear from an old, black man's gravelly voice. "I'm O.G. Welcome to Palm Hall."

My *celly,* John, who, at first glance, doesn't seem particularly interested in murdering or raping me, shares: He's here on a *ridiculous* parole violation for testing dirty; for what, he does not say. From the looks of him, my guess is mass quantities of anabolic steroids. He's up for release by the end of the week. I tell him my story in brief. Even the redacted R-rated version is shocking, but he doesn't ask any questions, doesn't even do the *you're a lawyer?* bit. He just lays back and hands me an apple. *Something's amiss. This is too easy. Hmmm.* I know the whole razor-blades-in-the-apple thing on Halloween is an old wives' tale, but I never eat an apple without the thought popping up, and if there was ever a situation where I actually *could* bite into a razor-bladed apple this would be the time. I bite cautiously. Crunch. No razor blades. It's not like I thought there *would* be, just an outside possibility. I'm quite aware at this moment in time that anything is possible, especially the *worst* anything.

This cell would barely pass for a walk-in closet. Ten feet deep and just a tad wider than my wingspan, it has two bunks that fold up into the wall, a little built-in desk, and the ever-present stainless steel toilet-sink combo. The wall opposite the bed is a canvas of sloppy angular gang tags, *Nuestra Familia, Mara Salvatrucha, Trece XIII, Nortenos, MS 13,* framing the masterpiece: a large, intricate, white power montage featuring an angry, glaring eagle—apparently eagles hate minorities—atop a slightly incongruous swastika with *NLR* crested below. The wall has been painted so many times, the last several dozen institutional beige, the etchings are the texture of palette-knife oil paintings.

I climb up to my bunk. I'm relieved, and it's not terribly uncomfortable albeit about a half foot too short. This is as safe as I've been since I sat in front of the judge twelve days ago. Unless I've misread John greatly, I think I'm going to be okay for a minute. It's incredible: the noise hasn't stopped or even dipped. I figure there are 150 inmates in this cavernous hall with the acoustics of a squash court, and it sounds like half of them are rattling their bars or screaming. I'm so exhausted. I wasn't this tired after my first kickboxing bout, when I could barely move from the beating my legs took. I pull my paper-thin pillow tight over my face and ears, but it's like I just turned the volume down from ten to nine. *Thank God*, whatever that means, for getting me here safe. I think of Vinny. Then I say it under my breath, the prayer he told me to say, *God, I offer myself to thee, to build with me and do with me as thou wilt* ... Even though I know no one can hear me, I still feel embarrassed praying, but it does calm me. I fade knowing I'll sleep hard and that my dreams are going to be quite the ride.

I feel a tug on my arm. I'm in the midst of a stress dream, something about being late to court in Long Beach with a client waiting and Tito and my dad and Beth and Keri, all mad, all disappointed. I rise abruptly. It's another cell, I'm wearing orange, the smell; a toilet flushes. The angry noise is rising. *Yes, okay, here I am. I'm in Chino.*

"It's chow time, get ready for unlock," John says.

A prisoner walks by and hands him something through the bars. John stashes it somewhere around his pillow. I'm not ready for this. I'm not ready for the prison chow hall scene. I've seen it in so many movies. This is the part where Danny Trejo or that giant black guy with the wandering eye that was in *Friday* stabs my hand to the table with a fork.

"Just follow me," John says, reassuringly, apparently sensing my fear.

The cell doors of the entire tier rack open, one by one, from front to back. *Click, slide ... clack! Click, slide ... clack!* The energy pulses. It's recess for cons. I follow John's hulking figure out to and down the catwalk closely. The orange uniforms file along and down the stairs. Some mill a bit. One has his shirt in his hand, showing off his colorless prison tats on his thick, ripped body. There isn't a patch of skin unillustrated. The biggest piece reads, *SUR 13*. There are raised puncture wound scars near his kidney and slash scars from his ear to Adam's apple. The volume crescendos. There are no guards to be seen. John approaches the big tatted Mexican and clandestinely hands him something. I trail behind.

Everyone quiets upon entering the chow hall. Two black and green uniformed COs oversee the crowd of inmates. One is a middle-aged Mexican man with a smile and a paunch. The other is tall, white, and muscular, wears dark, sport sunglasses, and seems ready to beat some-one down with his baton upon the drop of a canned green bean. I'm sandwiched in line between O.G. and John. Inmates in clear plastic hair-nets and loose, clear plastic gloves ladle soupy, gray chicken-something, green beans, and roughly plop down a roll and a carton of milk onto each inmate's partitioned, orange, plastic tray. We eat with thick, dull, plastic spoons at spider tables like the ones at Twin Towers. There are about twenty tables. The talk is hushed.

"You want yo milk, homey?" O.G. asks me.

"Damn, O.G. He ain't givin' you his *gat damn* milk, Ohhh ... Geee!" John says lightheartedly with a mock-black accent.

"Ise just axin. Damn, ain't nothin'," O.G. responds.

"*Essssooo.* You ain't punkin' Clark Kent, O—Geeee," a wiry young Mexican inmate seated next to O.G. says with a wry smile. I recall the Mexican shot caller and his homeys at the sex pod at Twin Towers say-ing *esso.* Must be a thing. *It sounds awfully cool.* I wonder if Woods have a cool word like that. We all laugh quietly, except the skinhead next to me, a thick, white guy with sloppy *SS* Lightning Bolts tattooed on the left side of his neck. *This is good,* I think, *Clark Kent is better than Harry Potter.*

After about three minutes, the big Nazi-esque guard taps his baton on the top of an empty spider table. The loud, tinny rap interrupts the con banter. The first table of inmates, all black, stand and walk in single file toward the tray drop, each shows his tray and spoon to the older guard and drops it in the bin. Another *tap-tap* rings out from the CO's baton, and the next table rises, and then again and again until the line has reached the end of the room. The line forms between the tables through the middle of the room right past our table. I try not to look, but I feel the eyes staring at me, some comment, usually something with the word *fish* or *Wood* in it. I stare down at my empty plate and wait for our *tap-tap.* The chicken-something wasn't so bad. *Tap-tap* another table of six rises and lines up.

In my periphery, I see the last inmate in line, a lanky Mexican with an edgy tweeker's face, stalling to make room between himself and the inmates in front of him. He doesn't look right. Something's amiss. The tweeker makes eye contact with me and sees me seeing him. His eyes dart down. He walks forward slowly, and then lurches toward our table, raising a fist like a hammer. He's coming right at me. *Freeze.* I can't move. I can't speak. *Release.* I lean away, toward John to my left. Nazi Lightning Bolts sits to my right. They are both still unaware. Everything is slow and quiet, just like in my DUI wreck. The incoming orange blur hammers down at Lightning Bolts' head and hits him square on the side of the neck. Lightning Bolts falls back to the ground. *Oh fuck. This is happening.* I watch as the tweeker rabbit punches Lightning Bolts in the neck, *one-two-three.* I'm stuck in time, locked up with a mixture of excitement and panic and yet thinking, I can't believe he punches like that. *Who punches like that? A girl—a girl who doesn't know how to punch.* A wailing siren sounds. A shot of blood spurts out of Lightning Bolts's neck.

Everyone flees the spider tables and huddles against the exterior wall, *except me*. The scene is at my feet, and the black and green COs rush in, spraying streams of liquid from their canisters, and yelling, *Get down! Get the fuck down! Get down!* A guard thumps the tweeker on his back with his baton—*thook, thook, thook*. It sounds like a well-struck, sand bunker golf shot. The tweeker goes limp and crumbles face-first. The end of a blood-dipped pencil protrudes out of a crude, papier-mâché handle and drops from the tweeker's hand to the floor. I'm ripped off my stool by the back of my shirt. The hard fabric chokes me. I'm dragged fifteen feet across the floor to the wall. My eyes never leave the scene. Lightning Bolts is in a pool of oil-black blood. He's unconscious; his mouth is agape. The pool laps into his mouth like ocean water edging forward as the tide comes in. The blood puddle expands to his chest.

"Cover your face with your shirt," John whisper-shouts at me.

I do what he says and instantly notice the sting in my eyes and nose. *It occurs to me: I was wrong. The tweeker doesn't punch like a girl; he stabs like a killer.* John and I sit shoulder-to-shoulder against the wall. *My God.* There are holes in Lightning Bolts' neck, one of which must have pierced his jugular. The siren quits. The roar from the other two tiers in the cellblock, obviously aware that something fantastic is happening, fills the space the siren has freed up. One gas-masked CO presses his boot down on the back of the tweeker's neck, while another cuffs him with a zip tie like a rodeo star. They lift him up unnaturally by his arms and walk him out. He's stunned but conscious and smirking. Several minutes go by. Lightning Bolts is still bleeding, and the pool of blood has expanded below his waist and an arm's length beyond his head. His body jerks as if he's about to go into seizure but then stops. His eyes are shut. If he's still alive, he won't be for long. The body is a blood container. I know this, but now I really *understand* this. We are all just blood-filled water balloons hoping not to get popped. The COs just stand there and watch Lightning Bolts bleed; they keep us down. We all watch him bleed.

Finally, prison medics arrive and carry Lightning Bolts away on a stretcher. After a long meeting of the COs and some apparent dissension from the older Mexican guard with the paunch, those of us remaining are strip-searched one at a time in front of each other and the several remaining guards. It's clearly meant to be humiliating, and it is.

❖   ❖   ❖

John gives me a little golf pencil, and I write the prayers Vinny told me to say every night on the wall next to my bunk. They are long and annoyingly Christian, but I have them memorized, and if they can help me survive for three more months like they did all last year, I'm going to say them all day every day, whether I believe God is a sea anemone or a muscular, bearded guy on a cloud. I meditate, too, again, because that's what Vinny told me to do, because that's what the guy who helped him survive life after addiction told him to do, because that's what the guy before him told him to do and that's what everyone is supposed to do. It's in the 12-stepper's recovery manual. I've been doing it sporadically for a year. Sometimes my mind churns like a washing machine of horrible thoughts, but sometimes I get a certain absence of self: The constantly chattering, nonsense part of my brain turns off. When that happens, I feel this weird synthesis that I've never really felt before, except maybe when I used to lose myself past the abject pain of Muay Thai training or when researching in the law library for hours that felt like minutes. I've got plenty of time. It seems impossible to meditate with the constant noise, but I just do it. *God, your will, not mine, be done; God, your will, not mine, be done.* I repeat it until I lose count. And then I do fifty more. It fades into lights-out, when the cellblock goes dark. After a few minutes, it gets quieter; only a few shouts, bangs, and toilet flushes persist. I fade to sleep.

❖   ❖   ❖

Someone's yelling. I pop up, fumble for my glasses. The voice is familiar.

"Guard! Man down! Man down! Guard, man down, man-fucking-down!"

It's O.G. next door, shouting urgently.

"Joseph, Joseph, eh man, c'mon."

"Yeah, what's up?"

I jump off my bunk. John is sitting up on his bunk in his boxers. His eyes are glazed, and his arms are extended out like Frankenstein's monster.

"I'm alrigh' ... I'm oaaa, I ooh," John slurs his words, mouth agape.

He tries to stand but he's stiff and just rocks and falls back as if his entire body is in an invisible cast.

"What's going on?" I ask O.G., whose shaky reflection I can see in the little mirror he's holding out into the catwalk.

"Guard, *Gat dammit*! Man motha-fuckin' down!" O.G. yells desperately. Other inmates farther down the tier, closer to the guard station, are yelling for the guards, too.

"Why don't you shut the fuck up and mind yo own business ol' man. That's *they* problem not yo's," O.G.'s celly barks viciously.

O.G. pauses, as if to contemplate whether he should respond, and then defiantly says, "Fuck you, nigga. You ain't got the common decency God gave a rat."

I hear a guard clanking down the steel gangway. He drags his baton across the railing.

Someone yells, *keys on deck*.

John's head is swiveling atop his giant, stiff torso. He's trying to tell me something.

A CO stands in front of our cell.

"He got the sugar, boss," O.G. says.

"I know. I know. Third fucking time this month," the CO says.

John begins to cough, choke, and drool.

"The sugar?" I ask the CO.

"It's diabetes ... dumb niggers call it *the sugar*," the CO says, rolling his eyes. "Put him on his side."

I stand in front of John. He tries to fight me with his stiff arms, as I grab his shoulders and push him sideways onto his bunk. He's too big. I duck around his arm and sit next to him and lean into him.

"Now clear his mouth," the CO orders.

Why isn't our cell opening? Why am I doing this instead of a medic? I tilt John's chin back, as he tries to push me away with his arms. I pull his tongue flat. It's cold.

"Good, now here." The CO holds out a plastic tube that looks like travel-sized toothpaste. He cracks off the top and hands it to me through the bars. "Squeeze this onto his tongue, and if he doesn't swallow, you'll have to cover his mouth and hold his nose."

I dodge John's arms again. He fights me like a giant baby that doesn't want his smooshed carrots, so I hold the back of his head and thrust the tube into his mouth and squeeze it all out in one motion. We all watch anxiously, O.G., via his little round mirror. After a five count, John's eyes light up, his arms relax, and he comes to. He sits up as if he just woke up from a little nap, as if he wasn't the subject of a medical emergency seconds ago. *Jesus Christ.*

"Hey, Joseph," John greets me groggily, his eyes still adjusting.

"*Hey, Joseph*, hey, Joseph?" O.G. says, mocking John through the mirror. "You dumbass. I tolds you. How you not gonna tell yo celly you got the sugar? Man, that just stupid. You coulda died on our ass. What if that CO didn't come?"

"Sorry. I didn't think of it," John says as he rubs his eyes. "I'm discharging. I should be out of here already. I thought ..."

"You *were* almost out of here—in a *motha fucking* pine box," O.G. snaps.

"Old man. Shut the fuck up, and let me sleep," O.G.'s celly viciously barks. "You wake my black ass up again on some bullshit, I'm gonna break you off a piece. You understand?"

"Fuck you," O.G. retorts boldly but with just a dash of fear at the end.

John and I go quiet. I can feel the tension, and John's saucer-eyes confirm my instinct that O.G. could be in trouble.

"Oh, *Fuck me?* Say it again, nigga. Say that *shit* again. I cut you slack cuz you old and decrepit and shit, but say it again nigga. Say, fuck me. Say it, nigga!"

"Take it easy, Lo-Lo. He was just lookin' out," John says, trying to de-escalate the situation.

"Not *yo* cell, not *yo* business. This between me and this dumbass ol' country-ass nigga here," Lo-Lo says.

Like an after-school fight, inmates are on the bars egging them on. Among the bar rattling and other instigators, I hear a Wood taunt, *fuck that nigger up Ohhh Geee!*

In his silence, I can feel O.G.'s pride debating against self-preservation. The eggers-on press harder, yelling and rattling their cages. For several moments, I think O.G. has used his better judgment and decided to stay quiet.

"Fuck. You. Lo-Lo! Fuck you, nigga!" O.G. says loudly and defiantly for everyone to hear.

The surrounding cells go berserk. John cringes, and sticks his little makeshift circular mirror through the bars to see into O.G. and Lo-Lo's cell. We see and hear the gist of the violence *cinema verite* via the little, shaky circle. It's more like watching a medical procedure than a movie's fight scene.

John shouts *man down!* before man is down. His shouts are drowned out by the uproar of the entire hall. I hear the crunch and the slap and the squishing and the heavy breathing for a few moments. Then it's just strike after strike and intermittent desperate partial words—*no ... pleas ... c'mo... da ... fu*—as O.G. is beaten far past the point of defeat. John keeps shouting, *man down!* In the murky, shaky, little mirror, I can see the general form of O.G., faceup with his head jammed against the bars. Lo-Lo has him pinned and is choking him out.

The crowd turns against Lo-Lo.

"You like that, nigga? You like that?" Lo-Lo says as he let's go of O.G.'s neck. O.G. gasps for air. "I can kill you right now, nigga." He chokes him further, then lets go. O.G. gasps like a drowning man coming to the surface just before his lungs fill with water.

Other inmates have joined John in calling, *man down!* and *guard!*, but there is no response. Lo-Lo keeps choking and then letting go of O.G. John pleads with him to stop, but Lo-Lo just keeps it up. *Choke ... gasp, taunt, choke ... gasp, taunt.* This goes on for several minutes. I wonder if Lo-Lo is actually going to kill O.G. Then he stops, and there is a long silent pause, and all I can hear is heavy breathing.

"Jesus Christ, old man!" Lo-Lo shouts in disgust.

Lo-Lo dismounts O.G. The most wretched smell fills the air. O.G. has shit his pants. Lo-Lo makes a show of it, "Old man shit his pants ... fuckin' disgusting."

I can hear the humiliation in O.G.'s silence. John lies down in his bunk. A couple minutes later, I hear a loud plop of O.G.'s shit-filled pants hit the concrete of the bottom tier. The inmates on the bottom tier go nuts, yelling out in disgust and anger.

No guards come.

TWENTY

I'm alone in my cell. John has gone back to the world. That's what he said, *back to the world*, like Chino was another planet. I think I hear my name, and then it's repeated, "Naus, prepare for unlock." My heart races. I'm not supposed to pray for myself, only that I be given the strength to do God's will, but I'm making an exception.

"God, please keep me safe, God. Amen."

My cell door slides open and pops into place. It's loud. Kites on strings bob up and down all around me like I'm at a fly-fishing demo. Inmates yell at me, the usual, *Wood, Nazi, fuck, homey, faggot.* I walk tall and briskly and keep my eyes in front of me. I get *burned*—a black guy holds his cock out for me to see as I walk by. I don't flinch. I bounce down the stairs. The inmate tier tender—a kind of inmate janitor—waits for me at the bottom of the stairs. He wears plastic gloves and holds a broom and a long-handled dustpan. He rests his leg across the railing to block my path.

"Mongrel," he says and extends his mitt-like hand.

He's thick and muscular with tattoos covering every exposed piece of skin below his neck. His hair is long and pulled back in a ponytail.

"Joseph," I say as I shake his hand. "It's a pleasure to meet you Mongrel."

It's actually not nice to meet him. It's quite scary, in fact.

"What are you in here for, Wood?" he asks.

"Felony Assault and Criminal Threats."

"Nah, you ain't PC-upped for that shit," he says bluntly.

Mongrel gets in my face. Time slows down. But I don't move back. I'm so close I can feel his eyelashes. I want to beg him to let me pass, but I also want to wrap him up with a two-legged takedown and see if he knows how to defend a full-mount. Instead, I stay silent but stand my ground.

"Why you PC-upped?" he asks and backs up a few inches.

"Because I'm an attorney."

"Naus, get over here," I hear.

Mongrel and I turn toward the voice. It's a CO standing in the entryway.

"I'm gonna get your jacket, and we'll see if you're lying," Mongrel says to me in a hushed voice.

He moves aside. The CO points me to the empty cafeteria. We've been on lockdown and cell-fed since the cafeteria shanking, so I haven't been in here since my first day. A man in a tan, corduroy jacket is sitting at a spider table. He has a leather attaché case and papers spread across the table.

"You want him cuffed?" the CO yells across the cafeteria.

"No, that's quite alright, officer. Thank you."

I walk to him, and he stands and offers his hand. He looks over his half-glasses.

"Dr. Driscoll."

Dr. Driscoll explains that he is a psychiatrist that sometimes works for the state doing psychiatric evaluations, that he's here to speak with me, that he's read my file, that he'll be submitting a report to the court. It's a bit canned, and he doesn't look at me while he goes through his introduction. Then he stops.

"I've never seen anything like this, Mr. Naus," he says. "How bizarre. What a tragedy."

My chest opens up, and I can feel space in there. I didn't know how badly I wanted to hear someone say that.

"I've read Dr. Rothberg's report. As I'm sure you are aware, he's highly regarded in the field. His report was thorough. Obviously, he was paid to write it, but the facts are the facts."

Dr. Driscoll pulls out the police report. I immediately recognize it. I've read it so many times.

"My take is basically the same as Rothberg's," he says and then asks, "Do you have anything you want to add?"

I clench my face to keep from crying. I've been staying in the present to stay alive, but this has brought the whole of the last eighteen-month nightmare back like a giant wave. I remember that not long ago the story of my life wasn't a patent tragedy.

"I just ... I'm so sorry. I'm so *so* sorry. I'm sorry for what I did to Winston, a complete stranger. I'm sorry I ruined my law partner's business. I'm sorry I caused pain for my family and the few friends I still had ..." I can't hold it back any longer. The tears rain down. It feels so good. Finally, tears.

After a few moments, Dr. Driscoll hands me a few tissues from his attaché.

"I still have a hard time believing I'm here," I say. "I can't believe I'm not going to be a lawyer, that I'm a felon and that I'm going to be a registered sex offender for life."

"Frankly, I can't either," Dr. Driscoll says.

A group of inmates walk into the cafeteria with a CO.

"Don't let them see me crying," I say through my teeth. I turn my back to the door and try to gather myself.

"Officer, we'll be done in a minute. Please ... some privacy," Dr. Driscoll says with surprising authority. They all turn and head back out.

"Anything else?"

I'm drizzling tears. I haven't cried like this since ... since ever.

It takes me a half-minute to get my sobbing under control. Dr. Driscoll makes notes in a yellow legal pad.

"I'm sober, I'm clean. I don't do the things that got me in here any-more. That's all I can do ... live my life differently. I wish it didn't hap-pen, but maybe I'm lucky not to be dead. I have to think that way or I can't go on, you know?"

He finishes writing and then looks up at me. "As far as I'm concerned you shouldn't be here in the first place, and you definitely shouldn't be coming back. But, it's up to the judge. I'm just one of three people who will be evaluating you—so, be careful in here."

❖   ❖   ❖

I'm alone in my cell again. I hope it stays this way. The cart comes around and I'm given my Wellbutrin. As I've been doing since Twin Towers, I tongue it and then spit it out. Sometimes they crush it up before they dump it into my hand from the little pill cup. It depends on which CO and which medical assistant is assisting. Today the CO makes me open my mouth and say *ah*. It doesn't change anything. I've still got it stashed behind my right lower molars. The Lexapro, then the Wellbutrin did the trick for sure while I was in triage mode for the first year after my arrest. It trimmed my life's sheet music off at the highs and the lows, probably kept me from actually taking that trip to Las Vegas, then to the Grand Canyon, then to the Grand Canyon floor. The only reason I submitted my prescription in here and Twin Towers was in the hope it'd keep me safer, because I'd be in some medical unit, but that didn't happen. *So why should I take this crap? Wasn't that what all the alcohol and cigarettes and prostitutes and porn were about? Wasn't I just medicating my-self? Why am I going to all these meetings and praying and meditating and implementing all these spiritual principles into my now-ruined life if I'm still going to have to use a chemical to feel okay? Fuck that.* I spit them out into the sink.

After my meditation, and after the release of crying, I feel aglow, just like after my fifth step *confession* to Father Terry. It's bizarre. Here I am in a five-by-ten cell in a deadly prison. My material life, all that I worked for, is gone, maybe forever. But, *it* is gone, too. I didn't know *it* was so absolutely always there, until I came to a place where *it* couldn't be fed. I have nothing but the here and the now. No TV, no porn, no prostitutes, no coffee, no fast food, no alcohol, no cigarettes, no coke, no sugar, no nothing, not even masturbation. For my safety and for my sanity, I've let it all go. And in here, *in here*, in this barrenness, it isn't really available to me anyway. And that part of me that chases it, constantly chases it, has turned off. The bear that lives inside me is convinced that there is nothing to eat in here, so it has gone into hibernation, and I feel as if every cell in my body has been infused with an extra bit of lightness. Maybe this is my spiritual experience. I've taken every layer off, and I can finally be with me and me alone. I can't remember ever feeling like this. I can hear acutely. Things are clearer. My lungs breathe free and deep. My hands and feet are relaxed. My thoughts are crisp and undistorted. I'm observing without judgment. Right here, right now, I'm completely alive. Yes, this is bizarre.

❖   ❖   ❖

"Back to Chino!" my new celly shouts out over the blare of the hall and through the bars of our cell just after the gate slides closed and clicks shut.

Several voices I recognize shout back, *Thaaaaattt's riiiight! Shot caller on the bars!*

Jimmy is, apparently, notorious. After a few minutes of frenzied catching-up with the Wood contingency over the bars, Jimmy turns his attention to me and starts talking as if we were in the middle of a conversation.

"I knew I'd test dirty, so I didn't show—picked me up in Colorado with this fine-ass bitch. We were *on one*, ran out of money, so I took this punk for his watch and wallet. He says I hit him. I didn't even hit that bitch. I roughed him up. Don't matter none. They didn't even file charges. Punk-ass parole officer swooped me up and violated my ass. *Bam!* Back in Chino on lockdown in fucking Palm Hall. I'm x'ing out my number anyways. Fuck all that parole shit."

Jimmy is a specimen: tall, with golden skin; his face and body are chiseled. He has short, blonde hair and eyes the color of Maui ocean water. But for his teeth and tats, you might think he was a Ralph Lauren model. Jimmy's teeth—some blackened, some crooked, a missing bicuspid, several fillings—give away his white trash lifestyle, presumably one involving a good amount of methamphetamine. And if his mouth were shut—so that you couldn't see his teeth or hear him talk—a body blotted in poor-quality prison tats, the most notable, twin *F.T.W.s*, for *fuck the world*, above each eye with little iron crosses for periods, exposes Jimmy's felonious tendencies.

Jimmy tells me his story matter-of-factly. He speaks in jarring bursts: Senior in high school, played on the football team, had been in some minor trouble, but nothing big. One night he goes on a meth bender, goes crazy, walks into a pawnshop, stabs the pawnshop owner, a former cop. Next thing he knows, he's seventeen years old, and he's looking at the ten years of calendars on the wall of intake at Pelican Bay.

"I'm seventeen. I'm putting work in for the Aryan Brotherhood. I end up in the SHU, supermax, high power. Doesn't get any worse," Jimmy says.

"Yeah?" This is the first thing I've said to Jimmy. I only know his name because I heard it shouted out by him and others over the bars. I'm picturing a seventeen-year-old kid that was playing high school football a couple months earlier going into prison. *Seven-fucking-teen.*

"I look at the wall," Jimmy recalls, "1993, 1994, 1995, 1996, 1997, 1998 … 2003 … ten years. I'm looking at ten years. Ten *fucking* years."

Jimmy sits on the desk stool as he tells me his story. Kites are coming in. He opens them, examines the contents, and yells out thanks.

"Good lookin' out, Menace," he shouts happily. Jimmy sets the green, plastic lid of a container for instant coffee onto the desk. He unwraps a white cloth kite tied up with strips of orange cloth. He pulls out a skin-toned, plastic glove and an empty potato chip wrapper. "Good looking out, Devin, you crazy motherfucker," Jimmy yells.

Devin barks back, "At your service, *dawg*."

"Where was I?" Jimmy asks, "Oh yeah, motherfucker violates me, *again*. Ain't no more violations." Jimmy pulls out his green, laminated CDC card. "I done discharged this motherfucking number."

Another kite comes in, this one in a milk carton. He opens it, but it's empty but for a note. "Just in case," he reads aloud and shouts, "Just in case of what, Derelict, crazy *Brand*-ass motherfucker."

"That don't play in Palm, Jimmy. Ain't no Brand in here, brother, just Woods," Derelict shouts back.

"I know," Jimmy yells, "I know. I'm just playin'. What's with the empty fish kit, motherfucker?"

"Keep digging, Grasshopper," Derelict shouts back.

Jimmy dissects the carton carefully. I see his eyebrows rise. "*Thaaaattt'sss riiighttt!*" Jimmy shouts above the cellblock hum. "Good lookin' out, Derelict." Jimmy holds out a razor blade between his thumb and forefinger, displaying it to me like a prize butterfly. "Slip and slide," he says.

"Slip and slide?" I repeat.

He runs his finger at an angle across the microblade.

"Dull as fuck. We'll swap it out. You ain't got one?" Jimmy asks me.

I shake my head. He slides it into a flat crevice on the bottom bunk.

Jimmy goes back into his story. "I'm putting in serious work. *Down for mines.* Taking care of business. To be endorsed, you know?"

I don't really know, but I've got an idea *endorsed* is what it sounds like: getting jumped into a gang. I nod.

"Shit, I'm in the SHU, supermax, high-fucking power. Seven years in. I'm about to get out on parole in like a week. Them motherfuckers want me to put work in on some *Paisa* on some bullshit. I mean *work*. Some fucking Mexican needed to get got. I mean *get got*. Nah, fuck that. I already got away with shit that coulda got me fucking bonus time. He points to his teardrop tattoo. "I ain't doin' it. No way. *Fuck that*. I'm a soldier, but it ain't like that."

Another kite comes in from next door. O.G. hands it over. Jimmy unwraps a couple wads of tissue, each with enough for half a cigarette. The smell is delicious, especially in contrast to the constant waft of gas and shit that emanates from the hundred-plus toilets in smell range.

"Mad love, Stripes," Jimmy shouts over the bars. "That's what I'm talking about. Good looking out, Wood! Where's that other bitch, Lucy?"

"Not yet," Stripe hollers back from way off. "I'll let you know. You know I got your back, Wood."

"*Thaaatttt'ssss riiiiggght!*" Jimmy shouts back. A few other Woods join in.

Jimmy leans in close to me and shows me the scar running along his hairline above his forehead, then twists around to show me the several puncture wounds on his back near his right side.

"Almost got me. Almost got," Jimmy says. "But I ain't going out like that. So, I'm a dropout. I'm in the *hat*—PC for life." He goes to the bars and yells, "In the motherfucking hat!" Several voices call back.

"Fuck yeah."

"*Thaaaatttt's riiiightttt!*"

"In the hat," Devin, a constant voice on the bars, begins to rap, "at Palm, with the chesters, the molesters, the motha-fuckin snitches and the bitches, uh, uh. *Thataa'tttts riiiightttt!*"

Jimmy turns his attention to me and asks, "So why you PC-upped?"

"Because I'm a lawyer. Felony assault, criminal threats while on probation for a felony DUI. I'm here on a ninety-day evaluation."

"Get the fuck out-uh-here," Jimmy says, grinning, "You ain't no lawyer."

"I certainly am. I graduated from Pepperdine Law in 1997, passed the Bar in July of the same year. My bar number is 192487, and until I broke into a guy's house that I didn't even know and attacked him in the middle of the night in an alcohol-induced blackout, I was a fine upstanding citizen, at least as far as the California State Bar was concerned."

"Lucy!" Stripe shouts.

Jimmy turns the potato chip bag inside out and stretches the shiny chrome surface taut across the instant coffee lid. He takes the razor and cuts the wrist of a rubber glove into a rubber band, and secures it around the perimeter of the lid. He pulls and stretches and pulls and stretches and *voila*, a hand mirror. Jimmy sticks it out the cell bars, and I can see Mongrel walking toward our cell with a purpose.

"What's up, Wood?" Mongrel says. He glares at me and turns back to Jimmy. He pulls out a small battery, sheathed in magazine paper with a wire protruding from it. Under his hand, he uses it to light a piece of rolled-up toilet paper. Mongrel also hands him several pages from a Bible. Jimmy takes the fire—*Lucy*—and hands it to me. I cup it. It's about to go out. Jimmy expertly blows at the base of it, and the fire expands. He rolls two tiny cigarettes with the Bible paper, takes the fire back, and lights the minicigs. He takes a drag. He's purely satisfied. I'm happy just watching him.

"You want a hit?" Jimmy asks me.

"No thanks. I don't smoke." I lie. I do want a hit. I want a hundred hits. *Damn.*

❖   ❖   ❖

Jimmy and I *program*. I get it. I'm only in here for a few months, and I can see that I'd go insane if I didn't have a routine. I wake, I meditate, I pray, I read, I write letters. We aren't supposed to be able to get books or full-length pencils, but Vinny sent me twenty pencils and two books, *Alcoholics Anonymous* and *12 Steps and 12 Traditions*. I wasn't that surprised that these items got through until I saw Jimmy's reaction. You'd think I'd received a kilo of dope and twenty heroin rigs. After the mess hall shanking, I know why CDC doesn't want full-length pencils sent in, but I don't get why books are a problem. Jimmy explains that the binding, even on the soft-cover books, are used to fashion shank handles. Between Jimmy's slip-and-slide razor blade and my dozen full-length pencils and two books, I'm sure Jimmy could make a battle-ax. Maybe the books got through, because the CO that brought me my mail to open in front of him because it was addressed from the law office where Vinny worked and by law couldn't be opened by a CO because it was attorney-client privileged, was sympathetic to 12-step programs, or maybe he was in a 12-step program. But then a book from my mom got through, too. Jimmy was nearly flabbergasted when I opened the envelope up—which had been opened and resealed—and pulled out a hard-bound book. For whatever reason, I was the only guy in the entire hall who had new books.

After breakfast, in our closet-sized cell, we work out. I've always worked out hard. Before I started going to the gym and lifting weights, I'd been kickboxing with David, and David didn't think it was a good workout unless we bled, vomited, or passed out. When I thought if I threw one more punch or kick I'd die, David would say we only had a half-hour left. He pushed me physically far past where I thought I could ever go. I often had to lie down in the gym for fifteen minutes before I could safely drive home. I'm not as strong as Jimmy, but I stick it out. Jimmy works out as if he's possessed, and if he could just eke out those last ten reps, he could finally get rid of the demon inside him. He screams at the top of his lungs after a set of fifty burpees.

Jimmy made a deck of cards out of milk cartons. We pull cards and do the number of reps indicated on the card—through the entire deck, twice. By the end I can barely do one or two reps of whatever exercise is called out. Jimmy finishes up with a final, straight, fifty push-ups. We stand in our soaked boxers and shoes. The concrete floor is drenched with sweat. We mop up all the sweat and clean the floor. We each birdbath in the sink. Jimmy has created a curtain out of old sheets for privacy. Each day we get stronger. I haven't been in this kind of marine-boot-camp shape since training for fights with David. Jimmy and I are bonding over the workouts. He loves that I work out so hard, that I actually want to work out. I'm glad for it. It takes a chunk out of the day, and it tires me so I can sleep.

After our workout, I write letters and I read the detective book my mom sent me and the books Vinny sent me. It's so bad, I can only read the detective book twice, but I read and reread *Alcoholics Anonymous* and *Twelve Steps and Twelve Traditions* over and over. I stay up on my bunk. I receive letters from people I've gotten to know a little in the recovery meetings. I'm sure Vinny has something to do with this. It's good. They keep me busy reading their letters and writing them back. While I'm up on my bunk, reading and writing, Jimmy starts his hustling and fiending.

When Jimmy sees that I am tonguing my twice-daily dose of Wellbutrin and spitting it in the sink, he goes nuts. It's as if he'd found somebody who was using hundred-dollar bills as kindling. Jimmy loves speed. So, now, I give them to him, and he crushes up my little aspirin-sized pills, chops them up with his razor, and snorts them. At the same time, he is collecting apples from his own lunch and various other inmates for a batch of *pruno*, prison alcohol. After every meal, especially when we go to the chow hall, Jimmy runs all over the tier collecting apples. He sends a shipment of nearly twenty apples down to Devin's cell in one day. It's been three days, and Jimmy is crazy with anticipation. Jimmy came in to Palm Hall with nothing. Now, between my Wellbutrin and his various hustles, he is snorting up to four Wellbutrin a day, getting shots of coffee, and even an occasional cigarette. The *Wellbys*, as he calls them, must burn like hell. Every time he does a line, his eyes water, and he raises his head with that surprised look cokeheads always get after they do a line. Then he yells, *fuck!* Or *goddamn!* just like Ms. Mia Wallace in *Pulp Fiction.*

What Jimmy really wants is the pruno Devin is brewing. I tell Jimmy my story, minus the whole naked-with-a-hard-on-accused-rapist part, but he is so entranced with getting wasted it doesn't register a bit that I am no longer a big fan of alcohol. When he gets out, Jimmy tells me, he is going straight to the liquor store to buy a bottle of Jack. And then he is going on a *run*, he even calls it that, a *run*, just like the dope fiends in 12-step meetings call it. I learned that word in rehab. A *run* is like a road trip of destruction and debauchery for addicts. The primary focus of Jimmy's run would be meth, but he'd venture into women and alcohol, and, I imagine, eventually, assaults and robbery.

"Fuck yeah!" Devin yells. His nasally voice is instantly recognizable. He's Palm Hall's comedic DJ. *Fuck yeah!* is his catchphrase. It's how he kicks off his rants. He's the penal version of Howard Stern.

"Fuck yeah! Fuck yeah, Devin's on the bars," his co-host-slash-side-kick, Kyley, announces. "I repeat: Devin is on the bars."

A good chunk of Palm Hall stops and listens. It's a daily half-hour event.

"What do you know about Rodney on the Roq?" Devin asks.

"Fucking-Rodney-on-the-motherfucking-Roq. Classic," Kyley says.

Devin goes into his imitation of Rodney on the Roq, a DJ that's been on the air on KROQ, an alternative radio station in Los Angeles, for the last twenty years. Devin talks softly and slowly and takes the harshness out of all his consonants. It's a spot-on impersonation.

"Hi, you're listening to K-Fucked here at Chino State Prison, a.k.a., the California Institute for Men. It's really *really* hot here and, believe it or not, we'll be without air conditioning all summer long. Draconian. I know, right? What's up with that? So we are going to serve up some '80's rock, and who better than the Elvis of new wave, modern Casanova, Morrissey?"

"What do you know about some *goddamn* Morrissey?" Kyley shouts.

Devin does Morrissey as Elvis and Kyley jumps in with his own version of, *Shyness.*

Quite a few inmates join in. I really want to, but I have a policy of staying off the bars. It's part of my stay-alive program.

"Thaaaatttt's riiiiggght" Devin shouts out, ending his Morrissey rendition with the Wood's official call.

"And what do you know about ...," Devin pauses for dramatic effect and then begins singing another Morrissey song, something about a double-decker bus crash.

I feel a sense of normalcy listening to Devin's shtick. It's just like hearing the same radio DJs, Kevin & Bean, also on KROQ, in the morning on my daily commute nearly every day from the time I was in high school until the night of my arrest. Hell, I think, I've been listening to those fools for fifteen years, and they aren't much better than Devin and Kyley.

Devin tells stories about his myriad arrests. This morning he tells the story of how he was arrested for stealing watches from a department store so he could trade them for dope. Yesterday it was a story about stealing his grandfather's boat in Newport Harbor and getting drunk and being chased by the coast guard and capsizing his grandfather's boat after ramming a jetty. Then he went on a fifteen-minute rant about the futility of the coast guard. *We already have a goddamn navy. We need a coast guard?* It's pretty clear that Devin feels more comfortable being the Palm Hall DJ than living in *the world.*

Through the bars of our cell and out the wall of windows, some broken, Jimmy and I have a view of Birch Hall's yard. Birch's yard is solid concrete, double-fenced, and not much bigger than a basketball court. Birch Hall houses supermax gang members and is segregated by race and gang affiliation. While smallest in population, the white supremacists are the

ss and regimented. Jimmy is an expert and explains to me
-on of Birch Hall with great detail.

the blacks come out, they mill around and talk and work out.
Same with the Mexicans, who come out in two separate groups, the
Mexican-Mexican's: *Paisas*; and the American-Mexicans: *La Eme*. When
the whites come out, it's a show. Jimmy knows all about it, because he
lived it for nearly ten years. There is a series of gates that ensure the
prisoners never have access to the COs. Inmates come out one at a time.
They walk down a chain-link hall wearing only their boxers, socks, and
prison shoes. They are handcuffed. The CO opens a gate and lets them
into a chain-link box. They turn their back to the CO, and another CO
uncuffs them through a steel-framed slot in the gate. All of them have
shaved heads and are tatted up, some, like Jimmy, even have tats on
their faces, necks, and hands. Unlike the blacks and Mexicans, when
they enter, they walk into a formation line all facing the leader, who is
the first man let into the yard. Once all thirty inmates are released into
the yard, which takes about a half-hour, the leader of the white supremacists calls out, *Ready* and everyone calls back *Yes, Sir!*

Then they do 123 reps of burpees. They call out each rep loudly. W
is the twenty-third letter of the alphabet, hence the 123 reps. Some days
they do two sets of different exercises of 88, *H* being the eighth letter of
the alphabet and 88 signifying *Heil Hitler*. Nearly all of them complete
all 123 reps, and the ones that don't, stand dead-still in place until they
can continue. At the end, the leader hollers a long drawn-out *Thank you!*
and they all respond back, *Thank you, Sir!* Then they shake hands like it's
the end of a little league game.

"Come here, come here, watch," Jimmy says to me. It must be something special because Jimmy stopped *getting his money*—exercising—to
watch. He narrates it like he's already read the script. He pulls me in so
I'm right next to him, so he can show me exactly what he sees. "Look,
look … okay," Jimmy says. He wants to make sure I don't miss anything.
"Now see that guy, see him? Okay, okay. He's talking to that one—the

one on the right ... okay ... okay. Wait. You see? He's going to start trouble. PEN1 have a 'no hands policy'."

"Huh?" I ask.

"Blood in, blood out."

"What?"

"It means they don't touch skin-to-skin. They use a tool and stab you. They don't fight. *They kill.*"

"Oh."

"Penitentiary Death Squad PEN1," Jimmy explains. "Penitentiary Number One, one of the baddest white-power prison gangs," Jimmy continues without looking away from the scene some twenty yards away. "Watch, watch ... see? He's starting to get in his face. It'll be no-hands, no-hands policy. No skin-to-skin. Just tools."

"How do they get weapons out?" I ask, which seems like a pretty good question, seeing that they all come out only in their boxers.

"Keistered," Jimmy answers plainly. "See how they are yelling, starting an argument? See the two guys coming up from behind?"

Jimmy is entranced, and so am I. It's *going down* just as Jimmy describes. Sure enough, two skinheads walk toward the two others having the shouting match.

"Here you go ... wait ... watch," Jimmy instructs.

It happens so quickly. Two guys arguing. Two other guys come up from behind. They stab the victim in the back with quick, little jabs to the kidney. *Nak, nak, nak.* It's over, and all three all walk away. The victim acts like he's been stung by a bee. Then he drops. The siren goes off, and both of the attackers and some of the skinheads near them are blasted from the guard tower with block guns. There are four bodies on the ground. All the Skins dive to the concrete to avoid being shot. Then one by one, each skinhead places his hands on his head and walks backward toward the gate, this includes the three hit with the block gun, who both hobble. They are cuffed, and let into the chain-link hall. The skinheads' victim lies in a puddle of water near a shower drain. The puddle turns dark with blood. He's dead for sure. It takes fifteen minutes before all the skinheads are led out, and the victim is taken away on a stretcher. Jimmy and I finish our workout, and when we are done, we peer out the window. It's a rapture for sinners. The only thing left are several pairs of prison shoes and a couple black shower sandals, and a puddle of watered-down blood.

A week goes by without being let out of our cells even once. But then we start getting yard-time for a couple hours every few days. After seeing the shanking, I've skipped the first two yards, but I haven't been outside in so long I think I might go albino if I don't have direct sunlight soon. I'm going to go this time. I figure I'll just stick close to Jimmy. He's champing at the bit, like the school bell is about to ring. We of Palm Hall are led out one tier at a time. We go through metal detectors, are patted down, and then we are let into an actual yard. It has two handball courts, a little basketball court, a few wall-mounted showers, several steel benches with matching awnings, and a tiny track framing a patch of grass and three sets of pull-up bars. Two sets of high fencing topped with spiraling razor ribbon enclose the yard, and a CO in a tower oversees it all, rifle in hand. I can't believe it. I thought that was only in movies. There is actually a guard in a tower with a rifle. *The novelty!*

Jimmy heads straight to the bars and gets in line with Menace, Devin, Kyley, and Flathead. Jimmy doesn't have a nickname. They all treat him like royalty. He introduces me to his *boys*. He says about me: *he's straight*, and they all air-bump fists with me and give me the nod—no physical contact is allowed on the yard. They are all tatted-up, white gang dropouts like Jimmy, in here on a parole violation, except Devin, a six-foot-nine illustrated man. He's going to be shipped out to another prison to do some real time. I know this from his daily radio show. Menace has *737* tatted over one eye and has another tattoo bust of Hitler that looks more like Moe of The Three Stooges. The only reason I know it was intended to be Hitler and not Moe is because of the swastika crest.

When my turn arrives on the bars, I crank out twenty wide grip front pull-ups. I'd been doing them at the gym in Silverlake prior to turning myself in, and my adrenaline is off the charts, so it's easy. When I get back in line, Menace comments on my pull-up prowess, and he and Devin re-nickname me *Clark Kent.*

It's a beautiful day here in the Inland Empire, one of those Chamber of Commerce days in May just before it goes smoggy and unbearably hot for the long summer. I feel good. Jimmy and the boys sit in the grass on the edge of the track and reminisce about Nazi-gang shit. I don't want to get drawn into any questions, so I decide to take a jog around the track, careful to keep one eye on Jimmy and to not get too close to anyone. I stretch a bit, and then walk a bit and then trot into a medium-paced jog.

Get down! Get the fuck down! I hear. The voice is coming from a bullhorn. Guys behind and in front of me dart away. The two COs in the yard trot toward me with their Mace cans out. I look to Jimmy and his crew. Jimmy is mid pull-up, and Devin and Menace are looking at me laughing. I look up toward where I thought the bullhorn sounded, and I see it. The CO on the tower has a rifle with a scope aimed at me. I put my hands in the air. *Fuck.*

"No running in the yard," one of the COs, trotting toward me and pointing a canister of Mace, says through a bullhorn.

The COs turn away, and the rifleman goes back to scanning the yard with his binoculars. Scene over. My heart is pumping out of my chest. I didn't notice no one else was jogging.

"Clark Kent, what the fuck are you doing?" Jimmy asks as I walk back to the group.

"This ain't a track meet, homey," Devin jabs.

I'm embarrassed a bit, but feel safe in my role as the straitlaced, naive newbie. I jump up to the bar and crank out thirty underhand pull-ups, probably the most I've ever done in my life. I think of fourth-grade PE class, being tested on field day at the pull-up bars and not being able to do a single pull-up. It was so embarrassing. The teacher had to time how long I could hold onto the bars, like he did with the girls. It couldn't have been more than thirty seconds. *Look at me now, Teach,* I think, *I'm hanging with the Nazi convicts —doing so many pull-ups.*

Jimmy and his boys head toward the showers. I'll stick to the bird-baths. I've seen *American Me.* I've heard the stories. I'm not going near any group showers if I can help it. Not far from the showers, there is a raucous basketball game going on. I love basketball, and there are brothers playing, and they aren't too bad. I miss basketball. Ever since Pepperdine, I haven't played ball. Maybe I could actually have some fun in here after all, I think—not that playing craps for push-ups with hardened, toilet-paper dice and watching narrated yard shankings isn't a blast. I am standing about twenty feet behind the game when a black guy walks over.

"What up, *peckerwood?*"

"I'm just watching," I say defensively. I look over to the showers to make sure Jimmy is still in sight.

"You play ball, homey? Do you shoot underhand?" he asks and laughs.

I want to tell him I'll dunk on him, but the truth is I don't know if I could even touch the rim. It's been so long since I'd played, let alone dunked.

"C'mon," he says, "we'll get you in the game, peckerwood."

I think about how much fun I've had playing basketball. It's been so long. I haven't smoked, and I'm in great shape. I reluctantly walk over, as the game ends.

"Hey Crip, peckerwood wants to ball. He gotta mad crossover."

"It's *like that,* nigga," one of the other black guys playing says to me animatedly. "Fucking peckerwood all up in the mix in *my* yard on *my* court."

A black guy is in my face cussing at me. I can't even understand what he's saying. He has cornrows and smells of oil. Just like that, I'm sur-rounded by black guys, cussing at me and asking me questions. I hear the word *chester,* and I start to look for a way out, but short of tackling through one of them and making a scene, I'm trapped. *Fuck. What was I thinking?* I'm about to get my ass kicked.

"What up, Crip!" I hear Jimmy shout angrily. He charges into the circle with Devin and Menace and another skinhead. His shirt is off, and he's flexed and pissed, eyes inflamed, like he's ready to kill. It's that look he gets when we're working out, and he's trying to get those last twenty reps in.

"Clark Kent is *rollin' with us!*" Devin shouts.

Jimmy has taken my place and is right in the black guy's face, *mad-doggin'* him with his wild eyes. "We cool? We cool? Or do we have a problem?" Jimmy threatens.

"Nah, Jimmy," the black guy says defensively. "This ain't mainline. Ain't no problems. We straight, *may-n*. Just ballin'. He wanna play, cool. He straight."

I walk off with Jimmy and the crew. *Jesus. I'm not wandering off again. If Jimmy climbs the fence, I'm going with him.* Ten minutes later, yard is called. We stand on yellow-painted lines, waiting to be marched back in. I stand in formation between Devin and Menace, and Jimmy is in front.

"Superman had one hell of a yard. Almost gets gunned down after deciding to go on a little run," Devin says.

"He thinks he's Jesse Jackson!" Menace snickers.

They both laugh.

"Jesse Jackson?" Devin says to Menace. "You dumbass motherfucker. *Jesse Jackson?* You mean Jesse *Owens.*"

"Fuck you," Menace responds.

"Then Clark rolls over for a little pick-up basketball with them *ka-ra-zy* niggers from C-town," Devin continues, ignoring Menace and then begins to rap, "Foe life, foe life ... Clark Kent's rollin' through the hood with strife. Foe life, foe life ..."

Ice Cube, I think.

❖   ❖   ❖

Jimmy handles a slip-and-slide like a magician handles a deck of cards. He grins at me and says, "Check this out," and tosses the razor blade into his mouth.

An inmate trustee and a CO are going cell to cell and passing out orange, plastic, shaving razors so the inmates can shave. Jimmy has a plan to swap out his dull *slip-and-slide* for a new one.

"Check my mouth," Jimmy says to me.

He opens wide and I look in. I can't see the blade, just a dental nightmare.

"That's how you get to the yard with a slip-and-slide," Jimmy says with a grin. "Metal detectors don't pick it up."

Jimmy is getting manic. The flow of *Wellbys*, Tina—cigarettes—and shots—coffee—is not keeping up with his increasing tolerance. Jimmy is going insane. Sometimes he just grabs the bars and shakes them and screams. It's a little scary, not because I think he's going to intentionally attack me. In fact, he goes out of his way to protect me. It's that I can picture him losing it and turning into a tornado. I'd be the small town in his path. I stay up on my bunk. Yesterday, Jimmy read me the sweetest letter from his high school-girlfriend, replete with Bible quotes. He says he wants to change his life, settle down with her, and then a couple minutes later, he's telling me he's got plans on building his own meth lab. He needs a drink, *so badly*. And today, it comes. The pruno he's been contributing to has fully fermented. Mongrel delivers three milk cartons-full of the foulest liquid I've ever smelled. It's like Bacardi 151 and gasoline blended with rotten fruit. Jimmy declares that he is taking the day off from our usual workouts. He offers me some of the concoction. I politely decline. I sit atop my bunk and read my favorite personal story from *Alcoholics Anonymous*, the one where the full-blooded Cherokee pilot is arrested and goes to prison for flying drunk, gets sober, and then years later gets his pilot's license back.

Jimmy sips the pruno and can barely keep it down, but he couldn't be happier. He's on the bars with Devin and Menace and a couple others that are partaking. They are like kids in the back of their mom's minivan on the way to Disneyland—just waiting for the fun to start. Jimmy has saved up several Wellbys. He takes a swig out of the little, white and pink milk carton and chops a rail of the white pill with his new slip-and-slide. He's in pure bliss, and I'm jealous. I'd like to disappear for a while, too.

A kite comes down the tier, and O.G. hands it over to Jimmy.

"It's for Clark."

Jimmy hands me a piece of paper, tightly folded. It's my first kite, and I don't want it. I think of throwing it away without reading it, but I open it anyway.

I got your jacket. You're PC because you're a fucking rapist. Give me your Wellbys and Jimmy doesn't find out.

It's from Mongrel, the inmate trustee that fucked with me at the bottom of the stairs.

"What's it say? Who's it from?" Jimmy asks.

"Clark Kent going to have some and turn into Superman?" Devin yells out over the bars.

"Nah, Clark don't drink," Jimmy shouts back.

"You sober, huh?" Menace asks me.

I shake my head yes for Jimmy to answer for me.

"He don't go on the bars," Jimmy yells, "but he's shaking his head yes," Jimmy slurs.

"I'mma get back in the Program and get sober again as soon as I get out of here, and as soon as I get a couple bags of smack," Devin yells out. He's starting to get saucy from the pruno.

Jimmy forgets about my kite. For the next three hours, the screaming escalates as the several imbibers get drunker and drunker. Devin turns funnier. Menace gets emotional. Jimmy turns into an animal. Some other Wood sings pop hits. They're on the bars constantly. It's a loud raucous bar with the full spectrum of personalities. Someone tells Jimmy to shut up. It's a black voice I don't recognize, but Jimmy does.

It's Spencer. Jimmy is furious. Within ten minutes Jimmy has vowed to murder Spencer the next time the cells open. Spencer backs down.

"Man, be cool. I wasn't trying to disrespect you. You just be hollerin' constantly for hours."

Jimmy doesn't back down a bit: *I told you I was going to kill you, and I meant it.* Even a drunken Devin and Menace try to chill Jimmy, but he's enraged. All he can talk about is how he's going to kill Spencer. I pretend I'm asleep. A CO shows up and asks Jimmy what the fuck is going on. He asks Jimmy if he's been drinking. Jimmy laughs and tells him, *Yes, I went to a liquor store and picked up a few 40s. Do you want some?* I'm up on my bunk trying to look Protestant-sober. I see the rage in the CO's eye at Jimmy's disrespect, and for a moment I think, for sure, he is going to open the gate and beat Jimmy to death, but he doesn't, he just tells Jimmy to shut up and then walks on. Jimmy must have been coming down because he did shut up, and soon after he passed out. It's the first time I've ever seen him sleep. After the other drunk Woods quiet down, the hall is half the deafening madness it usually is.

I soak Mongrel's note in water until it dissolves. I pray and meditate. My meditations are becoming more and more surreal. I float away. Time bends. I can feel my organs. I can feel everything. I focus on sliding down a perfect Malibu Surfrider wave on a beautiful warm summer day, a Santa Ana blowing in. I picture all the details. My toes, the smell of wax, that sway, that salty dryness, straddling my board looking out onto PCH, the feeling of weightlessness and joy of having a perfectly shaped wave unfolding in front of me for a hundred yards to the pier. I don't know how long I was in meditation, maybe twenty minutes, maybe an hour or more. I feel at peace. Right here, right now, everything is okay. I know exactly how to handle Mongrel. For this moment, my fear has left. I'm not buying in to this. I don't belong in here, and I'm not playing the game.

Surprisingly, we aren't going to be cell-fed dinner, even though there was a lockdown earlier from a stabbing in Birch Hall. I get ready for unlock. It's always a shock when the cells open. Jimmy does a bunch of push-ups to get his muscles *on-swole*. He looks at me and somberly pops the slip-and-slide into his mouth. He takes off his shirt. I've gotten to know him, so his swath of white pride tattoos don't look quite so intimidating. I don't know what Spencer looks like, other than black, but I hope he's on another tier and gets in his cell quickly.

Spencer must have been on the first or third tier because chow went off without a hitch. Not more than five minutes after we got back from dinner, a bag of several apples arrive on a line with a kite. Jimmy opens the kite and reads it.

Jimmy shouts over the bars, "We straight, Spencer. Thanks for the fruit. I'm just a drunk peckerwood."

"It's all good," Spencer hollers back.

That's it. Nobody on the block says anything, not even Menace or Devin.

Jimmy immediately starts to go to work on his own batch of pruno. He already has a dozen apples and a couple oranges, some sugar and a couple plastic bags. I try to talk him out of it. The last thing I want, given my reason for being in here, is to have the COs catch him making pruno, and then having it end up in my evaluation report to the judge. But, there is no stopping him. He wants to be drunk again desperately.

Night meds are passed. The CO with the med assistant passing them out doesn't make sure I swallow and doesn't make the med assistant crush the pills, so I'm able to give a whole pill to Jimmy.

"Here you go, Jimmy, a full one," I say, mocking pride.

He holds it out as if it's a rare ruby.

I decide this is a good time to deal with my Mongrel situation.

"Here's the thing, Jimmy. Remember I told you I'm in here on a felony assault, and that I'm a lawyer?"

He nods.

"Well, I'm PC not only because I'm an attorney but also because I was charged with a felony assault—assault with intent to commit rape."

Jimmy stands up.

"I'm not a rapist, Jimmy. There wasn't even a girl in the room ..."

Am I going to have to fight him?

I look Jimmy in those crazed, blue eyes of his, and I can tell before he speaks that I'm okay.

"I know you had an 'R' on your jacket, Joseph," Jimmy says. "I don't know what happened, but I know you don't belong in here . . . I stabbed a guy in the neck. He had a wife and an eight-year-old daughter. I *belong* in here."

"Yeah?"

"Yeah," he says and nods sullenly. He fades off for several moments as if he's recalling something, then snaps out of it. "Fuck Mongrel. He's a piece of shit," Jimmy declares.

Indeed, fuck Mongrel.

TWENTY-ONE

I'm escorted by a CO to the giant hallway along with three other in-mates, two of whom are being transferred to the gym. Usually, the COs make us put our nose to the wall while we wait, but this one, an older, black CO, is content to let us stand uncuffed. Through a security door window, I see the inside of the gym. It's just that, a gymnasium with basketball backboards retracted to the ceiling. Every inch is filled with three-high bunk beds. There must be five hundred. The CO fills out paperwork to transfer two inmates to the gym. It's Halloween in there, all orange uniforms and black skin.

Across the hall are rectangular steel coffins, just big enough for an inmate to stand up. Their mesh fronts are too tight to slide a pencil through, and these little people-containers are so narrow the inmates in them can't sit; they can only halfway down. Although I've passed them a half dozen times now, this is the first time I realize what they are. I thought they were just storage lockers.

"Clark," a voice I recognize says, "it's me, Menace."

"Hey," I say quietly so as not to attract the wrath of the guard. I can't see Menace, but I recognize his voice. He's in for making pruno.

"Tell Jimmy to send a care package," he whispers and presses his face to the mesh. I recognize the outline of his face.

These cages remind me of the photos of chickens in tiny, stacked cages in factory farms in the book, *Diet for a New America.* I read it my first year of undergrad and went vegetarian for two years. I think: if there were cows in these cells, PETA would storm this place in black ski masks and spray paint, "Meat is murder," on the walls.

The CO leads me into an office, just off the main hall. He taps on a door and asks whether he should leave the cuffs on. Apparently, the answer is, *yes.* He sits me down in front of a desk and leaves. A woman swivels around and faces me. It looks like she spun in place on her own, because she's so fat she envelops the chair I presume is beneath her. She doesn't look at me, just stares into a file.

"Joseph. Naus. How are you enjoying your stay here?" she says sarcastically.

Is that really what you want to say to me? I think.

She has a coffee mug on her desk that reads, *You want that when?* and below is an animated laughing face. Next to it is a picture of a sickeningly cute kitten wrestling with another sickeningly cute kitten.

"Frankly," I say, "I'm shocked at how brutal the conditions are, but by the grace of God, I'm still in one piece."

I want to connect with her on this, because I want her to think I'm normal. A normal person would think this place is horrific. Only someone that has grown up in this system could possibly think these conditions are humane.

"People end up here for a reason," she says.

Behind her are a couple more cat-motific cartoons and a cat calendar. She's a month behind. May is a big, fat Maine Coon with a perturbed look on its face.

What a stupid thing to say. What does that have to do with the fact that the conditions are unacceptable? Haven't you ever heard that a society is to be judged by how it treats its worst, not its best?

"How long have you been sober?"

"It'll be two years July 24," I answer. "I've been sober since the night of my arrest. I went to rehab as a condition of my—"

"Yes, I know," she interrupts me. "I have it all here in my file. Just answer the questions I ask."

Clearly, I disgust her, and the feeling is mutual.

"You attempted to rape someone ... Are you remorseful?" she asks and tilts her top chin down and looks at me over her nose.

"The victim was a man, so I couldn't have raped him, but, yes, I'm very sorry. I'm glad that he didn't get hurt. He had every right to beat me up the way he did. I'm lucky he didn't kill me."

She stares at me and purses her lips for several moments.

"So you feel like he took revenge on you? Is that what you are saying?"

This bitch clearly has it out for me. Just be nice and don't say anything stupid.

"No, I'm just saying that—you know, I broke into his house, and he defended himself, and then he and his friend ended up beating me up pretty bad. I mean, I did a terrible thing, and I hope he doesn't have nightmares or anything, but he *didn't* get hurt. I *did* get hurt pretty badly, and I pretty much had to forfeit my entire life because of what I did."

She stops listening to me after the first couple words. I might as well be reciting baseball box scores. She thumbs through my file.

"According to the report, he *was* injured," she says proudly, as if she's a lawyer at trial who just caught a hostile witness in a lie.

"The report says he had some bruising on his neck and a scrape or two, but it was so minor that it didn't even show up on camera when they tried to photograph it. He went to the hospital just to make sure. Nothing was wrong. They gave him a bandage and sent him home. I mean, I think the real damage was psychological, someone breaking into his home in the middle of the night."

"Naked," she adds.

"Yes, I was naked," I agree.

"With an erection," she says.

"Yes, indeed," I respond.

She probably sees a dozen inmates a day, and they all claim innocence, so her reaction to me shouldn't surprise me, but it does. I want to say, *Can't you see me? Can't you read? Does that file look like the file of a marauding midnight rapist?* Maybe the answer is, *yes*, but I don't think so.

It doesn't matter. For the rest of the interview she lectures me on the psychological and emotional damage endured by rape victims and how someone with my advantages should be particularly ashamed of my behavior. I nod sincerely. There is no use doing anything else. My mind wanders for a moment. I picture her imbedded in a couch, blanketed by a dozen cats. I wonder how many calories it takes to maintain her weight. *Five thousand? Six thousand?* She finishes lecturing me and calls the CO back in.

Back in the cell, Jimmy is nurturing his plastic bag of fruit that will soon become pruno. He carefully releases the gas from the billowing plastic bag, concealed in the toilet. Like a TV chef perched over a stew of *coq au vin* and talking into the camera, Jimmy explains to me, with his head hovering over the toilet, that the warmth of the toilet water quickens the fermentation process. This is good, he says. I agree, because the sooner it ferments, the sooner he will drink it, the sooner he'll get the psychotic episode that goes along with drinking it over with. I want to get it over with. I know there is a possibility that Jimmy will get caught like Menace did, and that there is a possibility that I will be guilty by association, and it will end up on my evaluation report. There is nothing I can do. I couldn't convince Jimmy to flush his batch of pruno down the toilet in exchange for a governor's pardon. Jimmy's relentless pursuit of Wellbys, *Tina*—cigarettes—and the perfect pruno has supplanted his, and thus, *our* workout routine. We *get our money* less and less. Today, I had to do a little workout on my own. Otherwise, I can't sleep.

The lights go off. It actually sounds like when someone shuts off the power in an old movie with one of those giant lever switches. I haven't seen it, but I've heard it. I picture Bugs Bunny pulling down the giant lever, causing some catastrophic event for Elmer Fudd. *Or was it the Road Runner and the Coyote?* In here, things get quieter when the lights go off. Just before lights-out, the COs often announce it over the archaic loudspeaker, *lights off in ten*. That's when I start to meditate. Tonight, like most nights, this is when the Paisas start chanting. I love it when the Paisas chant. They are declaring, if only to us and each other, that their spirit is not dead. They may be locked up in cages, but they are still alive. Every Paisa in the cell knows the chant and joins in wholeheartedly. I understand a little Spanish, but I can't make out a word of it. The chanting is accompanied by a giant bass drum via flat-handed slaps on the base of the stainless steel toilets, which sound like an orchestral bass drum. The verses end with a triumphant, *Hey!* and then the constant bass line, *boom, boom, boom.* The closest thing I've ever heard is that European football chant at the World Cup, *ayyy ah ay ya ay yaa ah yaa ah ya ah ya.* It ends abruptly with one last triumphant, *Hey!* and then all the Paisas and their fans, probably some La Emes and Surenos holler out *Esss-Oohhh!* That is usually the finale of the evening, but tonight an inmate belts out a perfect Journey rock ballad. It's so perfect, for a second I wonder if it might not actually be Steve Perry. It's beautiful. The entire hall quiets down to listen.

He sings about a small-town girl living in a lonely world taking the night train ...

. . .

. . .

. . .

He hits the last note, and it's as quiet as a dark desert night. I hold my breath. Several moments go by and then whistles, claps, *bravos, essos* from the Mexicans and *that's rights* from the Woods fly into the silence with the reverence of a black-tie crowd after the last note of a flawless symphony performance. The response is more soulful than raucous. Even for us outcasts, there is no denying beauty. I can't imagine Journey being anything other than kitschy in any other context, but tonight it was like we'd been served *crème brûlée* on Tiffany silver. I go to bed in peace, strangely satisfied.

Dear God, whatever you are, I'm grateful for the inmate who sings '80's Journey ballads like tonight's his last night.

I fall off to sleep.

❖   ❖   ❖

I awake from a dead sleep to a booming noise.

Bad Boys, Bad Boys ...

Jimmy is already up, ripping at the bars. I gather myself and come to realize a CO has placed the speaker of the TV in the control room in front of the microphone for the loudspeaker, and we are hearing the theme song to a reality show about police officers. At first, I'm startled, but then I figure out that, yes, this is what's happening; this is where I am in my life; I am one of several hundred captive recipients of a prison guard's practical joke; and, *goddammit* if it isn't hilarious!

The CO laughs his head off into the loudspeaker and then announces deadpan, *fucking criminals.*

The whole cellblock is in a fury, screaming and cussing and rattling the bars. This isn't the usual chaos of hell noise; they really want to kill this guy. I, on the other hand, am trying to recall if I ever experienced anything funnier. After a while, things quiet back down, but then the CO reappears over the loudspeaker and says, deadpan *fuck you criminals.* The entire block goes insane and begins chanting *fuck you, fuck you, fuck you.* After fifteen minutes, things quiet down again, and then it comes again,

Bad Boys, Bad Boys ...

This guy is hilarious, I think. I love this guy. The block explodes with noise. It's deafening. I stuff my ears with the little paper earplugs Jimmy made me, and I fade off to sleep.

❖   ❖   ❖

I wake early to Jimmy's tormented screams. He has a toothache. He *just* has a toothache the way I *just* have a couple legal problems. He's inconsolable and has half the cellblock screaming for a guard, if for nothing else than to shut him up. *Man down* is used judiciously around here, but I even hear a couple of those being thrown around. Finally, an irritated CO shows. He is quickly convinced that Jimmy is in real pain. Soon after, our cell gate slides open, and Jimmy's prison number is called over the loudspeaker, and I'm left alone. Not having Jimmy in the cell is like taking off a pair of shoes two sizes too small. The constant nervous energy is gone. The cell feels three times as big. It's just me and a big bag of fermenting pruno. It's now a proper walk-in closet. I work out hard and think even harder. It's nearly time to go back to LA. I want this to end, but I'm dreading the trip back to Twin Towers, and I'm especially dreading going back to the sex pod. I'm ultimately dreading going to court because, as much as I want to believe that society is done kicking me in the balls, I can't stand the idea that I may be coming back here, or somewhere worse. Three months—I've submitted to this without a fight because it's only three months. If I don't get hurt, it'll just be a really, really bad summer, but if the judge sends me back for two years, it'll be more than a bad summer, and I doubt I can survive two years without becoming a gladiator.

I finish my last set of a hundred push-ups without much of a struggle. I couldn't even do that when I kickboxed. There is that: I'm now a calisthenics master.

Jimmy reenters dejected. He doesn't even have his shirt off. He shows me where the tooth they removed used to be, near the back molars. He asks if I can see it when he smiles. I can, but I tell him I can't. Jimmy explains, in prison, if you have a tooth problem, the dentist only has one solution: *pull it.* Jimmy tried to wait it out, so a dentist who has tools other than pliers could look at it after he is released, but the pain became simply unbearable.

"The air hitting the bare nerves," Jimmy says, sounding like a deaf man, because he has a wad of cotton stuffed in the hole in his mouth, "I thought I was going to faint. I've never been in so much pain."

I hand him this morning's Wellby, a nice unbroken full pill.

"A couple more days …," Jimmy says after inspecting the pruno.

Jimmy crushes up the Wellby on the desk and snorts up a line. The draw of air through his nasal cavities must hurt like hell, because he screams as if his balls are in a vice. Jimmy sticks his hand in his mouth and presses down on the cotton swab and snorts the rest of the Wellby rail.

He comes down off the Wellbys, and he's visibly depressed. It's the tooth. He didn't want to give it up, but he had no choice, and he knows he's not getting it back. For some reason, losing that tooth has brought it all home for him. He keeps looking at his smile in the little makeshift mirror, trying to figure out a way to convince himself it hasn't affect-ed his smile. When the view of his maligned grill gets too much for him, he reinspects the pruno. It'll be ready tomorrow, he mumbles. It'll be perfect tomorrow. Absolutely perfect. Much stronger than the last batch and more of it, and, he says, he's going to keep four milk cartons for himself. Wow, I think, he was murderous with just two cartons last time. I can't imagine what it'll be like this time. Maybe he'll pass out before he dies of alcohol poisoning.

Chow hall is particularly tense. I presume it's because of the *Bad Boys* prank. I'm not sure, but the way the other inmates glare at the big, blonde, Aryan CO with the defiant smirk on his face, I'm pretty certain it was him. Jimmy tries to eat on one side of his mouth and grimaces as if he's chewing a mouthful of tacks. Chow goes on longer than usual. The COs aren't dismissing tables with the tap of the baton as usual. I can tell Jimmy knows what's going on, and he's pissed. I half expect him to jump up and smash someone's face in. Ten minutes pass, and the chow hall is getting so loud that we've been ordered to shut up twice. Finally, a CO walks in, and they start releasing us back to our cells in the usual order. When Jimmy and I reach the entryway, the Aryan CO stops us and orders us to stand against the wall. After everyone leaves, he pats us down roughly. He squeezes my balls so hard I have to stifle a yelp. He dismisses me and keeps Jimmy.

As I walk back into the hall, I see the entire cellblock is up in arms. There are sheets and bedding and lines and kites thrown to the floor on the bottom tier. Mongrel and another trustee are sweeping it all up, while a CO monitors them. Trash rains down from the upper tiers. Jimmy runs past me to our cell. When I reach the cell, he has his face in his palms and is rocking angrily. Our cell is completely tossed, and the pruno is gone. Even my letters, papers, and books, all of which I keep in a manila envelope that Vinny sent me, have been paged through and tossed all over. I start to gather my stuff, careful not to disturb Jimmy. Jimmy wanted that pruno so badly, especially after losing his tooth. I feel sad for him. I know how badly he needs his medicine. I think something I haven't thought in a while: how damn good a Jack and Coke with a cigarette would be. Then I realize what just happened *to me:* They just found alcohol in my cell. *Fuck.*

Our workouts have been grueling since the cell search. Summer has hit Chino, and it's stifling. There is one industrial fan for the whole cellblock, and the only ventilation is through the intermittent, broken window squares in the wall of windows opposite the tiers. The fan is fifty yards from our cell. Jimmy and I are both drinking a gallon of water a day. Our workouts are so intense they are like a meditation. I go so far into pain and exhaustion that I reach a runner's high. Our workouts go on for two hours, and I'm so exhausted that afterward I can take a nap and still sleep through the night. I get a hold of a tattered softbound book that looks like it's been passed around Chino since the 1930s, *The Old Curiosity Shop,* by Dickens. I'm so grateful.

Jimmy has calmed down and has even been reading Bible passages that his girlfriend mailed him. I meditate, pray, read, workout, eat three perfectly balanced meals a day. I haven't eaten junk, smoked, or drunk in three months. I haven't even jacked off. I feel incredible. I've never felt this strong and serene in my entire life. When I pray—and I don't even know what I'm praying to—I feel like I have a beam of light shooting out of my head. And when I meditate, it's like I go into a serenity cocoon. I lose track of time, but Jimmy tells me I'm gone for nearly an hour sometimes.

We are cell-fed dinner. Jimmy starts collecting fruit again. The kites are coming in from everywhere. Jimmy hands me a frightening pencil drawing he's been working on. It's what's called prison *cheese*, a shaded, intermingled collage of bones, skulls, calendar sheets from '97-'05, a little Viking ship with an Iron Cross on its masthead, flames, melting prison bars, and a blank face with its mouth sewn shut. At the top, Jimmy has drawn his face with sad eyes, with an enlarged version of his *fuck the world* tattoo above his right brow and his teardrop under his right eye. In the middle of the page is a skull with deep-set, radiating eyes.

On the back Jimmy writes,

Joseph, May you always feel and claim just how much our heavenly father, "Jesus Christ" loves you. Let this be a valuable lesson as well as learning experience to you because this has been my life for many years my friend. I wish you the best in your journey when you get out stay strong and stand tall through it all out there.

God Bless you, your family, recovering friends always.

All My All, Through It All, Full - Blast.

Jimmy"

That afternoon, just after Jimmy gave me his drawing, he said that I'll be leaving very soon. That night I lay in bed just before lights-out while the Paisas chanted. I read the three prayers I'd penciled in on the wall. I love that part from the Lord's Prayer, *take away my difficulties that victory over them may bear witness ...* Indeed, God, plenty of difficulties to choose from. *Grant me the courage to change the things I can* ... Florence in rehab, she said courage isn't about being a superhero. It's about doing the thing you know is right even when you don't want to do it. And that seems about right to me. I've been trying to do that for the last two years. I don't always do it, but I really have been trying to try. And I heard Vinny say, spirituality has nothing to do with spirits or God, it has to do with acting consistent with basic principles that all religions and cultures recognize: kindness, fairness, love, respect, diligence.

I wish I'd known these things, *really known* these things, before I lighted my life on fire with a blowtorch.

And then there is, *We don't regret the past or wish to shut the door on it.* I've heard this so many times in so many 12-step meetings. I've no idea how that could ever be possible for me.

"Naus, Joseph Naus. Prepare for unlock," sounds over the loudspeaker.

Jimmy is carving an iron cross into the desktop with a slip-and-slide. I gather my stuff. I give him a hug.

"Thanks for looking out for me, Jimmy," I tell him. "I don't know if I would have made it in here without you."

"Fuck. You know I take care of mine," Jimmy says, beaming with pride.

The cell door slides open, such a familiar sound now. As I walk out Jimmy hollers loudly over the bars,

"Clark Kent has left the building! Clark Kent has left the building!"

Bars rattle and I hear Menace and Derek and O.G. and many voices, *Thaaaatttt'ssss riiiighhht! ... Get yours Clark! ... Esssssoooo ... Fly on out of here motherfucker!*

I turn back. I try to capture it all in my memory. I won't regret my time here.

❖   ❖   ❖

Judge Von Silkman has been transferred from LAX court to the LA downtown court, and thus, so has my case. I'll be in Twin Towers until my hearing within a few days. I call Vinny and Keri from the pay phones in the sex pod. Vinny tells me I'm going to be alright. I halfway believe him. Keri tells me that two of the three evaluation reports came back recommending more prison time. *Surprise*: the fat lady didn't like me, thinks I'm unremorseful. The Assistant Warden, who I never even met, says I could use some more time in his facility because of the egregiousness of my crime. And let me guess, Keri jokes, the prison union wants another raise! The good news is that the guy with an actual legit degree says I shouldn't have been in Chino in the first place. I *love* that guy: *so* smart. Keri says it isn't unusual for all three 90-Day Eval reports to recommend prison time, so mine isn't so bad. I try to keep a stiff upper lip, but I know I've used up everything I have to make it through this far. I don't know how I'll survive if the judge sends me back for two years. I can't do two years. *I just can't.*

I'm wide-awake when my name is called at 5:00 a.m. for unlock. Today is the day. I was hoping I'd feel serene like during my meditations at Chino, but I don't. I'm churning inside. Today a man in a black robe is going to decide whether to send me to prison for two years or whether to set me free.

I'm buzzed out of the sex pod. I walk the maze, then through the turnstiles with all the other excited inmates, but I feel like I'm in a bubble, like everything and everyone is moving faster than me and orbiting around me. Nobody says a word to me, and I don't feel scared. I know what's going on. I go to the little PC cell on the corner, and I'm the only one in here. My name is called, and I board a loud, crowded bus and am placed in the little one-man cage behind the driver—the VIP cage. The deputies play classic rock, and so I think of my dad. The bus ride is short, since the court is only a couple miles away. I'm in the staging area with my nose to the wall, and I hear my name over a crackling walkie-talkie. *Get Naus up here now.* A sheriff takes me solo in the elevator.

"What are you, a celebrity or something?" the CO asks.

I don't answer. I just shrug.

I'm handed off to the bailiff and placed in a large cell by myself next to the courtroom. I can feel the energy from the courtroom. It adds to my tension. I'm nearly hyperventilating. The cell has three built-in benches. I pace atop the benches. I clean my glasses. I clasp my hands between my knees to stop them from shaking. I get on my knees. I take a deep breath and begin to pray.

God, I know who you are. You're the one that let me survive the last hundred days, the last two years. You are the one that made me decide not to kill myself. I know I'm not supposed to pray for myself, and I don't usually ... but please God, please, please, please let me go free today. I don't think I can survive in prison for two years. Please do this for me and I'll never drink again, or take another drug or sleep with another prostitute. I'll go to meetings, and I'll help others. I promise. Oh, God, please help me. I promise. Please.

I hear the exterior door unlock, then the keys rattle.

"C'mon, Naus."

I stand up, and the bailiff handcuffs me and walks me into the courtroom. Everyone goes silent and stares at me. The courtroom is packed. Keri and Mark are at Defense Counsel's table, and DA Villa and some other attorney are at the DA's table. The judge is reading papers. I look to the audience, and there must be sixty people filling every seat, and then some are standing. There's Vinny and Tito's son, Tomar, and several of my exes. And my sponsee, Todd, and Florence and Bob from PRC. And Kib is here, and my client, Ken, from Flyer Motor Homes. And, of course, Will is here. And my dad is here. I can't believe it. And the rest are all 12-steppers I've met over the last two years and some from the *Other Bar*. I make eye contact with my dad. He smiles softly. I scan for my mom, grandpa, Uncle Billy, and Aunt Suzie, and none of them are here.

They all see me like this, in my orange jail suit, handcuffed. I'm overwhelmed with emotion. I can't believe they are all here. I can't believe my mom and Aunt Suzie and Grandpa aren't here.

"Honorable Samuel T. Von Silkman, presiding. Calendar item number 1, People versus Naus, Number SA049492-01," the court clerk announces.

The courtroom goes silent.

DA Carmen de Villa opens the hearing by lambasting me, per her usual. I watch Judge Von Silkman to try to get a read, but he is poker faced. Villa says what she always says: *If there were a girl in there, Mr. Naus would have raped her*; that the DA's investigators showed a picture of me to the massage parlor manager and workers, and they didn't recognize me. Carmen's a fucking shill. I wonder if I'll ever be able to say her name in prayer and not feel anger course through me.

"Again, Your Honor, the state's psychologist makes a cogent point," Villa says, referencing the evaluation report that the fat lady at Chino wrote, "had a woman been in that bed, there is a high likelihood that she would have been overtaken by the defendant and raped."

Villa relishes in saying that in front of all my supporters. She's aglow.

"He was naked," Villa continues. "He intended to have a sexual encounter with the person who was inside."

To my amazement, DA Villa actually turns her back to the judge to see the gallery's reaction. I wonder if there are any of the people in the audience here for me that didn't know the details of my story. Well, they do *now*. Judge Von Silkman remains stone-faced.

Villa continues in earnest about the report of the Associate Warden who didn't even see me, "Dr. Tennison also said that the community would be absolutely protected from Mr. Naus's severe, rough behaviors caused by substance abuse if he is incarcerated."

Judge Von Silkman raises his eyebrows at that comment. *For God's sake*, I think, *did she just quote someone that said that I wouldn't harm society during the time I was locked up if I were locked up?*

"That's all I have, Your Honor," Villa closes.

I look back over my shoulder. Tomar, Tito's son, smiles at me. I'm shocked he's here, and I'm so glad Tito isn't. Tomar is a judge now, has two kids and a wife. I remember I was at his party at the country club when he passed the Bar. Tito had an ice sculpture of the scales of justice made for him. Tomar was so embarrassed. Larisa is sitting next to him. She looks so beautiful dressed up. She has her hair up in a bun, and her eyelashes are tipped with tears. She wipes them away and forces a smile for me.

"Mr. Ackerman," Judge Von Silkman announces.

Mark places his hand on my shoulder as he stands to address the court. *C'mon Mark, hit a home run for me. I really fucking need it.*

I know I haven't been the easiest client for Mark. I know he and Keri have been doing everything they can to help me, and I've been a dick to him more than once. Mark took it in stride. Keri had gotten my hopes up a bit because she didn't want me to slit my wrists, and when I came to realize my hopes for the outcome of my case were completely unrealistic, I called Mark and took it out on him.

I'm breathing too deep and too hard. Things are getting blurry, like I'm going to pass out. I blink. I slow it down. *Think positive. Please God.*

I've read the sentencing memorandum that Keri wrote, so I know basically what Mark is going to say. *Poor, poor boy.* Mom was a junkie, my alcoholic-junkie dad left when I was a baby, my mom and I lived in poverty, and that I picked myself up by my bootstraps and became a successful lawyer. But then the seeds of my past, planted by my parents, finally bore fruit and I snapped, but I'm *actually* a *really* good guy. My sentencing memorandum included letters from friends, family, and colleagues, all attesting to my fine character. Some were actually very touching.

[VERBATIM OFFICIAL COURT TRANSCRIPT]

MARK ACKERMAN: YOUR HONOR THERE'S NO WAY TO PUT A HAPPY FACE OR POSITIVE SPIN ON THE CRIMINAL CONDUCT IN QUESTION. AND I WOULDN'T ATTEMPT TO DO SO. PART OF MR. NAUS' RECOVERY IS EXHIBITION OF REMORSE. HE TAKES FULL RESPONSIBILITY FOR WHAT HE DID. WE ARE NOT GOING TO STAND HERE AND TRY TO MINIMIZE OR TRIVIALIZE WHAT HAPPENED. HOWEVER, HE DID IT IN A DRUNKEN STUPOR AND THROES OF ALCOHOL ABUSE. WE LEARNED FROM THE VICTIM AT THE PRELIMINARY HEARING THAT MR. NAUS WAS OUT OF HIS MIND AT THE TIME. BUT WHAT HE DID WAS HORRIBLE AND DESPICABLE, AND THAT IS THE END OF THAT STORY.

I ASK THE COURT TO CONSIDER WHAT HAPPENED SINCE THESE UGLY EVENTS OF TWO YEARS AGO.

Mark puts his hand back on my shoulder for a second. It makes me feel good, like something a dad would do. Mark summarizes the gist of the sentencing memorandum. I'm the portrait of sobriety.

YOUR HONOR, HE'S BEEN STONE COLD SOBER SINCE THAT FATEFUL NIGHT AND HAS MADE EVERY EFFORT TO REHABILITATE HIMSELF AND TO OVERCOME HIS DISEASE.

Disease. I don't feel so uneasy about that word anymore. Someone in a meeting asked me, would you rather have diabetes or alcoholism? Given my circumstances, it seems I'd be a hell of a lot better off taking insulin daily.

THE CLINICAL PSYCHOLOGIST THAT SAW MR. NAUS AT
CHINO RECOMMENDED PROBATION AND NO FURTHER IN-
CARCERATION FOR MR. NAUS. THE ASSOCIATE WARDEN
NEVER EVEN SAW MR. NAUS, NOT FOR TWO MINUTES.
[READING:]PROBATION IS A SUITABLE PUNISHMENT,
AND MR. NAUS WILL LIKELY SUCCEED ON PROBATION IF
HE HAD ALCOHOL AND DRUG TREATMENT AND CONTINUE
TO ATTEND RECOVERY MEETINGS AND OBTAIN FURTHER
PSYCHOLOGICAL COUNSELING. THAT WAS THE OPINION
OF THE PSYCHOLOGIST WHO ACTUALLY SPENT SOME TIME
WITH MR. NAUS.

The judge remains stone-faced. When I argued civil motions, I could
almost always tell what the judge thought within a few seconds. I knew
whether I was going to win or lose the motion, or whether the judge
thought my client and my case was bullshit. But not with Judge Von
Silkman—he's not giving himself up at all.

Mark turns to the gallery.

YOUR HONOR, THESE PEOPLE ARE HERE TO SUPPORT
MR. NAUS. THESE ARE THE PEOPLE THAT HE WILL
BE LIVING WITH AND AMONG AND WORKING WITH AND
TALKING TO AND SEEING DAILY IN THE COURSE OF HIS
EFFORT TO COMPLETELY REINTEGRATE HIMSELF INTO
SOCIETY AFTER THIS DISASTROUS SITUATION IN WHICH
HE ACKNOWLEDGES AND HE SEEKS FORGIVENESS AND LE-
NIENCY.

Mark turns back to the judge and places both hands on my shoulders.

HIS FATE IS IN YOUR HANDS . . . WE HAVE NOTHING
FURTHER, SUBMITTED, YOUR HONOR.

Mark sits. There is dead silence in the court. My ears are red-hot, and the pulse in my wrists flutter. *Oh, God, please.* Judge Von Silkman looks out over the gallery.

THE COURT: I APPRECIATE ALL THE PEOPLE WHO HAVE COME TO SUPPORT MR. NAUS. WE DON'T GET THIS MANY PEOPLE . . . HARDLY EVER.

He looks at Mark, then me, and Keri.

I'VE READ THE SENTENCING MEMORANDUM THAT WAS SUBMITTED ON BEHALF OF MR. NAUS AND ALL THE SUP-PORTING DOCUMENTS. I'VE READ THEM THOROUGHLY. AND I HAVE TO SAY, I DISAGREE . . .

He disagrees. Oh, God, no! I feel my mind and body drop. If I could, I'd run out of here and jump out the window. It's happening again. They won't let me out. I blink to stay conscious. I'm going to pass out.

. . . THE FATE OF MR. NAUS IS NOT IN MY HANDS. IT IS IN HIS HANDS.

What?

HE IS VERY FORTUNATE TO HAVE THE HANDS OF ALL OF THE PEOPLE WHO HAVE COME HERE TODAY, SUPPORT-ED AND THOSE WHO HAVE WRITTEN LETTERS TO THE COURT, BUT WHETHER HE'S GOING TO STAY SOBER AND PRODUCTIVE FOR THE REST OF HIS LIFE, THAT IS UP TO HIM, NOT ME.

Mark leans in and Keri looks over at me. I can feel my entire body vibrate, like when I smoke a whole pack of cigarettes in an hour.

WHEN I READ THE PRELIMINARY HEARING TRANSCRIPT AND THE REPORTS, I HAD TROUBLE WITH THE INTENT ISSUES HERE. I'M CONVINCED BEYOND A REASONABLE DOUBT THAT MR. NAUS INTENDED TO HAVE SEX WITH SOMEBODY THAT NIGHT WHO WAS A FEMALE, NOT A MALE. AND HE WENT INTO A HOUSE WHERE A MAN WAS SOUND ASLEEP RIGHT NEXT DOOR TO A MASSAGE PARLOR. I COULDN'T FIND ANYWHERE IN ANY OF THE INFORMATION A MOTIVE TO BREAK INTO THIS APARTMENT. HE DIDN'T KNOW THE VICTIM WAS SOUND ASLEEP WHICH MAKES IT UNLIKELY THAT MR. NAUS SAW HIM BEFORE HE BROKE IN. AND, IT IS REASONABLE, I THINK, GIVEN THE WITHDRAWAL OF $100 AHEAD OF TIME TO BELIEVE THAT IN THIS STUPOR HE FELT IN SOME CRAZY WAY THAT HE WAS GOING INTO THE MASSAGE PARLOR. I THINK IT WAS CLEARLY ALCOHOL RELATED ALCOHOL MOTIVATED, ALCOHOL GENERATED AND ALCOHOL INDUCED.

This is good. Thank you, God.

BUT, WHAT HE DID WAS BAD. BREAKING INTO AN OCCUPIED HOUSE IS JUST ABOUT AS BAD AS IT GETS SHORT OF A HOMICIDE OR RAPE OR SOMETHING LIKE THAT. A HOME BURGLARY WITH SOMEBODY IN THE HOUSE AT NIGHT IS VERY, VERY BAD. BUT HE KNOWS THAT . . . HE'S A LAWYER.

I was a lawyer.

AND MR. NAUS WAS BORN TO YOUNG PARENTS WHO ES-
SENTIALLY SADDLED HIM WITH ALL THE HEREDITARY,
GENETIC PROBLEMS OF ADDICTS WHO ARE PARENTS. I
READ THE LETTER FROM JOSEPH'S MOM, AND I KNOW
SHE'S BEEN SOBER FOR A LONG TIME. IS JOSEPH'S MOM
HERE? CAN SHE PLEASE STAND UP?

Mark looks at me. I shake my head. *No, my mom didn't show up to my sentencing hearing. It was too much of a hassle.*

NO, YOUR HONOR. SHE COULDN'T MAKE IT.

Judge Von Silkman quickly moves on as if my mom's absence is so odd that he can't process it.

WELL . . . UH OH. IN ANY EVENT, I KNOW ON A
PERSONAL LEVEL THE STRUGGLES OF ALCOHOLISM. I'VE
BEEN SOBER FOR SEVEN YEARS . . .

Wait, what? I think. *Did he just say he's been sober for seven years?*

. . . AND I KNOW ABOUT THE DISEASE AND BLACK-
OUTS AND WHAT IT TAKES TO STOP . . . IN ANY
EVENT, MR. NAUS, GIVEN HIS FAMILY HISTORY, WAS
DESTINED TO BECOME AN ALCOHOLIC AND THE VOLCANO
ERUPTED THAT WAS BRIMMING AND BREWING FOR MANY
YEARS ON THE NIGHT THAT HE BROKE INTO THAT HOUSE.

Jesus fucking Christ! Oh my God. I may get to go home today.

I DON'T THINK PRISON IS GOING TO SOLVE ANY
PROBLEMS IN THIS CASE. I'M GOING TO PLACE YOU

ON PROBATION FOR FIVE YEARS AND MAKE SURE YOU
GET COUNSELING AND INSIST THAT WHILE YOU'RE ON
PROBATION FOR THE NEXT FIVE YEARS YOU GO TO FIVE
RECOVERY MEETINGS A WEEK, AND YOU WILL BE TESTED
AND IF THERE IS EVEN A HINT THAT YOU ARE DRINKING
AGAIN, YOU ARE GOING TO PRISON. DO YOU AGREE TO
THAT -- DO YOU AGREE TO THOSE TERMS?

THE DEFENDANT: YES, YOUR HONOR.

Judge Von Silkman thanks all the people in the audience and closes
the hearing. I watch my friends funnel out of the courtroom. They are
joyous, like sports fans that just rooted their team on to victory in a
close match. The court empties. After a while, it's just Keri and me, and
a few court staffers attending to their business. Keri is gathering her
things. I'm shocked that this is over. I don't know what to do or what
to think. And suddenly, I feel a gathering from all parts of my mind and
body, and all my emotions suck into my chest. I try to hold it in, but my
whole body heaves, and I begin to shake uncontrollably. The skin on
my nose creases, and I clench my jaw and squeeze my eyes to fight it off.
But it's no use. It rushes like floodwater. I sob with my entire body. It's
everything all at once. It's too powerful to stop, so I just let it go. It feels
so good. My eyes are blurry, and my nose runs, and when I hear Keri
and the bailiff hover over me to usher me out of the courtroom, it looks
and sounds as if I'm underwater looking up at them.

TWENTY-TWO (EPILOGUE)

"You new?" I ask.

I know the answer. He has that shaky wide-eyed look of a newcomer. I sat next to him at the recovery meeting that just ended. He didn't stop tapping his right foot and wringing his hands the entire meeting. The moment the meeting was over, he bolted out the door for a cigarette, just like I used to do.

"Yeah, I got a DUI two nights ago," he explains to me after a long drag off his cigarette. "My lawyer says I'm going to lose my driver's license. My girlfriend's all pissed. You?"

"Me," I say, "I haven't drunk in over two years. Amazing, right?"

"Two *fucking* years, seriously?"

"Yeah, right? So, which way are you going?"

Brandon pulls out another cigarette and answers, "Way down Sunset. I'm taking the bus. *The fucking bus.* Jesus ... anyway, my car is wrecked ... DUI ... so, yeah, the bus."

"I can relate," I say. "I'm parked on Sunset. I'll give you a ride."

We cross Sunset at Silverlake Boulevard and walk east down Sunset. I'm still in a state of wonderment. Ever since I got out, it's been like when I was a kid, and all of Los Angeles is Disneyland. Food tastes better, and even the air smells good. When I walk I'm mentally skipping.

Brandon is rambling at warp speed about his girlfriend, about how he's *totally fucked*, and how in the fuck is he going to keep his job at the ad agency if he has a suspended license? And how much money the DUI is going to cost him, and how his car insurance is going to go up. He can't be a day over twenty-five. He's in the zone. I've been there. There are no spaces between his sentences, and I don't even try to get a word in. I'm listening only vaguely as I watch the giant, podiatrist's office sign at Sunset and Benton rotate slowly. The *happy foot* is a smiling cartoon foot with white gloves and white shoes giving the thumbs-up. The *sad foot* has a sickly face with red eyes, a bandaged toe, and crutches. Brandon and I walk closer to the sign. The giant foot rotates slowly: *happy foot, sad foot, happy foot, sad foot.*

Brandon keeps rambling on. He's background noise.

Vinny lives right down the street. I recall him saying that the superstition around the neighborhood was that you knew how your day was going to go depending on whether you first saw the *happy foot* or you first saw the *sad foot.* For the longest time, the sign was broken, and it was stuck so that whenever I drove to Vinny's, I'd see the *sad foot.* I'm not superstitious, but given how shitty things were, a couple times I took another route.

"... and I had to spend the night in jail," Brandon says. "I was in a cell with a guy who pissed himself. You can't imagine what it's like in there. I blew over a two-point-zero, so my lawyer says I'm for sure going to lose my license. What am I supposed to tell my boss? I don't have a car, so I can't pick up the clients ... *sorry* ..."

Brandon keeps talking, and we are right under the sign, and from this angle, I can see the sign in great detail like I've never seen it before. It occurs to me: It's not two different feet. It's just two different sides of the same foot. Fuck, I always thought *happy foot* and *sad foot* were two different feet.

We keep walking, and Brandon hasn't stopped talking yet, "... and all I want to do is drink. And I'm smoking twice as much. I just want a beer. What? I can't drink a beer now? I have to go to stupid meetings for the rest of my life and sit around drinking coffee, praying and meditating ... It's ridiculous. But I keep on getting in trouble when I drink, but I can stop whenever I want to; so I just want to, you know, not drink so much."

Happy foot, sad foot, happy foot, sad foot.

I'm finally able to a wedge a word in: "If you can quit anytime you want, why not just quit for a while, and see how it goes?" I ask casually, as if I'm curious and not suggesting something. "I mean, if drinking isn't a big deal, then *not* drinking for a while shouldn't be a big deal either, right?"

We hop into my car. I wait for his answer.

"I guess," Brandon says, "but that isn't the issue. I mean I'm not going to drink and drive ever again. My problem isn't alcohol; it's the DUI, my girlfriend, my job, living without a car for two months. Those are my problems."

"Hold that thought," I tell Brandon. "I need to concentrate."

I'm still not used to the breathalyzer I had to have installed in my car. In order to start the car, I'm required to perform a series of blowings of my breath, done in nearly perfect sequence. The damn thing even goes off while I'm driving. I blow and get it right on the first try.

"Which way?" I ask.

"Down Sunset," Brandon says. "*Fuckin' A.* You got a breathalyzer in your car? Damn. I thought you had over two years sober?"

"I do," I say. "Things got pretty bad out there for me. It's what we call the *wreckage of your past.* Anyway, you were saying about your problems not being alcohol?"

Brandon rolls down the window and lights a cigarette as we stop at the light on Benton Way. I do mind, but I know he needs a cigarette a hell of a lot more than I need him not to smoke in my car. I open the sunroof. It's one of those warm summer evenings in Los Angeles, the kind that blow my mind, the kind that make me appreciate living in southern California, even though I've never lived anywhere else.

"Just stick around the meetings and don't drink," I tell Brandon. "Things will get better. They will."

"I'm one of the top associates at SKG," Brandon says. "I drive clients to meetings and out to lunch sometimes. What am I going to tell my boss? We have work events with alcohol. What am I supposed to say? Fuck, my attorney said that it isn't totally out of the question that I might have to wear an ankle bracelet. Can you believe that?"

"Yeah, I can," I respond flatly.

Brandon flicks his cigarette out the window. I use extreme restraint and don't react. He doesn't need a lesson about littering, not right now at least.

"It's right here on the left," Brandon says and points at a new pink-trimmed condominium complex. "My girlfriend's waiting for me. We are going to have a talk, you know *a talk*. My whole life is *shit*, and I'm not supposed to even be able to go get a drink? I can't believe this. How could it get any fucking worse?"

Brandon folds in half in the passenger seat so that his head is in his knees. He cradles his face with his hands. He's breathing hard, likes he's about to hyperventilate or break into sobs. It's a move I'm not unfamiliar with. After a few moments, he rises back up and stares out the windshield. He takes a deep breath.

"It could be worse," I say. "You could be an unemployed, two-strike felon, registered sex offender for life, disbarred lawyer with two hundred grand in student loans and tax liability."

Brandon drags his fingers dramatically back through his thick dark hair.

"I'm sorry," he says. "I can't even pay attention. My head's all over the place."

"It's alright man. Just take it easy," I say.

"Yeah, okay," Brandon says. "Sorry, I'm kind of caught up with all this stuff that's happening. You said something about student loans? You still owe student loans?"

"Yeah ... student loans, wreckage of the past. Never mind. I was just saying that we all come in with problems, but no matter how bad they are, there is nothing that drinking can't make worse."

Brandon turns toward me, confused.

"Here is my cell number," I say and hand him one of my old business cards with my cell number written on the back. "Just don't drink, okay? And give me a call tomorrow, and I'll pick you up, and we'll go to a meeting."

Brandon reads the business card under his breath, "Yi & Naus, Attorneys at Law, Joseph W. Naus."

"My cell number ... it's on the other side," I say.

"You a lawyer?"

"Nah," I say, "not anymore ... *wreckage of the past* .... You can make it without drinking until I pick you up tomorrow, right?"

"Yeah, I can do that. Okay," Brandon says. He's dazed, thinking about the confrontation he's about to have with his girlfriend. He gets out and shuts the door and leans in through the passenger window. "Thanks, Joseph. I'll see you tomorrow."

I drive back toward Sunset. I glance back in the rearview mirror until I lose sight of Brandon. I take a right on Sunset. The breathalyzer beeper goes off. I take a deep breath and calmly blow in perfect sequence. It beeps low and long with my breath and then goes silent in submission. I drive toward the giant podiatrist's sign, stare at it, and think, *It's just one foot. Happy foot, sad foot, happy foot, sad foot.*

An Excerpt from Joseph W. Naus's
follow up memoir *The Palsgraf Revelation*

ONE

A perfectly neutral female voice commands me, "Enter your seven-digit code and press the pound key." I follow her instructions, pressing each button with breathless caution, as if clipping the wires of a time bomb.

"C'mon, c'mon, c'mon," I plead aloud, "not today, baby."

There's a long pause as if the recorded woman is contemplating her decision. I imagine she's twisting her face up in deep thought. After an excruciatingly long silence, a man's stern recorded voice reveals my fate, "Minnesota Vikings, I repeat, Minnesota Vikings."

"Ah fuck."

Yesterday, Oakland Raiders, today, Minnesota Vikings. That's the way it goes. The Probation Department's random phone-line drug testing system has chosen the Vikings group of probationers to test today. I close my eyes, take a deep breath, hold it, and let out a long sigh. Man, I had solid plans today. I was going to re-re-watch the entirety of Season One of *The Office*, breaking between each episode for cigarettes and coffee.

I hate Santa Monica. It's where it all went terribly wrong for me. I hate driving to Santa Monica, too. It's only 15 miles away, but it can take a couple hours to get there. It usually doesn't, but I can't be late, so I usually end up arriving an hour early. When I moved out of Keri's place on the Westside of Los Angeles, bordering Santa Monica, to Echo Park on the Eastside of Los Angeles, I begged Maya, my probation officer, not to transfer my case to the downtown Los Angeles Probation Office.

Maya told me she doesn't think I should be on formal probation and she treats me more like a colleague than a criminal. I'm on three probation tracks simultaneously—sex offender, drug/alcohol, and violent offender—so she could have me jumping through hoops like a circus dog, but she only makes me do the things she can't avoid. She even fudges the weekly home visits. But she can't get around the drug and alcohol testing. Judge Von Silkman was unequivocal at my sentencing hearing. "For the next five years you are going to five AA meetings a week, and you will be tested, and if there is even a hint that you are drinking again, you are going to prison."

Prison. Nope, not me. If I decide to drink again, I'm buying a handgun with my bottle of Jack Daniels so I can blow my head off when I hear that knock on the door. "Knock, knock. LAPD, Open Up!" Ain't happening. I've got my cigarettes and I've got my coffee. Those'll do just fine. I don't really think about drinking anymore. Instead I think about that quick trip to the bottom of the Grand Canyon. Suicide. It's like a back-up parachute, but if I pull the chord on it, it ejects a pair of scissors so I can cut the strings. Why would anyone do that? Maybe because they are descending upon an alligator swamp and they'd prefer to die from the fall than from being eaten, maybe that's why.

I'm on the 10 Freeway, halfway there. Downtown Los Angeles is miniaturized in my rearview mirror. I've got the radio on just loud enough to drown out any unwanted engine noise, but not enough to drown out the noise in my head.

Santa Monica is breezy and sunny, below a flame blue sky, as it was when I moved here four years ago, as it was when I cruised through here on my way to Pepperdine Law in Malibu in the summer of 1994. Across the street from my destination is an ultra-modern building that houses one of the world's most prestigious neoliberal think tanks. Young, trim, smart people, men with better-than-typical khakis, and women with black rayon palazzo pants and cream silk blouses walk briskly, shoulders squared, backs straight, in and out of the think tank's custom glass doors.

I join dozens of others in the snaking security line to enter the Los Angeles County government building that houses several courtrooms and the Probation Department. As I get closer to the entry, my anxiety rises to a steady hum just below my skin. I have the same thought I had the last time I was here to see my probation officer, and each time before that. Am I going to get arrested going through security for possessing contraband? Did I leave one of those knife-like envelope openers I don't even own in my pocket or that money clip with the tiny pocket knife Grandpa gave me that I haven't seen in years? Or maybe someone slipped a tiny baggy of crystal meth into my pocket?

I place my papers, wallet, cell phone, keys, and sunglasses into a blue rubber basket and set it on the conveyor belt. This will go smoothly. I have nothing to hide. I watch my stuff move down the conveyor belt. It stops under the x-ray, it's seen on the monitor for what it is—nothing—and then the conveyor belt jerks my stuff forward. I walk under the metal detector arch. I wait for the beep, but there is no sound. I smile at the security guard carefully.

I walk down a long hallway past several women sitting on benches tucked away in little alcoves, past the domestic violence service window, and through double doors into a large waiting room. I sign in and sit down. The fluorescent lights are oppressively bright. There is an outdoor smoking area through a sliding glass door. Through the glass, I observe a uniformed bailiff conversing with a detective. The detective wears a chrome revolver holstered below his armpit and stands quartered to me. He speaks so demonstratively that his cigarette bounces, leaving little trails of smoke behind each intonation. I imagine the bailiff saying to the detective, "Really, you beat him to death with the butt of your pistol, and you weren't even sure he stole the packet of ramen noodles?"

A couple walks in. They are tatted and slinky in an American Apparel kind of way. He's the criminal. She's here because he's here. She sits several chairs to my right and he saunters up to the counter. He stands and rocks back and forth, hands forcefully stuffed into his ultra-tight jeans. He occasionally glances back at her, apologizing with his face. A probation officer bursts through the door.

"Hands up!" the officer orders.

"What's up?" the young probationer says.

The probation officer doesn't respond. He grabs his charge's wide boney shoulders and whips him around, presses him to the wall, and kicks each foot out wide. He whips cuffs out from a leather holster attached to his belt at the small of his back and slaps them on the probationer's wrists. It's all one big, bad, pro move.

"You tested dirty again. Opioids."

The officer holds the boy out toward his girlfriend. She begins to cry and then shouts.

"You fucking asshole! You fucking fuck. I came here with you—"

Despite being handcuffed, the boy lurches forward as if he's going to embrace her, but the officer turns him away and marches him back toward the door into the inner probation office. The boy cranes his neck and yells to her. "I didn't, baby. I didn't!"

The girlfriend marches out of the room. Her tear-diluted mascara and eyeliner bring a raccoon to mind. The waiting room is now silent and empty.

I've got nowhere to be, I just don't want to be here. These notoriously overburdened probation officers, they press one wrong button on their county-issued laptops and we probationers, we the presumed guilty, return to jail.

Officer Maya steps into the room. I hope she doesn't have handcuffs. Maybe a false-positive drug test came through and the boy and I are both victims.

"Quickly, Joseph," Maya says. "Let's get this done and get you out of here." She beckons me to follow.

I hand her my court cards—little green index cards indicating which AA meetings I've been to, the date, and a signature from each meeting's secretary. Maya slaps them down on the copy machine, prints them out and then leads me through a maze of cubicles to hers, back by the window facing the people waiting in the security line to enter the building.

"Ok, you are testing today, right?" Maya asks.

"Yep."

"You got your most recent registration for me?"

"Yep. Here you go," I say, handing them over.

She examines my sex offender registration papers.

"Hey look, you even got my name right," she says, and keeps scanning. "No job yet?"

"Uh, yeah, not yet," I report.

"Restitution?" Maya inquires.

"I paid it a long time ago."

"Oh yeah," she says, apparently recalling.

Officer Maya is a pretty, light-skinned black woman around my age. She's got two kids, both young teens. She must be a single mom. She wears no wedding band, and the photos of her and her kids are sans partner.

A head of blonde hair pops over the grey cubicle wall, followed by a woman's bulging eyes.

"Maya, you want to go to Third Street for lunch?" she asks, then sees me. "Oh, sorry, didn't know you were working."

"I'm almost done," Maya replies and taps away into her computer keyboard. "You gotta start looking for work, Joseph. And I don't know how long my supervisor is going to let me keep you. But today, just test and I'll see you next week."

"Thank you," I say, and smile at her. She smiles back in a way she wouldn't if she thought anyone could see us. It's nothing much, just a little kindness. I follow her back out to the waiting room. She asks a male probation officer to test me since she can't. He gives Maya a mild ration of grief but agrees, and I follow him out to the waiting room bathroom and smile a goodbye to Maya. She stands next to her blonde friend and responds to me formally, "Goodbye Mr. Naus. Remember, I'll need employment progress next week."

I stand at the urinal trying to pee into a pill-bottle-sized container without touching its edge with the head of my penis. The man stands over me. He's not casual about it. He stares at my cock, completely asexually, I presume to thwart the possibility of me cheating on this pee test. I stall out.

The probation officer sighs dramatically and says, "We doin' this or not?"

"I got it. I got it," I reply.

I close my eyes and imagine a wooded mountain stream, flowing steadily. After a few beats, urine begins to flow. I feel the plastic container heat up from my pee. I cap the sample, initial the sticker that seals the cap, and sign a form. I thank the man and hurry out of the building.

As I alight into the God-kissed meteorological perfection that is Santa Monica, I mumble a prayer, "Thank you, God," acknowledging my gratitude for completing such an unpleasant task without incident. I jump into my car, pull onto the street and am immediately sandwiched between two shiny Santa Monica Police cars. My anxiety returns. It says: Cops to Jail to Prison to Death. Cops to Jail to Prison to Death. I strangle my steering wheel, grit my teeth, and breathe deeply through my nose, until a couple blocks later and I'm loosed from the cop cars and back on the freeway. Relieved again, I crawl along the jammed 10 Freeway, one tire rotation at a time.

"Jesus fuck!" I say to myself. It has become my custom to think aloud in my car. "It's a design for living that works in rough going. Rough going? Who talks like that? An alcoholic stock analyst in the 1930s with a penchant for womanizing, cigarettes, and eventually, hallucinogenics.

Okay, okay. Don't kill the messenger. I'm the messenger now. Just call your sponsor and go to a meeting. Just call your sponsor and go to a meeting, Joseph."

I call my sponsor and he answers the phone, "Vinny, here."

"I'm going a little crazy here, Vinny," I say as if trying to prove my statement.

"Okay, okay. Take it easy, Joseph. I feel you man, but do you got a roof over your head?" he asks.

"Yeah," I answer.

"A little money in the bank?"

"Just a little, but yeah," I say.

"Food in the fridge?" Vinny asks.

"Yes," I admit.

I can hear office noise in the background. Vinny works at a giant downtown civil litigation firm.

"Then you're alright, today. Just do today. Right?"

"I guess, man. I don't feel alright."

"Jesus, Joseph. You made it through prison. This is cake. But you go home, read pages 86 and 87. Pray, meditate, go to a meeting. Take some steps to get a job. That's all you can do. You made it this far. Love you man, but I gotta go."

Vinny hangs up. I keep my eye on the car bumper in front of me. I'm traveling 10 m.p.h.

Vinny is right. I'm okay. Read the Big Book, pray, meditate, go to a meeting. Take some action to get a job. It's all I can do. I know the routine. I've been doing this, under great duress, for over two years now. "Lack of power," the Big Book says, "that was our dilemma." Was. It was my dilemma, but now I don't want to drink, and I sure as hell don't feel like going to a prostitute or massage parlor. Actually, the idea of relapsing terrifies me.

But what am I going to do? What do I want to do? How am I going to make a living?

No good comes of these questions. I'm not ready to answer them. I've got some time. I've got a few bucks in the bank from Yi & Naus, my law firm that existed what seems like a long, long time ago.

I turn up the radio as loud as I can stand it, to drown me out.

Acknowledgments

First and foremost, my enduring gratitude to my dearest friend through it all, Kelly C. Quinn, Esq.

Tracy M, for showing me how to love little Joseph and for leading me to God.

For the gift of safe port: Ryan and his mom, Elizabeth and her parents, Sheri and Buddy, and Grandpa Bill McAdams (R.I.P.).

Vince Grant, for going beyond the call of duty.

David "Wild Thing" Morrow (R.I.P.) for teaching me how to fight and be an athlete.

Florentino "Tino" Garza, Tom Garza, Robert V. Fullerton (R.I.P.), Larry Lushanko, Jack Marshall, J. E. Holmes, III, Mike Marlatt, "Les" Werlin, lawyers that acted in the great legal tradition of mentorship, asking nothing in return.

Dr. Lee Blume, (R.I.P.), Mark Werksman, Esq., Nina Daly, Esq., Michelle Michaels, Esq., all professional heroes.

Scott Wu, Esq., a great family man and loyal friend.

Bill Myers, Christine Quinn, and Chris Lloyd, for going out on a limb for me.

Allison Palmer, storyeditor extraordinaire, Christine Van Zandt, copyeditor and Allie Paull, cover design.

Theresa Saso at KMP.

Thank you: Francis S, Paul F, Sean C, Robin D, Larisa C, Jana T, Irene W, Jana & Peter, Rob & Stephanie, Todd S, Robert Q, Jordan S, David B, Vincent J, Gen Max, Tom F, Robert S, Tim and Aleathea, Charlie S, Dez, Gabby O, Paul C, Gabe, Dad, Mom & John; all the 12-steppers that showed up for me in court.

Reverend Michael Bernard Beckwith and Rickie Byars Beckwith of Agape International Spiritual Center, channels for God.

About the Author

J oseph W. Naus was born in Riverside, California, in 1971 and now resides in Los Angeles. *Straight Pepper Diet* is his first book.

Made in the USA
Columbia, SC
20 March 2021